CAREERS *in* INTERNATIONAL AFFAIRS

CAREERS *in* INTERNATIONAL AFFAIRS | EIGHTH EDITION

MARIA PINTO CARLAND
CANDACE FABER

EDITORS

GEORGETOWN UNIVERSITY PRESS / Washington, D.C.

Georgetown University Press, Washington, D.C. www.press.georgetown.edu
©2008 by Georgetown University Press. All rights reserved. No part of this book may be
reproduced or utilized in any form or by any means, electronic or mechanical, including
photocopying and recording, or by any information storage and retrieval system, without
permission in writing from the publisher.

Careers in international affairs / Maria Pinto Carland, Candace Faber, editors—8th ed.
    p. cm.
   Includes index.
   ISBN-13: 978-1-58901-199-1 (alk. paper)
   1. International relations—Vocational guidance—United States.
  2. International economic relations—Vocational guidance—United States
  I. Carland, Maria Pinto, 1944–   II. Faber, Candace.
  JZ1238.U6C37   2008
  327.023′73—dc22

                                        2007027135

This book is printed on acid-free paper meeting the requirements of the American
National Standard for Permanence in Paper for Printed Library Materials.

15   14   13   12   11   10   09 08   9 8 7 6 5 4 3 2

Printed in the United States of America

Contents

Preface

Careers in International Affairs is a book about career options for young professionals. Compiled by a career counselor, a student, alumni, and friends of the School of Foreign Service at Georgetown University, it is designed for men and women who want to serve their country or the international community in business, government, world organizations, and nonprofit groups. Thus, our intention is to introduce and demonstrate the variety of global employment opportunities available and to provide

- understanding of international careers and what they offer,
- insight into the skills and knowledge employers seek,
- awareness of individual career potential, and
- guidelines for career choices.

Alumni make up the heart of this book. We have watched them transition into, and out of, public, private, and nonprofit sectors; into and out of not one but several careers; always learning, growing, and contributing. Their essays in this book, however, are more than simply descriptions of the trails they have blazed—they represent efforts to return and widen the path for others to follow them. It is individuals such as these who serve as mentors and create the networks necessary to provide options power for those seeking international careers.

Young people today are well aware of the essential elements of a job search: education, internship, resume and cover letter, interview, and contacts. However, more than twenty years of observing students move through these steps reveal several aspects of the career search that receive short shrift:

- the importance of self-knowledge,
- the ability to communicate that knowledge, and
- the need for networks and mentors.

After all, if you do not know what you want, how can you choose where to send your resume? If you are not aware of your abilities, how can you describe your skills to an interviewer? And if you do not have reliable sounding boards, how can you be sure you are moving in the right direction, and, as always, where do you turn for help? To emphasize this, we have included chapters on three topics—interviews, mentors, and a new chapter on networking—all critical elements of a job search.

Each subsequent chapter begins with an essay by an alumnus or friend of the School of Foreign Service and, in some cases, contains a shorter commentary by a recent graduate. Their reflections come from one of two sources: either the broad perspective, resulting from one or a series of careers, or the more focused view of a young professional just starting his or her career. In addition, for the first time we have included a new chapter devoted to choosing the graduate program that not only meets your needs but also suits you best.

This new edition contains nearly three hundred organization profiles, all of which have been updated since the last edition. Though it may appear that there are many new entries, in fact, some are the result of downsizings, mergers, and acquisitions. Each entry provides a thumbnail sketch of the organization's activities in the United States and abroad. Whenever possible, we include notes on the skills and background desired in applicants. Also provided are telephone, fax, and/or website contact information. The profiles we list are of selected organizations that best represent the field and that also have a history of hiring international affairs graduates. There are some exceptions. On one hand, the U.S. government and international organization listings are not just a sampling of agencies and organizations, they are comprehensive; on the other hand, the development chapter has no listings at all because work in this field ranges across nonprofits, government agencies, businesses, and international organizations. Our purpose is to convey a sense of the options but not to create exhaustive lists.

The knowledge and skills that international professionals bring to first jobs can carry them into other fields and other careers. International careers often morph into one another, to be sampled and explored sequentially. The international professional must recognize and be ready for each option as it appears.

The first edition of this book was published in 1967. The current edition, like those before it, has a unique architecture. Its blueprints were based on our students' experiences. Its design arose from our interactions with those same students. It was built with the wise words of our graduates and was developed by a team of colleagues and friends. We hope that this edition provides powerful options for those who will become the architects of their own international careers.

We would like to acknowledge here individuals who were with us at the beginning and stayed with us until the end: Blaise and Raphael Carland, who actually took their mother's career advice with them into the worlds of social work and the U.S. Department of State—and who now advise her; and also Matthew and LauraLee Faber, who have always known that there is a place in the big world for those who hunger to know it.

And finally, we must recognize our alumni, whose progress we have watched with confidence, and whose successes we have accurately anticipated. They do not disappoint. Having blazed a trail, they return to us again and again, with gifts of information, insight, and inspiration. And after each return, they widen the path ahead and lead us on.

PART I

STRATEGIES

1

Introduction to the International Affairs Job Market

MARIA PINTO CARLAND

Maria Pinto Carland *is the counselor of the Master of Science in Foreign Service Program in the School of Foreign Service at Georgetown University. Before joining the school, she was an administrator at the Patterson School of Diplomacy and International Commerce and in the University of Toronto Graduate History Department. She has been a curatorial assistant at the Metropolitan Museum of Art in New York, the Art Gallery of Ontario, and the University of Kentucky Art Museum, and a program officer at the United Nations Association and the Foreign Policy Association. She is also a career counselor for men and women of color in the International Career Advancement Program at the Aspen Institute, which works to bring greater diversity to the staffing of senior management and policymaking positions in international public and nonprofit careers. She holds an MA from Georgetown University.*

A PHRASE that has crept into our vocabulary is "My first job was. . . ." We no longer speak of a single career in a single organization, and no one expects us to do so. For example, one of our Georgetown alumni started in the private sector after graduation with a major bank, overseas. He returned home to join the staff of a senior U.S. senator. Then, several years later, he left to head up a nonprofit group. He now runs a small think tank / educational organization and is a member of the board of a well-known foundation. So it is only natural that when we speak of the international job market, we are really talking about not just a range of fields from which to choose but also all the fields that you might one day work in or deal with—at a negotiating table, in a boardroom, or on a consulting team. The path our alumnus took through the international arena is quite typical of international affairs professionals today, and your path may well be like his. As a new international affairs professional, you are in demand!

Agencies, corporations, nonprofit groups, and international organizations around the world now expect the new hire to have not only cross-cultural experience but also cross-disciplinary skills. The corporate interviewer expects a job candidate to have the ability to articulate and defend ideas on paper and in person. The nonprofit director wants a staffer who can read budgets and understands fund-raising. Government agencies want managers as well as analysts, and international organizations look for all these things.

Graduates of international affairs programs today are being urged to "step up" to the global challenges that require education and experience. They have received an education that allowed them to have several concentrations and therefore multiple options. They have spent time overseas—studying, living, working. They want to integrate foreign policy and business, law and economics, medicine and human rights. They not only combine disciplines but also expect to move in and out of sectors and specialties. Creative career combinations and sequences are more and more common. The joint degree—international relations and law, international relations and business, international relations and medicine—is extremely popular. The interest in and need for cross-cultural studies is as important, if not more so, than ever.

EDUCATION AND EXPERIENCE

Information about careers has become such an integral part of the American educational system that even many children in elementary schools have a day set aside to learn what firefighters and farmers do. We are a can-do country, and we are urged early in our lives to discover what we want to do and whether we have what it takes—in interest, skills, education, and experience. To this end, effective career guidance and employment services are essential. Most educational institutions recognize this and offer students preparation and training, insights and advice, and opportunities and contacts as well as encouragement and assistance. What they do not offer is jobs. Indeed, experience at the School of Foreign Service at Georgetown shows that our students' achievements are supported by our career services but their accomplishments come through their own efforts. We believe that career achievement is the result of interaction between a student's character and our curriculum, a student's intelligence and our instructors, and a student's skills and our services.

Thus, it is crucial for you to realize that the responsibility for finding a job is basically yours. And it is critical for you to understand that the most difficult part of any job search—and of life in general—is knowing who you are and what you want. The answers to these questions will assist you in choosing a sector, will help you explain why you want to join a particular organization, and will enable you to convince others that you have something to contribute to the field. *You* must create and seize opportunities for yourself. *You* must be able to present yourself as an asset to potential employers and to those whose placement assistance you seek.

PREPARATION FOR THE ENTRY LEVEL: EDUCATION

Today it is no longer sufficient or satisfying to study a single discipline in isolation. Just as the line between domestic and international has blurred, so too the line between disciplines is disappearing. Historians must understand economics and science; political scientists must appreciate budgets and finance. Furthermore, educated individuals must be able to combine technical and cultural skills not only to expand their knowledge but also to apply it. We have already begun to assume that the physical and behavioral sciences, the humanities, and cultural and ethical studies will be part of every person's body of knowledge. And yet studies reveal that employers place the highest value on skills not usually associated with specific training: generic cognitive skills and social skills. Nonacademic training and experience are rated as highly as the knowledge, principles, and practices of a particular academic discipline or trade. Cross-cultural competence is the critical new human resource requirement created by the global environment.

This integrative approach of interdisciplinary, intercultural, and multilingual education is infiltrating and informing all the traditional fields. However, a number of enduring requirements continue to stand out:

- knowledge of history and awareness of patterns in international relations;
- a thorough grasp of what determines foreign policy priorities and realities;
- grounding in economics and familiarity with basic business and accounting;

- a high comfort level with technology;
- an understanding of policy development and implementation;
- clarity and accuracy in speaking and writing;
- awareness of and commitment to ethical standards and personal values;
- self-awareness: comprehension of leadership and teamwork skills;
- logic and objectivity in thinking and the ability to project consequences of decisions;
- a talent for skillful time management; and
- personal qualities of poise, humor, imagination, compassion, intellectual curiosity, judgment, and openness to new ideas.

The utility of specialization is perhaps one of the more common questions posed with regard to educational requirements and concerns. Specialization and sophistication of knowledge and analytical techniques can be crucial to the knowledge and work of the international professional. However, the isolation essential to scientific study or specialist investigation is a severe handicap in policy prescription and in the successful implementation of a given strategy. Coping in policy situations with the multidimensional interactions that characterize international affairs requires a holistic, conceptual approach. The requirements of a new era in international affairs demand generalists capable of understanding the work of specialists and able to synthesize knowledge from various fields. Thus the liberally educated generalist is prepared to wrestle with complex issues, to sort them out, and to produce logical and responsive conclusions.

The ability to communicate is the essence of international relations. It is the capacity to resolve communication difficulties among specialists that distinguishes the international policymaker.

Practitioners of international affairs must recognize the importance of interpersonal relations in affecting the outcome of any decision-making situation. The circulation of knowledge is already one of the most significant aspects of the twenty-first century. The ability to communicate is the essence of international relations. Students will need experience with both the theory and practice of international affairs to be able to communicate and collaborate across disciplines. It is the capacity to resolve communication difficulties among specialists that distinguishes the international policymaker. Students eager to prepare themselves must understand that whereas practical training will help them land their first job, their theoretical training will ensure promotions and a long and successful career.

Preparation for the Entry Level: Internships

Most entry-level job seekers in the international field face an experience dilemma: They need a job to gain experience but cannot get a job without experience. One solution is to find a job for a few years between undergraduate and graduate school. This is an ideal time to explore the world of work, to travel, to make mistakes, to test yourself, and then return to the classroom. However, if this is not possible, there is a middle way: internships. Many students obtain an internship while in school. The term "internship" loosely refers to a part-time or temporary position (paid, unpaid, or for academic credit) involving some relevant professional experience. Ideally, it should be a training experience that involves mutual learning and screening by both the intern and the employer. It should be an occasion for the student to take academic knowledge out of the classroom and apply it in the professional world and to use real-world experience to complement academic courses.

Internships offer several advantages:

- insights into and an understanding of a particular career field;
- exposure to, and experience in, a professional environment, enabling the intern to make contacts and get a feel for the working world;
- the potential for an inside track to an unadvertised full-time position.

An internship's major disadvantage is the risk that off-campus involvement during the academic year may undermine academic performance, given the tendency of employers to emphasize their priorities over the intern's. The ability to handle an internship depends on the ability to manage one's time. In seeking an internship, several points are worth considering:

- Consult a variety of sources for leads. It pays to cast a wide net, but be discriminating—do not apply for every opportunity you come across.
- It takes time to arrange an internship, because they are not high on the list of an employer's priorities. Be persistent. Be patient.

- You may be able to take on more responsibility than an internship description would first indicate. Many employers will want to test you on the job before rewarding you with pay or substantive responsibilities. Remember that if you have a particular interest, you can sometimes convince an employer to create an internship where none exists.

THE EMPLOYMENT SEARCH

Job hunting is a testing, matching process. What makes it challenging and stimulating is the way you use your self-knowledge and your knowledge about the world of work. It is especially important that you do the necessary preparation or homework to acquire this knowledge. Your goal should be to learn about a career field and about your capabilities and interests in that area. Generally, the most successful job seekers have researched various job sectors; have done a good deal of reading; have made many contacts, phone calls, and consultations; and have skillfully used their academic base. They have done considerable internal preparation, self-assessment, and thinking. They know their personal characteristics, their desired job environment, their long-range goals, and what they can offer an employer. How do you go about this?

The most successful job seekers know their personal characteristics, their desired job environment, their long-range goals, and what they can offer an employer.

There are two kinds of preparation: internal and external. Internal preparation involves some soul searching about who you are, what you have accomplished, what you do well, and what makes you happy. Career guidance and testing will help you here, as will workshops on resume and cover letter writing. The process of putting together your resume will help you define your accomplishments and experience. Be honest with yourself about who you are and what you want.

External preparation involves investigating career fields in general and firms and agencies in particular. You already possess the tools necessary—by virtue of your education, you are a researcher and analyst. You should approach career planning in the same way as you approach your studies. Just as you attend classes, attend workshops offered by your school's career office. Just as you use the library and the Internet for research, consult them for information on career planning. In the same way you strive to write clear and concise prose, you should learn how to prepare an impressive resume and write a targeted cover letter. Just as you may interview various individuals for term papers and other projects, interview them for career information. Just as you expend considerable effort analyzing competing worldviews, historical interpretations, and philosophical tomes, analyze your own aspirations, skills, and credentials.

You may also wish to consult one of the many books that have appeared in recent years covering the mechanics of locating a job. Though there are many witty and engaging manuals on the techniques of job seeking, the basic components of the employment process can be stated simply:

- Identify your interests.
- Prepare an effective resume.
- Develop leads and contacts.
- Prepare for interviews.

We have, of course, already been discussing the first of these. It is useful to briefly examine the other three.

Resumes

Resumes are useful for one purpose only—to get an interview. Job-hunting manuals all have sections on the preparation of a resume, but the suggestions for form and content vary significantly. There is no standard way to do a resume, but for young people, a chronological approach is ideal. It is critical to keep it brief (one page) and neat and make sure that an employer can easily and quickly discern your assets and skills. Your resume should be technically perfect—with no errors and no typographical errors, and in an easy-to-read font that can be scanned into a computer database. The resume should convey to the employer where you studied, where you worked, and what results you achieved, so that he or she can determine what you have accomplished and what you have to offer.

Your cover letter should be more specific than the resume. It should emphasize why you wish to join that particular organization instead of another, clearly state what attracted you to the open position, and *demonstrate* why your skills and knowledge would be a good match by briefly describing a relevant accomplishment. Both the resume and a short, properly worded cover letter are important, but you can waste time rewriting them. Instead, the best use of your time would be to hone your interview skills.

Contacts

An overwhelming majority of jobs—85 percent—are never advertised. Additionally, many companies have decided that on-campus recruiting is an inefficient use of resources. Instead, many employment opportunities are passed on by word of mouth. Thus, it is important to establish a wide circle of acquaintances who know your interests and abilities, so that when they hear of a position, they will think of you. If you wish to tap into the "hidden job network," you need to consult with a variety of people of different ages and experience who are willing to help you (e.g., faculty or university staff members, alumni of your school, family friends, relations, and interviewees for past research projects).

Networking is an overused word, but with good reason. Networking is often the most important component in a job search. However, do not overuse your network—contacts are a valuable yet delicate and perishable resource. You need to cultivate them carefully. Be appreciative, reasonable, and courteous—particularly about their time. Most people you will meet and speak with have full-time jobs that require their attention and energy. They are doing you a favor by giving you some of that attention. Do not ask for an information interview if you really plan to ask for a job. Honesty and forthrightness are essential elements in maintaining this valuable access. Contacts, used properly, can provide you with excellent information about their own and other organizations. They may suggest job search strategies that will assist you, they may share stories about what they did right or wrong with their education and their career decisions, and they even may find a job for you or refer you to one. Remember, an information interview provides a showcase for your ability. Use it wisely.

Because networking is critical and a critical component of networking is a mentoring relationship, this book includes brief chapters on what networking relationships involve and on how to find mentors and work with them (chapters 3 and 4, respectively).

Interviews

Interviews are the key to receiving employment offers. Thoughtful preparation and participation are the key to a successful interview. Despite the lengthy and sometimes convoluted path that an interview may follow, there are really only three essential questions posed: Why are you interested in our organization? What can you offer this organization? What type of a person are you? If you cannot answer these questions, you should not be there. If you cannot give specific examples to support and illustrate your answers, you will not be convincing. Chapter 2 is devoted to helping you prepare for and participate in an interview.

The Realities of Seeking a Job

In conclusion, this advice should be considered carefully:

- Take the time to evaluate your education, experience, and abilities. Though you may be short on experience, you are long on the ability to analyze issues and make judgments in an intense, competitive atmosphere. You know how to organize your time, meet deadlines, and define and defend your ideas and interests orally and in writing. In a tight job market, you must be able to present your assets intelligently and to distinguish yourself. This means knowing what results you have produced.

- Employers may ask what have you done, but they really want to know what you can do for them. Make sure you have examples ready that illustrate what you have done in the past.

- Job search manuals, career officers, and college deans all emphasize the value of focusing interests. This does not mean closing doors to other opportunities but, rather, choosing which door to open first. You must be focused. But this does not mean your focus can never change. You can still keep your options open.

- The overwhelming majority of people who fail in a job do so as a result of personality, not skill, problems. You can master most jobs. The way you handle interpersonal dynamics, however, will make all the difference between acceptable and superior performance.

- Remember that one of the most highly valued experiences these days is teamwork. Make sure you can cite experiences—in the classroom, as a volunteer, or on the job—when you played a meaningful role on a team. Be prepared to explain the results of that teamwork—not only in terms of success or failure but also in terms of what you learned about yourself and the situation.

- At the entry level, be willing to "pay your dues." It is simply a way of demonstrating not only ability but also an appreciation for the on-the-job culture.

- There is no forward movement if risks are not taken. You are young. You can afford to take calculated risks—do not apply only for jobs you know you can do without effort. Apply for the jobs that will make you stretch.

With these comments in mind, we hope that the international career information that follows will lead to a fuller understanding of the available opportunities and facilitate your career campaign. You will soon find that there are unlimited opportunities for those whose international, interdisciplinary education has prepared them for the twenty-first century.

2

Interviewing

MARIA PINTO CARLAND

THIS CHAPTER is designed to make you think about interviewing and its elements: about how to present yourself, who you are, what you want, why you are interviewing, and where you want to go. You must think about and know these things because, in an interview, you choose what to reveal, and you are the source of all information about yourself. So you need to have that information prepared and polished ahead of time.

Just as in your favorite seminar, in the best interview you listen, you share what you know, you ask questions, you learn, and you strive to make a good impression. What occurred in that favorite seminar to make it work? Everyone was at ease with themselves, comfortable with one another, glad to be there, familiar with the topic, and, ideally, interested in and enthusiastic about the discussion. A successful interview requires the presence of these very same elements.

To arrive at this happy juncture, you need to be clear about the purpose of the interview, how it is structured, what to expect, how to prepare, and how to participate. Remember, interview skills can be learned, should be practiced, and can always be improved.

Although two categories of interviews exist—informational interviews and job interviews—here we focus on the job interview (chapter 3 covers information interviews). There are various kinds:

- between an interviewer and a candidate,
- with a series of different interviewers and a single candidate,
- between a single interviewer and a group of interviewees, and
- with a panel of interviewers and a single candidate.

Participation in each of these is different, but the preparation for all of them is the same.

PREPARATION

Interview preparation requires the completion of two distinct tasks: a personal assessment of yourself and a professional assessment of the organization you are approaching. A word of advice before you even begin: Everything you read and everyone you speak with will emphasize the value of focusing your interests. However, doing so does not mean closing doors to other opportunities. Focus means, simply, that you choose which door to open first. You *will* be able to open the other doors later—count on it. Being focused now does not mean that your focus will never change. Opportunities will arise that you are not even aware of at this stage in your life. Think of the bodybuilder from Austria who became governor of California!

Personal Assessment

Do you know who you are? Do you know what you want? Are you comfortable talking about yourself? You have given presentations, spoken up in class, and responded confidently to questions on current events. However, to your surprise, you may find yourself hesitating when answering questions about yourself. The questions may seem simple, but your answers must be in polished, thoughtful sentences. For example: *Why did you choose your university? What was your most significant accomplishment on your last job? Who was your best boss?* An interviewer might use these questions to discover how you make decisions, what your priorities are, and what your work style is—but also to determine your ability to clearly articulate your ideas. You do not want to find yourself searching for something to say about yourself during an interview. You need to start formulating and polishing your ideas and answers now. To do so, you must become aware of and structure the ongoing self-assessment in which you have been participating all your life. *What are you capable of, and where do you want your education and experience to take you?*

Start with your resume. It outlines the professional facts about your life. Familiarize yourself with it as if it described someone else. You should be able to produce three sentences about any fact on your resume. For example, what your undergraduate thesis was and what you learned from it, why you were made captain of the tennis team, where you traveled as a backpacker and how it influenced you. In addition, you should be able to identify a consistent theme that runs through your education and experience and leads to your goal. Be sure that your resume emphasizes what is most pertinent to the career you intend to pursue. Review the projects you initiated and the problems you solved. Make certain you understand how your course work, internships, and jobs interconnect, and how they all relate to your goals. Know what you have been responsible for and what you have achieved. Be able to quantify your accomplishments. Be able to relate your achievements to the needs of the organization to which you are applying, and focus on what you have to offer that organization.

Take the time to actually imagine yourself working:

- Do you know your work style? Do you value routine, prefer flexibility, or some combination of the two? Do you prefer to work alone or in a group, or are you comfortable in both situations? Do you want to be working with clients or researching in the library stacks?
- Reflect on your last job or internship—what did you enjoy most? Did anything about the experience bother you—the way the office was managed? The training or lack of it? The work itself?
- Are you able to cite your strengths and weaknesses clearly and professionally? If you do not enjoy writing or do not write well, you should be prepared to say that you are working on improving your writing and how.
- Have you developed a sense about the work culture you prefer and the colleagues with whom you are most compatible?
- What are your priorities and values? If you care deeply about the environment, the opportunity to manage a lumber camp in the Amazon may not be for you. The interview is not the time to suddenly wonder out loud what your opinion is on an issue or on some aspect of your experience. "Eureka!" moments ideally should occur *before* the interview!

Interviewees often mistake an interviewer's pleasant attitude and willingness to listen for appreciation and concern. Remember that no matter how sympathetic your interviewer, he is not your career counselor! This is not the time to detail your anguish over whether you should use your accounting skills to work on microfinance in Latin America or take those same skills into an investment bank on Wall Street. Your interviewer expects you to be focused like a laser on the job he is offering. Otherwise, why are you there?

After reviewing your resume several times, get together with a friend. With his or her help, formulate statements that convey your opinions about your experience and education. Remember: An actor can learn lines but will be booed if she has not rehearsed. Once you have clarified your ideas and become comfortable with the vocabulary and phrases that describe them, you are ready to present them to an interviewer. Not all the questions for which you prepare will arise in your interviews. But knowing the answers to them will inform and enhance all your responses. The process will produce a bonus: You will have created a menu of responses to hold you in good stead in a variety of circumstances.

The most common complaint from interviewers is that interviewees have not done their homework.

Professional Assessment
When you identify an organization you wish to join and are offered an interview, you need to make a professional assessment of the organization. Now you utilize the skill every good student has mastered: research and analysis. Find out what you can about the organization. The most common complaint from interviewers is that interviewees have not done their homework. Interviewers have been describing their organization for years and may be tired of doing so. They will always welcome an interviewee who is clearly familiar with the company and has already targeted areas of interest within it. Furthermore, studies show that nearly 70 percent of an interview tends to be spent describing the company and only 30 percent on the interviewee. Change that so more interview time is focused on you, and what you have to offer. And of course, if the company is making a presentation, or a representative of the organization speaks on a career panel in your area, be sure to attend. At your interview, they may ask if you were there, or you can volunteer that information. It makes a good impression.

Your research can start at the organization's website—find out about its philosophy and objectives, products or projects, subsidiaries or alliances, growth plans, board members, and so on. But go beyond the website. Conduct a wider search online and or in the reference room of your library to see what has been written about the organization. (If you can refer to an article you have read recently about it, you will make a strong impression.) Read the relevant journals so that you are familiar with the major issues in the field. And especially, speak with friends or alumni who work in the organization or in that field. You will want to know what the organization's reputation is, not just what its employees say about it. An information interview with an alumnus or friend knowledgeable about the organization can give you insight into how it is set up, as well as what its various jobs involve, what the typical new-hire profile looks like, and the salary range. If you can arrange a site visit, even better—you will see how the office is laid out, what employees wear, and how they interact.

Next, you need to prepare your questions. There are many ways to discover what you need to know without being overly blunt or obvious, and if an alumnus or a friend will answer them, you will be ahead of the game. If not, prepare similar questions for the interviewer. If you want to know what the career ladder is like, ask where your predecessor is—if you are told that he was fired after the third day or retired after thirty-five years or was promoted, you have learned something. If you hear that there were six people in the job in the last year, you have learned something. If you are concerned about quality of life (and you should be!), ask about a typical day, and if you are told there are none (which says something about routine), ask about any one day. Ask the interviewer to start with when he arrives at work. Does he come in early or right at 9 a.m.? Does he travel a great deal? Does he delegate? Are there training sessions to attend? Does he eat lunch at his desk, or with clients, or with colleagues? Is he expected to entertain clients after five? Does he stay late, how often does he speak to the boss, and how are decisions made?

These questions may elicit useful data about attitudes, culture, and responsibilities—all things you need to know before you make a decision about the organization. With this information, you can plan how to express and illustrate your interest in the job. If the organization is an aggressive investment bank, you need to demonstrate that you are a can-do type. If the company is very structured, you need to be able to give examples of how you work well within a system.

Finally, you need to consider how you present yourself. Ask for feedback from professors and friends about your presentation style. You must be able to look people in the eye and give a firm handshake (sound like a cliché?—you would be amazed how many people still have not mastered that simple social exchange!). Your voice should be firm and clear—do you lower your face when you speak? Does your voice trail off at the end of the sentence or rise as if you are asking a question? Identify and correct any little idiosyncrasies that interfere with your ability to look, sound, and act confident, competent, and professional.

The next step is to put together what you intend to bring with you. First, always bring extra copies of your resume. Inevitably, another staff member will stop by or be called in and will ask for another copy. Have it ready. You can also bring an extra copy of your transcript and writing samples as well as a neatly typed list of references. A note here: If you are planning to use someone as a reference, have their correct name, title, and address, of course, but even more important, send them a copy of your updated resume, ask permission to use their name, and *ask if they feel able to give you a good reference*. If they agree, be sure you keep them up-to-date on what job you are applying for and why, so that they can sound informed and in touch when the interviewer calls. And make no mistake: The interviewer *will* call. It is the best way to elicit an immediate, unrehearsed response.

Take a small notebook and a pen with you, in case you are required to make notes during the interview. Put all this is a neat, professional-looking briefcase or portfolio. And of course, be sure you have a good suit, tie, shirt or blouse, shined shoes, clean hair and hands, and a nice handbag ready for the interview, so that you look prepared, polished, and appropriate. At this point, you move beyond preparation to participation.

PARTICIPATION

The communication tools you will use to arrange the interview will be the telephone and/or e-mail. The first thing to remember is that no one can see you when you use the phone or send e-mail, so use notes! Before you pick up the phone, create an outline of what you wish to convey. That way, whether your make the call or receive the call, you will sound precise and professional. If you find you must leave a voice mail message, you will be succinct and coherent, because of the notes in front of you. You will say who you are, why you called, how and when you will call again, and/or where the person you are calling can reach you. And you will not leave out anything important or find yourself hesitating or, worse, repeating yourself.

When you call, be formal—that way, if there are any adjustments to be made—that is, from addressing someone as "Mr. Smith" to calling them "John"—the change can be seen as a compliment to you, not a correction. If you write an e-mail message, be as formal as if you were writing a business letter. Begin with "Dear Mr. Smith" and give your name and home address. Be brief. Make every effort to keep your message within the space of a single screen. In a busy office, no one has time to read more. This is a good rule of thumb, for it forces you to edit your letters and demonstrates that you know their time is valuable and, by extension, so is yours. Remember, the organization's assessment of you begins the minute they receive something from you: your resume, your first call, or your e-mail.

When an organization calls to invite you to a job interview, be sure you are clear about all the details, and if you are not, ask: when; where; with whom; what, if anything, should you bring; and how to get there. Plan your schedule so that on the day of the interview, you are rested and alert. Be prompt—even if it means arriving early; allow plenty of time for the unexpected, for example, a rainy day and no cabs, long delays to get through building security, confusion about which floor your interview is on. You want to be on time and unflustered. Take your coat off in the reception area, and leave it there if possible. You do not want to arrive with your arms full, and you do want to be ready to shake hands and perhaps accept a packet of material. Smile, repeat the name of the individual aloud so you get it right, look them in the eye, and give a firm handshake. The strongest impression you make is usually in that first thirty seconds. In spite of that, do not be nervous or nonchalant.

Never underestimate the interviewer. Assume he has a reason for all the questions asked. Even if he is not a human resources professional, he has no doubt interviewed many men and women, and has developed an eye and a method for determining character, skills, and abilities. In other words, he can learn, and intends to learn, from everything you say and do.

Be prepared for stress. On the one hand, experiencing stress before and during an interview is only natural. You are putting yourself and your abilities on the line before a complete stranger who may or may not offer you something you want—definitely a stressful situation! On the other hand, it can be exciting and interesting if you are comfortable enough to you allow your enthusiasm to shine through. Keep your sense of humor. No one wants to hire someone who comes unglued over small incidents. If you spill your coffee, mop it up, apologize for the interruption, laugh about it, and keep talking. You will be the person they want on their team when things are difficult, as well as when everything is going smoothly. Think of it as an opportunity to demonstrate grace under pressure.

Provide examples of your skills rather than simply stating them.

Above, I mention the importance of preparing responses to possible questions about your resume. But if you do so, that does not necessarily mean you can use them no matter what the question! You do not want to sound preprogrammed, so pause and think before you speak. Ask for clarification if you need it. Provide examples of your skills rather than simply stating them. If you cannot give specific examples to support and illustrate your answers, you will not be convincing. Never respond by simply saying yes or no. Say yes, and elaborate. If they ask whether you are good with statistics, say yes, and go on: Tell them about a class you took that prepared you for a project and how that project contributed to obtaining an internship, and you will present the image of someone competent, interesting, and well prepared. Or say no, but. . . . Or agree and qualify. For example, if you are told you are "too young, too inexperienced," respond diplomatically. Acknowledge the remark, and then provide alternative information:

> Yes, that's true. However, when I was twenty-one, I spent a summer interning at an American embassy abroad. Most of the staff were on vacation, so I was given the work and responsibilities of a junior foreign service officer. I wrote cables and interviewed visa applicants, and learned a great deal about making judgments, articulating my opinion, and defending it in a fast-moving, high-powered environment.

The trick is to juggle several notions at the same time: You do not want to brag, you do not want to appear uninterested, and you do not want to drone on about yourself! Keep it short and honest, and be realistic with yourself: Be sure you can do the job, even if it is a stretch, because once you are hired, you will have to perform and produce!

You can almost assume that certain questions will be asked in a first interview. This session, often called a screening interview, focuses on reviewing your resume and making certain that you can speak to everything listed there. If the interviewer asks you to tell him a little bit about yourself, do not immediately assume he has not read your resume. He is really asking you to package for him the important things he needs to know about you. Do not ever say "as you can see on my resume." Instead, use three sentences to describe yourself and your potential in a manner that will not only catch his attention but also give him a handle for the next set of questions. For example, if you are applying for a position in a nonprofit that does work on conflict management, remember your theme and say:

> My education in French and American universities has focused on the field of international relations, and I chose work experience in Washington and

in Africa that would complement my course work and increase my specific knowledge of refugee issues. My accounting class enabled me to prepare budgets as a volunteer at a small nonprofit, and my experience as assistant editor of our journal was helpful when I wrote cables at our embassy in Togo this summer. I have been following your organization's work in Rwanda and want an opportunity to contribute to and learn more about refugee assistance, as I hope to build a career in refugee relief.

In just three sentences you have made yourself, your work, and your goals sound interesting and complementary. While linking your education and experience, you have simultaneously highlighted your skills and goals. By suggesting that you carefully choose, as opposed to drift into, your internships and jobs, you have also hinted at your decision-making skills. You have explained why you want to work for this organization and made it easy for the interviewer to imagine where you could be placed. Because you have the potential to do many things well, you are probably looking at a range of possibilities. You may not be as clear about your goals, and your education and experience may not perfectly match the position. But do not worry.

The interviewer may ask about your accomplishments. If so, mention projects or experiences that highlight your abilities: a paper, a publication, an award. Some interviewers, more straightforward than others, will simply ask: "Why should we hire you?" This is not the time to rattle off a string of skills but rather to illustrate them. This is when you make use of the examples you have prepared. And if you are not asked, work them into the conversation anyway!

There are some old saws to avoid. Do not say you are a "people person." A sharp interviewer will ask you what you mean. In fact, do not say anything about yourself—"I'm honest and hardworking" or the like. Instead, describe a situation that demonstrates that attribute. What have you done that makes you think you are a people person? Tell the interviewer that.

At the same time you should be prepared to discuss one or two failures (everyone has them) and place a positive spin on them. Failures often come from taking risks. Perhaps you attempted too much, too soon. Remember that a risk taker can be valuable in a company, particularly if he or she learns from mistakes, so review your "experience of not succeeding." Work out a satisfactory description of the event in question and provide insights to demonstrate not only what you did and why but also how you incorporated the lessons you learned from that "failure" into who you are today. No matter how you describe a disaster, you must reveal that you learned from it.

It is a given that you always highlight your best in each answer. If you are asked whether your grades are an indication of your achievements, you have several options. If you are a straight-A student, you will want to say "yes," of course, but do not stop there. Mention that you worked hard to earn the high grades and go on to briefly describe what excited you enough to work so hard. If you are a B+ student, mention that you felt you learned how to balance study and work because you complemented your course work with an internship each semester. If some of your marks were less than ideal, emphasize that you got your best ones when you developed a focus and moved away from general courses into your concentration. If there is one question you dread—about the year you failed all your classes or something equally catastrophic—face it head on, *before* the interview.

In the midst of all this preparation, it is easy to forget that you will be in the interview room with another human being, not just The Interviewer. You must be aware of the interviewer as a person, not just an observer of your performance. He is prepared to like you; in fact, he wants to like you, just as he wants to be impressed by your achievements and ability, so that he can hire you. Therefore, your aim should be to create good chemistry between yourself and the interviewer. Sometimes that is possible, sometimes it is not. If, for example, he comes unprepared, contribute to the success of the interview by jumping in with additional information or insights about yourself and your experience. Remember, he wants to form favorable judgments about whether you can do the job, get along with his colleagues, manage people, and be realistic about your own skills and the requirements of the job. Do your best to help him come to such conclusions.

**If there is one question you dread, face it head on,
before the interview.**

Most interviewers are professionals who know the rules and are familiar with the law, written and unwritten, governing what is permissible and what is not in an interview. Because it is their job to represent their organization well and to attract new hires, they are not likely to do or say anything that is inappropriate or, worse, illegal. You, too, should be aware of what is illegal—such as questions regarding age, race, or religion, and so forth. Still, there is always the possibility that an unfortunate question will arise. You should not allow it to throw you off stride. There are several ways to respond: Keep in mind that you do not have to answer if you do not want to; but if you do, you can do so in a civil manner: "Perhaps I have misunderstood your question, but I don't believe it is appropriate for me to respond to it here." Or you can simply turn the question aside; for example, if they ask if you are planning a family, you can reply, "I assure you that I make every effort to keep my personal and professional life separate, so you needn't have any concern about my private life." Of course, there is a third alternative: You can leap up and threaten to sue. We recommend the first or second alternative!

You might also consider volunteering some information. The choice is yours. For example, if it is clear you have the job and you are talking comfortably about benefits, and the interviewer mentions day care or health care for spouses, you can certainly say, "Marvelous, I have a three-year-old." Or: "My husband will be pleased to hear about the health care benefits." But remember, you decide whether to share this information. If you are anxious about such questions, there are many publications available to help you determine what is or is not legal in an interview setting.

Ordinarily, salary as an issue does not come up in a screening interview, but it might when you are asked to fill out an application. If the application form has a space for salary, do not agonize about it. Instead of a figure, just write "open." As a general rule, it is better not to discuss salary until you have convinced the interviewer that you are a good fit for the position and until he and his colleagues decide they want you to fill it.

If the interviewer asks for a salary figure, once you have advanced beyond the screening interview, you might say that you would expect a salary that would enable you to live comfortably in that particular city, and you could even mention—if necessary—your need to pay off education loans (this might become a bargaining tool later on). Then ask what the range is for the position. Whether or not he provides a range, he will probably press you for a ballpark figure, so you must be prepared to respond. You can research benchmark salaries (see *The American Almanac of Jobs and Salaries* for a guide). Be realistic. Presumably, you are applying for an interesting, exciting job along with a number of other excellent candidates. Most organizations are able to give a 10 percent increase over their original offer. But keep in mind that if you ask for more than their budget allows, they will not hire you because they will fear that you will be unhappy with the salary they can afford. They may want to establish your salary history, so you should indicate your previous salary and current expectations. If there is a significant difference between the two, you will need to defend that difference. In short, you want to ask for a good amount—the Goldilocks salary: not too high, not too low.

Ideally, you will have decided beforehand what you want, what you will settle for happily, and what is unacceptable. You might say you are flexible (if, in fact, you are) and give yourself room to yield gracefully if they do not meet your demands, but you still want the job. Always preface any comments about a position by enthusiastically stressing how interested in it you are. Then if you have to accept less than you had hoped for, you still have room to say that you are eager for the experience and thus willing to accept the lower figure.

But do not stop there. This is a negotiation. Ask if there is a possibility for a review and a bonus, or a raise or new title at the end of six months if you have proven yourself. And always remember: Though salary is at the heart of the matter, benefits can be critical to your decision making. Benefits can amount to as much as an additional one-third of your salary. Consider health benefits—and dental and optical plans. If the organization cannot give you the salary you want, but you still want the job, see if it is willing to give you something else that is valuable. Inquire about parking and flexible hours, and do not forget that day care! Ask if they fund further education or relevant training. And do not forget vacation time—perhaps you could negotiate an extra week. Once you start to think about it, you may realize there are other things that are important to you.

All interviews have a beginning, a middle, and an end. At a certain point in the process, the interviewer will probably ask if you have any questions. You should have some prepared, because they make you appear engaged and interested, but you should also interpret this to mean that the interview is drawing to a close. The last question you ask should be about the next step in the process. When might you hear from them? After hearing the answer, it is time for you to leave. Shake hands with and thank the interviewer. Tell him you are interested and you want the job and, if you are in the early stages of the interview process (before negotiations), you can truthfully say that if they offer it you will accept! Do not be shy about doing this if you really want the job. Occasionally, people feel that expressing interest and offering a commitment puts them in a vulnerable position. That is not the case. You are affirming the interest that brought you to the interview and sending a message the interviewer can factor in as he makes decisions. This does not mean that at a later date you cannot change your mind. After all, they may not make an offer, or the offer may come in a package your find unacceptable. But until that happens, you have not only demonstrated in the interview that you are qualified but have also reinforced the notion that you are ready and willing.

When the organization actually makes an offer, ask for time to think the offer over. Both you and the interviewer may have deadlines to meet. Just as you can ask for time to consider, they can set a deadline for your answer. The time frame may be flexible—or not. If you want the job but are considering other offers (and want them to know that they have competition), you might mention that you have a deadline as well. It might speed up their response, or it might not. You have to judge the situation.

Thank the receptionist on the way out. Remember, she has already been hired and is no doubt a valued staff member. If she has anything to say about you, her boss will listen carefully. You want to always make a positive impression on the staff you hope to work with because they, too, want to know if you are collegial, and they may have a say in who gets the job. Immediately after leaving, you should take a moment to jot down the main points discussed, or any material you promised to send as a follow-up.

Follow up with a written thank-you, again expressing enthusiasm about the job. In the note, you might include additional information as well as a recap of a certain skill or experience of yours that is particularly applicable to the job. But keep it short! This can be done by e-mail, with a handwritten note (plain white card or paper and legible handwriting), or a typed business letter. Do it immediately.

If you have not heard from the organization in two weeks, or within the time period mentioned if that is shorter, then you may telephone to ask if a decision has been made. In the meantime, evaluate your performance—note what was easy or difficult for you, and what you did well or where you might improve. Keep your perspective, and keep looking. In the end, you will have developed a sharper image of who you are, what you want to do, and where you want to go—and you will be able to better articulate it. Three final pieces of advice:

- Forward movement often requires taking risks. You can afford calculated risks—do not only apply for the jobs you know you can do without effort. Interview for the job that will make you stretch.

- Every conversation has two sides: One is the ability to speak; the other is the ability to listen. Do not forget to listen.

- Prepare well, and practice, practice, practice!

3

Networking

MARIA PINTO CARLAND

A T SOME POINT, we lift our heads, leave our books, and abandon the library in search of good conversation. This is because a great deal of our learning comes from questions and answers, talking and listening. The information we accumulate in this fashion is valuable, precisely because it is not in the books and papers on our desks. Because you are the one who elicited it, the information you collect is unique to you. But that is not all. Conversations that involve learning and teaching are a means to form relationships, and they create an image of ourselves in other people's eyes. This is networking. And when it comes to careers, networking is absolutely necessary. This chapter is about networking: how to do it, what you get out of it, and what to do with it.

WHAT IS IT ALL ABOUT?

Career networking begins when you move beyond reading about a career field and begin relating to the people in it. This should start before your actual job search, when what you need is not only information but assistance. You need to reach out. You need contacts who can provide advice and details, some of whom may eventually become mentors and friends. Learning about a career from someone who is actually doing the job, and having the chance to ask questions as you listen, is very different from reading a text. You are no longer in the library, you are out in the world— introducing yourself, meeting people, and especially listening and deciding how you can use what you learn.

Networking is like advertising and marketing a product that is needed but that no one knows about. You are the product, and as we discussed in chapter 1, you need to know exactly who you are and what you have to offer before you can start selling. Then you need to be clear about what field (or fields) you want to enter and which employers in that field are

27

hiring. Next, you need to choose a marketing strategy and plan your advertising. You will learn from your networking that certain employers need you—your skills, education, and experience. But they have never heard of you, and they are not looking for you—and if they were, they might not even know where to find you. Networking is the solution to their problem and yours.

Learning about a career from someone who is actually doing the job, and having the chance to ask questions as you listen, is very different from reading a text.

You want to learn about international careers, and you have narrowed it down to several—say, development nongovernmental organizations (the nonprofit sector) and development consulting firms (the private sector). You have read about them, and you are ready to get to know them—and, equally important, ready for them to get to know you. The latest statistics say that only 4 percent of new hires are unknown to the employer. Your goal, like that of any good advertiser, is for your name—the product—to be on everyone's lips and on everyone's minds, especially when there is a job opportunity that is right for you! What they think and say about you builds an image of you: you solving a problem, serving a client, saving the day.

At the same time, you are gaining "street savvy"—learning what is going on in your field of interest; what the latest trends are, what has changed recently, and what the major issues are. You are also accumulating assurance that your interest in the field is appropriate for your background, and your new insights allow you to change your focus as you learn. As any successful advertiser can tell you, sometimes a good product is marketed to the wrong audience. When this happens, you need to readjust your strategy and find the right audience. This is not a defeat or even a setback, because in the process, you learn a great deal—about both yourself and the field you thought you were interested in—and that information can be saved for when it is needed later. . . . And rest assured, it will come in handy some day. In the words of the old song: *Pick yourself up. Dust yourself off. Start all over again!*

How Do You Do It?

How do you understand the product, plan a marketing strategy, advertise, and sell? The first thing is to always remember that you are more than simply a product—you are an individual with a personality and a passion about international affairs. And the audience to whom you are selling yourself is composed of individuals with personalities and passions, as well as power, but also with time constraints and commitments. Some will find you interesting, some will not. Some will respond to you, some will not. And of course, the reverse is also true: You are not going to be interested in or responsive to everyone. Never forget that networking is, at its core, human interaction and is therefore always complex, sometimes confusing, and usually fascinating.

So, how do you do it? Before you begin:

1. Know who you are and what you have to offer. If you have already read chapter 2, you know the drill: a three-sentence introduction, examples of your accomplishments, good listening skills, and practice.

2. Do your homework. Read up on the fields that interest you and see what strikes a chord and what does not.

3. Start strategizing. Consider which organizations you want to target, who you can talk with about the field and your target organizations, and who you know at those organizations or who can introduce you to people there. Begin to compile basic questions and lists of organizations you feel are worth exploring.

4. Become better known. You want to develop access and give as well as get input. If you are in school, speak with your classmates, but do not stop there. They cannot be your main source. Speak with the staff and professors about your interests. Whether you are in school or not, demonstrate your interests by joining relevant clubs and committees so you will meet more people and raise your profile. Attend conferences and find ways to introduce yourself to the attendees, speakers, and organizers—and, to those last, say thank you! People seldom do, and they will definitely remember you. Attend church or community events and share your interests. And finally, be sure your family and their friends know what those interests are. I cannot tell you how many parents have said to me, with a laugh and a shrug—"We have no idea what our son is looking for these days!" Even when they do not hear from you, parents will not forget you—but professional contacts will, unless you keep in touch. Be sure that when you call to ask a favor, they know who is calling!

Getting Started

Now, to begin. Implicit in this type of networking is that you are looking for a job. However, you are *not*, just now, asking for a job; you are exploring to find a fit that combines your interests and career opportunities. In short, you are asking for information. That removes possible tension from the interaction. It is never easy to walk up to someone you have never met after a speech, during a reception, or at a conference. Even if you are not a shy person, you may feel a little intimidated by a famous speaker or be afraid of being brushed aside—or worse, of seeming pushy and feeling foolish. Stop and think of all the other people you see introducing themselves as they enter a party or approaching total strangers at a meeting. They are no different from you, except that they have made the decision that the information they will gain is worth the risk that they will not say something fascinating. You can do it, and, frankly, no one will recoil in horror at your temerity! They will simply answer your question, or introduce themselves, or just listen to you—and then give you a chance to listen. You need to do just enough talking to introduce yourself and interest the speaker. What you want is to hear what he or she has to say. If you did all the talking, you would have missed the point, which is to make a connection and learn. After all, if you are shy, you are probably a great listener and can remember what was said. And very possibly, while listening to someone discuss what interests you, you will forget yourself and jump right in. Try it!

When you attend a lecture on a topic that interests you, listen carefully. And then, during the question-and-answer time, stand up, give your name, and ask a succinct question. After the lecture, go up, introduce yourself, say you enjoyed the lecture, and perhaps ask another straightforward question. Ask for the speaker's card; give her yours. Then follow up with e-mail or phone with another question, or perhaps, modestly, with some information she might not have. Then stay in touch. Try it. Practice it. And once you become comfortable doing it—or at least learn that the sky does not fall when you do—you will see that it is well worth it.

Have you ever watched an experienced businessman enter a reception? Nine times out of ten he is there for two reasons: to be seen at this event and to carry out an agenda. There are probably several individuals he came to speak with, and he will head straight for them. For him, this is work; chance meetings with other pleasant, interesting people are a plus, but it is not a party.

You need to think in similar terms. If you attend a reception or a conference, check the guest list, if you can, and decide with whom you wish to speak. Then find those individuals and introduce yourself. If it is a professor, mention a book that you have read (if possible, one she wrote), ask her opinion, and give yours. Then listen. If it is an executive, ask about the greatest success or worst event in his field. Then listen. If it is an alumnus, be prepared to say something positive and enthusiastic about what is happening at your university. Ask about the experience he had there, and then listen. Pose a question, listen carefully, ask for his card, and move on. Or better yet, introduce a friend and then move on. If the conversation went well, you wish to follow up, and feel that the alum or executive does, too, make a note of the topic you discussed, and send an e-mail to pursue the topic and solidify the impression you made.

One more tip: Do not head for the food first. By the time you turn around to case the room, your hand and mouth will be full. Wait until you have spoken with the individual you were looking for, then ask if you can get her a drink. That gives her a breather and a chance to talk with someone else but also gives you a chance to return to the conversation or break into the group that will have formed around her. However, if you find you are caught in a lengthy conversation you want to end, you can interrupt to say, "Ah, I see you don't have a drink / need a refill. Let me get one for both of us." Then, when you return, bring a friend with you, introduce him or her as someone eager to speak with this person, thank them for their time, and leave.

If you are at a table, make a point before you sit down to walk around and introduce yourself to each person. But do not give each of them your card. Wait until the meal or session is over, and be selective. If there is no general conversation at the start, ask the person to your right or left why she came, and what she hopes to gain from the event. Then listen, but be prepared to share your opinion, briefly.

Also, do not think that when you approach a stranger that you are making them uncomfortable. If you are clear and courteous about exploring rather than requesting a job, there will be no awkwardness. If you say, "I was particularly interested in what you said, and I would like to learn more because I am doing a paper on the topic / interning with a firm working on that issue / exploring that particular career field," you are asking for information. If she has time, she will give the information to you. If she does not, trust me—she will say so, and you will be none the worse off. You can respond by asking if she might suggest someone else with whom you can talk. Then tell her it was a pleasure speaking with her, and move on. No harm has been done, and it was not that terrible an experience.

You will have noticed the frequency with which the words "introduce yourself" occur in this chapter. This is really important. You are introducing the product—the audience has to remember the brand name, that is, *your name.* Make sure you pronounce it slowly and clearly, especially if it is one people have trouble pronouncing or remembering. Then hand them your card, so they can also read it. This holds true both in a one-to-one introduction and in a situation where you stand to ask a question. Give your name. You want the speaker to remember you, John Doe, as the one who asked the brilliant question!

Your network should include people who view the world differently and who do things differently. These people know about and hear about things that you might never come across otherwise.

One thing to keep in mind: Networking is not about moving in a circle of likeminded people. Your network should include people who have networks that you do not. It should include people who view the world differently and who do things differently. These people know about and hear about things that you might never come across otherwise. Knowing them will broaden your view and expand your reach. They will provide the kind of cross-fertilization that results in new perspectives and new ideas. Think of the major figures in the world. They have been in and out of the public, private, and nonprofit sectors. They are often on the boards of cultural organizations, relief groups, and corporations. They advise government officials (and are sometimes seen with movie stars!). They interact in overlapping circles—intellectually, socially, politically, and economically. These circles form a web of interaction and support in ways that enhance the performance, and raise the profiles, of those who move easily around and among them.

Having read this far, you are no doubt thinking: This networking can take a lot of time and effort. Networking can take time, and all too often, people will say they were just too busy with a current project or pressing deadline to take the time and make the effort. When I hear these excuses,

I remind our students that they need to distinguish between the urgent and the important. The urgent is the deadline; the important is finding a job. You need that perspective so that with good time management you can meet deadlines regularly and still have time for networking.

Networking keeps you on people's minds. Here are some useful tips:

- Tell everyone you are looking—so the people who know you will refer you to people they know.
- Tell everyone what you are looking for. Make it short and sweet, and they will be more likely to remember and help you. Do not make it any more complicated than it needs to be. As Einstein said, "Everything should be made as simple as possible, but not simple." Emphasize only what is relevant—do not give too much background or detail.
- Be enthusiastic: "It was a great experience." "I really enjoyed it." "I'm having fun."
- Attitude counts. People will believe you are having a good time if you say you are. They will also believe you will fail if you always sound discouraged. So do not.
- Get a helping hand; remember, some employers award bonuses to those who refer successful applicants. And do realize that a referral puts your resume on or near the top of the pile. However, this also means that an employee has put himself on the line for you and thus will be judged by your performance.
- Use alumni! And remember, alumni are more than they seem. They may have once been at a company you are interested in. Find out, and follow up.
- In fact, always follow up. Make sure it is worth it to help you. If someone offers to help, do not leave that offer lying there. If she asks for your resume, the temptation might be to just drop it in the mail. Instead, mail it, but attach a little note. It makes you look eager, and positive. Then follow up to ask who she sent it to and if you could meet that person to follow up with him or her. That is proactive and acceptable behavior.

DIFFERENT APPROACHES

You should spend a healthy amount of time on networking every week. There are four main ways to do this. *The first way is cold calls on the telephone.* Call when you are feeling your best and when you are most optimistic. Know what you want to say, and have it ready in your mind or, if necessary, in a prepared script. Do not ramble; be crisp, and be prepared. Whether the person you are calling answers the telephone or his assistant does or you only get voice mail, leave a message with your name, why you called, and when you will call again. That is easier than asking him to call you—easier for him, I mean! It also either reminds him that he already received your resume or that a friend said you would be calling. And, what is more, doing all this creates an image in his mind of someone who is professional. It is all about making it easy for someone to want to meet you, because you will sound as if you know what you are doing.

The second way is to strike up a conversation. You never know what will come of a casual conversation. If you introduce yourself and add a few salient remarks, you may have a pleasant exchange that goes nowhere, or you may make an interesting connection. At a think tank library recently, a friend of mine visiting from Bosnia struck up a conversation with a researcher there, only to discover that they had been working on some of the same issues and were both returning to Bosnia, where they agreed to meet to discuss an article she was writing. A recent graduate struck up a conversation with an executive while waiting for her flight at the airport. She boarded her flight, and when her plane landed, she received a call and a job offer from him to work in her home country. That job eventually led to a position, first in the Trade Ministry and then advising the foreign minister! That is not going to happen every time, but it does happen.

The third way is to write letters and e-mails. In this wired age, it is very easy to shoot off an e-mail. But first, think about who you are sending the e-mail to and whether they are likely to read it. Everyone is spammed these days by unsolicited e-mails. If they do not know you, they may well delete your message without reading it. Sometimes, a letter is better. A letter, literally and figuratively, carries more weight.

Both e-mails and letters should be short—do not waste the addressee's time repeating everything in your resume, and do not waste their time with clichés such as "I will be graduating this spring from . . . with a concentration in . . . and have taken a course in. . . ." Cut to the chase. You were referred by, or met them at, or heard them speak, and would now like twenty minutes of their time to talk about such and such because. . . . Then tell them you will call to follow up, and do so. This way, you have given them a heads-up that you are coming, so they will recognize your name when you call, can be prepared to discuss the issue you mentioned, and, having been suitably impressed during the ensuing conversation, will give you referrals.

The fourth way is to do information interviews. These form a crucial part of networking because they are face-to-face occasions. They represent the ideal opportunity to make a good impression and an excellent chance to ask about the field. Be frank and say you are looking for the field and the firm that best fits your interests, abilities, and desire to make a difference. This is where your poise, your intelligence, your interest, and your inquiries will help the individual you are speaking with to decide whether to assist you. Some of the questions you might ask are:

- How did you get into the field?
- What are your responsibilities?
- If you were doing it over, what would you do differently?
- Which skills are most necessary now?
- Does my resume show a person suited for this field? If not, what is it lacking, and can I correct it, or should I be looking elsewhere?
- What are the biggest issues or trends in your organization and your field?
- Which companies on my list of ten are the best? Are any good ones missing from my list? Should any be dropped?
- Which firm is your toughest competitor or the best in the field?
- Are there other firms besides those on my list that might be right for me?
- Who do you know in that organization(s) to whom you could introduce me?

On occasion, networking involves e-mail correspondence with someone who is on the other side of the country or the world. If you are approaching an individual who is far away, acknowledge this in your approach, and ask if he would respond to questions by e-mail. But if he agrees, this does not mean you should send a laundry list of questions and ask him to fill in the blanks! Ask one question, and see whether, and how much, the person questioned replies. Make sure to send a thank-you note and, if possible, a few sentences reflecting on the answer. Then wait a while before writing again. You want to be interesting, not irritating. Remember, this person's time is valuable. And do not forget that, for your own part, you need to take a break from all this every once in a while.

FINAL TIPS

Because individuals are so understandably focused on the job search, they often forget to show appreciation, and I do not just mean thank-you notes. So often people ask me: "Whatever happened to so-and-so? We had a great conversation about his career plans; I gave him some contacts, and then I never heard from him." You can be sure that if that young man ever asks for help again, he will not get an enthusiastic response. If someone refers you to another person, do not decide on your own that that individual is not worth contacting. Get in touch with him. To be sure, he may not be useful, but you will not know that unless you meet him. There is nothing more discouraging for the person doing the referring than to learn that a valuable referral was never contacted. And it is equally discouraging to see a student's real chagrin when he realizes too late that the referral could have provided timely assistance. Believe me— the original contact will ask her friend if you ever got in touch. If you did not, they will both conclude that you were not listening and that you wasted their time. Neither will be happy to hear from you again. So, make use of the referral, and then write to the individual who gave you the name in the first place, tell her you met, what transpired, and thank her. If you could not get in touch with that person, tell the person who referred you, and still, thank them, again. When I give a referral, I want feedback. Was the person I referred a friend to responsive and helpful, or should I stop sending people to him? I want to know, and the person I sent should be the one to tell me.

You can, and should, give more than feedback whenever possible and appropriate. For example, if you are a student, you may have access to scholarly advances in history, political science, regional studies, international relations theory, and economics, to name just a few areas. Individuals in your network may not have heard of a new book or its reviews, a major lecture, or a new academic opportunity. Share that information with them. It might be of interest, it will keep you in mind and in touch, and it will move your relationship to a new level on which you feel more comfortable requesting assistance because you have shown yourself able to return the favor.

Now that the search is over, sit down with your list or spreadsheet of contacts and write each of them a thank-you note.

After you have successfully landed a job, it is time to thank everyone who has helped you. If, during the job search process, someone talked with you about the field you are interested in or your own career plans, then he or she helped your job search. Now that the search is over, sit down with your list or spreadsheet of contacts and write each of them a thank-you note. Tell them that the conversations you had with them, the advice they shared, the referrals they gave, and so on, all helped you find and win the job you are about to start. . . . And tell them about your new job and where it is. Then, say that if there is any possibility that you might one day be of assistance, you are eager to do so. End by saying that you hope your paths will cross again and that you look forward to keeping in touch. And trust me; your paths will cross, because your networking has drawn you into the same circles.

Networking is necessary before starting a job search, during a job search, and for the rest of your life. As you advance in the international arena, you will move into various circles of friends, colleagues, and supporters. Initially, networking will prepare you for your job search, and then it will help you find the right job. And once you are employed, networking will continue to be of value. It will help you learn a new job more quickly, assist you in finding a mentor, and aid you when you need to reach out and collaborate with other departments and agencies. Networking will continue to raise your profile and sharpen your image so that you gain responsibility and enjoy promotions. It will also enhance your value to your employer, get you noticed in your field, and eventually attract other job offers, often from sectors you had never considered. And along the way, you will find not only mentors and role models but also good friends.

4

Finding and Working with a Mentor

Maria Pinto Carland

W E HAVE ALL BEEN involved in a mentoring relationship at one time in our lives—with family, friends, or colleagues. Mentoring can be part of a formal program, a situational connection, a friendship, or a casual relationship without any formal structure. In this instance, however, we are discussing a professional relationship. Although you may find that this chapter simply confirms what you already know, it also seeks to provide a framework for your ideas and future actions as you form and establish mentoring relationships.

In ancient times, young men and women were sent to other families to learn, through observation and imitation, how to behave and succeed in society. To be sure, sometimes they were hostages, but an old Irish word for such situations sounds more like what we have in mind: *fostering*. In modern times, this concept—in schools, businesses, and the public sector—has become known as *mentoring*.

Mentoring is almost invariably a beneficial relationship. It provides a sounding board for plans and strategies, it initiates a mental or physical move to another point in life, and it establishes a ritual of seeking and finding advice and support. Typically, mentoring is a relationship in which information and insights are shared by a more experienced person with a less experienced one. By listening to and observing the more experienced person, the less experienced individual receives personal attention and learns through precept and example. The more senior partner gains prestige and satisfaction from the junior partner's progress and success. Interestingly, the experience also lends itself to introspection and self-awareness. That is, the mentor herself must have a clear image of who she is, what she is good at, and what she has learned from life before she can know what she has to share.

When seeking a mentor, a distinction should be made between a mentor and a confidant. A mentor is usually someone on the inside—at school, at work, in a volunteer group, at a church—who can influence events. A confidant is someone on the outside, who may listen sympathetically without either involvement or the ability to influence. As a matter of prudence, it might be unwise or unfair to discuss some issues with an individual within your organization. For example, in the wake of a difficult experience, you might wish to share your immediate feelings with a confidant who could listen sympathetically. Later on, you might go to your mentor for advice and suggestions about the experience. However, whether the relationship is with a mentor or a confidant, your relationship must be one of trust and confidence.

When seeking a mentor, a distinction should be made between a mentor and a confidant.

You should keep in mind that your role model may not always be an appropriate choice for a mentor. For instance, you might identify an individual in your field whose career path impresses you and whose skills you wish to emulate. At the same time, you also realize that you will probably never get to know that person, and that he would never have the time or energy to provide you with the kind of one-to-one guidance you would expect from a mentor. Therefore, this is not the person you should approach to be your mentor. You should select someone with whom you are comfortable, probably not a direct supervisor but someone more senior, who knows you (or is willing to get to know you), understands your situation, and is in a position to be of assistance. Your mentor need not be the same sex or race, but you should always stay within your comfort zone. And of course, remember that there is no rule that limits you to only one mentor!

Look for these qualities in your mentor:

- good powers of observation, and a willingness to listen;
- the talent *and* time to guide and educate;
- a sense of tact, generosity, and understanding; and
- a knowledge of the playing field and the players.

Look for these qualities in yourself as a mentee:

- the ability to initiate and cultivate;
- clear goals and skill in articulating them;

- the ability to offer something, make a request, and give back; and
- the knowledge that most people enjoy helping and are flattered by requests but also appreciate those who return favors.

When Mentoring Goes Well, What Is Going On?

In a good mentoring relationship, the partners must establish the basics about each other's background, especially with regard to education and experience, on the path to a solid relationship. The junior partner must know what she wants. At the least, she should be able to identify a career goal, and perhaps outline the route she might take to get there, so that her mentor can indicate alternate paths and suggest important sites to see and things to do along the way. The senior partner should be thoughtful, capable, and articulate. She also should be able to provide perspective and insight into her field, describe her career path, share examples of her successes and failures, demonstrate what she has learned and show how she has integrated that knowledge, and discuss what she reads to expand her expertise in her field. The mentor should be able to offer advice about her field tailored to the mentee. For example:

- Does the mentee's resume appear appropriate for her field of interest?
- What skills should the mentee obtain and emphasize?
- How should the mentee view the field and position herself in it?
- What are the hot issues, organizations, and people, and what are future trends?

Both partners in a mentoring relationship should listen to and observe one another and be willing to give feedback on what they see and hear.

Both partners in a mentoring relationship should listen to and observe one another and be willing to give feedback on what they see and hear. Both must also be aware of what they have to offer each other: One partner may provide advice and insights; the other may bring a fresh eye and a youthful perspective. One may offer contacts, invitations, and opportunities; the other, university contacts—faculty, lectures, conferences, articles, books. Remember, mentoring is a process, and a dynamic one at that. To work, this relationship must be a two-way street.

What Can You Expect?

A successful mentoring relationship demands that you know what you want from the relationship. Is it advice? A good listener? Assistance? A professional friend? All the above? Be clear about what you are willing to contribute to the relationship. Some of what you should offer is openness to criticism, a willingness to share information, a sense of humor, and, always, behavior worthy of your mentor. Be sure that your expectations are in line with both your capabilities and your mentor's. Be realistic and be professional. Use your time with a mentor wisely; it is a precious commodity for each of you. Be a promise keeper—if you promise to be somewhere or do something, be there and do it.

In any relationship, you can create a comfort zone by negotiating a set of guidelines. You should reach an agreement on these points:

- How will you get in touch? By e-mail or phone? Day or night? At work or home?
- Where will you meet? At the university or office? At home or in public? For coffee, drinks, or a meal?
- When will you meet? Once a month? Twice a year? What suits both partners' needs and schedules?
- Why will you meet? Always have a purpose, a goal, an agenda for discussion or activity.

Make use of a variety of learning styles: discussion, observation, shared experience. Conversation is the most obvious and common style. However, observation of a mentor in action, by visiting her office or attending her staff or client meetings, can be equally rewarding. Shared experiences might include attending together a professional conference or a university class, joining the audience when your mentor gives a speech, and attending a reception and being introduced to her colleagues.

But remember: This is not an action adventure—doing things together is not the objective; doing something constructive while together is. There should be time for reflection and feedback for both partners. Each of you should make time for discussion of what you have observed in and heard from one another, so that it will be a learning and growing experience. After all, mentors do not just provide advice and support; they provide inspiration, too. And if you are fortunate enough to have such a mentor—someone who not only meets your expectations but also inspires you—remember that those who are mentored today are obliged to mentor tomorrow.

5

Choosing a Graduate School

CANDACE FABER

Candace Faber *is a 2007 graduate of the Master of Science in Foreign Service (MSFS) Program at Georgetown University, where she served as editor-in-chief of the* Georgetown Journal of International Affairs. *She is a Pickering Foreign Affairs Fellow with the U.S. Department of State and began her career in the Foreign Service in September 2007. She holds a BA in political science and a BA in Russian from the University of Washington in Seattle.*

"I AM A STUDENT in the Master of Science in Foreign Service Program at Georgetown University." These sixteen words, whether they have been spoken or written, have opened more doors in the past two years than any other sixteen words in my vocabulary. Attending graduate school is still one of the best ways to broaden your horizons, develop your professional network, and gain invaluable experience in a short period of time. As a graduate student I have had more opportunities than time to explore them. The decision to come to Georgetown was the most significant of my life so far—and one of the best I have ever made.

But it was also very stressful. As a prospective student, you are about to spend two years of your life and thousands of dollars to earn an advanced degree that will take your professional career to the next level. Most people only earn one advanced degree—and the decision about where to do it is critical. During the past two years I have come to realize just how significant this decision was for my personal, social, and professional life. This chapter is the product of my own experiences as well as conversations with current and newly admitted students about what graduate school really means and how to make the best decision.

The obvious starting point for assessing the quality of a graduate school is the academic curriculum, but graduate school is about far more

42

than that. In the field of international affairs, equal or perhaps greater weight should be given to a number of other factors, including the quality of extracurricular and professional opportunities that will be available to you and—what, I believe, is most important—how well the program fits you personally as well as professionally. It is never enough to know the programs inside and out if you do not know yourself as well.

ACADEMICS

Most of the careers described in this book require a specific kind of graduate education—a professional master's degree in international affairs, much like that offered by the School of Foreign Service at Georgetown. Joint degrees in business or law can also serve you well in such positions, as can backgrounds in fields like economics, engineering, or computer science, depending on your interest. Some careers are a good fit for those who have studied international affairs exclusively; other careers require a graduate degree to build on the professional or vocational skills developed in undergraduate education and professional life.

The best starting point for exploring international affairs programs is the Association of Professional Schools in International Affairs (APSIA). All these schools offer two-year master's degree programs that are focused on academic and professional preparation for top careers in international affairs. To meet membership criteria, APSIA programs must be diverse; specifically, at least half the students must be female and 30 percent must be international; have an impressive faculty composed of both scholars and practicioners; and offer a multidisciplinary program focused on applied concepts. APSIA recognizes the importance of the makeup of the student body and the faculty for the overall educational experience, and this should inform your decision as well. There are twenty-nine member schools in APSIA, eleven of which are overseas in either Europe or Asia, and several affiliate members. All meet rigorous criteria and send graduates to top positions in their fields, and all are worth considering. The programs are high in quality but do differ in their focus and character.

Although I am finishing this chapter during a year when my own program was ranked number one among its peers by a group of respected intellectuals and practitioners in *Foreign Policy* magazine, I caution against relying too heavily on rankings when choosing a school. Rankings may tell you how far a program's reputation will take you in policy circles, which can be very important, but you need to know more. No one program can do everything—each has a different character and sends alumni down a variety of career paths. The program that offers you the specific advantage you are looking for—a joint degree with public health, for example, or a focus on environmental studies—may be another excellent program that is further down the list. Choosing among APSIA programs is like picking a mate from *People*'s list of the one hundred most beautiful people; they are all exceptional, but you just need the one who you can love (and who will love you back).

Other academic aspects of APSIA programs are the required courses, the diversity of the coursework, the faculty, the class and program size, and the extracurricular educational opportunities provided by the school or university. The programs differ in some ways. Some, like the Paul H. Nitze School of Advanced International Studies at Johns Hopkins University, have a strong focus on economics. Others, such as the Fletcher School at Tufts University, require a thesis demonstrating in-depth knowledge in one particular area. And Fletcher, like many schools, offers a program in international business. The program at the Woodrow Wilson School of Public and International Affairs at Princeton University includes workshops, which often include firsthand field research overseas that is integrated into a final team report. The MSFS Program at Georgetown combines a small program size with a location in the center of the policymaking world; most students take five core courses and then spend their electives fulfilling concentration requirements and taking other courses of interest from across the programs of the School of Foreign Service. Thus, each APSIA program is unique, and what may be an advantage in one place can be less than ideal in another. To accurately evaluate programs, prospective students should know what they want to get out of the experience.

PROFESSIONAL OPPORTUNITIES

All APSIA programs offer substantial professional opportunities as a supported component of academic work. For example, the summer internship is a key part of each program. However, the opportunities can vary. If you wish to intern during the academic year, for example, you will want to be in or near organizations that meet your interests—this is a strength of programs in Washington and New York City. However, programs with less emphasis on internships during the academic year often provide other opportunities that are integrated into the curriculum. Your choice should depend greatly on the degree to which a particular program can advance your career goals through its reputation, its network, its location, and the internship opportunities available to its students.

My own experiences as an intern—first with the Department of State in Washington and then at the U.S. embassy in Moscow—helped me to refine my personal and professional career goals. In Washington I saw the interagency process firsthand as my office coordinated projects and positions with the Department of Defense, members of the intelligence community, and the National Security Council. This was valuable for my later study of the U.S. policymaking process. My internship in Moscow was nothing short of transformative. I rotated through three sections—consular, public affairs, and political—gaining insight into many of the ways the U.S. government develops relationships overseas; lunches with heads of other sections, including non–State Department agencies housed at the embassy, provided another window.

But the most exciting part of my internship in Moscow was being at the embassy during the Group of Eight (G-8) summit in Saint Petersburg. Although I rarely worked directly on G-8 issues, there was plenty of activity at the embassy and particularly in my political portfolio, which focused on internal politics and civil society. By attending conferences, meeting and talking with influential figures, shadowing experts in my section, and assist-ing several high-level policymakers visiting from Washington, I gained a deeper understanding of the issues in the relationship between the United States and Russia. The experiences of that summer, and the professional network I began to build, took my preparation to the next level and, I believe, made my second year of the program even more substantial. Between developing a substantial portfolio of work, attending cultural events at the ambassador's residence, and befriending the extraordinary people—Foreign Service officers, military personnel, contractors, and oth-ers—who serve at U.S. embassies, I got a strong sense of what the Foreign Service is all about. And I fell in love with my future career.

Depending on your interests, you can also review the types of confer-ences and events sponsored by the school to which you are applying, or at least those that take place in the same city. Many of my most valuable contacts have come through attendance at conferences and events on campus or in town and not always through my professors (although the words "I am taking a class with . . ." have been helpful as well). However, despite being well positioned to take internships on Capitol Hill and with various federal agencies, I decided that the best preparation I could get for a career in the U.S. Foreign Service was hands-on management training. As a result, I chose to devote my time during the academic year to editing the *Georgetown Journal of International Affairs*, a respected and widely distributed publication of the School of Foreign Service that is run entirely by students. Working with faculty and soliciting articles from experts made me a quick study on how to identify key issues in international affairs, and as chief of an organization of over sixty students from across programs, I learned valuable management and leadership skills while forming meaningful relationships with an impressive group of people. It also helped me to feel like a contributing member of the Georgetown University community at large. This choice was absolutely right for me, but it was not a traditional one.

It is impossible to weigh this aspect of the APSIA schools against one another just by reading the materials they provide. Talk with faculty and any professionals you know about the school's strengths and the reputation of the program in the field you are trying to enter. Perhaps more important, talk with current students about the kinds of opportunities they have had and whether they feel that they have been able to maximize their experience. Finally, remember that the admissions process and the career-advising process are two different things—just because you are admitted to a program and will pay its tuition does not mean that its staff can simply put you on the fast track to the World Bank presidency. You need to be able to make the most of the professional opportunities that are offered, and this will depend on you. Know what environment you thrive in, and you will have a strong sense of whether the program will help you make the most of your own talents.

PERSONAL AND SOCIAL LIFE

This is a book on careers, not personal happiness, but I strongly believe that it is impossible really to succeed professionally if you are not happy personally. Furthermore, graduate school can be an intense experience, which is also an opportunity to bond with your colleagues.

As a young, single person, I was afraid that graduate school would foster competition rather than camaraderie. However, I have found—both at MSFS and in other programs I have visited—that quite the opposite is true. Whether we have depended on one another for help with homework assignments, to get us through our exams, or simply to help us relax and enjoy life, my class has established a bond that is unlike anything I have ever known and that will carry us far into the future. My first day in the MSFS Program was intimidating. I introduced myself to a room full of future colleagues who I thought outshone me in every respect. They were older, they were very well traveled, many already had graduate degrees of some kind, they spoke many more languages than I did, and they were, on the whole, very good looking!

Know what environment you thrive in, and you will have a strong sense of whether the program will help you make the most of your own talents.

But what I discovered after a matter of weeks was that this was not just a group of star students, but a class. The diversity of backgrounds and experiences was tremendous, and all my coursework since has benefited from the variety of strengths and knowledge bases that my colleagues have to offer. I came in very young and inexperienced but with a strong academic background that has helped me contribute to courses in my own way. I represent a particular kind of American (politically independent, from the West Coast, from the suburbs, with strongly religious and traditional family roots) and a particular way of thinking (grounded in academics and theoretical analysis). There are a handful of others like me. There are also international students from Norway to Uganda, a strong contingent of Peace Corps volunteers, former attorneys and entrepreneurs, a handful of triathletes, a PhD dropout, and a former car salesman. I have learned as much from them as I have from my coursework, if not more.

I am happy with my small, intimate class and the opportunities for genuine networking that it provides. Others prefer large programs where they can specialize in a particular region or function. Some enjoy seminar-style courses; others prefer to take at least one or two lecture-style classes each semester. At Georgetown, the School of Foreign Service is home to my program plus four regional programs, the Security Studies Program, and two certificate programs—one in refugees and humanitarian emergencies and the other a rigorous honors certificate curriculum in international business diplomacy. Many other institutions offer equally varied choices.

For me, the small Georgetown program has been something of a crucible, enabling me to form friendships under intense pressure that go well beyond work and play. These include people from my class but also those in classes ahead of and behind me as well as graduate students from the various other programs in the School of Foreign Service who have become part of my life. I have been happy to have this small community even as I engage with the urban life of Washington—extensive support from my friends and colleagues has helped me perform at my best professionally. Others may find a larger program or a smaller city better suited to their personality and their needs. Among the APSIA schools, there is a program for everyone. I consider myself lucky in all respects to have found the program that was best for me, and I hope that other prospective students will likewise consider the importance of the social and personal aspects of graduate school and end up just as happy.

Making Your Decision

Even if you go into the search with all the above factors in your mind—the academic, professional, social, and personal aspects of education—it can be hard to sort through your choices. When making your decision, I strongly suggest the you consider the following.

First, talk with faculty and professionals for their opinions. My undergraduate advisers and contacts at various universities were able to give me a more robust sense of the academic quality of different programs and whether they truly fit my interests. Then, talk with current students, who can tell you more about what life in the program is like. One caveat: talk with more than one student if you feel you need to. When I found myself on the line with someone who did not share my interests, I asked to talk with a student who understood what I was looking for—and that feedback was decisive in the end. Finally, if you can, visit the campus. It can be expensive to travel there, but not nearly as expensive as the education you are about to pay for! It is worth it—for so many reasons—to go get a feel for what the program will be like and where you will fit in it—and among your future peers.

I am always amazed by the things that prospective students ask about. The questions they ask before getting to know the program are inevitably the ones we later find to have been least essential to our experience. Newly admitted students are always very concerned about rankings—which is number one, which has the most Presidential Management Fellows, what kinds of salaries graduates receive, and so forth. They miss the boat. Even in the strongest program, not every student who wants one gets a fellow-ship or a position in a corporate leadership program.

Second, newly admitted students tend to focus on financial aid to an extreme degree, allowing a few thousand dollars in the present to determine their experience of the following two years and to have a significant impact on their professional future. Money is important, but you only get one master's degree—think through the opportunity costs of picking your second choice as well as the financial ones.

Third, students often focus on the status of one or two key faculty or courses at the expense of examining the overall program. Course schedules can vary greatly from year to year, particularly at institutions that rely on a large number of adjunct professors, and not everyone gets the courses they want.

Fourth and finally, leave room for yourself to change—many students think that they know precisely what they want to do after graduation before they have even had a chance to attend orientation. Many return from their summer internship changed, or otherwise alter their course of study based on new understandings of themselves and of the professional world that they gain in a graduate program.

Remember, your academic experience will not be defined by any one aspect of graduate life but by the total package. Forget about trying to figure out which program is the best, and look for the one that is right *for you*. A recent study concluded that when there are a number of complicated factors, people make the best decisions when they gather information and let their subconscious sort it out—the much-lauded "gut feeling" that we often ignore. Choosing a graduate school can be overwhelming because of the number of factors. But in the end, you will feel right at one place or another. Your best choice of graduate schools will not be made using an Excel spreadsheet that weighs the various perceived strengths and weaknesses of the programs. It will be made when you narrow down your choices to the best fits, gather as much information as possible—through reading books like this, talking with current students and/or alumni, and visiting the campus—and then wait for your gut to tell you where to go.

No graduate program will be perfect, but most will offer you many opportunities. Wherever you go, your experience will be the best if you engage wholeheartedly in your coursework, lectures and conferences, networking opportunities, and extracurricular work. A master's degree will not guarantee you a fabulous position in any organization. But while you are in it and for many years afterward, it can open countless doors.

PART II

TYPES OF EMPLOYERS

6

The United States Government

Careers in the U.S. Government

MATTHEW MCMANUS

Matthew McManus *is a 1990 graduate of the Master of Science in Foreign Service Program at Georgetown University. He joined the U.S. Department of State as a Presidential Management Fellow and is currently the division chief for energy producer country affairs. The views presented here are his own.*

GOVERNMENT SERVICE should be irresistible. It offers a chance for personal and professional growth, and these days it is well paid. But most of all, it offers the opportunity to have an impact on your country and your fellow citizens. You can make a difference in government service. It remains as true in both your job search and your life that "timing is everything." Given demographics, there has never been a better time to look for work in the federal government!

As one makes the long-awaited transition from student to twenty-first century knowledge worker, many catchphrases come to mind. In the movie *The Graduate*, "plastics" was the future, and indeed that was good advice in the 1960s. Today's advice might be "energy"—careers in biofuels; or, more soberly, biowarfare or avian flu epidemiology, energy, national and homeland security, genetically modified agriculture, international trade, the Internet, or nanotechnology. Globalization is no longer a buzzword; it is here, and all federal agencies, no matter how domestic their mandate, are approaching their issues with an international dimension and with cadres of international staff to guide them. No matter what your educational background, expertise, or interests, the U.S.

government can offer you a wealth of experience, responsibility, and job satisfaction as it seeks to promote, regulate, enforce, or shape the future of our economy and the safety and well-being of our citizenry. You will work on key issues and participate in policy debates central to our nation and its ideals.

All this is available in an employment sector that is changing rapidly. The "new normal" for the twenty-first century workforce will bear little resemblance to that of the late twentieth century, in which many current federal managers spent the majority of their careers. This is being exacerbated by several compelling trends that are converging to make immediate planning and action imperative, including:

- A significant retirement wave among current federal employees has begun—40 percent of the government workforce is expected to retire between now and 2015.
- Competition for talent is increasing throughout the national economy.
- Differing expectations among applicants need to be accommodated; their needs and interests have shifted from past generations, which means government must offer a wider variety of employer–employee relationships.

One interesting result of all this is the potential for rapid promotion! Consider the traditional view of a federal career: An entry-level employee joins an agency and spends the next thirty-plus years coming to work five days a week, in an agency office, on a traditional schedule to provide valuable public service and meet that agency's mission. That view will continue to describe many positions. However, more and more of the needed and available talent will be interested in something other than this traditional arrangement. To compete successfully for those potential employees, the government is adapting to their expectations to create an environment that will support their success. The federal government must cultivate, accommodate, and advertise the broad range of opportunities and arrangements that will characterize federal careers in the future. In short, it is developing a new mindset. It is dealing with a twenty-first-century challenge that requires a twenty-first-century approach.

The Office of Personnel Management's "Career Patterns Approach"

Creating the environments to attract a wider range of potential employees will require planning and investment in equipment and training. Among other things, the government is working to make sure that managers and leaders have the specific competencies to supervise and manage in nontraditional work settings. That is where the Career Patterns initiative comes in. Using this new approach, federal human capital managers will be able to shape their workforce planning efforts to build and operate in a broad range of employer–employee arrangements where, for example:

- Retirees from private-sector firms bring their skills to a federal agency as a commitment to public service.
- Recent graduates form a cadre of mobile talent that deploys to wherever the need is greatest.
- Midcareer experts spend a few years on a groundbreaking federal project before rotating back out to work in the private or nonprofit sector.
- Employees work from home at any hour of the day or night.

Many of the alternative work arrangements that will attract and retain talent are already permissible and in use in many agencies. With a Career Patterns mindset, we will come to think about those different arrangements—telework, flexible work schedules, and varied appointment types—as natural and regular ways of getting work done and not as aberrations. Ensuring that the federal government continues to have an effective civilian workforce is an achievable goal. But success will be greatest if human capital managers throughout the government take a proactive, twenty-first-century approach—the Career Patterns approach—to hiring.

CAREER PATTERNS DIMENSIONS

To meet this challenge, the Office of Personnel Management (OPM)— which in most cases sets the overall tone and approach for the human resources departments of the U.S. government—has developed the Career Patterns initiative, a new approach for bringing the next generation of employees into federal government positions. Career Patterns is a way of viewing recruiting and presents techniques for identifying opportunities and crafting action plans to ensure that employment efforts are successful. OPM's focus on Career Patterns recognizes that employer–employee relationships will increasingly vary across many dimensions. OPM is considering such determinants as

- time in career (early, middle, late, and returning annuitants),
- mobility (among agencies, between public and private sectors),

- permanence (seasonal/intermittent, long-term, revolving, temporary, students),
- mission focus (program-based, project managers), and
- flexible arrangements (detached from office, job sharers, nontraditional time of day, part-time, irregular schedule).

These dimensions offer insights to both individuals and to work situations. Each employee—or potential employee—can be characterized by identifying the point in each dimension that best matches his or her description or interests. Similarly, each civil service position can be categorized by identifying the range within each dimension that could characterize an effective working arrangement for an employee who fills the position.

Unlike my own job search, which I will admit began slightly before the advent of the Internet, one no longer has to roam the corridors of power to paper the offices there with resumes and cover letters (although of course that tactic is helpful in identifying opportunities and tracking down leads!). So before pounding the streets, the best way to begin the process is to log on to the websites below, such as USAJOBS.gov and www.opm.gov or the website of any federal agency, to begin your search. Even before you set fingers to keyboard, there is one important piece of information to keep in mind: The United States is constantly involved with nations throughout the world on many levels and in many forums, influencing international discussions and protecting American interests. Thus nearly every agency and department of the U.S. government has an international division, even the Department of the Interior. Make sure you do not overlook a bureau that is doing international work in an area of interest to you.

In 2006, OPM announced the rollout of a major media campaign to draw attention to the unparalleled range of opportunities the government offers. The goal is to raise the awareness of potential employees around the country of the exciting and rewarding careers they can find in the federal government. This national initiative is also promoting USAJOBS .gov, the government's web-based clearinghouse for federal jobs spanning the globe. Updated daily, you can view up to 30,000 jobs and customize your searches by criteria including agency, job title, and location. Is your passion working with supercomputers? Or is it preserving environmental wonders like the wilderness lands in national parks? Maybe you are driven by the desire to make the country more secure at the borders or airports.

All over the world, U.S. government employees do exciting jobs on behalf of their country. I encourage you to log on to USAJOBS.gov.

I found this website to be very user friendly, with job search engines by agency, by occupational series code, and by categories—for example, searches for veterans or specialists. And a wide surf of the site, with its expansive job descriptions, will certainly give you a feeling for how the government is staffed and how to tailor your own search. The site is also updated with links to the most topical job listings, for example, Special Opportunities to Protect Democracy in Afghanistan and Iraq. As the federal government modernizes its job selection and categories, it is still helpful to recall the overall structure of most federal jobs, and a discussion of these follows below.

HOW FEDERAL JOBS ARE FILLED

Many federal agencies fill their jobs by allowing applicants to contact them directly for job information and application processing. Most federal agencies are responsible for their own hiring actions. Resumes are preferred when applying; however, the Optional Application for Federal Employment, Form OF 612, is also accepted. Also, most positions do not require a written test. Though the process is similar to that in private industry, there are differences due to the laws, executive orders, and regulations that govern federal employment.

Competitive and Excepted Service
There are two classes of jobs in the federal government: those in the competitive civil service, and those in the excepted service. Competitive service jobs are subject to the civil service laws passed by Congress to ensure that applicants and employees receive fair and equal treatment in the hiring process. A basic principle of federal employment is that all candidates must meet the qualification requirements before they can be accepted into the position.

Excepted service agencies set their own qualification requirements and are not subject to certain statutes; however, they are subject to veterans' preference. Some federal agencies, such as the Federal Bureau of Investigations (FBI) and the Central Intelligence Agency (CIA), have or offer excepted service positions. Other agencies may have both types of positions.

Position Announcements

Agencies are required to post their competitive service positions on OPM's USAJOBS system whenever they are seeking applicants from the general public and outside their own agency. Although agencies are not required to post their excepted service positions on USAJOBS, many do, so they can get additional applicants. Remember, an agency is under no obligation to make a selection. In some instances, an agency may cancel the posting and choose to reannounce the vacancy at a later time.

USAJOBS is the federal government's official employment information system. On USAJOBS, you can explore over 15,000 jobs on any given day; build and store up to five resumes for applying to federal jobs; and access a wide range of information about federal agencies and various federal employment issues. USAJOBS is also accessible by telephone at 703-724-1850 or TDD 978-461-8404. The USAJOBS phone system affords job seekers the same access to job and employer information as the USAJOBS .gov website.

Applying for Positions

Most federal agencies do their own recruiting and hiring. Agencies post their announcements on USAJOBS, along with all the instructions and procedures for applying to that particular position. Because agencies do their own hiring and have different requirements, procedures and information requirements often vary among agencies. All agencies require basic resume information, but they vary as to how much additional information they need to process your application. Examples include transcripts, forms, narrative descriptions of competencies, and questionnaires. Follow the agency's instructions very carefully. Missing or incomplete information can result in your application not being evaluated.

Many announcements allow applicants to apply online directly to the agency. Using the online method, you can decide which resume to submit for that particular job. Contact information is also given in the announcement. If you have questions, call or e-mail the contact person.

Frequently Asked Questions

The federal government has also done much to improve its overall pay and benefits in recent times, including addressing locality pay, as evidenced by the current federal pay scale given in table 6.1. For example, whereas those coming out of international graduate programs would typically receive a General Schedule level 9 (GS-9) salary, hiring agencies have recently been more flexible, based on experience before and during graduate work, in some cases offering GS-12 salaries.

Having said all this, the best time to search for a government job is not just after graduation but rather, while you are still in school. Your extra hours and summers may be just the ticket for honing your edge and finding out what your interests are. You can also obtain an expansive insight into a multitude of federal work environments. Internships have long been a staple of Washington student life, and the federal government has long been the most open place to intern in the country. It is true that some government internships may be unpaid, but in such cases, you are making a wise investment in your future. In my own case, an unpaid summer internship at the State Department's then–Bureau of Inter-American Affairs, which I held while an undergraduate student at Holy Cross College, was pivotal to my decision to accept a position as a Presidential Management Fellow upon graduation from Georgetown's Master of Science in Foreign Service Program nearly twenty years ago.

Have you ever applied for a job and been told that they are looking for people with "experience"? Have you ever wondered what it is really like to work in a particular career field? Have you ever been curious about how the federal government works? If your answer is "yes" to any of these questions, a government internship may be just the right experience for you.

Although, generally speaking, federal agencies are prohibited by law (Section 1342 of Title 31, United States Code) from accepting volunteer service, one exception to this prohibition is the employment of students to further their educational goals. Anyone enrolled full or half time in a community college, a four-year college or university, or an accredited educational institution is eligible. Individuals who are eager to volunteer their services to the federal government should contact the agency that interests them to inquire about specific opportunities.

These volunteer and internship opportunities can provide work experience that relates to your academic program, and allow you to explore career options early in your studies, develop your personal and professional skills, and enhance your ability to obtain jobs in the future. Internships enrich your future. As an intern, you are exposed to the federal work environment and can gain insight into the missions and responsibilities of various federal agencies and departments.

TABLE 6.1
General Schedule Salaries for 2007, Incorporating the 1.70% General Schedule Increase Effective January 2007

Grade	Step 1	Step 2	Step 3	Step 4	Step 5	Step 6	Step 7	Step 8	Step 9	Step 10	Within-Grade Amounts
1	$16,630	$17,185	$17,739	$18,289	$18,842	$19,167	$19,713	$20,264	$20,286	$20,798	Varies
2	18,698	19,142	19,761	20,286	20,512	21,115	21,718	22,321	22,924	23,527	Varies
3	20,401	21,081	21,761	22,441	23,121	23,801	24,481	25,161	25,841	26,521	$680
4	22,902	23,665	24,428	25,191	25,954	26,717	27,480	28,243	29,006	29,769	763
5	25,632	26,477	27,331	28,185	29,039	29,893	30,747	31,601	32,455	33,309	854
6	28,562	29,514	30,466	31,418	32,370	33,322	34,274	35,226	36,178	37,130	952
7	31,740	32,798	33,856	34,914	35,972	37,030	38,088	39,146	40,204	41,262	1,058
8	35,151	36,323	37,495	38,667	39,839	41,011	42,183	43,355	44,527	45,699	1,172
9	38,824	40,118	41,412	42,706	44,000	45,294	46,588	47,882	49,176	50,470	1,294
10	42,755	44,180	45,605	47,030	48,455	49,880	51,305	52,730	54,155	55,580	1,425
11	46,974	48,540	50,106	51,672	53,238	54,804	56,370	57,936	59,502	61,068	1,566
12	56,301	58,178	60,055	61,932	63,809	65,686	67,563	69,440	71,317	73,194	1,877
13	66,951	69,183	71,415	73,647	75,879	78,111	80,343	82,575	84,807	87,039	2,232
14	79,115	81,752	84,389	87,026	89,663	92,300	94,937	97,574	100,211	102,848	2,637
15	93,063	96,165	99,267	102,369	105,471	108,573	111,675	114,777	117,879	120,981	3,102

Note: Annual rates by grade and step.

Volunteer and internship opportunities allow you to explore career options early in your studies, develop your personal and professional skills, and enhance your ability to obtain jobs in the future.

Interns are involved in professional projects and work activities related to their academic studies. These activities run the gamut from developing computer skills to policy- or research-oriented projects involving such diverse topics as security initiatives, environmental concerns, and congressional issues. Depending upon the employing federal agency or department and the student's academic pursuits, internships will differ, but all promise to be stimulating and rewarding. Many interns develop a work agreement in collaboration with their school and host federal agency. Such an agreement outlines the responsibilities of each partner, the nature of the assignments, and the weekly work schedule. It may also identify the type of assignment and the conditions under which you will work. A typical internship means work for a federal agency or department for three to four months during a school semester and/or during the summer. If you are interested in an internship with the federal government:

- Contact the personnel office at the federal agency or department for which you wish to work. The Departments of Defense (Army, Air Force, and Navy), Commerce, Health and Human Services, Interior, Justice, State, Treasury, and Veterans Affairs use the largest number of student volunteers.
- The government also has an impressive website for student jobs, www .studentjobs.gov. This site has a direct link to each federal agency offering student jobs, and my review suggested that the list would be particularly helpful because it linked into an extensive list of federal jobs outside Washington as well.
- And of course, visit your school's career counseling or internship office for further information. Many of them receive notices of internship opportunities directly from government agencies.

Service in the federal government can and should provide you with a deeply fulfilling career and the opportunity to work on issues that matter, all while serving your country. In my nearly two decades of federal service, I have been lucky enough to serve as a negotiator for the North

American Free Trade Agreement; to travel to South America with a sitting U.S. president; to participate in bilateral meetings, multilaterals, ministerials, and even a few summits with countless foreign delegations; to negotiate as a member of many accredited U.S. delegations to international organizations; and to give plenty of speeches, write an ocean of memos, and travel abroad as a State Department adviser to several U.S. secretaries of energy. All in all, this is not bad for someone who started as an unpaid summer intern and returned to find a rewarding path to a life of interesting work.

RESOURCE LISTINGS

Agriculture, U.S. Department of

The United States Department of Agriculture (USDA) serves a wide range of international functions. USDA's **Foreign Agricultural Service** (FAS) is the lead agency administering the department's numerous agriculture-related activities and representing U.S. agriculture abroad. In this capacity, the FAS works to build and improve foreign market access for U.S. food and agricultural products, build new markets, and improve the competitive position of U.S. agriculture in the global marketplace. The FAS administers the USDA's export-financing programs designed to expand and maintain foreign markets for U.S. products and assists developing nations in the transition from concessional financing to cash purchases. The FAS carries out a broad array of international training, technical assistance, and other collaborative activities with developing and transitional countries to facilitate trade and promote food security. The FAS also helps enhance U.S. agriculture's competitiveness by providing linkages to global resources and international organizations.

A network of global attachés serves as the USDA's "eyes and ears" abroad, representing the interests of U.S. agriculture. Drawing on the resources of private-sector agricultural trade promotion groups, the FAS's overseas offices also help link U.S. and foreign buyers as well as provide trade services to U.S. exporters.

As a career field, international agriculture has excellent employment prospects for applicants with strong backgrounds in economics, agriculture, and trade. With a current staff of more than six hundred professionals based in the United States and more than one hundred overseas, the FAS hires a number of professionals each year. Most career opportunities are in the field of economics and international affairs, and require a graduate degree (or equivalent experience) with substantial economics course work. Other limited complementary opportunities exist for agricultural marketing specialists, management analysts, public affairs specialists, and other specialized disciplines. The FAS has both a competitive career civil and Foreign Service, and it thereby offers a broad range of activities and opportunities for promotion. For more information about the FAS, go to www.fas.usda.gov.

A number of other USDA agencies also are concerned with international affairs. For more information about these agencies, go to www .usda.gov. To find international affairs positions at the USDA or other U.S. government agencies, go to USAJOBS.gov—the official job site for the U.S. federal government, which provides information on thousands of U.S. government job opportunities worldwide.

U.S. Department of Agriculture
1400 Independence Avenue, SW
Washington, DC 20250
Tel.: 202-720-2791
www.usda.gov

Commerce, U.S. Department of

The U.S. Department of Commerce encourages, serves, and promotes American international trade, economic growth, and technological advancement. To fulfill its mission, the department provides a great variety of programs.

The **International Trade Administration** (ITA) carries out the U.S. government's nonagricultural foreign trade activities. It encourages and promotes U.S. exports of manufactured goods, administers U.S. statutes and agreements dealing with foreign trade, and prepares advice on U.S. international trade and commercial policy. ITA is divided into four main offices: the Import Administration, Manufacturing and Services, Market Access and Compliance, and the U.S. and Foreign Commercial Services. The **Import Administration** is ITA's lead unit on enforcing trade laws and agreements to prevent unfairly traded imports and to safeguard jobs and the competitive strength of American industry. Its primary role is to enforce effectively the U.S. unfair trade laws and to develop and implement other policies and programs aimed at countering foreign unfair trade practices. The **Manufacturing and Services** unit employs experts and economists to perform strategic research and analysis in order to shape and implement trade policy, create conditions that encourage innovation, lower the cost of doing business, and promote U.S. economic growth. **Market Access and Compliance** identifies and overcomes trade barriers, resolves trade policy issues, and ensures that U.S. trading partners fully meet their obligations under the nation's trade agreements. It resolves trade complaints and addresses market access issues ranging from intellectual property and piracy to transparency and contract security. The **Commercial Service** is ITA's trade promotion unit. It employs specialists in 107 U.S. cities and in more than eighty countries to help U.S. companies begin exporting to or increase their sales in global markets. Its employees conduct market research, host trade events, introduce companies to buyers and distributors, and offer counseling and advocacy through the export process.

ITA is headquartered in Washington. It employs about 2,500 people in various positions. International trade specialists should have a strong academic background in marketing, business administration, political science, sales promotion, economics, or related fields. Other professional positions at ITA include specialists in trade, industries, import and export administration, compliance officers, electronic engineers, trade assistants, and criminal investigators. All these positions require a bachelor's degree; however, a master's degree is helpful. In some instances, appropriate work experience (e.g., in market research, sales promotion, advertising, industrial production operations, commercial law, administrative law enforcement, and the application of investigative skills) can qualify a person for certain positions.

An important part of ITA with its own independent personnel procedures is the overseas component of the U.S. and Foreign Commercial Service (U.S. & FCS), known as the **Foreign Commercial Service** (FCS), which is part of the Foreign Service of the United States. The FCS is a career Foreign Service much like that of the Department of State and has officers stationed in over eighty foreign nations as well as in the United States. The mission of the FCS is to support and represent American trade and investment interests abroad, particularly in export expansion. The FCS pursues these goals in three primary ways: by promoting trade and facilitating investment, by developing market and commercial intelligence, and by representing the rights and concerns of U.S. commercial and investment interests abroad. The FCS's professional profile emphasizes three elements:

experience; commercial, policy, and linguistic skills; and behavioral characteristics. Junior officer entry is through the Foreign Service written examination. Competition for positions in the FCS is extremely intense, and many officers come from within ITA or the Department of State.

The Commerce Department's **Bureau of the Census** is the world's largest statistical organization and generates a considerable quantity of international demographic and foreign trade statistics. Approximately 105 professionals in the **Foreign Trade Division** compile current statistics on U.S. foreign trade, including data on imports, exports, and shipping. The **Center for International Research** has a staff of sixty-two and gathers in-depth current data on a broad range of socioeconomic and demographic indicators for individual nations as well as particular world regions. Employment with the Census Bureau requires a background in statistics, demography, mathematics, economics, or area studies combined with a reading knowledge of a foreign language.

The **National Oceanographic and Atmospheric Administration** (NOAA), part of the Department of Commerce, is involved in a number of international activities in connection with its responsibilities for the Weather Service, civilian satellites, ocean fisheries, charting and mapping, and oceanic and atmospheric research. Each of these activities has an office specializing in international affairs. The **National Marine Fisheries Service** collects extensive data on foreign fishing and acts as staff in connection with the negotiation of bilateral fisheries agreements. A small **Office of International Affairs** coordinates the work of the line organization, represents NOAA in certain international negotiations, and acts as a point of contact on international matters. A few positions with NOAA overseas also are available at weather stations and observatories for scientists with meteorological, electronic, or geophysical backgrounds.

The **Bureau of Economic Analysis** (BEA) monitors the state of the U.S. economy, including international transactions. The BEA's **International Investment Division** measures U.S. direct investments abroad and studies the economic impact of multinational corporations. Accountants and economists constitute the majority of the division's thirty-member professional staff. The bureau's **Balance of Payments Division** employs about forty-five professionals who prepare current statistics and analyses of the U.S. balance of international payments and international investment position.

International matters are dealt with by a number of other offices within the Commerce Department. The **Maritime Administration** compiles statistics on U.S. seaborne trade, manages U.S. maritime relations with foreign countries, and administers the development and operation of the U.S. Merchant Marine. The **National Bureau of Standards** represents the United States in several international standards-setting organizations, maintains contacts with individual agencies in policymaking on international science and technology issues, and offers technical assistance to nations wishing to engage in standards research. The secretary of commerce is advised on policy for the U.S. telecommunications industry by the **National Telecommunications and Information Administration**. The **Patent and Trademark Office** processes international trademark laws and regulations and represents the United States in international efforts to cooperate on patent and trademark policy.

> U.S. Department of Commerce
> Personnel Division
> 14th Street and Constitution Avenue, NW
> Washington, DC 20230
> Tel.: 202-482-2000
> www.doc.com
> www.ita.doc.gov
>
> Bureau of the Census
> Personnel Division
> Room 1412-3
> 4700 Silverhill Road
> Suitland, MD 20746
> www.census.gov
>
> National Oceanographic and Atmospheric Administration
> Personnel Division
> Silver Spring, MD 20910
> Tel.: 301-413-0900
> 301-713-3050 (Personnel)
> www.noaa.gov

Commission on Security and Cooperation in Europe

The Commission on Security and Cooperation in Europe (CSCE), also known as the Helsinki Commission, is a U.S. government agency created in 1976 to monitor and encourage compliance with the Final Act of the Conference on Security and Cooperation in Europe, which was signed in

Helsinki in 1975 by the leaders of thirty-three countries, the United States, and Canada. The addition of Albania, the Baltic states, the newly independent states of the former Soviet Union, and several of the former Yugoslav republics has increased the number of participants to fifty-six.

The CSCE consists of eight members from the U.S. House of Representatives and ten from the U.S. Senate, and one member each from the State, Defense, and Commerce departments. The posts of chairman and cochairman are shared by the House and Senate and rotate every two years when a new Congress convenes. A professional staff of approximately fifteen persons assists the commissioners in their work.

The CSCE carries out its mandate in a variety of ways. It gathers and disseminates to the U.S. Congress, nongovernmental organizations, and the public information about Helsinki-related topics. Public hearings and briefings focusing on these topics are held frequently. The CSCE also reports on the implementation of Organization for Security and Cooperation in Europe (OSCE) commitments by the countries of Central and Eastern Europe and the former Soviet Union, and the United States. Some meeting reports are published. The CSCE plays a unique role in the planning and execution of U.S. policy in the OSCE, including member and staff participation on the U.S. delegations to OSCE meetings and in certain OSCE institutions. Finally, members of the CSCE have regular contact with parliamentarians, government officials, and private individuals from OSCE-participating states.

Commission on Security and Cooperation in Europe
234 Ford House Office Building
Washington, DC 20515
Tel.: 202-225-1901
Fax: 202-226-4199
e-mail: info@csce.gov
www.house.gov/csce

Congressional Research Service

The Congressional Research Service (CRS) is a legislative branch agency that conducts nonpartisan policy analysis and research exclusively for the U.S. Congress. The CRS's Foreign Affairs, Defense, and Trade Division, one of five subject area divisions, provides information and analysis on foreign, defense, and trade policy. The division employs approximately eighty-five staff members, including seventy-five policy analysts, in several regional and functional sections: Asia, Europe/Eurasia, Latin America,

Middle East and Africa, foreign policy management and global issues, international trade and finance, defense resources, and military forces and threat reduction. Foreign affairs analysts follow political and economic developments in every region of the world. They provide analysis and information on U.S. economic and political relations with particular countries, U.S. foreign aid programs, international organizations, international financial institutions, and transnational issues such as terrorism and refugees. Defense policy analysts cover national security policy, military strategy, the U.S. defense budget, the defense acquisition process, weapons systems, military compensation, civil rights within the military, military research and development, and U.S. military bases both here and overseas, among other issues. Trade analysts follow trade-related legislation, policies, and programs and provide analysis of U.S. trade performance and investment flows. They provide analysis and information on trade negotiations and reciprocal trade agreements, export promotion, import regulations, tariffs, and the organization of trade policy functions.

The CRS employs a highly educated professional staff who are hired, retained, and promoted on the basis of merit and accomplishment. Positions are available periodically throughout the year.

> Congressional Research Service
> Library of Congress Madison Building
> 101 Independence Avenue, SE
> Washington, DC 20540
> Tel.: 202-707-9169
> Fax: 202-707-4094
> e-mail: employment@crs.loc.gov
> www.loc.gov/crsinfo

Council of Economic Advisers

The Council of Economic Advisers (CEA) is the president's key advisory panel on economic issues. The three CEA members, appointed by the president with the advice and consent of the Senate, are served by a small and highly professional staff. Ten senior staff economists, typically professors on one- to two-year leave, are assisted by ten junior staff economists, usually graduate students, and four permanent economic statisticians. The staff analyzes economic issues, provides economic advice, evaluates the federal government's economic programs and policies, and makes recommendations concerning economic growth and stability. The CEA's focus on international issues has grown over the years.

The CEA has a senior international finance economist and a senior international trade economist, both of whom have PhDs in economics and have published in peer-reviewed journals. The CEA generally hires two junior economists in the international area. Internships at the CEA are available for both graduate and undergraduate students.

> Council of Economic Advisers
> Old Executive Office Building, Room 314
> Washington, DC 20502
> Tel.: 202-395-5084
> www.whitehouse.gov/cea

Defense, U.S. Department of

The Department of Defense (DoD) and related components offer a variety of careers in the military and for civilians specializing in strategic and intelligence activities. Although many positions are filled by military personnel, a significant number of offices and agencies in the DoD are staffed by civilian employees. In fact, there are over 700,000 civilians in the DoD, making it the largest civilian federal employer. For the sake of simplification, the DoD's related components are treated here as distinct from the main department.

The DoD is responsible for providing the United States the military forces it needs for its security. The department's organization and civilian recruitment procedures are complex. For a better understanding of the structure of DoD, visit the website at www.dod.mil/comptroller/icenter /links/servstruct.htm#structure. The DoD and the military services (Army, Navy, and Air Force) have their own separate personnel offices that independently recruit civilians for domestic positions. In general, all the service components seek candidates with broad-based academic training. International affairs majors with a strong preparation in history, languages, and applied economics and an understanding of defense issues make attractive candidates. To search for these types of jobs at the DoD or its components, visit www.godefense.com.

The Office of the Undersecretary of Defense for Policy develops and coordinates U.S. national security and defense policies and conducts analysis and research in the fields of international political, military, and economic affairs. This office has four key advisers who help manage policy, finance, force readiness, and purchasing. They cover issues such as international security, force structure, counterproliferation, special operations, stability operations, homeland security, and similar subjects. The office administers overseas military assistance programs and arms sales to allied and friendly governments and provides policy guidance for U.S. military forces abroad and for U.S. representatives to international organizations and conferences. It also is responsible for negotiating and monitoring agreements with foreign governments concerning proliferation, counterproliferation, and transfers of equipment and services.

The Office of the Secretary of Defense (OSD) itself has limited occasions for hiring master's graduates with previous work experience. Typically, foreign affairs specialists are hired at the GS-13 or GS-14 levels. Positions filled at the entry level are done through the Presidential Management Fellows Program and through various other DoD recruitment programs.

There are other DoD offices with significant international responsibilities. **The Office of the Secretary of Defense for Acquisition, Technology, and Logistics** oversees the DoD's research and development activities and exercises export control responsibilities. The office is involved in export-licensing decisions, technology transfer policy, the review of foreign military sales proposals from a techno-military viewpoint, security assessments of proposed exports, munitions control cases, and technology training and sharing programs with allies. **The Office of the Assistant to the Secretary of Defense for Intelligence Oversight** (ATSD IO) is an independent organization reporting to the secretary and deputy secretary of defense, and is responsible to the secretary and deputy secretary for ensuring that intelligence oversight policies and regulations are carried out by DoD organizations that perform intelligence functions. To this end, they conduct inspections and investigations to ensure that all activities performed by intelligence units and personnel are conducted in accordance with federal law, presidential executive orders, DoD directives, regulations, policies, standards of conduct, and propriety. For more information on this office and its work, see the resource listings in the "Careers in Intelligence Analysis" section below.

Each of the military services has two offices where domestic employment opportunities in the international field are most numerous: intelligence and operations. Each service runs its own intelligence unit, which gathers information on the activities of foreign elements as they relate to the interests of the particular service. Each branch also has an office concerned with operating and planning. Within each of these offices are desk officers who follow political and military developments abroad and who prepare policy papers on issues confronting the particular service.

The DoD's civilian job search and application procedures are available online at www.godefense.com. In addition, the DoD offers a toll-free applicant assistance telephone number, 888-363-4872, which was developed to help applicants navigate the DoD employment process. General information about the DoD is available at www.defenselink.mil. This web page has links to other departmental sites that contain additional information about the DoD.

Defense Security Cooperation Agency

The Defense Security Cooperation Agency (DSCA) is at the forefront of America's National Security Strategy. The work done by the DSCA and its team advances America's interests all over the world and takes many forms—it can be seen in the modern equipment fielded by U.S. allies, in the ranks of technically armed forces of allied nations, and even in the provision of emergency relief supplies in the wake of a natural disaster. The activities of the DSCA span the spectrum of security cooperation, even as the United States' global reach spans the globe.

The DSCA's professional staff comprises more than 130 security staff assistants, program analysts, country program directors, comptrollers, budget analysts, and data analysts. Academic preparation in international relations, national security studies, or area studies provides good training for positions as security staff assistants and country program directors. Expertise or experience in defense issues, military sales programs, or weapons systems is an asset for any potential recruit.

> Defense Security Cooperation Agency
> Suite 203, 201 12th Street South
> Arlington, VA 22202-5408
> Tel.: 703-601-3731
> www.dsca.mil

Defense Threat Reduction Agency

The Defense Threat Reduction Agency (DTRA) protects the United States and its allies from weapons of mass destruction (WMD). The agency's work is wide ranging, from preventing the spread of WMD to deterrence to preparing for future WMD threats. Under DTRA, the resources of the Defense Department are used to ensure that the United States is ready and able to address present and future WMD threats through combat support, threat control, threat reduction, and technology development.

DTRA employs about 2,100 military and civilian personnel. Although its headquarters are in Fort Belvoir, Virginia, and most of its personnel work is in the Washington area, DTRA also posts personnel to Albuquerque; Darmstadt, Germany; Moscow; and the Yokota Air Base, Japan. Its employees have backgrounds ranging from nuclear physics and engineering to linguistics, accounting, policy analysis, treaty expertise, and management.

> Defense Threat Reduction Agency
> 8725 John J. Kingman Road
> MSC 6201
> Fort Belvoir, VA 22060
> Tel.: 703-767-5870
> Fax: 703-767-4450
> www.dtra.mil/be/employment_op

Drug Enforcement Administration

The Drug Enforcement Administration (DEA) enforces the controlled substances laws and regulations and investigates and prepares for prosecution those individuals suspected of violating federal drug-trafficking laws. It also regulates the manufacture, distribution, and dispensing of licit pharmaceuticals. On an international level, the DEA attempts to reduce the supply of illicit drugs entering the United States from abroad, conducts investigations of major drug traffickers, exchanges intelligence information with foreign governments, stimulates international awareness of the illicit drug problem, and assists foreign nations with the development of institutional capabilities to suppress drug trafficking.

In addition to the DEA's domestic field offices, the agency has special agents, diversion investigators, intelligence analysts, and support personnel stationed in offices in sixty-two countries. About half the agency's 10,000 employees are special agents. Minimum qualifications for these positions are a combination of work experience and a four-year college degree.

Students of international affairs may be particularly interested in the DEA's Intelligence Division and Operations Division. The Intelligence Division is responsible for constructing a complete picture of the international drug-trafficking situation and operations focusing on enforcing the drug laws; the Operations Division is responsible for conducting enforcement operations. Many employees in these divisions have investigative, computer, financial, foreign affairs, and intelligence backgrounds. For information on intelligence-related careers with the DEA, see the resource listings in the "Careers in Intelligence Analysis" section below.

Drug Enforcement Administration
Personnel Division
2401 Jefferson Davis Highway
Alexandria, VA 22301
Tel.: 800-DEA-4288
www.dea.gov

Education, U.S. Department of

The Department of Education's international activities are primarily the concern of two offices. The mission of the **Office of Postsecondary Education's International Education Programs Service** (IEPS) is to meet the national needs for expertise and competence in foreign languages and area or international studies. The IEPS administers ten programs supported under Title VI of the Higher Education Act and four programs supported under the Fulbright–Hays Act. These programs are complementary in nature and designed to benefit a variety of audiences through training programs, research, start-up or enhancement projects, and fellowships. These programs serve to develop and maintain high levels of expertise in foreign languages and area studies and increase the general understanding of other languages and world areas. Less commonly taught languages and related cultural and area studies are emphasized.

The **International Affairs Office (IAO)** is located in the Office of the Secretary and is responsible for the overall coordination of the Department of Education's international presence. The IAO works with the department's program offices, support units, and senior leadership as well as with external partners including other federal agencies, state and local agencies, foreign governments, international organizations, and the private sector. International education is an important aspect of the department's mission. The secretary of education has emphasized the significance of international education in preparing American students for citizenship and work in a global context. The department administers over forty international programs with annual budgets totaling over $120 million.

Department of Education positions are in the federal civil service. There are twenty-nine professional positions, and job openings are rare. When job openings occur, they are posted on OPM's USAJOBS.gov website. The Department of Education uses an automated web-based hiring tool (EdHIRES, www.edhires.ed.gov) to accept and evaluate applications.

International Education Programs Service
U.S. Department of Education
1990 K Street, NW
6th Floor
Washington, DC 20006
Tel.: 202-502-7700

International Affairs Office
Office of the Secretary
U.S. Department of Education
400 Maryland Avenue, SW
Washington, DC 20202
Tel.: 202-401-0430
Fax: 202-401-2508
e-mail: international.affairs@ed.gov
www.ed.gov/international

Energy, U.S. Department of

The Department of Energy (DOE) coordinates and develops national energy policy and administers the federal government's energy research and development functions. The DOE also prepares long- and short-range national energy estimates and plans concerning the supply and utilization of energy resources of all types.

International energy policy development and implementation are the principal responsibilities of the **Office of the Assistant Secretary for Policy and International Affairs (PI)**. Additionally, PI has responsibility for international energy activities, including international emergency management, national security, and international cooperation in science and technology. PI is divided into both regional and functional suboffices, such as the Office of International Science and Technology Cooperation, the Office of Oil and Gas Analysis, and the Office of Climate Change Policy. Fewer than thirty professionals staff the entire office. Professionals assigned to the office generally are trained as economists, analysts, and engineers. Individual backgrounds range from international relations and international economics to foreign area studies and contingency planning and business administration. A significant number of the staff have earned master's and/or doctoral degrees.

There are also a handful of foreign affairs-related positions in various offices throughout the DOE and within the National Nuclear Security Administration, which is also part of the DOE and runs several bilateral programs. The DOE has a jobs resource web page, chris.doe.gov, where applicants can view vacancies and sign up for e-mail notifications. For information on intelligence-related careers with the DOE, see the resource listings in the "Careers in Intelligence Analysis" section below.

> Personnel Division
> Department of Energy
> Forrestal Building
> 1000 Independence Avenue, SW
> Washington, DC 20585
> Tel.: 202-586-5000
> www.energy.gov

Environmental Protection Agency

Environmental Protection Agency (EPA) is responsible for executing federal laws for the protection of the environment. EPA's mandate covers water quality, air quality, waste, pesticides, toxic substances, and radiation. Within these broad areas of responsibility, EPA program efforts include research and development and the development, implementation, and enforcement of regulations. EPA is involved in many policy and technical aspects of transboundary, regional, and global environmental and health-related issues. These international activities also include information sharing within many international organizations and directly with other countries on common issues, problems, and solutions.

EPA's involvement in international efforts is coordinated by the **Office of International Affairs**, which runs bilateral programs with other countries. Qualifications for employment with the office may include education and experience in international affairs, environmental issues, or management, with a demonstrated ability to work on policy and technical issues that are the responsibilities of EPA. Internships for current students with the Office of International Affairs are available through the Environmental Careers Organization (see www.eco.org). EPA also runs a full-time employment program for recent graduates called the EPA Intern Program.

> Environmental Protection Agency
> Headquarters
> 1200 Pennsylvania Avenue, NW
> Washington, DC 20460
> Tel.: 202-564-0300
> www.epa.gov/ezhire

Environmental Protection Agency
Office of International Affairs (2610R)
1200 Pennsylvania Avenue, NW
Washington, DC 20460
Tel.: 202-564-6613
Fax: 202-565-2411
www.epa.gov/oia

Export-Import Bank of the United States

The Export-Import Bank of the United States (Ex-Im Bank) is an independent agency of the U.S. government that facilitates the export financing of U.S. goods and services. It supplements and encourages, but does not compete with, commercial financing. By neutralizing the effect of export credit subsidies from other governments and by absorbing risks that the private sector will not accept, the Ex-Im Bank enables U.S. exporters to compete effectively in overseas markets on the basis of price, performance, delivery, and service. The Ex-Im Bank's programs include the Working Capital Guarantee Program, the Export Credit Insurance Program, and several finance and loan guarantee programs.

The Ex-Im Bank is a small but dynamic agency with about 360 employees working nationwide. It offers career opportunities for engineers, economists, attorneys, and resource management specialists. Competition for jobs is keen. Staff vacancies generally are filled through individual vacancy announcements that outline specific job duties, salary, and qualification requirements. The announcements are widely distributed to colleges and universities, federal job information centers, professional organizations, newspapers, and the Internet. About twenty-five professional positions are filled annually. Most jobs at the Ex-Im Bank require OPM competitive eligibility. They are filled from a federal listing of qualified candidates, which is open to those with undergraduate degrees or significant work experience. For interested applicants with a graduate degrees or relevant experience, there are some trainee positions open to those with majors in finance, accounting, or economics. The bank also employs a small number of students during the year under various intern programs.

Export-Import Bank of the United States
Office of Human Resources
811 Vermont Avenue, NW
Washington, DC 20571
Tel.: 202-565-3946
www.exim.gov

Federal Bureau of Investigation

The responsibility for investigating violations of most federal laws and civil matters of interest to the U.S. government rests with the Federal Bureau of Investigation (FBI). In addition to these duties, the FBI provides the executive branch with information relating to national security and interacts with cooperating foreign police and security services.

The principal professional position within the FBI is that of special agent. Applicants for this position must be U.S. citizens who have reached their twenty-third but not thirty-seventh birthday and qualify under one of four entrance programs: the Law Program, for those with a law degree; the Accounting Program, for those with an accounting degree; the Language Program, for those with at least a bachelor's degree and fluency in a foreign language for which the FBI has a current need; and the Diversified Program, which covers any academic program. Applicants must possess a four-year college degree and three years of full-time work experience. There are currently more than 10,000 special agents within the FBI. All special agent applicants must pass a battery of written tests (Phase 1) and a structured interview and written exercise (Phase II) of the special agent selection system. Applicants must also undergo a drug test, polygraph examination, and physical examination. Besides special agents, the FBI employs language specialists who possess the ability to translate foreign languages.

Those interested in a position with the FBI should contact the applicant coordinator at the nearest FBI field office, listed under U.S. government in the telephone directory, or visit the FBI's careers website, www.fbijobs.gov. For more information on intelligence-related careers with the FBI, see the resource listings in the "Careers in Intelligence Analysis" section below.

Federal Communications Commission

The Federal Communications Commission (FCC) is responsible for U.S. telecommunications policy. The core functions of the **International Bureau** are to develop, recommend, and administer policies, standards, procedures, and programs for the regulation of international telecommunications facilities and services and the licensing of satellite facilities under its jurisdiction. The bureau also assumes the principal representational role for FCC activities in relation to international organizations.

The International Bureau currently consists of three divisions. The Policy Division has responsibility for the following key areas: (1) petitions for reconsideration addressed to the bureau, (2) international spectrum rulemakings, (3) international telecommunications policy development, and (4) service to the commission as experts on Section 310 foreign business and foreign government ownership issues in merger proceedings. The Satellite Division is responsible for (1) satellite policy development and rulemakings, (2) satellite licensing activities, and (3) service to the commission as consultants on satellite and satellite-related spectrum issues. The Strategic Analysis and Negotiations Division is charged with (1) economic and industry analysis of trends in international communications markets and services; (2) the bureau's consolidated intergovernmental and regional leadership, negotiation, and planning functions; and (3) research and studies concerning international regulatory trends, as well as their implications for U.S. policy.

> International Bureau
> Federal Communications Commission
> 445 12th Street, SW
> Washington, DC 20554
> Tel.: 202-418-0500
> www.fcc.gov

Federal Maritime Commission

The Federal Maritime Commission (FMC) was established as an independent regulatory agency in 1961. The FMC is composed of five commissioners appointed for five-year terms by the president with the advice and consent of the Senate. The president designates one commissioner as chairman, who is the chief executive and administrative officer of the agency.

The principal statutes or statutory provisions administered by the FMC are the Shipping Act of 1984; the Foreign Shipping Practices Act of 1988; section 19 of the Merchant Marine Act, 1920; and Public Law No. 89–777. All these were amended and modified by the Ocean Shipping Reform Act of 1998.

The FMC's regulatory responsibilities are as follows:

- Protecting shippers and carriers engaged in U.S. foreign commerce from restrictive or unfair foreign laws, regulations, or business practices that harm U.S. shipping interests or ocean-borne trade.
- Reviewing agreements between and among ocean common carriers and marine terminal operators to ensure that they do not have excessively anticompetitive effects.

- Reviewing and maintaining filings of service contracts between ocean common carriers and shippers, and guarding against anticompetitive practices and other unfair prohibited acts.
- Ensuring that common carriers' published rates and charges are just and reasonable and do not unfairly undercut their private competitors.
- Issuing passenger vessel certificates evidencing financial responsibility of vessel owners or charter boat owners to pay judgments for personal injury, death, or the nonperformance of a voyage or cruise.
- Licensing ocean transportation intermediaries and ensuring that they maintain bonds to protect the public from unqualified, insolvent, or dishonest companies.
- Investigating the practices of common carriers, terminal operators, and ocean transportation intermediaries to ensure that they do not engage in practices prohibited by the Shipping Act of 1984 or other FMC-administered statutes.

The FMC regulates the ocean-borne foreign commerce of the United States, assures that U.S. international trade is open to all nations on a reciprocal basis, and protects against unauthorized activities in U.S. ocean-borne commerce. The FMC's work includes attempting to eliminate the discriminatory practices of foreign governments against U.S. shipping and trying to achieve comity between the United States and its trading partners. The FMC employs about 125 people in its headquarters and field offices. Most of the professionals have backgrounds in law, transportation, business administration, and economics.

> Federal Maritime Commission
> 800 North Capitol Street, NW
> Washington, DC 20573
> Tel.: 202-523-5773 (Personnel)
> www.fmc.gov

Federal Reserve Bank of New York

The Federal Reserve Bank of New York (FRBNY) is one of twelve regional Federal Reserve banks that, along with the Federal Reserve Board in Washington and the Federal Open Market Committee (FOMC), comprise the Federal Reserve System, the nation's central bank. Although all the Federal Reserve banks have many responsibilities in common, the FRBNY has some unique responsibilities. At the direction of the FOMC, the top policymaking unit of the Federal Reserve System, the FRBNY conducts open market operations on behalf of the entire system. Open market operations—the purchase and sale of U.S. government, agency, and mortgage-backed securities in order to stabilize the federal funds rate at, or near, the level targeted by the FOMC—are the means through which the system conducts monetary policy. Uniquely within the Federal Reserve System, the FRBNY manages accounts, serves as an agent in foreign exchange and financial markets, and provides advice and training for foreign central banks. On the unusual occasions when the Treasury Department calls for intervention in the foreign exchange markets, the FRBNY carries out appropriate operations on behalf of the system and the Treasury. The presence in the New York region of many of the largest U.S. and foreign banks ensures that the FRBNY has an active and important role in bank supervision and regulation.

Many jobs with a significant international component exist at the FRBNY. For example, staff members of Emerging Markets and International Affairs evaluate risks, financial issues, and capital market developments in emerging and newly industrialized economies, and they collaborate with foreign central banks, official international institutions, and the private sector to address global and systemic challenges. The FRBNY recruits students with a variety of undergraduate and postgraduate degrees. The FRBNY places a high value on highly developed quantitative, critical reasoning, and communication skills, as well as the ability to work successfully alone and in teams. Many positions require a strong background in finance, accounting, and economics.

> Federal Reserve Bank of New York
> 33 Liberty Street
> New York, NY 10045
> Tel.: 212-720-6130
> www.newyorkfed.org

Federal Reserve Board

The primary function of the Federal Reserve Board is the setting of monetary policy to foster stable economic conditions and long-term economic growth. International career opportunities exist with the **Division of International Finance**. The division analyzes the international policies and operations of the Federal Reserve System, major economic and financial developments abroad that affect the U.S. economy and U.S. international transactions, and a wide range of issues connected with the working of the international monetary system and the balance of payments adjustment process. The staff produces both analysis and interpretation of recent developments and research projects of a longer-run nature. Staff members regularly serve on U.S. delegations to international financial conferences and maintain liaison with the central banks of foreign countries.

The division has a continuing need for economists who already have achieved or are working toward their doctorates and for exceptionally qualified economists holding a master's degree. In addition, many opportunities exist for applicants with a bachelor's degree in economics, strong quantitative skills, and a knowledge of computer programming to work closely with the economists and assist in basic research projects.

The supervision and regulation of foreign banks operating in the United States and of foreign branches of state member banks are provided by the **Division of Banking Supervision and Regulation**. The division also analyzes specific issues of monetary and international financial policies that have a bearing on regulatory policy. Individuals interested in pursuing employment opportunities as a financial analyst in Banking Supervision and Regulation should possess an MBA in a related field or an undergraduate degree with one to three years of relevant work experience.

The Federal Reserve Board, located in Washington, has a staff of more than 1,500. Most professional positions require formal education or specialized equivalent experience is such fields as economics, finance, law, and data processing.

Board of Governors of the Federal Reserve System
20th Street and Constitution Avenue, NW
Mail Stop 129 (Human Resources)
Washington, DC 20551
Tel.: 202-452-3880 (Personnel)
Fax: 202-452-3863
www.federalreserve.gov

Government Accountability Office

The U.S. Government Accountability Office (GAO) is an independent agency in the legislative branch of the federal government. Commonly known as the "investigative arm of Congress" or the "congressional watchdog," the GAO examines how taxpayer dollars are spent and advises lawmakers and agency heads on ways to make the government work better.

The GAO exists to support Congress in meeting its constitutional responsibilities and to help improve the performance and ensure the accountability of the federal government for the benefit of the American people. This agency provides Congress with timely information that is professional, objective, fact based, nonpartisan, nonideological, fair, and balanced. The GAO is unique among legislative branch support agencies in that its reports often present original data and professional analyses drawn from extensive fieldwork.

Of particular interest to those searching for an internationally oriented career is the GAO's **International Affairs and Trade Team**, which analyzes the effectiveness of U.S. foreign aid programs and assesses how trade agreements further U.S. interests, among other issues. Its oversight responsibilities include the State Department, the U.S. Agency for International Development, the Office of the U.S. Trade Representative, the International Monetary Fund, the United Nations, the World Bank, and some Department of Defense functions. Work in other GAO teams, such as the **Defense Capabilities and Management** and **Information Technology** teams, frequently involves international issues. In addition, the GAO's field offices increasingly are involved in carrying out work in an international environment.

The GAO employs more than 3,200 people. The GAO's professionals come from a variety of educational backgrounds, including public administration, public policy, computer science, business, political science, international affairs, and accounting. The GAO also employs specialists in the social sciences, economics, computer science, mathematics, and other specialties. Approximately 200 new professionals are hired each year to work in the GAO's Washington headquarters or in field offices. The GAO maintains a human capital system separate from the executive branch. Employment at the GAO requires a bachelor's degree or equivalent work experience as a minimum. Most candidates have master's degrees, and some have doctorates.

Talent Acquisition and Human Capital Consulting Center
U.S. Government Accountability Office
441 G Street, NW
Washington, DC 20548
Tel.: 202-512-6092
www.gao.gov

General Services Administration

The General Services Administration (GSA) leverages the buying power of the federal government to obtain the best value for taxpayers and federal customers. In this capacity, the GSA provides responsible asset management to deliver superior workplaces, high-quality acquisition services, and expert business solutions. The GSA's responsibilities include the construction and management of federal buildings, the procurement and management of supplies and services for the government, and the development of innovative and effective management policies. The GSA employs approximately 13,000 people in all fifty states, the District of Columbia, Belgium, Germany, Italy, Japan, Korea, Puerto Rico, the United Kingdom, and the Virgin Islands. The majority of the GSA's international work involves the procurement and distribution of supplies and services and the administration of a small amount of U.S. property located overseas. The majority of the professionals with the GSA have academic backgrounds in business, finance, economics, engineering, and computer sciences. Vacancies are posted daily on the GSA website.

> General Services Administration
> 1800 F Street, NW
> Washington, DC 20405
> Tel.: 202-501-0370 (Human Resources)
> Fax: 202-219-0149
> www.gsa.gov

Health and Human Services, U.S. Department of

The Department of Health and Human Services (HHS) is the U.S. government's principal agency for protecting the health of all Americans and providing essential human services, especially for those who are least able to help themselves. With more than 65,000 employees and a budget of $460 billion in fiscal year 2002, HHS administers more grant dollars than all other federal agencies combined. The department administers more than 300 programs, which are managed by eleven operating divisions, including eight agencies of the U.S. Public Health Service and three human service agencies. HHS's eleven operating divisions are the **National Institutes of Health (NIH)**, the **Food and Drug Administration**, the **Centers for Disease Control and Prevention**, the **Agency for Toxic Substances and Disease Registry**, the **Indian Health Service**, the **Health Resources and Services Administration**, the **Substance Abuse and Mental Health Services Administration**, the **Agency for Healthcare Research and Quality**, the **Centers for Medicare and Medicaid Services**, the **Administration for Children and Families,** and the **Administration on Aging**.

Within HHS, the **Office of Global Health Affairs** is responsible for:

- Representing the department to other governments, other federal departments and agencies, international organizations and the private sector on international and refugee health issues.
- Developing U.S. policy and strategy positions related to health issues and facilitating involvement of the Public Health Service in support of these positions and in collaboration with other agencies and organizations.
- Providing leadership and coordination for bilateral programs with selected countries, such as the U.S.–Russian and U.S.–South Africa Health Committee, in support of presidential and vice presidential initiatives.
- Facilitating cooperation by Public Health Service Operating Divisions with the Agency for International Development.
- Providing policy guidance and coordination on refugee health policy issues, in collaboration with Public Health Service Operating Divisions, the Office of Refugee Resettlement, the Department of State, and others.

Additionally, the mission of NIH's **Fogarty International Center** is to promote and support scientific research and training internationally so as to reduce disparities in global health.

U.S. Department of Health and Human Services
200 Independence Avenue, SW
Washington, DC 20201
Tel.: 202-619-0257
www.hhs.gov

U.S. Department of Health and Human Services
Office of Global Health Affairs
Office of the Director
5600 Fishers Lane
Room 18-105
Rockville, MD 20957
Tel.: 301-443-1774
Fax: 301-443-6288

Homeland Security, U.S. Department of
The Department of Homeland Security (DHS) was created by the Homeland Security Act of 2002 to coordinate and provide a base for the key national security efforts of various institutions. Upon its creation in 2003, the DHS absorbed or replaced a number of other offices and agencies by bringing them under four main directorates: the **Border and Transportation Security Directorate**, which combined the U.S. Customs Service,

part of the Immigration and Naturalization Service, and the Transportation Security Administration, among others; the **Emergency Preparedness and Response Directorate**, which coordinates the Federal Emergency Management Agency (FEMA) and other key offices; the **Science and Technology Directorate**; and the **Information Analysis and Infrastructure Protection Directorate**. The **United States Secret Service** and the **Coast Guard** also joined the DHS.

Now the third-largest Cabinet agency, the DHS employs over 180,000 men and women in a variety of areas, many of which have an international component. Of particular interest to students of international affairs are the **Office of Intelligence and Analysis** and the **Citizenship and Immigration Services**, whereas those interested in international law enforcement should explore the **Immigration and Customs Enforcement Service** and the **Secret Service**.

Citizenship and Immigration Services (CIS) is one of the largest services within the DHS, with approximately 15,000 employees in around 250 headquarters and field offices around the world. The CIS fulfills the service and benefit functions that were formerly part of the Department of Justice's Immigration and Naturalization Service. The CIS has an extensive overseas presence. It works with the Department of State to adjudicate immigrant visa petitions, naturalization petitions, and asylum and refugee applicants coming under either U.S.-legislated refugee programs or referrals from the UN High Commission for Refugees; among other functions. It also provides resources for new immigrants and refugees.

Immigration and Customs Enforcement (ICE) also has around 15,000 employees across 400 offices in the United States and 50 offices overseas. It is the DHS's largest investigative arm and is responsible for enforcing customs and immigration laws and providing security for federal buildings. Its work is primarily in law enforcement; most employees are therefore either law enforcement, security, or intelligence professionals or administrative support.

Most positions in these services are filled through OPM's USAJOBS .gov website. The number of available positions varies weekly. ICE criminal investigators (special agents) are not hired through the typical application process, but through "special agent recruiters" at the special agent-in-charge offices throughout the country. There are also several opportunities for students. For comprehensive information on the many career opportunities available through the DHS, visit www.dhs.gov/

careers. For information on intelligence-related careers with the DHS, see the resource listings in the "Careers in Intelligence Analysis" section below.

> U.S. Department of Homeland Security
> Washington, DC 20528
> Tel.: 202-282-8000
> www.dhs.gov

Inter-American Foundation

The Inter-American Foundation was established to promote social change and development in Latin America and the Caribbean. It provides support through grants and the financing of projects for private, community-level, and self-help efforts in solving basic social and economic problems. This approach springs from the belief that only the recipients themselves can define their communities' problems and needs. The wide variety of projects funded by the foundation has included workers' self-managed enterprises, peasant associations, informal education, credit and production cooperatives, cultural awareness programs, self-help housing, legal aid clinics, and worker-run bank and agricultural extension services.

The foundation has an average turnover of one or two positions per year. There is a tendency to hire social science generalists rather than people with specific, technically oriented backgrounds. The skills needed by the foundation are defined by its wide array of activities. Employees have backgrounds in such diverse fields as economics, rural and urban development, finance, agriculture, international affairs, education, statistics, and industrial management. Although a master's degree is not a prerequisite for employment, virtually all professionals on the staff have at least that degree.

> Inter-American Foundation
> 901 N. Stuart Street, 10th Floor
> Arlington, VA 22203
> Tel.: 703-306-4301
> Fax: 703-306-4365
> www.iaf.gov

Interior, U.S. Department of the

As the nation's principal conservation agency, the U.S. Department of the Interior (DOI) has responsibility for most of the U.S. nationally owned public lands and natural resources. The Department's **Office of Policy**

Analysis includes staff for international affairs and international trade. The international affairs staff provides oversight and coordination of bureau international activities. For almost a hundred years, the DOI has conducted international activities that facilitate its domestic responsibilities, including managing protected areas adjacent to international borders; sharing scientific findings, technology, and other information beneficial to domestic programs; protecting migratory wildlife; fighting cross-border fires; meeting the DOI's congressionally mandated international activities such as elephant, rhinoceros, and tiger protection and migratory bird preservation; supporting U.S. foreign policy objectives at the request of the White House or State Department, including providing technical and scientific advice on such issues as managing water and other natural resources and addressing environmental hazards; and meeting U.S. treaty obligations.

Of DOI's 65,740 employees, just 125, or 0.2 percent, work almost exclusively on international programs. Almost all these employees are located within the DOI technical bureaus (the U.S. Fish and Wildlife Service and the U.S. Geological Survey have the largest staff). Despite the many offices within the department with some form of international responsibility, employment opportunities for graduates in international affairs are extremely limited. In most cases, the professionals are trained in the particular discipline of the office involved rather than in international studies.

> U.S. Department of the Interior
> 1849 C Street, NW
> Washington, DC 20240
> Tel.: 202-208-3100
> www.doi.gov/hrm/doijobs.html

International Trade Commission
The U.S. International Trade Commission (ITC) studies and makes recommendations on international trade and tariffs to the president, Congress, and government agencies. The major thrust of the ITC's work is the analysis of all possible effects of imported products on U.S. industries. Special emphasis is placed on the effects of imports from countries with nonmarket economic systems. The ITC also conducts studies on a broad range of topics relating to international trade and publishes summaries of trade and tariff information. To carry out its responsibilities, the ITC must engage in extensive research and maintain a high degree of expertise

in all matters relating to the commercial and international trade policy of the United States.

The staff of the ITC, which numbers about 240 professionals, provides six commissioners with the expertise required to carry out the responsibilities of the organization. International economists form one of the primary groups of employees on the staff. They must have a minimum of twenty-one credit hours in economics and three credit hours in statistics earned at the bachelor's and/or master's level. Of particular importance are courses in microeconomics, industrial and labor economics, and international economics and trade. Other prevalent staff positions include international trade analysts, investigatory economists (both frequently require course work in accounting and international economics), and attorneys (especially patent, antitrust, and customs-related). Additional academic specializations of special interest to the ITC are marketing, international law, international trade, business administration, and regional studies.

> U.S. International Trade Commission
> 500 E Street, SW
> Washington, DC 20436
> Tel.: 202-205-2651 (Human Resources)
> www.usitc.gov

Justice, U.S. Department of

Within the Department of Justice, most international legal issues are handled by five of the seven department divisions: Antitrust, Civil, Criminal, Environment and Natural Resources, and National Security. The **Antitrust Division** is responsible for the enforcement of federal antitrust laws. The **Foreign Commerce Section** of the division is responsible for the implementation of division policy on issues of trade and international antitrust enforcement. The section is active in the interagency process of administering trade laws and assessing the competitive aspects of U.S. trade policy. The Foreign Commerce Section is the division's liaison with international organizations, including antitrust enforcement agencies of the European communities, Canada, and other countries. In conjunction with the State Department, the section exchanges information with foreign governments concerning investigations and cases that the division initiates involving foreign corporations and nationals.

The **Civil Division** represents the United States in virtually all types of civil proceedings. Litigation based on international maritime agreements is handled by the division's **Torts Branch. Commercial Litigation Branch** attorneys within the Civil Division represent the United States in virtually all cases initiated in the Court of International Trade. These cases include challenges brought by domestic and foreign producers contesting antidumping and countervailing duty investigations, as well as actions commenced by the government to enforce civil penalties for customs fraud. Attorneys in the Civil Division's **Office of Foreign Litigation** pursue claims on behalf of the United States and defend the government's interests in foreign courts. Foreign litigation attorneys frequently become involved in white-collar crime cases and the recovery of offshore assets. Decisions in this area often have significant foreign policy implications. The Civil Division's **Federal Programs Branch** handles the defense of challenged government activity ranging from domestic welfare programs to international agreements. The Federal Programs Branch's responsibilities include matters as diverse as litigation involving federal banking statutes and regulations to suits raising national security and foreign policy issues.

In enforcing most of the nation's criminal laws, the **Criminal Division** participates in criminal justice activities involving foreign parties where a centralized national approach is desired. The Criminal Division's **Office of International Affairs** supports the department's legal divisions, the U.S. attorneys, and state and local prosecutors regarding questions of foreign and international law, including issues related to extradition and mutual legal assistance treaties. The office also coordinates all international evidence gathering. In concert with the State Department, the office engages in the negotiation of new extradition and mutual legal assistance treaties and executive agreements throughout the world. Office attorneys also participate in a number of committees established under the auspices of the United Nations and other international organizations that are directed at resolving a variety of international law enforcement problems such as narcotics trafficking and money laundering. **The Office of Overseas Prosecutorial Development, Assistance, and Training** offers assistance and training and related support activities in a variety of international contexts.

The **Environment and Natural Resources Division** is the nation's environmental lawyer. The **Policy, Legislation, and Special Litigation Section** of the division coordinates and directs the division's legislative program, including representing the department on interagency groups that develop the administration's position on legislation and at meetings with congressional staff. The section's attorneys coordinate both the division's international environmental activities and environmental justice activities.

The new **National Security Division** has been established to deal with terrorism cases and matters as well as intelligence and other related issues. It will also supervise the investigation and prosecution of cases affecting national security, foreign relations, and the export of military and strategic commodities and technology.

The **Foreign Claims Settlement Commission** is an independent, quasi-judicial agency within the department, responsible for adjudicating claims of U.S. nationals against foreign governments that have nationalized, expropriated, or otherwise taken property of those nationals without paying compensation as required under international law.

Also, various **United States Attorneys' offices** from time to time handle cases or matters involving international matters. Finally, various departmental legal policy and leadership offices, as well as the General Counsel offices of the department's investigative agencies, such as the FBI and the DEA, may be called on to deal with issues, matters, or cases having an international association.

The bulk of the professionals employed by these offices and divisions are attorneys assisted by paralegals and other support staff. Attorneys and law students interested in employment with any departmental organization are encouraged to visit the Office of Attorney Recruitment and Management web page, www.usdoj.gov/oarm/, for detailed information about the department's legal employment programs and the legal responsibilities of each organization in the department. A listing of current department attorney vacancies is available at ww.usdoj.gov/oarm/attvacancies.html.

U.S. Department of Justice
Office of Attorney Recruitment and Management
Room 5100, 20 Massachusetts Avenue, NW
Washington, DC 20530
Tel.: 202-514-8900

General Employment:
Justice Management Division
Personnel Staff
Suite 1175, 1331 Pennsylvania Avenue, NW
Washington, DC 20530
Tel.: 202-514-6818
www.usdoj.gov

Labor, U.S. Department of
The Department of Labor's international activities are concentrated in the **Bureau of International Labor Affairs**. The bureau's major duties are in the areas of trade, combating child labor, trafficking and forced labor, and representing the United States in international organizations. The bureau also conducts research on international labor issues, and monitors international labor development. Specific duties include helping to formulate international economic and trade policies; implementing overseas technical assistance projects; administering the North American Agreement on Labor Cooperation (NAALC), the labor supplemental agreement to the North American Free Trade Agreement and other trade agreements; preparing reports on international child labor issues and management of international programs to eliminate child labor exploitation; conducting research and helping to formulate policy to eliminate trafficking and forced labor; arranging exchanges and programs for foreign visitors to the United States; providing guidance and information to labor attachés at U.S. embassies; assisting with the representation of the United States in bilateral and multilateral trade negotiations and in various international organizations; representing the United States in the International Labor Organization and the labor and employment components of the Organization for Economic Cooperation and Development, the Group of Eight, the Asia-Pacific Economic Cooperation forum, the U.S.–EU dialogue, the Inter-American Conference of Labor Ministers, the United Nations and the Organization of American states; and reporting on and analyzing international labor issues.

To handle these responsibilities, the bureau is divided into three offices: the Office of International Relations, the Office of Trade and Labor Affairs; and the Office of Child Labor, Forced Labor, and Human Trafficking. The majority of professional positions within the bureau require a strong background in economics (especially microeconomics and some knowledge of statistics), international trade and/or labor relations, or international relations and/or regional studies.

> U.S. Department of Labor
> Human Resources
> Room C5515, 200 Constitution Avenue, NW
> Washington, DC 20210
> Tel.: 202-693-7813
> www.dol.gov

Management and Budget, U.S. Office of

The Office of Management and Budget (OMB) performs a wide variety of functions. OMB prepares and administers the federal budget; analyzes proposed legislation and executive orders; reviews all major administration testimony and all legislation enacted by Congress; assesses federal program objectives, performance, and efficiency; and tracks the progress of government agencies with respect to work proposed, work actually initiated, and work completed.

The associate director for National Security Programs holds paramount responsibility for OMB's review of international programs. The director's staff is partitioned into two divisions: international affairs and national security. The **International Affairs Division** is concerned with trade, monetary, and investment policy and deals with such specific issues as international energy policy and commodity agreements. The division reviews all foreign aid, trade financing, grants of military assistance, and foreign military credit and cash sales programs as well as the budgets of the agencies primarily responsible for international economic activities and the conduct of foreign affairs. Reviewing and advising the Defense Department budget and national security policy is the task of the **National Security Division**.

OMB has a total staff of under 550 professionals and administrators, over 90 percent of whom hold career appointments. The majority of the staff have graduate degrees in economics, business and accounting, public administration and policy, law, engineering, and other disciplines. Analytic and quantitative skills, effective oral and written communication skills, strong interpersonal skills, and the ability to work under pressure and on deadlines are required. All potential recruits must meet OPM eligibility requirements. Paid summer internships are available for graduate students with the same qualifications.

Office of Management and Budget
725 17th Street, NW
Washington, DC 20503
Tel.: 202-395-7250
Fax: 202-395-3504
www.whitehouse.gov/omb/recruitment

National Aeronautics and Space Administration

The National Aeronautics and Space Administration (NASA) ensures that activities in space are devoted to peaceful purposes for the benefit of all humankind. In addition, the act that created NASA in 1958 charged the agency to conduct its activities "so as to contribute materially to . . . cooperation by the United States with other nations and groups of nations." In fulfillment of this mandate, NASA has entered into more than 3,000 agreements with more than 150 countries and international organizations. These relationships have covered a broad spectrum of collaborative endeavors, ranging from the development of major space hardware to the sharing of space data among scientists around the globe.

The Office of External Relations is responsible for all NASA's international activities. These includes liaising with foreign entities, international agreements, export control, and foreign visitor and foreign travel policies. The staff consists of about thirty-five professionals with backgrounds in international relations, political science, science, engineering, or related fields. A graduate degree is preferred, and communications skills are emphasized. The ability to speak a foreign language is helpful in many of the positions. The staff assignments include responsibility for relations with particular countries and/or space projects or functional areas, such as export control.

> National Aeronautics and Space Administration
> 300 E Street, SW
> Washington, DC 20546
> Tel.: 202-358-0000 (Public Information)
> Tel.: 202-358-0450 (Office of External Relations)
> www.nasa.gov

Overseas Private Investment Corporation

The Overseas Private Investment Corporation (OPIC) provides political risk insurance, financing, and a variety of investor services to encourage U.S. private investment in more than 140 developing nations and emerging markets around the world. Although wholly owned by the U.S. government, OPIC is organized along the lines of a private corporation.

OPIC's mission is "to mobilize and facilitate the participation of United States private capital and skills in the economic and social development of less developed countries and areas, and countries in transition from non-market to market economies, thereby complementing the development assistance objectives of the United States." To achieve this mission, OPIC focuses on four principal activities:

- insuring overseas investments against political risks,
- financing businesses overseas through loans and loan guarantees,

- financing private investment funds to provide equity to businesses, and
- advocating for the interests of U.S. businesses abroad.

OPIC employs approximately two hundred employees, of whom about 60 percent are professionals. OPIC's requirements for professional personnel generally include training in law, finance, business, economics, or international affairs. Depending on the job requirements, foreign language skills may be required. Computer skills are often important. OPIC has only occasional vacancies, but it welcomes applications for employment from qualified U.S. citizens.

> Office of Human Resources Management
> Overseas Private Investment Corporation
> 1100 New York Avenue, NW
> Washington, DC 20527
> Tel.: 202-336-8799
> www.opic.gov

Peace Corps

The Peace Corps seeks to promote world peace and friendship, to help the peoples of other countries meet their needs for trained labor power, and to promote mutual understanding and cooperation between Americans and other peoples. To meet these goals, the Peace Corps trains volunteers in the appropriate local languages, the technical skills necessary for the particular task they will be performing, and the cross-cultural skills needed to work with peoples of a different culture. Following successful completion of the two- to three-month training, volunteers are sent to various sites within another country, where they spend a period of two years aiding the country's economic and social development.

There are more than 7,749 Peace Corps volunteers in seventy-three countries. Assignments vary according to volunteers' qualifications and host-country needs. Volunteers work primarily in the fields of agriculture, forestry, fisheries, education, health, engineering, business, the skilled trades, and community development-related activities. In greatest demand are those with degrees and/or backgrounds in forestry, fisheries, mathematics, science, and agriculture. It is important to remember that education is not the only avenue to acquiring the background necessary for these positions; such backgrounds can be obtained through a variety of experiences.

Applicants to the Peace Corps must be U.S. citizens who are at least eighteen years of age. In view of specific requests, however, it is extremely rare that candidates under twenty have the skills or experience to qualify. Though specific skills or work experience and foreign language proficiency are highly desired in potential volunteers, the Peace Corps also looks highly upon those who demonstrate a desire to serve others, a sense of dedication, emotional maturity, and a great deal of flexibility and adaptability. The Peace Corps covers round-trip transportation from the United States to the country of assignment and provides medical care. It also provides each volunteer with a living allowance to cover basic necessities such as housing and food, including a modest amount of spending money. Upon completion of service, each volunteer receives a $225 readjustment allowance for every month he or she has served. The Peace Corps recruits approximately 3,750 volunteers per year.

Additionally, the Peace Corps has employees stationed in Washington, in eleven regional recruiting offices around the United States, and in Peace Corps offices abroad. These employees are involved in such fields as volunteer recruitment, program development, support, and personnel. The Peace Corps has tended to hire former volunteers for many of these positions. The Peace Corps prefers that applications be delivered through its website.

> Peace Corps
> Paul D. Coverdell Peace Corps Headquarters
> 1111 20th Street, NW
> Washington, DC 20526
> Tel.: 800-424-8580

> Peace Corps
> Office of Human Resource Management
> Room 2300, 1111 20th Street, NW
> Washington, DC 20526
> Tel.: 202-692-1200
> Fax: 202-692-1201
> www.peacecorps.gov

Postal Service, United States

The U.S. Postal Service (USPS) furnishes mail processing and delivery services to U.S. and foreign individual and business mailers. The USPS operates an **International Postal Affairs** (IPA) function that is responsible for coordinating relations and activities with foreign postal administrations, international postal organizations (e.g., the Universal Postal Union) and with U.S. government agencies concerning international postal issues. IPA supervises the exchange of mail with other countries based on multilateral and bilateral treaties.

IPA has fifteen professional positions for the following functions: developing overall USPS international mail policies, conducting bilateral and multilateral postal business negotiations, representing the USPS at international postal organization meetings, and coordinating technical cooperation and postal development activities with other postal administrations and international development institutions like the United Nations Development Program and the World Bank. Graduate degrees in international relations constitute the most relevant background for a career in IPA. Fluency in foreign languages, particularly French and Spanish, is extremely useful.

International Postal Affairs
475 L'Enfant Plaza, SW
Washington, DC 20260
Tel.: 202-268-2020
Fax: 202-268-7232
www.usps.gov

Science and Technology Policy, U.S. Office of
The Office of Science and Technology Policy (OSTP) serves as a source of input for the president on issues of science and technology policy. The office advises the president about scientific and technological considerations involved in areas of national concern, including the economy, national security, and foreign policy. In executing its mandate, the OSTP frequently deals with such issues as export controls, arms control, information technology, technology transfer, foreign aid, energy, space cooperation, transborder data flows, and ocean policies. Of the OSTP's total staff of about forty, about one-quarter deal directly with international affairs. Candidates must have strong technical backgrounds combined with relevant experience. Employment opportunities are limited.

Office of Science and Technology Policy
Room 360, Old Executive Office Building
Washington, DC 20506
Tel.: 202-456-7116
www.ostp.gov

State, U.S. Department of
For information on the U.S. Department of State—both the Foreign Service and Civil Service—see the "Careers in the U.S. Foreign Service"

section below. Specific information on the Bureau of Intelligence and Research is also given in the "Careers in Intelligence Analysis" section.

Securities and Exchange Commission

The Securities and Exchange Commission's (SEC's) Office of International Affairs has primary responsibility for the SEC's international initiatives. These include international enforcement cooperation and the negotiation of memoranda of understanding with the SEC's foreign counterparts, international regulatory initiatives and the promotion of high regulatory standards worldwide, and technical assistance and international training.

> Securities and Exchange Commission
> 100 F Street, NE
> Washington, DC 20549
> Tel.: 202-551-7500 (Personnel)
> www.sec.gov/asec/secjobs.htm

Trade and Development Agency, U.S.

The U.S. Trade and Development Agency (USTDA), an independent U.S. government agency, advances economic development and U.S. commercial interests in developing and middle-income countries. The agency funds various forms of technical assistance, feasibility studies, training, orientation visits, and business workshops that support the development of a modern infrastructure and a fair and open trading environment.

The USTDA accomplishes these objectives by providing grants for feasibility studies, training programs, and other project planning services for public-sector development projects that can be assisted by U.S. company expertise. The USTDA assists U.S. firms by identifying high-priority development projects that can be met by U.S. commercial goods and services. The USTDA's activities serve as a catalyst to encourage U.S. private-sector involvement in critical infrastructure projects. This approach helps position U.S. firms for follow-on contracts when these projects are implemented. Successful USTDA projects are measured by the agency's hit rate, the export multiplier, and developmental impact. These activities have led to more than $25 billion in U.S. exports—or approximately $43 in exports for every $1 invested in USTDA activities.

USTDA activities cover a wide range of sectors of high priority to host governments and international development efforts. U.S. technological expertise can help accelerate the development process in all these sectors.

A staff of fifty employees runs the program. Virtually all entry-level positions are at the higher grade levels and are usually filled by candidates with advanced degrees in international finance, trade, or business and with previous experience.

> U.S. Trade and Development Agency
> Suite 1600, 1000 Wilson Boulevard
> Arlington, VA 22209
> Tel.: 703-875-4357
> Fax: 703-875-4009
> www.ustda.gov

Trade Representative, Office of the U.S.

The Office of the U.S. Trade Representative develops and coordinates U.S. international trade, commodity, and direct investment policy as well as overseeing negotiations with other countries. Professionals negotiate directly with foreign governments to create trade agreements, resolve disputes, and participate in global trade policy organizations. They also meet with governments, business groups, legislators, and public interest groups to gather input on trade issues and explain the president's trade policy positions. The agency has its main office in Washington and small offices in Geneva and Beijing.

Employment opportunities are limited and highly competitive. Notable skill in economics with expertise in negotiations and trade is required of all applicants. A doctorate in economics or trade is preferred. The agency has a nonremunerated intern program for graduates and undergraduates with concentrations in economics, international relations, law, political science, business, and finance.

> Office of the U.S. Trade Representative
> Executive Office of the President
> 600 17th Street, NW
> Washington, DC 20506
> Tel.: 202-395-7360
> www.ustr.gov

Transportation, U.S. Department of

The Department of Transportation (DOT) is responsible for planning and administering the nation's overall transportation policy. The **Office of Aviation and International Affairs** provides departmental leadership for international transportation policy issues and assesses economic, financial, technological, and institutional implications. The office coordinates international transportation cooperative research; organizes technical assistance programs for developing nations; formulates and presents the U.S. position on transportation matters before international conferences; develops, coordinates, and evaluates international air and marine transportation policy in concert with various elements from government, industry, and labor; and negotiates and implements multilateral and bilateral aviation agreements.

The educational experiences of the office's staff professionals vary widely. The most common backgrounds are law, international relations, and public administration. Many of the professionals have joined the staff with previous work experience in areas such as bilateral negotiations, aviation and maritime policy, cooperative technical exchange programs, and technical assistance programs.

The **Federal Aviation Administration** (FAA) has an **Office of International Aviation** that promotes aviation safety and civil aviation abroad by managing the FAA's foreign technical assistance programs, providing training for foreign nationals in areas of the agency's expertise, developing and coordinating the FAA's international policies, and exchanging information with foreign governments. In addition, the office provides technical representation to international organizations and conferences and participates in cooperative efforts with other U.S. government agencies and the U.S. aviation industry to promote aviation safety abroad. The office's professionals stationed in the United States fall into two broad categories: international specialists and those with technical backgrounds. The international specialists have degrees or backgrounds in economics, international relations, or international marketing. For the people with technical aviation backgrounds, the emphasis is on experience. The majority are former pilots, air traffic controllers, flight safety inspectors, and the like. Some have engineering degrees, but many others have nontechnical degrees in areas such as the liberal arts.

There are three other major offices within the department involved in international issues. The **Federal Highway Administration** (FHWA) employs highway design, construction, maintenance, and bridge engineers and specialists to provide assistance and advice to foreign governments in various phases of highway engineering and administration. It also is active in a number of international organizations interested in road-related affairs. The FHWA's **National Highway Institute** trains foreign highway officials interested in American highway practices. The

Saint Lawrence Seaway Development Corporation operates that portion of the seaway within the territorial limits of the United States and coordinates its activities with those of its Canadian counterpart. International maritime and related U.N. matters are dealt with by the **U.S. Coast Guard**, which falls under DOT's jurisdiction during peacetime. The Coast Guard maintains an Office of Public and International Affairs. Additional Coast Guard offices are concerned with the enforcement of international laws and treaties, the international impact of environmental questions, and the operation of deepwater ports.

> U.S. Department of Transportation
> Departmental Office of Human Resource Management
> Room 7411, 400 7th Street, SW
> Washington, DC 20590
> Tel.: 202-366-4088
> Fax: 202-366-6806
> www.dot.gov

> Federal Aviation Administration
> Human Resource Management Division
> Attn: AHR-19
> 800 Independence Avenue, SW
> Washington, DC 20590
> Tel.: 202-267-8007
> www.faa.gov

Treasury, U.S. Department of

The Department of the Treasury is the primary federal agency responsible for the economic and financial prosperity and security of the United States, and as such it is responsible for a wide range of activities, including advising the president on economic and financial issues, promoting the president's growth agenda, and enhancing corporate governance in financial institutions.

In the international arena, the Department of the Treasury works with other federal agencies, the governments of other nations, and the international financial institutions to encourage economic growth, raise standards of living, and predict and prevent, to the extent possible, economic and financial crises. Treasury's **Office of International Affairs** protects and supports economic prosperity at home by encouraging financial stability and sound economic policies abroad. International Affairs performs constant surveillance and in-depth analysis of global economic and financial developments and then engages with financial market participants, foreign governments, international financial institutions, and in multilateral forums to develop and promote good policies.

The **Office of Economic Policy** is responsible for analyzing and reporting on current and prospective economic developments in the U.S. and world economies and assisting in the determination of appropriate economic policies. The assistant secretary for economic policy reports directly to the secretary of the Treasury and is responsible to him for the review and analysis of both domestic and international economic issues and developments in the financial markets.

With the dramatic expansion of trade in recent decades, the world economy is more connected than ever before. Successfully managing the U.S. economy is as important to the rest of the world as their success is to America. As the chief financial officer of the federal government, the secretary of the Treasury manages a diverse team of over 100,000 employees by promoting values that enrich their work environment and foster pride in their work. All Treasury Department jobs open to the public are announced on OPM's USAJOBS.gov website. For information on intelligence-related careers with the Treasury, see the resource listings in the "Careers in Intelligence Analysis" section below.

> Department of the Treasury
> 1500 Pennsylvania Avenue, NW
> Washington, DC 20220
> Tel.: 202-622-2000
> Fax: 202-622-6415
> www.ustreas.gov

U.S. Agency for International Development

The U.S. Agency for International Development (USAID) was created by Congress in 1961 to administer the foreign economic and humanitarian assistance programs of the U.S. government. It operates from headquarters in Washington through field missions and representatives in developing countries in Africa, Asia, the Near East, Europe and Eurasia, Latin America, and the Caribbean.

USAID's purpose is to help people in the developing world acquire the knowledge and resources to build the economic, political, and social institutions needed to promote and maintain national development. USAID works to provide this assistance in concert with the Department of State, Peace Corps, and other federal and private voluntary organizations. The assistance covers many diverse sectors, including but not limited to environment, agriculture, economic growth, strengthening democracy, health and family planning, education, disaster preparedness, and humanitarian assistance.

The New Entry Professional Program is USAID's program for bringing well-qualified applicants into its Foreign Service, which provides successful applicants with a career-long system of rotational assignments overseas. Like the U.S. Department of State and other agencies employing Foreign Service personnel, successful applicants are offered a clear path for planning their career from the intake level through the most senior executive positions.

Candidates for employment with USAID should have background in one or more of the following areas: political science, economics, government, public administration, international development, business administration, law, banking, international transportation, procurement, contracting, finance, agriculture, anthropology, biology, fisheries, food science, forestry, geography, natural resource management, resource economics, rural sociology, agricultural economics, the administration of justice, international affairs, comparative government, public policy, agribusiness, public health/nutrition, trade management, environmental engineering, urban planning, public health, medicine, nursing, midwifery, demography, social/behavioral science, material management, and marketing.

U.S. Agency for International Development
1300 Pennsylvania Avenue, NW
Washington, DC 20523-0056
Tel.: 202-712-4810
www.usaid.gov

Careers in the U.S. Foreign Service

Maura Harty

Maura Harty, *a 1981 graduate of the School of Foreign Service, is currently assistant secretary of state for consular affairs. Her initial assignment was to the American embassy in Mexico, then as watch officer in the Operations Center in Washington. She was a special assistant to then–secretary of state George P. Shultz, served as chief of nonimmigrant visas in Colombia, and then served as consul at the American embassy in Madrid. She was appointed managing director of the Directorate of Overseas Citizens Services, and then selected as deputy executive secretary of the Department of State. She subsequently served as executive assistant to Secretary of State Warren Christopher, and following that, became U.S. ambassador to Paraguay.*

I can assure you, public service is a stimulating, proud, and lively enterprise. It is not just a way of life; it is a way to live fully.

—LEE H. HAMILTON

I HAVE BEEN in the Foreign Service for twenty-five years. Short of being a multimillionaire, there is absolutely nothing I would rather have done with the last quarter century. The Foreign Service has presented me with great challenges, great joys, and tremendous personal satisfaction. I believe it also has transformed my life. It waits to transform yours as well.

I want to tell you why the Foreign Service was and remains the right career choice for me, what you might expect from a career in today's Foreign Service, and I hope why the Foreign Service can be the right career for you. In the process I hope to give you an understanding of why I love this job and feel so passionately about it. Frankly, it represents an opportunity to *do* good and to *be* good—virtues instilled in part by my Georgetown education.

When I joined the Department of State right out of college, I could not possibly have imagined what adventures awaited me, or what I would be asked to do. Some of it has been what you might think the life of a Foreign Service officer (FSO) would be. Yes, I have had the privilege of meeting national leaders on occasion—the great, the good, and the disappointing. I have attended a fair amount of fancy receptions, drafted classified reporting cables, and hopscotched the globe on pretty much every airline—even Air Force One! But I have also visited American citizens in foreign jails in the middle of the night. I have landed in a war zone during combat to help Americans there find their way to safety. I have scoured police stations and hotels searching for missing American citizens at the request of worried relatives far away. I have secured the return of abducted children to their anxious parents—a gratifying experience that almost defies description.

In hopes of being able to help Americans in a crisis, I went to Somalia when we still had an embassy there to conduct an evacuation exercise. I led a team that opened our embassy in Lithuania after a forty-year absence from that country, and was deeply touched to see Lithuanian officials welcome us back with tears in their eyes. As an ambassador, I had the incredible privilege of serving as our nation's representative to Paraguay, a fledgling democracy, and helping it find its way, despite a coup attempt and a vice presidential assassination, to a strengthened respect for its institutions of government and its Constitution.

My career has taken me from Mexico to Moscow and from Paraguay to Phnom Penh. Along the way, I have been fortunate to learn priceless lessons about leadership and public service working directly for three secretaries of state: George P. Shultz, Warren Christopher, and Colin Powell. But I can say with certainty that the greatest privilege I have enjoyed during this career is the opportunity to help people in need.

THE JOB DESCRIPTION

When talking about Foreign Service careers, I am often asked, "What does a Foreign Service officer do?" It is a good question, because the terms "Foreign Service officer," "consul general," and "diplomat" do not necessarily bring to mind the clear mental pictures that "lawyer," "journalist," and even "consultant" do. It can be a tough question to answer, however, because the answers are as many and varied as the countries in the world and the U.S. interests in those countries. The mission of the Foreign Service—"to create a more secure, democratic, and prosperous world for the benefit of the American people and the international community"—leaves room for a lot of different activities. And that is one of the great things about the Foreign Service: No matter what your interest, background, or expertise, there is a place for you.

That is one of the great things about the Foreign Service: No matter what your interest, background, or expertise, there is a place for you.

There are five career tracks, or what we call "cones," in the Foreign Service. *Consular officers* protect and assist American citizens living or traveling abroad, and exercise weighty border security responsibilities through the adjudication of visa and passport applications. *Management officers* oversee multimillion-dollar real estate portfolios, supervise the staffing and budgets for embassies and consulates, and help guide the career development of colleagues. *Economic officers* help promote U.S. commercial interests, work with U.S. and foreign business leaders, and analyze foreign economic developments in order to make policy recommendations. *Political officers* engage with foreign officials to influence their policies and positions and to analyze political events to predict their impact on the United States. *Public diplomacy officers* tell America's story to the world, explaining U.S. history and world events, interacting with foreign media, and organizing educational and cultural exchanges. Together, whether in Washington or at a post abroad, these five types of officers form one team with one mission: to promote and defend the national interests of the United States.

Each FSO is asked to choose one of these paths at the start of his or her career. But no FSO is limited to work in any single area—in fact, to be promoted an FSO *must* gain experience outside his or her career cone. The diverse nature of the work demands that each FSO master a broad range of skills. I would argue that we are all public diplomacy officers, sharing the example and inspiration of America with all we meet. In an emergency, everyone becomes a consular officer, quickly reverting to a core function enshrined as a sacred duty since the first consul was named in 1780. Moreover, the issues that FSOs confront every day—terrorism, environmental degradation, intellectual property rights, and HIV/AIDS, among many others—do not always fall neatly into the five cones. The Foreign Service's leaders encourage "out-of-cone" work because they know that leadership grows from having many different, challenging experiences, and that the service as a whole benefits from nurturing a wide variety of skills and competencies.

In addition to the generalist officer tracks, the Foreign Service has exciting opportunities for specialists, who provide critical technical, support, or administrative services in one of seven domains: administration, construction engineering, information technology, international information and English language programs, medical and health, office management, and security. Though specialists typically serve almost exclusively in their area of expertise, they bid on posts, serve overseas, and are integral parts of the Foreign Service family.

Getting into the Foreign Service requires commitment. The two-stage entrance examination includes both written and oral assessments. There is no cost to register for or take it. The standards are high; in 2006, 18,699 people took the exam, and the State Department admitted 385 new hires. For updated information on when the exam will be given, consult www.careers.state.gov.

The exams are rigorous, but open to all Americans. I am proud to say that the Foreign Service reflects the diversity of the America it exists to serve. A typical entry class—affectionately still called "A-100" after the room where it met many years ago—includes professions as diverse as attorneys, bartenders, city planners, English teachers, moms, writers, and freshly minted university graduates. When I came in, it was common for people to join right out of college or graduate school. Many still do. But for others today, the Foreign Service is a second or even third career.

Although most people who take the written exam have a bachelor's degree or higher, you do not have to have one. In fact, the only requirements are that you be between the ages of twenty and fifty-nine years and that you be a U.S. citizen. You do not have to already speak a foreign language; if you pass the exam, you will have the chance to learn one or even several. Similarly, there is no "one" subject in which you should have majored or that you should study to prepare for the exam. Though many FSOs majored in government or international relations—or even in foreign service—many more studied philosophy, chemistry, business, law, literature, or languages. What you do need is an open and inquiring mind, a sense of adventure, and a desire to serve your country and your fellow citizens.

Joining the Foreign Service means joining an extended family.

There is one more requirement to serve in the Foreign Service: You must be willing to serve at any of its posts worldwide. FSOs serve everywhere, from large missions like Mexico City and Cairo to smaller embassies and consulates like Chiang Mai and N'Djamena. Many of these places are what we call "hardship" posts: places where many of the standards and amenities that you are used to are available only intermittently or not at all. You can expect to serve in such a post, and perhaps several times. In January 2006, Secretary of State Condoleezza Rice outlined her vision for the future of the Foreign Service in a speech at Georgetown University, in which she stated that positions would be moved from Europe to critical countries such as India and Nigeria, and that FSOs would be increasingly expected to serve in places such as Iraq, Afghanistan, and Sudan. She said:

> More and more often, over the course of this new century, we will ask the men and women of the State Department to be active in the field. We will need them to engage with private citizens in emerging regional centers, not just with government officials in their nations' capitals. We must train record numbers of people to master difficult languages like Arabic and Chinese and Farsi and Urdu.
>
> In addition, to advance in their careers, our Foreign Service officers must now serve in what we call hardship posts. These are challenging jobs in critical countries like Iraq and Afghanistan and Sudan and Angola, countries where we are working with foreign citizens in difficult conditions to maintain security and fight poverty and make democratic reforms. To succeed in these kinds of posts, we will train our diplomats not only as expert analysts of policy but as first-rate administrators of programs, capable of helping foreign citizens to strengthen the rule of law, to start businesses, to improve health, and to reform education.

Joining the Foreign Service means joining an extended family. One of its great privileges and rewards is the chance to work with Foreign Service national colleagues, men and women who have dedicated their lives to serving the United States; to training and guiding new employees; to helping America promote its positions, goods, and values; and to protecting and assisting U.S. citizens. They work alongside us, often at great personal cost and sacrifice. Quite a few have been with us for decades, advising and assisting us, teaching us about their country and, more often than not, our work. From them I have learned many of the finer points of being a consular officer, and of humanity. Along the way, I have developed friendships that have stayed with me long after I departed post. We stick by them, and they by us. When Hurricane Katrina hit the Gulf Coast in August 2005, it devastated not only the city of New Orleans but also the lives of our colleagues at the New Orleans Passport Agency. I was moved that so many throughout the State Department assisted them by donating generously to the Employee Emergency Relief Fund. But I was especially touched that our Foreign Service national colleagues from Papua New Guinea contributed $189 to the fund. This humble group from a humble society opened their hearts and reached out to employees they will probably never know, but with whom they nevertheless share the bond of the Foreign Service.

Consular Service

Now I turn to my particular area of concentration: consular work. From the earliest days of our nation's existence, the mission of consular officers has been a constant one: to protect the lives and interests of American citizens overseas, and to enhance the national security of the United States through the proper adjudication of U.S. passports and visas. The Consular Service was founded in 1780—eight years before America would inaugurate its first president. Consular officers thus laid the foundation of the long and proud history of the Foreign Service.

Today's Bureau of Consular Affairs is an organization that might make the *Fortune* 1,000 list if it were a business rather than a bureau within the federal government. Revenues generated by consular services topped $1.3 billion last year. The bureau includes some 7,800 people working in sixty-five different languages at 211 branch offices—namely, our embassies and consulates overseas—as well as at the Department of State and at 17 domestic passport agencies and 2 regional visa processing centers.

The core consular responsibility—indeed, the State Department's fundamental responsibility—is to protect the lives and interests of Americans overseas. Consular officers provide services that address the very cycles of our lives: We certify the birth of new American citizens abroad, and we assist family members with the difficult task of arranging to bring home the remains of an American who has died overseas. We deal with issues that matter to people in deeply personal ways: citizenship, marriage, adoption, international child abduction, illness, destitution, evacuation in a crisis, and voter registration, to name a few. We offer support in times of trouble or tragedy, natural disaster, and political unrest. Often, when we are called upon for assistance, an American citizen is suffering through some of the worst moments of his or her life and desperately needs not just a helping hand but also a kind and understanding word. We do our work most effectively by knowing police officers and social workers, hospital workers and friendly hotel owners willing to give an American a room overnight on our word. We help our fellow citizens access the social safety net of a society not their own so that they can get back on their feet after misfortune has befallen them.

We do this work twenty-four hours a day and seven days a week, around the world, often under difficult and even dangerous conditions. In fact, consular officers often head *into* tough spots just as others are leaving. The terrible tsunami in the Indian Ocean that ravaged so many lives in December 2004 is a brutal reminder of how unexpected and arbitrary natural forces can inflict so much damage. Images of the devastation, the victims, and the anguish of the survivors touched and saddened all of us. In the midst of the chaos and the loss, consular officers were there to demonstrate our central commitment to providing assistance to American citizens.

Sadly, our crisis response capabilities are all too often tested by human acts. When fighting broke out in Lebanon in July 2006, we raced 120 officers from Washington and 40 posts around the world to help our posts in Beirut, Nicosia, and Adana move over 14,700 American citizens out of harm's way. And we were there in London to assist our citizens after the transit system bombings in 2005. I once received a note from a parent who told me that we had cared about her children, caught in a terrorist incident, before she even knew about it. She said she had no idea that her government would be there for her in that way.

This is what consular officers do. We touch people's lives, and in doing so we enjoy the incredible privilege of being touched in return.

The Foreign Service also plays a critical role in protecting our nation's borders. Consular officers are literally stationed on the front lines of the global war on terror. We are responsible, through proper adjudication of

U.S. passports as well as immigrant and nonimmigrant visa applications, for preventing those who seek to do us harm from reaching and entering the United States. Every day consular officers—from entry-level officers to ambassadors—must draw upon a detailed understanding of U.S. immigration law, host-country socioeconomic factors, and traits of human nature to make hundreds of decisions that can potentially affect U.S. national security.

At the same time, consular officers are equally vigilant in ensuring that access to America is not impeded for those whose presence we encourage and value. Engagement with the rest of the world is vital to our national security. The U.S. travel and tourism industry contributed some $104.8 billion to our economy in 2005, and foreign students contributed an additional $13 billion. Beyond the dollar signs, I believe that the best advertisement for America *is* America, and that there is absolutely no replacement for the personal experiences people have when they visit the United States. When they return home, they have a greater understanding of this country and its people, and I think we all benefit from the goodwill engendered by these exchanges.

The Foreign Service can also be dangerous. Indeed William Palfrey, the first consul general, never made it to his first post. In an early, pre-scient reminder of the risks of our profession, he died at sea in 1780. And it has never ceased to be risky. Today in the entrance hall of the State Department, on C Street in Washington, there are plaques on the wall with the names of over three hundred employees who have made the ultimate sacrifice for this country—the last name, David E. Foy, was added in 2006.

But something special draws people to sit for the Foreign Service exam, take the risks, and keep going despite power outages, coups, and natural disasters. It is not just the chance to see the world—although you do get to do a fair amount of that. Every job you will read about in a book on this subject offers the prospect of traveling, working, and living in other countries. So what makes the Foreign Service different from other careers in the international arena?

I think the answer can be found in the words of two of our greatest public figures. In his 1961 State of the Union address, President John F. Kennedy called for a reinvigorated public service, urging, "Let the public service be a proud and lively career. And let every man and woman who works in any area of our national government, in any branch, at any level, be able to say with pride and with honor in future years: 'I served the

United States government in that hour of our nation's need.'" His contemporary, Martin Luther King Jr., noted: "Life's most persistent and urgent question is 'What are you doing for others?'"

This is the essence of public service. This is why we do what we do. We do it for the chance to touch people's lives and to serve our country, and in so doing we add a little bit of extra meaning to our own lives. That hour of our nation's need is now. I consider it a great honor and privilege to heed that call to service. It is available to you. I hope you will join us by seizing it.

RESOURCE LISTINGS

State, U.S. Department of, Foreign Service Officers

Foreign Service officers help formulate and implement the foreign policy of the United States. They are an essential part of the frontline personnel at all U.S. embassies, consulates, and diplomatic missions, and they work at nearly 265 locations worldwide as well as in Washington.

Many FSOs have liberal arts or business degrees, and some have advanced degrees in specialized areas ranging from law to the social and hard sciences. Knowledge of a foreign language is not a requirement to join the Foreign Service, because FSOs receive language training required for overseas assignments. However, the U.S. Department of State welcomes applicants who have foreign language competence, especially in Slavic, Middle Eastern, and Asian languages. Each FSO must choose one of five career tracks: management affairs, consular affairs, economic affairs, political affairs, or public diplomacy. Increasingly, issues such as the environment, science, HIV/AIDS, international law enforcement, narcotics trafficking, and trafficking in persons have gained priority among American foreign policy objectives. This shift has opened fascinating new avenues in which FSOs are making major contributions on the cutting edge of foreign policy. While serving in Washington, offices in all tracks also participate in developing and implementing our foreign policies.

Management officers are creative, action-oriented leaders who think on their feet and respond with efficient, on-target solutions in fast-paced—sometimes mission-critical—situations. Their responsibilities include developing personnel; negotiating bilateral work agreements; reciprocal tax treatment; managing a multimillion-dollar real estate portfolio; managing financial assets; and providing supervision at U.S. embassies, consulates, and other diplomatic posts.

Consular officers solve problems for American citizens abroad. From crisis situations to lost passports, the objective of the consular officer is a quick response and creative solution in providing assistance to U.S. citizens. Wherever Americans are in residence or traveling abroad, consular officers are there as a support system for addressing the surprises that can arise. Consular officers also review visa applications and make decisions on whether or not to issue the visa. To excel in this challenging position, FSOs must demonstrate sharp attention to detail and exhibit a reassuring, agreeable nature.

Decision making, policymaking, and advocating American business interests are just a few of the objectives of **economic officers**. They apply their technical expertise to analyzing the effects of a country's economic situation on its political climate and on U.S. economic interests. They work with U.S. and foreign business leaders as well as government decision makers on some of the most cutting-edge issues in foreign policy, such as technology, the environment, and HIV/AIDS, as well as in the more traditional areas of trade and finance. Versatility, sound judgment, and strong business skills are all hallmarks of economic officers.

The career of a **political officer** lies in analyzing political events in the country or region of his or her post. Political officers are sensitive to political climates abroad, and they interpret events and situations as they relate to U.S. interests. They apply their expertise to the situations at hand, making recommendations on foreign policy. These members of the U.S. Foreign Service engage in negotiations, influence the judgments of decision makers, and advise on international affairs.

As the voice of the United States to the hosting country, **public diplomacy officers** strive to broaden the understanding of American values and concerns. They are congenial, diligent relationship builders who conduct public awareness services via press and media outlets to promote U.S. interests overseas. It is a significant responsibility that presents opportunities unique to educating foreign cultures about America while offering unrivaled experiences around the world.

FSOs must be well-informed and knowledgeable across many disciplines: current world and national affairs, economics, history, public affairs, and management, among others. And because FSOs represent the United States to the world, they must also possess an insightful understanding of American society and culture. This breadth of knowledge is usually gathered gradually over time. The best foundation is a solid education and a personal life habit of reading, learning, and expanding one's understanding of the world.

The Foreign Service Act of 1980 tasks the U.S. Department of State, and the Board of Examiners specifically, with the responsibility for the evaluation and selection of candidates for the Foreign Service. The department takes this charge seriously and has devoted significant resources to the development of a written test and an oral assessment with the goal of providing all candidates—regardless of socioeconomic background, education, or experience—an equal chance to demonstrate their potential to be an FSO. If you pass the written test, you will find that the Foreign Service oral assessment is designed to challenge you and give you the opportunity in three different settings (a group exercise, a structured interview, and a case management writing exercise) to demonstrate the thirteen dimensions that have been identified as the qualities necessary to become a successful FSO.

> U.S. Department of State
> Office of Recruitment, Examination, and Employment
> HR/REE/REC
> Suite 518-H, 2401 E Street, NW
> Washington, DC 20522
> Tel.: 202-261-8888
> Fax: 202-261-8841
> www.careers.state.gov

Foreign Service Specialists

Foreign Service specialists provide unique services in support of foreign policy at one of nearly 265 posts worldwide or in Washington. Specialists are an integral part of a team dedicated to representing America's interests in other countries. In all, there are nineteen different specialist jobs, which are grouped into several categories.

Administration specialists manage key resources, including facilities, finances, embassy operations, physical resources, logistics, and human resources:

- *Facilities managers* plan and direct operations, maintenance, repair, and improvement programs of overseas properties; direct facilities program resources; prepare cost estimates and equipment needs; and manage work schedules and priorities.

- *Financial management officers* manage financial activities of the post; develop budgets and financial plans; control obligations and expenditures; prepare and audit payment vouchers; administer payroll plans; approve salary and allowance payments; and monitor cashier operations.
- *General services officers* manage physical resources at post, logistical functions, space management, and travel and transportation. They also solicit, evaluate, negotiate, and award contracts, and develop budget and workforce requirements.
- *Human resources officers* oversee human resource function, supervise and ensure effective performance of the Human Resources Office staff, provide expert advice to managers and supervisors on human resource issues, and provide counseling and interpret regulations for Foreign Service and Foreign Service national employees.

Construction engineering specialists monitor and oversee contract work for new construction and renovation of existing properties. They are hired to work both domestically, to coordinate support for overseas construction projects, and internationally.

International engineers monitor and oversee contract work for new construction and renovation of existing properties. They also verify progress payments, manage safety programs, supervise budgets and funds, and prepare and submit reports and estimates. On project matters, they direct activities of other U.S. government officials and liaise with host-country authorities. They also develop and implement procedures to properly manage classified material and information.

Information technology specialists install, operate, and manage information technology infrastructure, including personal computer networks and telecommunications systems:

- *Information management specialists* manage, install, operate, and train users on worldwide information technology infrastructure, including computers, hardware, and software applications, and manage embassy/consulate mailroom operations.
- *Information management technical specialists* design, install, and maintain various telecommunications, land mobile radio, telephone, and computer systems; provide regional technical assistance; and perform technical site surveys to determine structural and technical requirements, and other related work.

Officers in **English Language Programs**, **Information Resource Centers**, and **Printing** oversee international programs:

- *English language officers* are responsible for Department of State–sponsored English teaching activities in a country or region. They use English language programs to introduce democratic institution building and international standards of business ethics. In doing so, they design and administer exchange programs; develop English teaching materials; conduct English language seminars or workshops; and promote greater understanding of American language, society, culture, and values.
- *Information resource officers* provide professional guidance and direction to Information Resource Centers located at U.S. embassies within a specific geographic region of assignment, counseling officials on effective Information Resource Center resources and services. They also assess staff development needs and carry out regional training programs, demonstrate and promote U.S. electronic information resources to mission and host-country audiences, and establish contacts with host-country library and information institutions.

Medical and health officers provide health care services, including community health, primary care, and laboratory and psychiatric services. These officers are considered "essential personnel" and are on call to provide services twenty-four hours a day, seven days a week:

- *Health practitioners* assume the role of primary care provider. They are responsible for administering a full range of community health care services, including preventive health education for the official mission community.
- *Regional medical technologists* perform routine visitations to regional area health units to evaluate and monitor the performance of local laboratory technologists. They maintain their own laboratories at their post of assignment as well as x-ray equipment.
- *Regional medical officers* work independently or in conjunction with other Foreign Service medical personnel to provide primary medical care and appropriate health information and disease prevention programs at each post of responsibility as well as a host of other medical and health-related responsibilities.
- *Regional medical officers / psychiatrists* work independently or in conjunction with other Foreign Service medical personnel to provide primary psychiatric care for each post in the supported geographical region as well as a host of other psychiatric and mental health-related responsibilities.

Office management specialists are called on to provide a variety of office support office functions through general office management, visitor support, and administrative support. This includes planning and coordinating official conferences and high-level visits, and preparing travel orders and travel vouchers.

Security personnel provide security services, including document delivery, security systems design and support, protection, investigations, and law enforcement:

- *Diplomatic couriers* safeguard and escort diplomatic pouches containing classified and sensitive material between U.S. diplomatic missions overseas and the Department of State.
- *Security engineering officers* manage technical and information security program, projects, and resources. They conduct technical security assessments and recommend upgrades; plan and conduct surveillance countermeasure surveys; identify and analyze computer and network security risks and recommend measures and system requirements; and specify, design, procure, install, and certify security equipment and products for technical security and information technology systems.
- *Security technical specialists* play a vital role in protecting Department of State facilities and personnel from technical espionage, crime, and terrorism. They install sophisticated security equipment including: intrusion detection systems, closed-circuit televisions systems, vehicular and pedestrian access systems, metal detectors, and explosive detection systems.
- *Diplomatic security special agents* manage a range of programs designed to protect Department of State personnel, facilities, and information. They advise ambassadors on all security matters, protect the secretary of state and visiting foreign dignitaries, investigate passport and visa fraud as an armed federal law enforcement officer, and conduct personnel security investigations.

Civil Service Personnel

Civil Service employees support the foreign policy mission from offices in Washington and across the nation. They help to shape a freer, more secure and prosperous world as they formulate, represent, and implement U.S. foreign policy. Jobs are available in several fields:

Business management / finance / economics / accounting

- *Contract specialist*: The U.S. Department of State must procure a wide variety of supplies, skills, and services to operate effectively and efficiently around the world. These specialists are involved in the procurement and negotiation of agreements in the best interests of the U.S. government.

- *Accountant and auditor*: The challenges for these employees are equal to the work being done for a multinational company. They determine the accounting and financial requirements to address the needs of the department's worldwide operations.
- *Economist*: Few positions offer such a wide array of challenging assignments. An economist could be involved in everything from the North American Free Trade Agreement to the World Trade Organization to environmental policy and its effect on the worldwide economy.
- *Financial management specialist*: For the U.S. Department of State to be fiscally responsible, it needs people who can identify and resolve operational irregularities and problems, provide financial advice and analyses, and be involved in a variety of financial management improvement projects.
- *Budget officer*: The Department of State needs people knowledgeable about the laws, regulations, policies, and techniques of federal budgeting. This is an exceptional opportunity to contribute to the management, development, and application of highly sophisticated budget administration systems.

Foreign Affairs and International Policy and Operations
For individuals with a background and interest in foreign affairs and/or policy, the U.S. Department of State offers unparalleled opportunities to contribute to U.S. foreign policy:

- *Foreign affairs officer:* The challenges these officers take on directly contribute to policymaking in Washington. They work with interagency partners, with Congress, or at overseas posts to help formulate and implement policy decisions and to manage foreign policy programs. Their assignments could relate to regional affairs or transnational issues such as arms control, drugs, terrorism, environmental issues, and humanitarian affairs.
- *Passport and visa specialist*: In this vital job of serving American and foreign citizens, specialists assist U.S. citizens in crisis situations, determine applicants' claims to American citizenship, issue passports, and adjudicate requests for visas based upon applicants' eligibility for admission to the United States.
- *Public affairs specialist*: These employees are the voice of the U.S. Department of State to the world. They are responsible for disseminating information about departmental programs through newspapers, radio, television, magazines, speeches, and briefings for audiences in Washington and throughout the United States.

International and Domestic Security

- *Intelligence analyst*: These employees have an ideal opportunity to utilize their expertise in a specific functional area or geographic region. Analysts at the U.S. Department of State advise, perform research, and provide analysis in support of the formulation and direction of foreign policy. Other analysts gather information on terrorist incidents and other criminal activities to determine potential threats to our employees and facilities.
- *Criminal investigator*: These employees have a career in the protection of America. They are qualified to carry weapons, have arrest authority, and provide a variety of security functions. Their responsibilities could range from conducting background investigations on personnel to passport and visa fraud investigations, counterintelligence, and other criminal investigations. Other responsibilities could also include investigating alleged espionage incidents and conducting damage assessments.
- *Security specialist*: These employees have the vital job of protecting U.S. and overseas personnel, property, buildings, and information against terrorists, foreign intelligence agents, and criminals. They develop and implement comprehensive security programs and procedures; and educate department employees on counterintelligence and vulnerabilities that might be exploited by foreign intelligence.

Engineering

- *Electronic engineers*: For the U.S. Department of State to operate effectively, it must make the most of highly advanced electronic systems and devices to communicate, remain secure, and operate worldwide. These employees are responsible for work related to the design, development, and enhancement of these systems and devices.
- *Architect / engineer / facilities management / real estate*: These employees apply their practical and creative problem-solving skills worldwide. They help to design, build, acquire, and maintain embassies, consulates, residences, office buildings, and compounds around the world.

Human Resources / Information Technology / Legal

- *Human resources specialist*: The U.S. Department of State takes a great deal of pride in its successful recruitment and retention of highly talented individuals with outstanding credentials. These employees are responsible for ensuring that the department continues to hire the right people with the right skills, in the right place and at the right time, both in the United States and overseas.

- *Information technology specialist*: Like any large organization, the U.S. Department of State runs on information. These employees are responsible for designing and implementing systems and procedures to meet daily goals for the rapid sharing and storing of information worldwide.
- *Attorney*: These employees represent an organization in which they use all their abilities, while making a difference in America and the world. They provide advice on international and domestic legal questions; negotiate treaties, agreements, and contracts; draft and interpret legislation; and handle other matters in support of the work of the U.S. Department of State.

The Civil Service also seeks office support professionals and senior executive service officers, who represent a variety of professional occupations. These executives work in managerial, supervisory, and public policymaking positions above the GS-15 level. For these leadership positions, employees must possess the essential qualifications to succeed in the twenty-first century. Executive core qualifications include leading change, leading people, being results-driven, having business acumen, and building coalitions/communications.

International Organization Affairs, U.S. Department of State, Bureau of

The Department of State's UN Employment Information and Assistance Unit in the Bureau of International Organization Affairs and other federal agencies assist U.S. citizens interested in considering employment opportunities with international organizations. While pursuing a rewarding work experience, such international civil servants also impart to their chosen organizations their standards of integrity, competence, and dedication to the needs of the world community. As the largest financial contributor to most international organizations, the U.S. government has a major interest in the composition of their staffs.

International organizations maintain high standards for hiring professional employees. Requirements generally include an advanced degree that is directly related to a particular position; a significant number of years of relevant and specialized work experience; some field experience in developing countries; relevant management experience; and, in addition to English, usually a strong working knowledge of a second UN language (French, Spanish, Arabic, Chinese, or Russian). A wide variety of backgrounds are sought, including aviation, drug/crime prevention, education, public health, science, and trade.

The Department of State's UN Employment Information and Assistance Unit compiles a biweekly listing of *International Vacancy Announcements,* which can be accessed at www.state.gov/p/io/empl.

Individuals who believe they meet the stated requirements for a specific position with an international organization and are interested in competing for it should send a detailed resume (or UN personal history form) directly to the organization, stating the specific vacancy for which they are applying. If a resume is used, it should be detailed and include the applicant's date of birth and citizenship. The final selection of the candidate, of course, is always the prerogative of the international organization and often is based on a desire to maintain a geographical balance among member countries. Because most agencies receive a very large number of applications from all over the world, competition is always keen. It should be understood that selection does not depend on U.S. government support, and sponsorship from the U.S. government is rarely required.

UN Employment Information & Assistance Unit (IO/S/EA)
U.S. Department of State
Room 4808, 2201 C Street, NW
Washington, DC 20520
Tel.: 202-736-4825
e-mail: employmentun@state.gov

Reflections on Joining the Foreign Service

Yvonne Gonzales

Yvonne Gonzales *is a 2003 graduate of the Master of Science in Foreign Service Program at Georgetown University. Her first posting was as a cultural affairs officer in Panama, and she has recently been assigned to Jakarta. Her previous experience includes both teaching and internships with U.S. Representative Loretta Sanchez and with the National Democratic Institute.*

GROWING UP in a working-class neighborhood in Southern California, I never met anyone who had a career in international public service. In fact, I was the only person in my family who ever owned a passport! I had been teaching high school for four and a half years, and I decided to study abroad. During a semester in Mexico, my Internet research for graduate programs revealed frequent mention of the Foreign Service on university websites. I did meet a former Foreign Service officer, who said he left the State Department to seek a higher salary in the private sector. But because money was not my primary objective, he did not discourage me. Instead, I was intrigued by the idea of learning foreign languages, traveling the world one country at a time, and carrying out diplomacy.

By the time I entered graduate school I knew I wanted to become a Foreign Service officer, and I set myself to the task of passing the Foreign Service examination. It was offered twice that year, but I was so intimidated by the exam that I postponed taking it until the second opportunity. (Having been through the process, my advice to anyone interested in this career is to take the exam as early and often as possible. It is free and there is no penalty or record of not passing.) I learned as much as possible about the exam from readily available State Department sources, including a test preparation booklet available on the State Department website (www.careers.state.gov/officer/join/examinfo.html). The most valuable test preparation, however, was talking to people who had taken the exam. The first part was a written exam that included essays, multiple choice questions on a wide range of domestic and international topics, and questions about my relevant experience and suitability for the job. I am certain that familiarizing myself with the format of the exam was a key factor in passing on the first try.

I was scheduled to take the oral exam about six months later. In the interim I did an internship in the political section of the U.S. embassy in Tegucigalpa. That experience gave me a close look at the daily functioning of an embassy, which I later drew upon for the oral exam. Another bonus of that internship is that I met a first tour Foreign Service officer, who spent several hours helping me to prepare for the exam. I also attended Foreign Service exam workshops offered at my graduate school.

On the day I took the oral exam, there were eighteen candidates at the testing site in Washington. We were divided into three groups. My group began with an exercise in which we were assigned roles as proponents of different projects and then observed as we negotiated which projects to fund with our limited budget. The next part of the exam was an individual writing test in which we were each given a binder full of information that we had to sort through to write a concise memo to a fictional supervisor. The last part of the exam was a structured interview that included questions used to assess compatibility with Foreign Service work and lifestyle as well as hypothetical questions to test our decision-making skills in some of the difficult situations that an officer might encounter.

At the end of the long day I was relieved to learn that I was one of the two candidates who had passed! I was immediately ushered into an office, where a Diplomatic Security agent interviewed me, beginning the security clearance process. After my medical and security clearances were granted, I was placed on a ranked list of candidates, based on my final score on the oral examination. Eight months later, I was called to join the 114th class of Foreign Service officers.

Although many first-tour officers spend their days interviewing visa applicants, my Foreign Service career began as the cultural affairs officer of the U.S. embassy in Panama. I managed the cultural and exchange programs, including the Fulbright Scholarship Program and the International Visitor Leadership Program. I particularly enjoyed the U.S. Speaker Program, in part because I had great influence over the topics—it was easy to develop programs that were both priority areas for our post and of interest to me personally. The speakers were experts in their fields, often university professors, and I learned a great deal from them on a broad range of issues, such as anticorruption, ecotourism, trade agreements, and judicial reform. It also gave me the chance to visit many regions of Panama in the implementation of these programs.

Work in the embassy offered me many exciting opportunities well beyond cultural affairs. I took lead roles on several important visits by U.S. government officials, including Secretary of State Colin Powell, a congressional delegation led by Senator Henry Hyde, and President George H. Bush and Mrs. Laura Bush. The embassy hosted several large, public events each year at which I also played a role. I also headed the International Women's Month event committee. This was a special initiative of the ambassador and involved nominating outstanding Panamanian women from all over the country. The nominees were brought to the capital for a luncheon in their honor, a digital video conference, and a ceremony in front of 150 of the most prominent women leaders in Panama. These experiences were simultaneously invigorating and exhausting.

I recently completed nine months of Indonesian language, consular, and political-economic training in preparation for my second tour in Jakarta. It will be my first time in Asia, and I am eager to see as much of the region as possible. I will spend one year in the consular section and one year in the economic section. Both the work and the country context will be extremely different from my first tour. For me, this variety—in the nature of the work as well as the issues—is one of the most attractive features of the Foreign Service.

There are significant trade-offs to keep in mind when deciding about this career. The most difficult aspect for me has been the distance and length of time away from my family. For instance, it has been hard to accept that my nephews are growing up without getting to know me. Some people, especially single people and the spouses of Foreign Service officers without children, struggle with loneliness in this lifestyle. In many places in the world, it can be difficult to make friends with local people because of the association with the U.S. embassy and cultural differences. For those with families, it can be extremely trying, for example, if a spouse who wants to work cannot find suitable employment or teenage children do not want to leave their friends when the tour is over. In addition, there is a real security threat to Americans working abroad, especially in an official capacity. Furthermore, promotion in the Foreign Service is increasingly tied to serving at posts categorized as "high danger."

I have had a rewarding professional experience, but it is not as satisfying for everyone. Two of my closest colleagues in Panama quit before ending their tours. One of them had done a consular tour in Ankara and was an economic officer in her second posting. She left the Foreign Service to go to business school. The other colleague spent two years in the consular section and was hoping for a management section position on her second tour. However, because the assignment system favors officers coming from posts that are categorized as dangerous or hardship, she faced a second straight tour of consular work. She made the decision to leave the State Department and returned to the United States, where she got a job at an international relations nongovernmental organization.

The Foreign Service offers a unique experience and a tremendous opportunity for those who feel called to represent the U.S. government and its interests in foreign countries. Though the degree to which U.S. embassy officials are embraced by foreign governments and populations varies greatly by country and time period, nevertheless, the U.S. embassy commands respect around the world. That respect allows Foreign Service officers to have a positive impact on governments and regular people in every corner of the Earth. It is an awesome privilege that few careers can truthfully claim.

Careers on Capitol Hill

Denis McDonough

Denis McDonough, *a 1996 graduate of Georgetown University's Master of Science in Foreign Service Program, is a senior fellow and senior adviser at the Center for American Progress. He was formerly a legislative assistant in the office of Senate majority leader Tom Daschle, where he was responsible for U.S. foreign policy. Before joining Senator Daschle's staff in 2000, he worked as a Democratic professional staff member on the House International Relations Committee. He is a 1992 graduate of Saint John's University in Collegeville, Minnesota.*

THE CONSTITUTION ensures that Capitol Hill can offer challenging career opportunities to those with expertise and background in foreign affairs and an interest in public service. Though the Constitution names the president as the commander-in-chief, it also ensures that Congress retains both the pursue strings on the nation's treasury and an aggressive role on oversight of the president's conduct of all policy, including foreign and defense policy. From the League of Nations to Vietnam to Central America, history has demonstrated that a successful U.S. foreign policy demands an informed, involved, and expert Congress.

To fulfill this important constitutional duty, every House member and senator has at least one staff person who spends his or her time on foreign policy issues, including defense, homeland security, intelligence, trade, and foreign policy. Committees such as the Senate Foreign Relations Committee, the House International Relations Committee, the Senate and House select committees on intelligence, the House and Senate armed services committees, and the House and Senate government affairs committees and appropriations committees have entire professional staffs devoted to foreign policy and defense issues. Other committees in both houses—Agriculture, Finance and Budget, among others—also have staff that devote a bulk of their time to international issues. (See the list of committees and placement offices at the end of this essay.)

In the twenty-first century, the demand for qualified people to handle these issues and advise members of Congress on international affairs has drastically increased, making this a remarkably interesting and challenging time to work on Capitol Hill.

Staffers enter an arena with the potential to influence national policy while opening up an array of further career development opportunities.

The pace is frenetic, the hours are unpredictable, job security is non-existent, and issues change from day to day, even hour to hour. However, Hill staffers are compensated for these uncertainties: They draft legislation, have access to top policymakers both foreign and domestic, have opportunities for foreign travel, and influence the national agenda—often unencumbered by the layers of bureaucracy found in the executive branch. Staffers enter an arena with the potential to influence national policy while opening up an array of further career development opportunities.

HILL JOB-SEEKING STRATEGIES

Hiring practices on Capitol Hill vary from office to office, and there is no magic formula for landing a Hill job. Some staff—those still in or recent graduates from college or graduate school—start off as unpaid interns or as paid support staff or legislative correspondents and work their way up through the ranks.

All around the Hill and in both parties, one will find examples of interns becoming top policy advisers. One key Senate staffer started years ago as a driver for a senator from New York. Another key Senate floor staffer worked in the Capitol parking lot as he earned his master's degree in Russian studies. In 1995, two members of my Georgetown class used unpaid internships to get to know the Hill and thus position themselves for permanent jobs—one in a committee and one as foreign policy staffer for a senior Republican senator from the Midwest—upon graduation a year later. Another graduate student, using her home state connection and foreign policy background, landed an entry-level job as a legislative correspondent with a committee after two years at the State Department. After several months, due to staff turnover, she was given increased responsibilities and, within a couple of years, also became a professional staff member.

Others at middle or senior levels with no previous Hill experience may make a lateral move by bringing to their new job a great deal of substantive experience in a particular field such as arms control, trade policy, or foreign aid. Still others manage to land professional Hill jobs as a result of their campaign or political work for state or national parties or for individual campaigns. As with any job search, finding a job on the Hill often boils down to talking to the right person or being in the right place at the right time. But to suggest that it is merely luck misses a key point—those who succeed in landing jobs, be they starting positions or midcareer assignments, know the substance of foreign policy and the workings of the House and Senate. Because there is a plethora of talented international policy experts in Washington, the successful job seeker may distinguish herself from other candidates by knowing parliamentary procedure, including, for example, how to file an amendment or draft a bill.

Equally important—as much for job satisfaction as for success in finding a job—are the politics of the Congress. Those seeking a job on Capitol Hill should have some sense of their own ideological persuasion—and on what core principles they will not compromise—before approaching members' offices. Several times individuals interested in jobs on the Hill have told me that they do not care if they work for a Democrat or a Republican. This is a mistake. If you do not share the bulk of your boss's convictions, your job will be very uncomfortable and unsatisfying. That may even be the case when you and a particular member are of the same party. There is such a diversity of views on foreign policy (e.g., multilateralists vs. unilateralists) and defense policy (e.g., hawks vs. doves) within parties that you may find yourself at odds with your boss about issues on which you have to spend many hours.

Identifying a potential boss's views is easy enough. Every vote cast and statement made on the floor of Congress is recorded in the *Congressional Record*. It is published daily and available through any number of websites. Before applying for a job in a particular office, job seekers should spend some time reviewing the *Record* for insider information.

Everyone Need—or Should—Apply

Although individual senators and representatives do their own hiring, both houses of Congress operate placement offices to which individual offices may turn for resumes. More often than not, the placement office helps fill offices for support staff, but anyone interested in a Hill job should invest the few minutes it takes to drop off a resume and take a typing test at the placement offices. When job hunting, leave no stone unturned.

The offices of the home state delegation should be one of the first stops of any job seeker, because many members prefer to hire natives of their home state. Even if members do not have an opening, they do want to be responsive to their constituents, so job seekers should take advantage of this resource, even if just for job tips. Constituents have an automatic "foot in the door" that is unavailable to others and should arrange a meeting with the administrative assistant, chief of staff, or legislative director as a first resort.

List of Committees and Placement Offices

House Committees:

Committee on Agriculture
Committee on Appropriations
Committee on Armed Services
Committee on the Budget
Committee on Education and Labor
Committee on Energy and Commerce
House Select Committee on Energy Independence and Global
   Warming
Committee on Financial Services
Committee on Foreign Affairs
Committee on Homeland Security
Committee on House Administration
House Permanent Select Committee on Intelligence
Committee on the Judiciary
Committee on Natural Resources
Committee on Oversight and Government Reform
Committee on Rules
Committee on Science and Technology

Committee on Small Business
Committee on Standards of Official Conduct
Committee on Transportation and Infrastructure
Committee on Veterans Affairs
Committee on Ways and Means
Joint Economic Committee
Joint Committee on Printing
Joint Committee on Taxation

Senate Committees:

STANDING:

Agriculture, Nutrition, and Forestry Committee
Appropriations Committee
Armed Services Committee
Banking, Housing, and Urban Affairs Committee
Budget Committee
Commerce, Science, and Transportation Committee
Energy and Natural Resources Committee
Environment and Public Works Committee
Finance Committee
Foreign Relations Committee
Health, Education, Labor, and Pensions Committee
Homeland Security and Governmental Affairs Committee
Judiciary Committee
Rules and Administration Committee
Small Business and Entrepreneurship Committee
Veterans Affairs Committee

SPECIAL, SELECT, AND OTHER:

Senate Select Committee on Intelligence
Senate Select Committee on Ethics
Senate Select Committee on Indian Affairs
Senate Special Committee on Aging

WITH HOUSE:

Joint Committee on Printing
Joint Committee on Taxation

Joint Committee on the Library
Joint Economic Committee

PLACEMENT OFFICES:

Senate Placement Office
Room SH-116
Hart Senate Office Building
Washington, DC 20510

Office of Human Resources
102 Ford House Office Building
Washington, DC 20515
Fax: 202-226-7514

Careers in Intelligence Analysis

Volko F. Ruhnke

Volko F. Ruhnke, *a 1986 graduate of the Master of Science in Foreign Service Program at Georgetown University, is a deputy group chief in the Central Intelligence Agency's (CIA's) Counterterrorism Center. Among previous assignments, he served as the CIA's deputy national intelligence officer for science and technology. The views expressed in this essay do not reflect the official position of the CIA.*

THE PUBLIC RETROSPECTIVES over the past several years on the failure to warn of the September 11, 2001, terrorist attacks and the mistaken assessments of Saddam Hussein's weapons of mass destruction programs have put the tradecraft of the intelligence analyst under the microscope. The examiners of pre–September 11 analysis spoke of the importance of analysts "connecting the dots" and guarding against "failures of imagination" while the Iraq WMD postmortem seemed to warn against straining too hard to imagine connections between dots that do not really connect at all. So what have we learned that all can agree on? First, we know that U.S. (and allied) intelligence analysis clearly could be more competent. There is no doubt that analysis failed in these cases, with serious consequences. Thus, second, intelligence analysis is worth the investment to make it better.

How? We have moved resources, reorganized, and strengthened connections across the intelligence community—as the country has done in response to past intelligence failures. But will those rearrangements be decisive? What is the element on which success or failure hangs?

I assert that the answer is, in a word, talent. Will the intelligence community attract to its ranks the talent it needs to succeed? For intelligence analysis, that talent includes the ability to think strategically: the dynamic kind of analysis that realizes that what you are studying is studying you back—and reacting!

This kind of analysis includes the tenacity to squeeze the most under-standing you can out of fragmentary information; unlike a commercial venture, intelligence analysis cannot invest in just the most profitable areas but must work on even the toughest and least rewarding problems when national security or the national interest demand it. Even when intelligence collectors are not finding much information, or the informa-tion is ambiguous, the intelligence analyst remains on the hook to make a call, to be as helpful and unambiguous as possible.

This kind of analysis also includes the knack for asking the right ques-tions. As policy consumers have told us, a good analyst answers their questions, but a great analyst answers the questions that they should have asked but did not. Classic intelligence analysis divides into policy support (answering the questions coming in the door, no matter how tough) and strategic warning (looking ahead at those difficulties or opportunities not yet on the policymakers' scope).

Finally, this kind of analysis includes the disposition to walk the fine line between policy relevance and policy prescription. . . . .

THE MINISTRY OF BAD NEWS

One of my favorite professors in the Master of Science in Foreign Service (MSFS) Program at Georgetown—who had had a long career in foreign affairs and was serving in a senior policy post downtown at the time—told our seminar the following story. Working in an embassy, he had become close to the host country's president. One day on the golf course, the president asked his opinion of the makeup of his Cabinet. The profes-sor responded that he was impressed with how the organization of the Cabinet included ministers covering all relevant issues of national policy and was filled with intelligent individuals. There was only one position in the Cabinet missing, said the professor to the president: a minister of bad news.

My professor was commenting on the age-old tendency in government (and other enterprises, for that matter) of those individuals in charge of an area of endeavor to tell their boss that things are going OK. Policymak-ers tend to be optimistic about their own policies—how else could they sell them to an interagency Principals Committee? So it is not a bad idea to have someone who is truly expert watching the policy-relevant issues for anything that may be headed off the rails, and whose job it is to bring such information forward. Intelligence analysts—policy-neutral experts on policy-relevant matters—often find themselves playing that role.

So what kind of mindset toward international affairs might make you someone who would *thrive* in that role? Do you believe you can offer the right answers to today's controversial foreign or national security policy questions? Or are you not so sure but fascinated by the strengths and weaknesses of the opposing positions? Well, if the former, intelligence analysis actually may not be the career for you.

If the latter, I am with you. As a new MSFS student in 1984, I experienced something that I called "intellectual vertigo"—I had just arrived from an undergraduate program in international relations elsewhere that, I was soon to realize, had spoon-fed me from only one end of the political spectrum. There I was in Washington with professors who had served in administrations from one side or the other, in power and out of power, challenging me to test the opposite case. In the MSFS Program I learned that I might not have the right answer. And so I dedicated myself not to pushing one side of the policy argument but to elevating the level of policy debate, and I found the right career. The most useful posture for the intelligence analyst is as the policymaker's referent, adviser, coach, "idea man" but—though often a deliverer of bad news—never a critic or a cheerleader.

Follow Your Bliss

Naturally, the success of U.S. intelligence analysis will depend not only on mindset, knack, or raw analytic talent but also on substantive expertise. Effective intelligence analysis often requires getting under the skin of an adversary. So immersion in one's topic is at least a huge plus, if not essential.

The success of U.S. intelligence analysis will depend not only on mindset, knack, or raw analytic talent but also on substantive expertise.

Such immersion requires the investment of time, typically before one's career even begins. An MSFS student once asked me: What topics should I invest in? What expertise is the intelligence community looking for? My first answer probably was unsurprising in ticking off the areas of key U.S. national security and foreign policy concern: terrorism, the Middle East, WMD, China, and so on. Sure, the community has a hiring focus on such topics. You could probably refine and complete that list as well as I could.

But what may surprise some is that analytic offices are looking for and hiring expertise well off that beaten track. Global coverage remains an important objective, and, as I write, most of CIA's regionally and functionally organized analytic offices are interviewing and hiring. My own group seeks Middle East and terrorism specialists, but it seeks in its recruiting to leaven that expertise with a diversity of perspectives. And in any event, the Middle East–based terrorist threats we follow are global in nature, as are our counterterrorist partnerships, so a mix of global expertise is needed.

My second answer to the MSFS student was to follow her bliss—to get deep on the international affairs topic that really grabbed her, whether it was Iranian diplomacy, South American economies, or new European institutions. Her best chance of impressing an interviewer would be to show the depth of her investment as proof not only of her expertise on but also her passion for her topic. Analytic managers know that it is such passion—and not pay incentives—that at the end of the day fuels excellence in intelligence analysis, so her interviewers would be looking for this passion in her.

In addition, though the intelligence community recognizes the criticality of and nurtures substantive depth in its analysts, for better or worse it must also be ready to shift its analytic resources in reaction to world events and its consumers' interests. The imperative for any analytic directorate to be both deep and agile means that opportunities for substantive mobility for individual careerists will remain legion. I began my career working on Soviet military issues (the "big fight" of the day) and am now helping to lead analysis of terrorism, and I am not atypical.

If you are interviewing for a job as an intelligence analyst, show your energy for research and your creativity in finding the reliable source.

Analytic managers know that they frequently will have to ask experts on one topic to "read in" on others, so the demonstrated ability to dig not only *deeply* but also *quickly* is a sought-after skill. If you are interviewing for a job as an intelligence analyst, show your energy for research and your creativity in finding the reliable source. Again, the intelligence community works on many questions whose answers are not only obscure but also on which adversaries are actively working to thwart the search.

THE BROADER PRESIDENT'S DAILY BRIEFING

Here, I will not go into the advantages or disadvantages of analytic careers in this or that agency. Most if not all agencies are building up their analytic services in response to an integrated approach to the threat of terrorism and the mandate—for example, from the WMD Commission, to ensure that senior policymakers receive intelligence analysis from all agencies that have expertise and views relevant to a given issue. Toward those objectives, the career opportunities for analysts are becoming broader across agencies, and the ability to move among analytic services is growing.

The creation of a director of national intelligence (DNI) and the National Counterterrorism Center (NCTC) are cases in point. The Office of the DNI is encouraging and adding incentives for joint or "purple" tours—meaning service outside one's own agency, particularly in organizations such as the NCTC that integrate work across the intelligence community and thus rely principally on analysts on detail from elsewhere. The NCTC is in the process of standing up its own career service as well and presents an excellent opportunity to help shape a new enterprise in the war on terror as that enterprise gets rolling.

In the past, each agency's analysts served their own dedicated customer sets almost exclusively—the CIA, the president, the Department of Defense Information Agency, and so on. Today, many agencies write for the *President's Daily Briefing*, which means not only that a broader group of intelligence analysts can reach the most senior audiences but also that their work all must "meet threshold"—that is, pass through the same fine-toothed quality control process managed under the DNI's office to ensure that the analytic tradecraft is sound and the material is of sufficient import.

How does such quality control work mechanically? In the intelligence analytic profession, we put a great deal of sweat, blood, and tears into a process of coordination and review. Coordination is the lateral check on an individual analyst's work: Every other analyst in an agency—and, increasingly, in the entire community or in outside institutions as well—with some substantive stake in an article or paper gets a chance to weigh in on it. That way, we have milked the tension among analytic perspectives for value and done what we can to provide a 360-degree look at any topic. Review is the vertical check; managers, editors, and others up the line act as reader advocates to ensure that the product stands up and hits the mark.

At the end of this process, an individual's work becomes a product of the corporate agency or the intelligence community and bears that agency's imprimatur—though possibly at the expense of an individual's pride of authorship. It is a process that can be grueling over months and years, especially when that passion for substance is engaged, when the nature of the mission means that critical issues are at stake in any coordination skirmish, and when there are deadlines to be met. We call it collaboration, but it is not for everyone.

We do it because the mission leaves our analysis, our writing, and our briefing little room for ambiguity, shortcuts, or errors. We are writing for the busiest people in the world, who are reading and already conversant with our source materials, and who are keenly focused on the questions we are addressing because lives and billions of dollars really are at stake. U.S. intelligence analysis has never been error free, but compare the community's attention to coordination and review to the quality control process in, say, today's news media.

For this reason, if you interview for a position in intelligence analysis, you will notice the interviewer's interest in hearing about your ability to collaborate, to work effectively even with difficult people and even when the pressure is on. The interviewer also is likely to be interested in how hard you have worked to improve your writing and oral presentation skills. He or she will be listening for clarity of thought, economy of words, and precision of language.

INTELLIGENCE ANALYSIS AND THE GLOBAL WAR ON TERRORISM

Along with the broadened opportunity for the career analyst to support policymaking at its most senior level, intelligence analysis in the global war on terrorism affords a greater role for the analyst than ever before in supporting not only policy but also operations. The old model of analyst–operations interaction in the intelligence community was dominated by the separation of the disciplines, and it limited analysts principally to providing their operations counterparts with collection requirements and feedback on reporting. Intelligence analysis today is shifting to a new model in which the operator—intelligence or military—is becoming as important a consumer as the policymaker, and the analyst is becoming a key asset for the development and support of operations.

Symptomatic of this shift is the recent creation of a new career track for CIA analysts alongside political, military, economic, leadership, and other long-standing analytic disciplines: the targeting analyst occupation. Targeting analysts also support policymaking but specialize in the tools and tradecraft of operations support, providing the deep and detailed expertise needed to help not only collect information but also thwart adversaries in the field. An imperative in fighting terrorist cells, this application of analytic talent has also become important to the fight against narcotics traffickers, hostile intelligence services, weapons proliferation networks, and a host of other threats.

This blossoming of the analyst–operator partnership is multiplying the potential for even the most junior analyst to have an impact. Consider the question of what the decisive capabilities will be in defeating an adversary in the Age of Terror. It will not be industrial power or bombing accuracy; capturing or killing a terrorist is easy—if you can find him. If we know who and where the enemy is, we can get him. And that will come down to analytic talent—perhaps yours.

RESOURCE LISTINGS

Federal Bureau of Investigation, Directorate of Intelligence

The mission of the FBI is to protect and defend the United States against terrorist and foreign intelligence threats, to uphold and enforce the criminal laws of the United States, and to provide leadership and criminal justice services to federal, state, municipal, and international agencies and partners. The mission of the FBI's Intelligence Program is to optimally position the FBI to meet current and emerging national security and criminal threats by

- aiming core investigative work proactively against threats to U.S. interests,
- building and sustaining enterprise-wide intelligence policies and capabilities, and

- providing useful, appropriate, and timely information and analysis to the national security, homeland security, and law enforcement communities.

To perform its mission, the FBI employs a number of core tools, including investigative techniques, forensics, information technologies, and strategic partnerships. Intelligence is also one of those core tools. As a core tool and competency, intelligence is an integral part of the FBI's investigative mission. It is imbedded in the day-to-day work of the FBI from the initiation of preliminary investigations to the development of FBI-wide investigative strategies.

The tool of intelligence is more important than ever in today's threat environment. The threats facing the United States are evolving. Threats are global, and they often emanate from transnational enterprises that rely on sophisticated information technology. As such, threats transcend geographic boundaries, as well as the boundaries of authorities in the U.S. national security infrastructure. In this threat environment, having the right information at the right time is essential to protecting national security.

The FBI has a mandate from Congress, the president, the attorney general, and the DNI to protect national security by producing intelligence in support of its own investigative mission, national intelligence priorities, and the needs of other customers. The FBI must serve the American people with an enterprise-wide intelligence program that makes its investigations most effective for national security, homeland security, and law enforcement purposes, while meeting external needs for FBI information and analysis. For more information, visit www .fbijobs.com.

Central Intelligence Agency

The Central Intelligence Agency was created in 1947 with the signing of the National Security Act by President Harry S. Truman. The act also created a director of central intelligence (DCI) to serve as head of the United States intelligence community, act as the principal adviser to the president for intelligence matters related to national security, and serve as head of the CIA. The Intelligence Reform and Terrorism Prevention Act of 2004 amended the National Security Act to provide for a DNI who would assume some of the roles formerly fulfilled by the DCI, with a separate director of the CIA.

The director of the CIA serves as the head of the CIA and reports to the DNI. The CIA director's responsibilities include

- collecting intelligence through human sources and by other appropriate means, except that he shall have no police, subpoena, or law enforcement powers or internal security functions;
- correlating and evaluating intelligence related to the national security and providing appropriate dissemination of such intelligence;
- providing overall direction for and coordination of the collection of national intelligence outside the United States through human sources by elements of the intelligence community authorized to undertake such collection and, in coordination with other departments, agencies, or elements of the U.S. government that are authorized to undertake such collection, ensuring that the most effective use is made of resources and that appropriate account is taken of the risks to the United States and those involved in such collection; and
- performing such other functions and duties related to intelligence affecting the national security as the president or the DNI may direct.

The function of the CIA is to assist its director in carrying out these responsibilities.

To accomplish its mission, the CIA engages in research, development, and the deployment of high-leverage technology for intelligence purposes. As a separate agency, the CIA serves as an independent source of analysis on topics of concern and also works closely with the other organizations in the intelligence community to ensure that the intelligence consumer—whether a Washington policymaker or battlefield commander—receives the best intelligence possible. By emphasizing adaptability in its approach to intelligence collection, the CIA can tailor its support to key intelligence consumers and help them meet their needs as they face the issues of the post–cold war world.

The CIA offers global employment opportunities in seeking a diversity of people for the important job of keeping America safe. These include Clandestine Service officers to be on the front line of human intelligence, as well as individuals skilled in science, engineering, technology, analysis, foreign languages, and administration for positions in the United States and overseas. Several career paths are available at the CIA.

Analysts are skilled subject matter experts who study and evaluate information from many sources. Information flows in from around the world, including satellite surveillance, foreign newspapers and broadcasts, and human contacts. This information varies widely in reliability, and often it is conflicting or incomplete. The analyst's role is to develop meaningful and usable intelligence assessments from all those sources.

Often this is like putting together the pieces of a puzzle, received at different times from different places, to form a picture that is complete enough to comprehend—even when some pieces are still missing. An intelligence analyst pulls together relevant information from all available sources and then analyzes it to produce timely and objective assessments, free of any political bias. This finished intelligence product, which may be in the form of a written report or oral briefings, could very well appear on the desks of the president and his key senior advisers. Each morning, the DNI delivers the *President's Daily Briefing*, an extremely sensitive intelligence document containing short assessments of current worldwide developments as well as anticipated events that will require the president's attention in the future. The assessment content represents a team effort by analysts across the community.

The **Clandestine Service** is the front-line source of clandestine information on critical international developments, from terrorism and WMD to military and political issues. The mission requires Clandestine Service officers to live and work overseas, making a true commitment to the CIA. This is more than just a job—it is a way of life that challenges the deepest resources of personal intelligence, self-reliance, and responsibility. **Operations officers** work with **collection management officers** to determine what kind of assets to seek and what information is needed. Living under cover, many operations officers also must work at their "day" job, a necessary challenge that is part of their clandestine role. **Staff operations officers** contribute to the Clandestine Service mission primarily from the CIA's Washington-area headquarters, providing fast-paced research and case management in support of colleagues overseas. This includes monitoring counterintelligence issues and providing support needed to deal with foreign contacts in the field. Staff operations officers must be knowledgeable on both operational tradecraft and international issues in order to enhance their interaction with field-based officers.

The Clandestine Service has a program for recent college graduates, the **Professional Trainee (PT) Program**, after which PTs may be considered for the Clandestine Service Training Program. The CIA also has a comprehensive program to foster the acquisition and maintenance of foreign language skills. The Central Intelligence Language Institute uses native speakers and the latest instructional technology to teach sixteen languages. All employees who attain tested levels of language expertise through full-time training, part-time classes, or self-study are eligible for monetary incentives. (For a description of each proficiency level, go to www.govtilr.org and consult the "Unabridged Version of the Interagency Language Roundtable Scale.") New employees who already possess excellent language skills may be eligible for a significant hiring bonus. The CIA has two language incentive systems: the **Corporate Language Hiring Bonus Program**—under which new employees can earn up to $35,000 in hiring bonuses for superior language skills—and the **Corporate Language Program**.

The CIA also hires qualified scientists, engineers, and technology specialists, as well as support staff for a range of positions. The **Graduate Studies Program** may also be of special interest. The program looks for bright graduate students who are focusing on international affairs, languages, economics, geography, cartography, physical sciences, and engineering. Other majors may be accepted on a case-by-case basis. Students selected for this program should be entering either their first or second year of graduate studies following this assignment. Selected students will become acquainted with the work of professional intelligence analysts through active participation in CIA projects with the potential to have selected pieces of their work disseminated throughout the intelligence community. The program allows the CIA to assess students' skills and knowledge as they relate to permanent employment opportunities.

Applicants for positions must be U.S. citizens. The CIA Recruitment Center does not accept resumes, nor can it return phone calls, e-mails, or other forms of communication, from U.S. citizens living outside the United States. The CIA recommends submitting your resume online in response to a specific position. The online resume submission link is found at the bottom of each position listed on the employment site. Multiple online submissions for a position are unnecessary and slow the processing of your resume. If you are contacted about a position, be prepared to undergo a thorough background investigation examining your life history, character, trustworthiness, reliability, and soundness of judgment. The CIA also examines your freedom from conflicting allegiances, potential to be coerced, and willingness and ability to abide by regulations governing the use, handling, and protection of sensitive information. The CIA uses the polygraph to check the veracity of this information. The hiring process also includes a thorough mental and physical medical examination in relation to performing essential job functions. More information about jobs at the CIA is available at www.cia.gov/careers, where you may also submit your resume online.

Defense Intelligence Agency

The Defense Intelligence Agency (DIA) is a Department of Defense combat support agency and an important member of the U.S. intelligence community. With over 11,000 military and civilian employees worldwide, the DIA is a major producer and manager of foreign military intelligence. It provides military intelligence to war fighters, defense policymakers, and force planners in the Department of Defense and the intelligence community, in support of U.S. military planning and operations and weapon systems acquisition.

The DIA is headquartered at the Pentagon in Washington, with major operational activities at the Defense Intelligence Analysis Center (DIAC), Washington; the Armed Forces Medical Intelligence Center (AFMIC), Frederick, Maryland; and the Missile and Space Intelligence Center (MSIC), Huntsville, Alabama. The DIA's workforce is as diverse as its missions; its people are skilled in the areas of military history and doctrine, economics, physics, chemistry, world history, political science, biosciences, and computer sciences, to name a few. Most of DIA's activities are performed at the Defense Intelligence Analysis Center at Bolling Air Force Base in Washington. The DIA employs a limited number of support assistants (secretaries and bilingual research technicians) in U.S. Defense Attaché Offices, located at U.S. embassies worldwide. For the adventurous few, these assignments (some requiring language proficiency) offer a unique opportunity to live and work in exciting overseas locations, primarily in Europe and Latin America.

Initial employment with the DIA is subject to completion of a satisfactory personnel special security background investigation or reinvestigation to ensure compliance with the agency's special employment criteria. This investigation will include verification of experience, education, and personal history to ensure that an applicant is eligible for access to Top-Secret/Sensitive Compartmented Information. Applicants may also be subject to a required medical examination, personal interviews, any required counterintelligence-scope polygraph examination, satisfactory completion of a urinalysis test to screen for illegal drug use, and such other procedures as are deemed necessary to assure that the agency's security, suitability, and overall qualifications standards are met.

The DIA recruits U.S. citizens, both civilian and military. To view current listings and apply online, visit diajobs.dia.mil. For employment questions, call 202-321-8228 or e-mail staffing@dia.mil.

U.S. Drug Enforcement Administration, Office of National Security Intelligence

The DEA's Office of National Security Intelligence (NN), a part of the DEA Intelligence Division, is a member of the intelligence community. DEA/NN personnel are assigned to analysis, liaison, and central tasking management functions. The designation of DEA/NN as a member of the intelligence community does not grant DEA new authorities, but it does formalize the long-standing relationship between the DEA and the intelligence community and gives the DEA and other members of the intelligence community the ability to work national security interests in an integrated fashion.

The Office of National Security Intelligence is responsible for providing drug-related information responsive to intelligence community requirements. DEA/NN establishes and manages the centralized tasking of requests for and analysis of national security information obtained during the course of DEA's drug enforcement. The Office also centrally manages requests from the intelligence community for information either reposited in the DEA pursuant to the authority the administration derives from Title 21 of the United States Code or that is obtained for the intelligence community through existing assets operating pursuant to DEA's law enforcement missions.

The DEA and the intelligence community have a history of partnering for purposes of identifying and disrupting illegal drug trafficking. This partnership has been successful in facilitating the exchange of vital information and the leveraging of expertise. DEA/NN's membership in the community helps optimize the overall U.S. government counternarcotics interdiction and security effort and furthers creative collaboration between the many organizations involved in countering the threats from narcotics trafficking, human smuggling/trafficking, immigration crimes, and global terrorism. It is at the nexus of these transnational threats that some of the most serious threats to national security exist. Having the DEA as a member of the intelligence community permits greater exploitation of its intelligence capabilities, particularly against transnational targets.

With analytical support from the Intelligence Program, DEA has disrupted major trafficking organizations or put them entirely out of business. The DEA Intelligence Division also cooperates a great deal with state and local law enforcement and will soon provide intelligence training for state, local, federal, and foreign agencies. This training will be held at the

Justice Training Center in Quantico, Virginia, and will address the full spectrum of drug intelligence training needs. The best practices and theories of all partners in working on the drug issue will be solicited and incorporated into the training. Academic programs; the exchange of federal, state, and local drug experience; and the sharing of and exposure to new ideas together will result in a more effective application of drug intelligence resources at all levels.

The DEA has the largest U.S. law enforcement presence abroad, with eighty-six offices in sixty-three countries, and it has over thirty-three years of operational experience in the foreign arena. In this light, the DEA has many unique contributions to make to issues of national security. The membership of the DEA/NN in the intelligence community better equips the community to face the global threats of the twenty-first century. For more information on this program, visit www.usdoj.gov/dea /job/intelligence/intelligence.htm. Applications for all positions at the DEA are accepted through USAJOBS.gov.

U.S. Department of Energy, Office of Intelligence

The Department of Energy's Office of Intelligence (IN) is the intelligence community's premier technical intelligence resource in four core areas: nuclear weapons and nonproliferation; energy security; science and technology; and nuclear energy, safety, and waste. Tapping the broad technology base of DOE's national laboratories and the international reach of the DOE complex as a whole, IN accomplishes a three-part mission:

- To provide DOE, other U.S. government policymakers, and the intelligence community with timely, accurate, high-impact foreign intelligence analyses.
- To ensure that DOE's technical, analytical, and research expertise is made available to the intelligence, law enforcement, and special operations communities.
- To provide quick turnaround, specialized technology applications, and operational support based on DOE technological expertise to the intelligence, law enforcement, and special operations communities.

DOE's intelligence program traces its origins to the days of the Manhattan Project, when the former Atomic Energy Commission (AEC) was tasked to provide specialized analysis of the nascent atomic weapons program of the Soviet Union. Since then, that program—like the functions of the old AEC—has come to reside within DOE. It continues to evolve in close concert with changing policy needs and the strengths of DOE's unique scientific and technological base, from the world energy crisis of the 1970s—and consequent demand for intelligence expertise in international energy supply and demand issues—to growing concerns over nuclear proliferation in this decade. Listings of current openings at DOE, including with IN, are available at chris.doe.gov/jobs.

U.S. Department of Homeland Security, Information Analysis and Infrastructure Protection Directorate

Congress provided the Department of Homeland Security with a clear statutory mandate to reduce the vulnerability of the United States to terrorism and to detect, prevent, and respond to terrorist attacks. The DHS is composed of five directorates, one of which (the Information Analysis and Infrastructure Protection Directorate, IAIP) is a member of the intelligence community. The IAIP's mission—to disseminate information analyzed by the Department to State, local government agencies and authorities, and private-sector entities—brings to the post–September 11, 2001, federal government a capability for the security and protection of the nation's domestic assets that did not previously exist.

The essential function of IAIP is mapping the vulnerabilities of the nation's critical infrastructure against a comprehensive analysis of intelligence and public source information. This function is unique to the federal government and fundamental to the nation's ability to better protect itself from terrorist attacks. The roles and functions of IAIP and the Terrorist Threat Integration Center (TTIC) are complementary and collaborative and enhance the national effort to detect, disrupt, and prevent terrorism. The TTIC makes full use of all the terrorist-threat-related information and expertise available to the U.S. government and provides comprehensive all-source threat analysis to the president, the DHS, and other federal agencies. The IAIP provides intelligence analysts to the TTIC, who participate with analysts from other federal agencies in analyzing this all-source terrorist information. The IAIP also provides the TTIC with threat information gathered and integrated from DHS component agencies, state and local government agencies and authorities, and private-sector entities.

The IAIP integrates all-source threat information and analysis received from the TTIC and other agencies of the intelligence community with its own vulnerability assessments to provide tailored threat assessments, including priorities for protective and support measures to other agencies of the federal government, state and local government agencies and authorities, and private sector entities. Finally, the IAIP administers the Homeland Security Advisory System to include exercising primary responsibility for public advisories.

Together, the DHS's IAIP and the TTIC fulfill all the requirements called for in Sections 201 and 202 of the Homeland Security Act of 2002. Applications for all positions at the DHS should come through USAJOBS.gov.

U.S. Department of State, Bureau of Intelligence and Research
The Bureau of Intelligence and Research (INR), drawing on all-source intelligence, provides value-added independent analysis of events to department policymakers, ensures that intelligence activities support foreign policy and national security purposes, and serves as the focal point in the department in ensuring the policy review of sensitive counterintelligence and law enforcement activities. The INR's primary mission is to harness intelligence to serve U.S. diplomacy, and it also analyzes geographical and international boundary issues. The INR is a member of the U.S. intelligence community.

The nation requires more from its intelligence community than ever before because the United States confronts a greater diversity of threats and challenges than ever before. Globalization, the defining characteristic of our age, requires global intelligence coverage. Globalization is not a "threat" in and of itself—it has more positive than negative characteristics. But globalization contributes to the array of U.S. national security challenges, which are shaped by dramatic advances in telecommunications, technology, new centers of economic growth, and the consequences of crises within traditional cultures. National security challenges for the United States include

- terrorist threats to the United States, to its national security interests, and to its allies;
- challenges in Iraq, Afghanistan, and Pakistan;
- The proliferation of weapons and delivery systems in states of key concern, such as Iran and North Korea;
- regional conflicts, instability, and reconfigurations of power and influence in the Middle East, major African states, Latin America, Asia, and Eurasia; and
- energy security and the competition for supplies.

The INR is located at the Department of State in Washington. It is staffed by a permanent cadre of civil servants and by foreign service officers on a rotating basis.

> U.S. Department of State
> HR/REE/REC
> Suite 518-H, 2401 E Street, NW
> Washington, DC 20522
> e-mail: careers@state.gov

Office of Intelligence and Analysis, U.S. Department of the Treasury
The Treasury Department is a Cabinet-level agency whose mission is to promote the conditions for prosperity and stability in the United States and encourage prosperity and stability in the rest of the world. The Treasury's Office of Intelligence and Analysis (OIA) is a member of the U.S. intelligence community. The OIA is headed by an assistant secretary in the Office of Terrorism and Financial Intelligence (TFI).

The TFI was created in 2004 to marshal the Treasury Department's unique policy focus, financial intelligence, global network, regulatory responsibilities, tools, and authorities to safeguard the financial system and counter the financial underpinnings of national security threats. The TFI's priority areas are terrorist financing, proliferation financing, rogue regimes, and money laundering / narcotics.

The OIA was established by the Intelligence Authorization Act for Fiscal Year 2004. The act specifies that the OIA shall be responsible for the receipt, analysis, collation, and dissemination of foreign intelligence and foreign counterintelligence information related to the operation and responsibilities of the Department of the Treasury. The OIA's mission is to support the formulation of policy and execution of Treasury authorities by providing

- expert analysis and intelligence production on financial and other support networks for terrorist groups, proliferators, and other key national security threats; and
- timely, accurate, and focused intelligence support on the full range of economic, political, and security issues.

Applications for all positions at the Department of the Treasury should come through USAJOBS.gov.

Military Intelligence Service Organizations
Each military service has an intelligence organization that focuses directly
on the needs of that service. However, some services do produce intelli-
gence for branch use and for sharing across the intelligence community.
You may search for jobs within the Department of Defense by exploring
nonmilitary positions with the Department of Army, Department of
Navy, Department of Air Force, U.S. Marine Corps, and other Defense
Department organizations at www.godefense.com.

National Geospatial-Intelligence Agency
The National Geospatial-Intelligence Agency (NGA) is a major intelligence and combat support agency of the Department of Defense. It supports U.S. national policymakers and military forces by providing timely,
relevant, and accurate geospatial intelligence derived from the exploitation and analysis of imagery and geospatial information to describe,
assess, and visually depict physical features and geographically referenced
activities on the Earth. As the intelligence community's functional manager for baseline geospatial intelligence, the NGA provides critical support to the national decision-making process and the operational
readiness of America's military forces. The exclusive business of NGA is
intelligence.

The agency centralizes responsibility for imagery and mapping, representing a fundamental step toward achieving the Department of Defense
vision of "dominant battle space awareness." It exploits the tremendous
potential of enhanced collection systems, digital processing technology,
and the prospective expansion in commercial imagery.

The NGA makes its contribution to intelligence through the National
System for Geospatial Intelligence, the integration of technology, policies,
capabilities, and doctrine necessary to conduct Geospatial Intelligence in
a multi-intelligence environment. The NGA workforce is in fields such as
cartography, imagery analysis, the physical sciences, geodesy, computer
and telecommunication engineering, and photogrammetry.

With headquarters in Bethesda, Maryland, the NGA operates major
facilities in the northern Virginia, Washington, and Saint Louis areas as
well as support and liaison offices worldwide. As of July 1, 2006, the
NGA no longer accepts applications in hard copy, via fax, or via e-mail.
Only applications submitted through the NGA's online application
process on nga.mil/careers will be accepted. You may e-mail questions
to recruitment@nga.mil.

National Reconnaissance Office
The National Reconnaissance Office (NRO) provides America with its eyes and ears in space. The NRO was established in 1960 to develop the nation's revolutionary satellite reconnaissance systems. The NRO ensures that the technology and space-borne assets needed to acquire timely intelligence worldwide are always available to national policymakers and military war fighters. Intelligence is the exclusive business of the NRO, and as such, the NRO in its entirety is considered a member of the intelligence community.

The NRO's mission is to enable U.S. global information superiority, during peace and through war. The NRO is responsible for the unique and innovative technology, large-scale systems, engineering, development and acquisition, and operation of space reconnaissance systems and related intelligence activities needed to support global information superiority.

The mission of the NRO has become even more essential now than perhaps at any time in recent history. The nation is engaged in multiple alliances while simultaneously addressing major changes in traditional threats. New emerging dimensions in national security strategies include energy, the environment, and economic competition.

The NRO is a separate operating agency of the Department of Defense, managed jointly by the secretary of defense and the DNI. The DNI establishes the NRO's collection priorities and requirements.

The NRO is an intelligence community agency that employs personnel from within the Department of Defense and the CIA. As such, the NRO does not directly hire employees; rather, they are assigned by their respective agencies. If you are interested in seeking employment with these agencies, contact the following:

Department of Defense
Washington Area Service Center
1900 E Street, NW
Washington, DC 20520
Tel.: 202-606-2700

National Security Agency
The National Security Agency / Central Security Service (NSA/CSS) is America's cryptologic organization. It coordinates, directs, and performs highly specialized activities to protect U.S. government information systems and produce intelligence information on foreign signals. A high-technology organization, the NSA is on the frontiers of communications

and data processing. It is also one of the most important centers of foreign language analysis and research within the government.

Signals Intelligence (SIGINT) is a unique discipline with a long and storied past. SIGINT's modern era dates to World War II, when the United States broke the Japanese military code and learned of plans to invade Midway Island. This intelligence allowed the United States to defeat Japan's superior fleet. The use of SIGINT is believed to have directly contributed to shortening the war by at least one year. Today, SIGINT continues to play an important role in keeping the United States a step ahead of its enemies. As the world becomes more and more technology oriented, the information assurance mission becomes increasingly challenging. This mission involves protecting all the classified and sensitive information that is stored by or sent through U.S. government equipment. Information assurance professionals go to great lengths to make certain that government systems remain impenetrable. This support spans from the highest levels of the U.S. government to the individual war fighter in the field.

The NSA conducts one of the U.S. government's leading research and development programs. Some of the these programs have significantly advanced the state of the art in the scientific and business worlds. The NSA's early interest in cryptanalytic research led to the first large-scale computer and the first solid-state computer, predecessors of the modern computer. The NSA pioneered efforts in flexible storage capabilities, which led to the development of the tape cassette. The NSA also made groundbreaking developments in semiconductor technology and remains a world leader in many technological fields.

The NSA employs the country's premier cryptologists. It is said to be the largest employer of mathematicians in the United States and perhaps the world. Its mathematicians contribute directly to the NSA's two missions: designing cipher systems that will protect the integrity of U.S. information systems; and searching for weaknesses in adversaries' systems and codes. Technology and the world change rapidly, and great emphasis is placed on staying ahead of these changes with employee training programs. The National Cryptologic School is indicative of the NSA's commitment to professional development. The school not only provides unique training for the NSA workforce but also serves as a training resource for the entire Department of Defense. The NSA sponsors employees for bachelor and graduate studies at the nation's leading universities and colleges, and selected NSA employees attend the various war colleges of the U.S. Armed Forces.

Most NSA/CSS employees, both civilian and military, are headquartered at Fort Meade, Maryland, centrally located between Baltimore and Washington. Its workforce represents an unusual combination of specialties: analysts, engineers, physicists, mathematicians, linguists, computer scientists, and researchers, as well as customer relations specialists, security officers, data flow experts, managers, administrative officers, and clerical assistants.

Career fields at the NSA include business management, mathematics, cryptanalysis/signals analysis, intelligence analysis, foreign languages, and information assurance research. **Intelligence analysts** prepare written and oral assessments of current events based on the sophisticated collection, research, and analysis of classified and open source information. NSA intelligence analysts demonstrate an understanding of world history; its past and current relevance; and the geographic, social, economic, and political aspects that have influenced steady global change. They also expertly write reports that reflect outstanding critical thinking and a comprehensive grasp of world events.

NSA **language analysts** have a powerful impact in providing the most complete and accurate SIGINT picture to U.S. policymakers, military commanders, and intelligence community members. Working directly with the original written or spoken language, they are the first people to determine the relevance of the intelligence collected, to analyze it, and to put the information into context. They may even be called upon to research and understand a culture in which a specific language is spoken. Language instructor positions are also available.

The NSA recruits civilian and reserve military personnel. Candidates should apply online at www.nsa.gov. Civilian Recruitment and Staffing can be reached at 866-672-4473 or customercare@nsa.gov. Reserve Recruitment can be reached at 800-304-0512 or rfd_all@nsa.gov.

Introduction to the Presidential Management Fellows Program

ROBERT F. DANBECK

Robert F. Danbeck *is the associate director of the Human Resources Products and Services Division of the U.S. Office of Personnel Management and oversees the Presidential Management Fellows Program. He has held several senior management positions since joining OPM in 2003. Previously, he had a thirty-five-year career with the IBM Corporation in top personnel management positions in the United States and overseas.*

FOR THE PAST twenty-nine years, the Presidential Management Fellows (PMF) Program has been attracting outstanding master's, law, and doctoral students to the federal service. The PMF Program is your passport to a unique and rewarding career experience with the federal government. It provides you with an opportunity to apply the knowledge you acquired from graduate study. As a PMF, your assignments may involve domestic or international issues, technology, science, criminal justice, health, financial management, and many other fields in support of public service programs.

On November 21, 2003, President George W. Bush signed Executive Order 13318, "modernizing" the Presidential Management Intern (PMI) Program, in keeping with his emphasis on the strategic management of the federal government's human capital. The executive order renamed the PMI Program as the Presidential Management Fellows Program to better reflect its high standards, rigor, and prestige. It is designed to attract to the federal service outstanding graduate students from a wide variety of academic disciplines who demonstrate an exceptional ability for, as well as a clear interest in and commitment to, leadership in the analysis and management of public policies and programs. The executive order charges the director of the U.S. Office of Personnel Management with developing, managing, and evaluating the PMF Program:

- *Eligibility*: Students who complete a graduate degree (master's, law, or doctoral degree) during the current academic year from an academic institution formally accredited by an accrediting organization recognized by the secretary of the U.S. Department of Education are eligible to be nominated by their schools.
- *Nomination process*: Students must be nominated by their school's dean, chairperson, or academic program director, otherwise known as the nominating official, of their graduate program to be considered for the PMF Program. Applicants go through the school's competitive nomination process and must demonstrate breadth and quality of accomplishments, a capacity for leadership, and a commitment to a career in the analysis and management of public policies and programs.
- *Selection process*: Nominated students are invited to participate in an assessment process to determine finalists. Selection as a finalist is based on the student's performance in a proctored assessment process.
- *Appointment*: Federal agencies appoint fellows to a specific excepted service position under a Schedule A hiring authority. Agencies may make initial appointments of fellows at the GS-9, GS-11, or GS-12 level (or their equivalents), depending on the candidate's qualifications. Full-time paid fellows serve for two years. Additionally, fellows may have promotion potential up to the GS-13 level (or equivalent) during the two-year fellowship.
- *Career development*: Training has always been considered a fundamental part of the PMF Program. For each fellow, the appointing agency provides a minimum of eighty hours per year of formal classroom training that addresses the core competencies required of the occupation or functional discipline in which the fellow will most likely be placed upon completion of the program and conversion to a full-time, permanent position. Hiring agencies are also to provide fellows with at least one developmental assignment of four to six months in duration in the occupation or functional discipline in which the fellow will most likely be placed, with full-time management and/or technical responsibilities consistent with the fellow's Individual Development Plan.
- *Conversion or appointment to permanent positions:* Fellows who successfully complete the program are eligible for conversion or appointment to a permanent position with the federal government at the conclusion of their fellowships.
- *Citizenship*: Opportunities for federal employment for non–U.S. citizens through the PMF Program are extremely limited. Federal agencies are prohibited by law from hiring anyone who is not a U.S. citizen for positions

in the continental United States. There are certain exemptions to this restriction. A noncitizen may be eligible for employment if the individual is (1) permitted by a federal agency's appropriation act or agency-specific statutes covering the hiring of noncitizens, and (2) eligible to work under U.S. immigration laws. PMFs must possess U.S. citizenship by the conclusion of the two-year fellowship.

Regardless of the agency or type of position you choose, through selection and appointment as a PMF, you will be able to put your knowledge and experience to work in the service of your country. Graduate students interested in applying to the PMF Program can visit www.pmf.opm.gov for more information.

A Presidential Management Fellow Looks Back

BETH FLORES

Beth Flores *is a 2004 graduate of the Master of Science in Foreign Service and Master of Business Administration Joint Degree Program at Georgetown University. She is a former Presidential Management Fellow who joined the Department of Defense and, after several rotations, is currently working in the Office of Stability Operations Capabilities in the Office of the Secretary of Defense. Her previous positions included a Coro Fellowship in Public Affairs and internships with the Overseas Private Investment Corporation, Procter & Gamble, and the Carnegie Endowment for International Peace.*

THE QUESTION that most inspires fear in graduate students is, "So, what are you going to do after graduation?" Little did I know then that my answer would be: "Become a Defense Department bureaucrat!"

Now, two years after graduating from Georgetown University's School of Foreign Service, I am a bona fide civil servant in the Office of the Secretary of Defense at the Pentagon. I entered civil service through the two-year Presidential Management Fellowship, a fast-tracked leadership developmental program sponsored by over ninety federal agencies. My own experiences over the past two years reflect the breadth of exposure that the PMF provides.

My job search was simplified because a PMF position in government was my main objective. I sought a nomination from my graduate school, completed a written PMF application, and attended a full-day interview at the Office of Personnel Management. (The application process has since been changed, but the entire process still takes approximately six months.) Then I—along with four hundred others from across the country—received a PMF. The next challenge was confirming an appointment from one of the federal agencies advertising openings, which I was able to do after a daylong interview with the Office of the Secretary of Defense.

156 • *The United States Government*

A few notes from that job search:

- *Keep an open mind*: Do not refuse an interview or dismiss an opportunity because you assume you will not be interested.
- *Book yourself silly*: Schedule in-person information interview in offices where you would consider working. Face-to-face meetings are best, but telephone conversations will do.
- *Keep track of your growing network*: Follow up with everyone. Build a spreadsheet of names and contact information. Maintain a log of conversations.

During my first month at the Pentagon, I was assigned a desk, a computer, a phone, and a member of the senior civil service. My sole task was to learn as much as feasible about the scope of the Defense Department, both within the Office of the Secretary of Defense and across the whole department. To do this, I scheduled informational interviews with as many people as possible, often relying on the incredibly helpful PMF alumni network but sometimes picking up the phone and making a cold call. My interviews focused on rotations that would give me a mix of substantive work and practice in bureaucratic policymaking.

It soon became clear to me that getting things done in a bureaucracy is truly an art form, and that it takes more than a stellar academic record to be a smooth operator in the bowels of the Pentagon. I tried to get a sense of how strong a mentor my would-be supervisor might be during the rotation, that is, whether he or she would include me in meetings that would improve my situational awareness about the work or about the Defense Department as a whole. Finally, I sought rotations in areas of national security about which I knew the least, such as military capabilities and culture. I took to heart the fact that I had two years of relatively free access to all parts of the Pentagon, and I was determined to make the most of the PMF. By the end of my first month in the "five-sided puzzle palace," as the Pentagon is affectionately called, I had created a smorgasbord of rotational options to choose from. This was precisely the kind of rich learning environment I had sought.

Two years of rotational assignments, each lasting three to five months, exposed me to the DoD's breadth of work and schooled me in the machinations of policymaking in a complex bureaucracy. One of my early assignments was on the core team leading the Quadrennial Defense Review (QDR), a top-level strategic document that operationalizes national and military strategies. As a "reward" for my hard work on the QDR, my boss encouraged me to accept a position as the special assistant to the commander of U.S. and Coalition Forces in Afghanistan during Operation Enduring Freedom.

Never in my wildest dreams (or nightmares) had I expected the PMF to send me to live and work on a military base in Afghanistan . . . during a war! The experience was a personal and professional challenge, because I was thrust into an operational military environment and asked to translate the commander's daily business—to include meetings with Afghan ministers and provincial governors, regional warlords, and U.S. and Coalition military commanders—into strategic-level guidance for the command staff as well as senior leaders in Washington policy circles and at U.S. Central Command headquarters in Tampa. Finally, as a regional desk officer in the Office of Western Hemisphere Affairs, I prepared senior Pentagon leadership to participate in the Defense Ministerial of the Americas held in Nicaragua, a biannual gathering of ministers of defense from across the Western Hemisphere. I attended the ministerial as a member of the official U.S. delegation, and I even flew on Secretary Donald Rumsfeld's jet! Two rotations in the acquisition and analytical divisions of the Pentagon allowed me to contribute to a study of electronic warfare capabilities and perform due diligence on the urgent logistical and matériel needs of military commanders in Iraq and Afghanistan. All in all, the PMF allowed me to earn another degree—a master's in "DoD"—and it provided me with the breadth of experience that allows me to be a proactive and productive civil servant today.

7

International Organizations

Careers in International Organizations

JORGE CHEDIEK

Jorge Chediek, *a citizen of Argentina, is a 1989 graduate of George-town University's Master of Science in Foreign Service Program. He joined the United Nations Development Program in 1990 as a program officer and later served as assistant resident representative in Turkey. His additional assignments have included New York City, Montevideo, Havana, and Managua. He is currently the resident coordinator and resident representative in Lima.*

VERY OFTEN my friends and relatives ask if I am satisfied with my decision to have a career with the United Nations. Throughout the past sixteen years, since joining the organization, I have always given a positive answer. After all, I am part of an institution created to promote the best values and ideals of humankind: peace, development, and universal rights, achieved through collaboration among nations and peoples. At the same time, being an international civil servant can be very demanding at many levels, so someone planning to join the United Nations should be aware of the many dimensions of this great challenge.

JOINING THE UN SYSTEM

There are many different ways to initiate contact with the United Nations. Although some UN agencies have recruitment mechanisms for young professionals, it is more likely that a young person's initial experiences will not necessarily have the makings of a career path. Early assignments in the system can be as a consultant, volunteer, intern, short-term assistant for a project, or support staff for an event. Access to these opportunities is generally obtained through contacts with people on the inside, but there are a surprising number of openings available to external candidates through public sources. These temporary or part-time assignments for students and recent graduates can be very useful. They give a flavor of how and what the UN does, and they help make contacts and establish a track record. As with most career paths, success feeds into itself.

Sometimes the opportunities are related to hardship duty stations, where willingness to put up with difficult conditions and work under pressure compensates for lack of experience. Such situations can test you to the limit, because they can entail difficult work assignments entrusted to very junior people together with the risk of operating in a complex living environment. A typical recruitment mechanism for these positions is the Junior Professional Officer (JPO) Program, in which candidates are funded by their national governments in entry-level positions with the UN. Most developed countries sponsor JPO candidates for their own citizens, and occasionally, for citizens from developing countries. The usual duration of the assignments is two years, and many JPOs move on to join the ranks of the international civil service.

Once you have established a record you will also have access to recruitment opportunities within the system for international professional posts. Most organizations now have open and fair hiring mechanisms, mainly web based, and one can use short-term experience and contacts to enhance an application. Most positions in the professional category require advanced academic degrees at the master's level.

Citizens from developing countries also have the opportunity to join professional staff with UN operations within their own countries. Many of these professionals have higher education degrees from top academic institutions. These men and women have a different career path, and though there are some limits to their advancement, their jobs are highly sought after for their prestige and remuneration. They can also on occasion serve as an entry point to the international career track.

The Nature of the Job

No single job description can encompass the broad scope of UN work. The system is at once hierarchical and formalistic, and at the same time it can entrust serious responsibilities to junior staffers in the early stages of their careers. In my case, just a few months after joining the United Nations Development Program in Turkey in late 1990, I was actively involved in one of the largest humanitarian operations in history, in northern Iraq in the aftermath of the first Gulf War.

To make the most of your work for the UN, you must first have a predisposition to work in a large organization. Once within the system, there are ample opportunities for a junior staffer to make concrete contributions. Most of those opportunities, however, are in the field.

UN work requires many competencies, and the more you have or acquire, the more quickly you will move up within the system. Success requires strong interpersonal skills, the ability to work under pressure in a multicultural environment, a knowledge of languages and communication ability, and an eagerness to take on difficult assignments. The consistent deployment of these multiple competencies is crucial to a successful career. A degree of patience and understanding of the constraints within which a large organization operates is also required, together with the commitment to the goals and values of the United Nations.

Some UN jobs are subject to geographical representation, so nationals from certain countries have a greater likelihood of obtaining certain positions, although there are no formal quotas. It should be noted that the UN is actually a relatively old organization. As a result, due to different hiring freezes and restrictions over the years, a very high proportion of UN staff members are close to retirement age. This demographic reality, together with the intention expressed by senior management and member countries to rejuvenate the organization, may well open career opportunities at an earlier stage in the short term. In addition, the recruitment of women at every level of the organization is being strongly promoted, with the goal of achieving gender balance as soon as possible, particularly at the senior level.

BECOMING AN INTERNATIONAL CIVIL SERVANT

It should be kept in mind that, once you join an international organization, you legally become an international civil servant. From that perspective, you commit yourself to the goals of the organization and set aside personal preferences and national interests. A job with an international organization certainly does not demand that one discard personal ideals or renege on one's patriotism, but one must subordinate those personal views to the goals and policies of the organization.

In particular, the United Nations is rightly committed to a strong ethical behavior internally and in relation to operations. This commitment requires a strong personal discipline and ethical values, because international civil servants live very exposed lives, particularly in the context of field operations. Most colleagues certainly live up to these very high standards, but unfortunately, there are always exceptions. Such incidents can be demoralizing for those working to good effect within an organization affected by scandal. Such incidents may cloud, but can never obliterate, an international organization's reputation for major contributions to peace, development, and security in the world.

REMUNERATION

The remuneration package of international civil servants is established by the UN General Assembly. The basis for determining the conditions of work is the Noblemaire Principle. This rule, named after a committee chairman in the League of Nations, stipulates that UN civil servants should be remunerated at the same level as the highest-paid national civil service in the world. Thus UN salaries and entitlements are closely tied to those of the U.S. Civil Service.

This means that the overall remuneration structure is acceptable, if becoming rich is not your goal in life. UN salaries allow a decent standard of living, and the package includes good insurance and education support allowances. The pension plan is a valuable feature of UN employment, for it includes a defined benefit package related to grade and time of service. Such pension plans are increasingly difficult to find these days.

At the same time, the UN is not the best paying of all the international organizations. A recent study from the International Civil Service Commission found that UN salaries trail those of the World Bank and the Organization for Economic Cooperation and Development by almost 30 percent. The good news is that the gap is somewhat narrower than it was a decade ago. For a complete description of the employment rules and conditions, there is ample information at www.icsc.un.org.

THE PERSONAL DIMENSION

A successful career generally involves mobility across duty stations. About 60 percent of all UN staff serve in the field. For example, I am in my sixth post in sixteen years. These changes enrich your professional perspective, for the rotations require keeping one's mind open and prepared for new and different professional challenges every few years. If you are more comfortable with predictability and consistency, concentrating on a single issue over a long period of time, a UN job might not be the best choice.

Constant change has an impact on your personal as well as your professional life. Your spouse may be of a different nationality and culture; your children may be born in different corners of the world. This multicultural life is enormously enriching, and children tend to be at ease in international lifestyles from their earliest days. My eleven-year-old son has already lived in five different countries and attended five different schools.

This multicultural life is enormously enriching, and children tend to be at ease in international lifestyles from their earliest days.

However, this lifestyle can also be very taxing. There is a great deal of pressure on home life, arising from being away from home in difficult living conditions, with long working hours, and too much travel. In addition, long-term career opportunities for spouses are very limited. Many colleagues and their families suffer for it. And of course, some assignments are nonfamily duty stations, which can involve separation from your family for long periods of time. In addition, field assignments are generally not open to nationals of that particular country. As a result, one tends to become separated from one's own culture. Children grow up with only occasional contact with their extended families—a downside of interculturalism is that your children may not readily identify with your native country. This uprooting poses challenges at many stages, and it is very common to find colleagues who are undecided where to retire after a UN career, unless they have planned that stage of their lives well in advance.

Finally, security has now become a major concern. The United Nations is no longer considered the impartial outsider, respected by all parties. In some quarters, the values of the organization and its actions attract not only criticism and threats but sometimes outright violence, such as the terrible attack that took the life and health of many of our colleagues in Baghdad in 2003.

CONCLUSION

If the paragraphs above make the reader think that I have had second thoughts about my career, that is certainly not the case. There may be shortcomings and limitations, but the UN is a superb career choice:

- Where else can your work and professional achievement be so directly tied to making the world a better place?

- Where else can you serve under a flag that provides hope and opportunity to millions of people around the world?

- Where else do you wield the moral authority to bring rivals and enemies around a table to reach agreements for a better future?

- Where else can you put your values and your professional skills to better use than in the most international of international organizations?

After all is said and done, and I end my conversations with my colleagues and friends, I thank God for the best job in the world.

RESOURCE LISTINGS

African Development Bank

The African Development Bank (AfDB) is multilateral development bank whose shareholders include fifty-three African countries (regional member countries, RMCs) and twenty-four non-African countries from the Americas, Asia, and Europe (nonregional member countries, non-RMCs). It was established in 1964, with its headquarters in Abidjan, and it officially began operations in 1967. However, due to political instability in Côte d'Ivoire, the Governors' Consultative Committee, at a meeting in February 2003 in Accra, decided to move the AfDB to its current temporary location in Tunis. The AfDB has been operating from this Temporary Relocation Agency since February 2003.

The AfDB's primary objective is to promote sustainable economic growth in order to reduce poverty in Africa. It achieves this objective by financing a broad range of development projects and programs through (1) public-sector loans (including policy-based loans), private-sector loans, and equity investments; (2) technical assistance for institutional support projects and programs; (3) public and private capital investment; (4) assistance in coordinating RMC development policies and plans; and (5) grants of up to $500,000 in emergency support. The AfDB prioritizes national and multinational projects and programs that promote regional economic cooperation and integration.

The AfDB provides loans to its clients on nonconcessional terms. In October 1997, it introduced three new loan products to meet the needs of its clients: a single-currency variable-rate loan, a single-currency floating-rate loan, and a single-currency fixed-rate loan. The interest rate for the single-currency variable-rate loan is based on the quarter's average cost of all outstanding AfDB borrowings specifically allocated to fund these loans. The interest rate for the floating-rate loan is based on the six-month London Interbank Offered Rate in the basket of currencies offered by the AfDB. The rate for fixed-rate loans is based on the AfDB's cost of borrowing to fund them.

The AfDB offers an internationally competitive remuneration and benefits package, which includes a tax-free salary, generous education grant for children, annual leave, home leave every two years, medical care, staff retirement benefits, group accident and life insurance policies, and diplomatic immunity and privileges. Women are strongly encouraged to apply.

Division Manager
Staff Planning and Recruitment Division
Human Resources Management Department
African Development Bank
Temporary Relocation Agency
Angle des trois rues, Avenue du Ghana
Rue Pierre de Coubertin, Rue Hedi Nouira
BP 323 1002 Tunis Belvedere
Tunisia
Fax: 216-718-314-72
e-mail: recruit@afdb.org
www.afdb.org

Asian Development Bank

The Asian Development Bank (ADB), headquartered in Manila, is an international financial institution created in 1966 to help in the planning and financing of high-priority projects in the developing countries of Asia and the South Pacific. Its stockholders are the governments of sixty-seven countries in North America, Europe, and the Asia-Pacific region. The bank is not an organization within the United Nations system.

The ADB extends loans and equity investments to its developing member countries for their economic and social development, provides technical assistance for the planning and execution of development projects and programs and for advisory services, promotes and facilitates the investment of public and private capital for development, and responds to requests for assistance in coordinating the development policies and plans of it developing member countries.

The ADB's Young Professionals Program was established in 1983 to recruit and assimilate annually into the ADB a small number of exceptionally well-qualified younger personnel. Candidates must be less than thirty years old; a citizen of a member country; hold at least a master's degree (or equivalent professional training), with advanced training in economics, finance, and business administration or in other fields relevant to the ADB's work; and preferably have work experience in areas related to the activities of ADB.

> Asian Development Bank
> 6 ADB Avenue, Mandaluyong City
> 0401 Metro Manila
> Philippines
> Tel.: 632-632-4444
> Fax: 632-636-2444
> www.adb.org
>
> Mailing Address:
> P.O. Box 789
> 0980 Manila
> Philippines

Caribbean Development Bank

The Caribbean Development Bank (CDB) serves to contribute to the harmonious economic growth and development of its member countries and promote economic cooperation and integration among them. Its mandate also includes paying "special and urgent regard to the needs of the less developed members of the region." The CDB promotes the orderly expansion of international trade; provides technical assistance to members; promotes public and private investment in development projects; and assists efforts to promote financial institutions and regional markets for capital, credit, and savings. The CDB has twenty regional members and five nonregional member states.

The CDB's recruitment policy is to attract and retain staff of the highest caliber appropriate and gives due regard to recruiting staff on as equitable a geographic basis as is possible from among its member countries. The CDB employs people with a wide range of skills, including technical specialists in environmental science, engineering, banking, finance, human resource management and development, information technology, macroeconomics, law, general management, public administration, and project management. The CDB looks for mature individuals who understand the development process and possess sound interpersonal and communication skills. The CDB does not have a junior professionals program but offers indefinite, fixed-term, and temporary appointments.

The CDB has very special needs in light of its international nature; competition is keen and employment opportunities are limited. Applications should be sent in the form of a letter with a resume in English attached, stating nationality and including the names, addresses, and telephone numbers of three references, to this address:

> Deputy Director
> Human Resource and Administration
> Caribbean Development Bank
> P.O. Box 408
> Wildey, Saint Michael
> Barbados
> e-mail: recruit@caribank.org
> www.caribank.org

Consultative Group on International Agricultural Research

The Consultative Group on International Agricultural Research (CGIAR) is a strategic partnership of countries, international and regional organizations, and private foundations supporting fifteen international agricultural centers that work with national agricultural research systems, civil society organizations, and the private sector to reduce poverty, foster human well-being, promote agricultural growth, and protect the environment. The CGIAR generates global public goods that are available to all.

The CGIAR-supported centers are independently constituted, each with its own charter, international board of trustees, director-general, and staff. As of December 2006, there were over 1,100 international positions in CGIAR centers, all but one of which are located in developing countries. Positions filled through international recruitment are in the fields of agricultural sciences, social sciences, financial management, organizational management, human resource management, development communications, public awareness, and information technology.

Internationally recruited staff normally possess advanced academic degrees, have extensive experience in their field, and are fluent in at least two languages. Employment opportunities in the CGIAR are posted on the respective websites of the CGIAR centers (see www.cgiar.org for detailed information on and links to the centers). Interested parties are invited to write directly to the center of specific interest to them.

European Bank for Reconstruction and Development
The European Bank for Reconstruction and Development (EBRD) was established in 1991 to support Eastern European and ex-Soviet countries to nurture a new private sector in a democratic environment. Today the EBRD uses the tools of investment to help build market economies and democracies in countries from Central Europe to Central Asia.

The EBRD is the largest single investor in the region and mobilizes significant foreign direct investment beyond its own financing. It is owned by sixty-one countries and two intergovernmental institutions. Despite its public-sector shareholders, it invests mainly in private enterprises, usually together with commercial partners. It provides project financing for banks, industries, and businesses, both new ventures and investments in existing companies. It also works with publicly owned companies, to support privatization, the restructuring of state-owned firms, and the improvement of municipal services.

The EBRD's organization is articulated in three major areas: banking, where core-business activities are carried out; finance and risk management; and corporate functions, including legal, human resources, administration, and communications. The EBRD organization comprises its London headquarters and a network of thirty-three resident offices in its countries of operation. In 2006, the EBRD employed 1,279 staff members, 1,018 at the headquarters and 261 in the field.

In the same year, the EBRD employed 822 professional staff members and had 116 openings for professional staff positions. Over the last five years, the EBRD had an average of 74 openings for professional staff positions.

The EBRD recruits professionals with a minimum of three years' experience in project-financing-related activities. Professional experience in and knowledge of the EBRD countries of operation (including a command of Russian as a working language) are highly appreciated. A smaller number of professionals are recruited for jobs in specialized corporate activities, including counsels, controllers and accountants, human resources specialists, and the like. A few opportunities are available to less-experienced professionals, including those who have completed young professionals programs and internships.

The EBRD only hires nationals of its sixty-one member countries, and its recruitment is linked to advertised vacancies. The whole hiring process is carried out through the EBRD's electronic recruitment system at www.ebrdjobs.com. The system allows individuals with an interest in the EBRD to apply for vacancies, register for job alerts, and in general manage their interaction with the EBRD recruitment team.

> European Bank for Reconstruction and Development
> Recruitment Team, Human Resources Department
> One Exchange Square
> London EC2A 2EH
> United Kingdom

European Free Trade Association

The European Free Trade Association (EFTA) is a group of small European countries (Iceland, Liechtenstein, Norway, and Switzerland) working for the removal of import duties, quotas, and other obstacles to trade in Europe and the upholding of liberal, nondiscriminatory practices in world trade. EFTA, headquartered in Geneva, keeps watch on developments that could restrict or distort trade flows and ensures the observance of EFTA's rules for fair competition in matters such as the use of subsidies. Within Europe, EFTA works to strengthen and develop its special relationship with the European Union. In world trade, EFTA works with larger organizations such as the Organization for Economic Cooperation and Development and the World Trade Organization.

The EFTA Secretariat in Brussels employs a staff of fewer than a hundred professionals. It offers preparation and servicing of all EFTA and EFTA–European Economic Association meetings. The staff provides appropriate research and analysis of all questions dealt with by the association. The working language of the secretariat is English. A preference is given to nationals of the member states of EFTA.

> European Free Trade Association
> Headquarters, Third Country Relations
> 9-11 rue de Varembé
> CH-1211 Geneva 20

Switzerland
Tel.: 41-22-332-26-00
Fax: 41-22-3-26-77
e-mail: mail.gva@efta.int
jbs.efta.int

Brussels Office:
(EFTA EEA matters)
12-16, rue Joseph II, B-1000
Brussels, Belgium
Tel.: 32-2-286-17-00
Fax: 32-2-286-17-50
e-mail: mail.bxl@efta.int

European Union
The European Union, formerly the European Coal and Steel Community (ECSC), was created in 1951 by six Western European countries. The integration deepened as the community gained more competences; the ECSC became the European Economic Community (EEC) and the European Atomic Energy Community (EURATOM) in 1957. Today, as EU, it has twenty-seven member states: Austria, Belgium, Denmark, Finland, France, Germany, Greece, Ireland, Italy, Luxembourg, the Netherlands, Portugal, Spain, Sweden, the United Kingdom, Bulgaria, Cyprus, Czech Republic, Estonia, Hungary, Latvia, Lithuania, Malta, Romania, Slovakia, Slovenia, and Poland.

The European Commission is represented in the United States by a delegation in Washington. The Office of Press and Public Diplomacy is responsible for providing information on the activities, policies, and publications of the European Union. It does not have information on specific job opportunities or prospective employers in Europe. General information on EU personnel rules and competitive exams are available on the Commission's website.

The European Communities Personnel Selection Office (EPSO) was established on July 26, 2002. Its mission is to organize open competitions to select highly qualified staff for recruitment to all institutions of the European Union, namely, the European Parliament, the Council of the European Union, the European Commission, the Court of Justice, the Court of Auditors, the Economic and Social Committee the Committee of the Regions, and the European Ombudsman. Jobs are open to women and men who are nationals of an EU member state. Permanent officials are selected mainly by open competition. The full details and application forms are published in the *Official Journal*, "C Section." An annual subscription to *Notifications of Open Competitions* can be placed with EU sales agents. The agent in the United States is

Bernan Associates
4611-F Assembly Drive
Lanham, MD 20706-4391
Tel.: 800-274-4447 (toll free)
Fax: 800-865-3450 (toll free)
e-mail: query@bernan.com
www.bernan.com

Further information on EU institutions can be found at

European Parliament
Centre European
Plateau de Kirchberg
L-2920 Luxembourg
Tel.: 352-43001
Fax: 352-4300-4842
www.europarl.europa.eu

Council of the European Union
Rue de la Loi 175
B-1048 Brussels
Belgium
Tel.: 32-2-285-6111
Fax: 32-2-285-7381
www.consilium.europa.eu

European Commission
Rue de la Loi 200
B-1049 Brussels
Belgium
Tel.: 32-2-299-3131
Fax: 32-2-295-7488
ec.europa.eu

Court of Justice
Boulevard Konrad Adenauer
Plateau de Kirchberg
L-2920
Luxembourg

Tel.: 352-43031
Fax: 352-4303-2600
curia.europa.eu

Court of Auditors
12 rue de Alcide de Gasperi
L-1615
Luxembourg
Tel.: 352-43981
Fax: 352-439-342
www.eca.eu.int

Economic and Social Committee
Rue Ravenstein 2
B-1000 Brussels
Belgium
Tel.: 32-2-546-9011
Fax: 32-2-513-4893
www.eesc.europa.eu

Committee of the Regions
Rue Belliard 79
B-1040 Brussels
Belgium
Tel.: 32-2-282-2211
Fax: 32-2-282-2325
www.cor.europa.eu

European Investment Bank
100 Boulevard Konrad Adenauer
L-2950 Luxembourg
Tel.: 352-4379-3142
Fax: 352-4379-2545
www.eib.org

European Central Bank
Postfach 16 03 19
60066 Frankfurt am Main
Germany
Tel.: 49-69-13440
Fax: 49-1344-6000
www.ecb.int

Food and Agriculture Organization

The Food and Agricultural Organization (FAO) was established in 1945 to raise levels of nutrition and standards of living, to improve the efficiency of production and distribution of food and agricultural products, and to better the conditions of rural populations, which make up 70 percent of the world's poor and hungry. Today, the FAO is one of the largest specialized agencies in the UN system and the lead agency for agriculture, forestry, fisheries, and rural development.

The FAO's main activities are to provide information through its website, publications, and other forums; to share policy expertise with member countries; to serve as a neutral meeting place for nations to discuss common concerns; and to bring its knowledge to the field. In crisis situations, it works with other organizations to help people rebuild their lives.

The FAO has approximately 3,600 employees, 1,600 professional and 2,000 general service. About half work at the FAO headquarters in Rome, with the others spread across its field projects and decentralized offices. Most professional positions concerned with other than administrative functions are in technical fields related to the FAO's work.

> Food and Agricultural Organization
> Liaison Office for North America
> Suite 300, 2175 K Street, NW
> Washington, DC 20437
> Tel.: 202-653-2400
> Fax: 202-653-5760
> www.fao.org

Inter-American Development Bank

The Inter-American Development Bank (IDB) helps foster sustainable economic and social development in Latin America and the Caribbean through its lending and guarantee operations, leadership in regional initiatives, research and knowledge dissemination activities, institutes, and programs.

The IDB assists its Latin American and Caribbean borrowing member countries in formulating development policies and provides financing and technical assistance to achieve environmentally sustainable economic growth and increase competitiveness, enhance social equity and fight poverty, modernize the state, and foster free trade and regional integration. By the end of 2006, the IDB had approved over $145 billion in loans and guarantees to finance projects with investments totaling $336 billion, as well as $2.2 billion in grants and contingent-recovery technical cooperation financing. Public entities eligible to borrow from the IDB include national, provincial, state, and municipal governments, as well as autonomous public institutions. Civil society organizations and private companies are also eligible.

Most applicants for professional positions at the IDB possess at least three to five years of relevant work experience in addition to a graduate degree in such fields as economics, finance, engineering, business administration, and environmental sciences. Only citizens of the IDB's member countries are hired to work at its headquarters and country offices. Most positions require fluency in at least two of its official languages: English, Spanish, French, and Portuguese.

The IDB operates a summer internship program for students who are under thirty years old, enrolled in a graduate-level program, and fluent in two of its official languages. For career opportunities, it is important to contact the relevant department in which you have interest; for more detailed information, see the website.

> Inter-American Development Bank
> Human Resources Department
> 1300 New York Avenue, NW
> Washington, DC 20577
> Tel.: 202-623-1000
> www.iadb.org

Inter-American Institute for Cooperation on Agriculture
The Inter-American Institute for Cooperation on Agriculture (IICA) is the specialized agency for agriculture within the inter-American system. Its mission is to provide innovative technical cooperation to its member states, with a view to achieving their sustainable development in aid of the peoples of the Americas. In pursuit of its vision and mission, the IICA focuses its actions in six strategic areas: contributing to the repositioning of agriculture and rural life and to a new institutional framework; promoting trade and the competitiveness of agribusinesses; promoting the development of rural communities based on a territorial approach; promoting agricultural health and food safety; promoting the sustainable management of natural resources and the environment; and promoting the introduction of technology and innovation for the modernization of agriculture and rural development.

The IICA's new style of technical cooperation calls for the broad participation of national authorities in the conceptualization, implementation, and evaluation of its actions. It also involves working with the member states and its strategic partners in preparing technical cooperation agendas at three levels: national, regional, and hemispheric. The **national agendas**, which are prepared jointly with the public and private sectors of the countries, are the basis for IICA's cooperation activities. The **regional agendas** address problems common to a group of countries and include the IICA's commitment to support integration processes through existing mechanisms that operate at the regional and subregional levels. The **hemispheric agenda** is developed through dialogue with major stakeholders of the community of agriculture and rural life. It focuses on issues and mandates derived from the Summit of the Americas process, the **Inter-American Board of Agriculture**, and other hemispheric forums.

The IICA has a network of offices in its 34 member states and a permanent office for Europe, located in Madrid, which promotes relations with strategic partners. It also has a trade office in Florida that directs the Inter-American Program for the Promotion of Trade, Agribusiness, and Food Safety.

The IICA has two governing bodies: the **Inter-American Board of Agriculture (IABA)**, comprising its thirty-four member countries, which meet every two years; and the **Executive Committee**, comprising twelve member states chosen on the basis of a system of partial rotation and equitable geographic distribution, which meets on a yearly basis. The **General Directorate** is the IICA's executive organ. It comprises the technical and administrative units through which IICA's activities are coordinated and executed. The **Special Advisory Commission on Management Issues** was created on the initiative of the General Directorate by means of an IABA resolution. The purpose of this high-level advisory body, comprising representatives of nine member states elected on the basis of a system of partial rotation and equitable geographic distribution, is to facilitate dialogue with the member states.

The IICA currently has 95 international and 223 national professional staff positions in country offices throughout North, Central, and South America, and the Caribbean, including its headquarters in San José. Applicants for professional positions should have degrees in agricultural sciences, development, or other related disciplines. Candidates should also have at least five years of relevant work experience and be proficient in no less than two of the IICA's official languages: English, Spanish, French, and Portuguese.

Instituto Interamericano de Cooperación para la Agricultura
Dirección General
Apartado 55-2200

Coronado
San José, Costa Rica
Tel.: 506-216-0222
www.iicanet.org

IICA Office in Washington
Suite 360, 1889 F Street, NW
Washington, DC 20006
Tel.: 202-458-3767
Fax: 202-458-6335
e-mail: iicawash@iicawash.org

International Atomic Energy Agency

Founded in 1957, the International Atomic Energy Agency (IAEA) serves as the world's intergovernmental forum for scientific and technical cooperation in the peaceful uses of nuclear energy. Its principal objectives under its statute are "to accelerate and enlarge the contribution of atomic energy to peace, health and prosperity throughout the world" and "ensure, so far as it is able, that assistance provided by it or at its request or under its supervision or control is not used in such a way as to further any military purpose." The IAEA pursues these objectives by—among other things—promoting the transfer of nuclear technology and know-how, encouraging the creation of an international culture of safety and reliability in the utilization of nuclear energy, safeguarding nuclear materials so as to ensure that they are used exclusively for peaceful purposes, and disseminating information on the peaceful uses of nuclear technology. In recognition of its efforts to prevent nuclear energy from being used for military purposes and to ensure that nuclear energy intended for peaceful purposes is used in the safest possible way, the IAEA and its director-general were jointly awarded the 2005 Nobel Peace Prize.

The work of the IAEA is carried out through six departments: Technical Cooperation, Nuclear Energy, Nuclear Safety and Security, Management, Nuclear Sciences and Applications, and Safeguards. The IAEA currently employs about 2,200 scientific, technical, and administrative personnel, about 900 of whom are in the professional and higher categories. In 2006, over 130 posts were advertised at the professional level.

Nuclear engineers, nuclear physicists, and nuclear safeguards inspectors constitute the largest groups of professional staff members. The other scientific and technical occupational groups include engineers, biologists, agricultural scientists, physicists, marine scientists, chemists, medical doctors, and mathematicians with a wider variety of specializations. The major administrative occupational groups include accountants, personnel officers, computer experts, procurement specialists, lawyers, translators, editors, project managers, and librarians.

Candidates interested in employment with the IAEA are expected to have a university degree and appropriate prior work experience in their chosen profession. The required minimum period of experience depends on the grade of the post stated in the vacancy announcement. Professional staff members should also have good analytical and communication skills and, for supervisory positions, proven management skills. Furthermore, they should be articulate, tactful, diplomatic, and flexible, as well as possessing sound judgment, integrity, and a drive for results.

The official languages of the IAEA are Arabic, Chinese, English, French, Russian, and Spanish, but the IAEA's business is conducted in English and a good command of spoken and written English is essential. Good computer skills are also necessary, in particular, a knowledge of word processing and spreadsheets and the ability to use databases. In most cases, an appointment to a regular position is initially made for a period of three years, with the understanding that, if performance meets the required standards during this period and if there is a continuing need for the services of the staff member, he or she may be granted a two-year extension, so that the overall tour of service is five years.

International Atomic Energy Agency
Wagramer Strasse 5
P.O. Box 100
A-1400 Vienna
Austria
Tel.: 43-1-2600
Fax: 43-1-26007
www.iaea.org

International Maritime Organization

The International Maritime Organization (IMO) is the specialized agency of the United Nations with responsibility for the safety of shipping and the prevention of marine pollution by ships. IMO's 167 member states and three associate members have adopted more than forty conventions and protocols relating to international shipping. In addition to a university degree or its equivalent, considerable experience and expertise in international shipping is required for appointment to the IMO staff.

International Maritime Organization
4 Albert Embankment
London SE1 7SR
United Kingdom
Tel.: 44-0-20-7735-7611
Tel.: 44-0-20-7587-3210
www.imo.org

International Monetary Fund
The International Monetary Fund (IMF) was created in 1944, along with the World Bank (also known as the International Bank for Reconstruction and Development), as a pillar of the international economy. Its membership has grown from the original 45 governments to 185 countries, all working to promote international monetary cooperation, exchange stability, and orderly exchange arrangements; to foster economic growth and high levels of employments; and to provide temporary financial assistance to countries to help ease balance-of-payments adjustments. Although its financial assistance activities are the best known, its surveillance consultations and technical assistance operations are key activities that help to maintain stability in the global economy.

The IMF has a staff of over 2,700 people from 165 countries. It continuously accepts applications for experienced economist and support-level positions, because there is an ongoing need to fill such positions. The IMF also accepts applications for the next intake of the Economist Program and Summer Intern Program. Experienced Economist Program candidates should have a master's or PhD in economics and five to fifteen years of economic policy experience at the national level. The Economist Program is extremely competitive, accepting only 20 to 30 candidates out of a pool of over 1,500 annually. Candidates must be under thirty-three years of age, fluent in English, have a superior academic record, and have graduate level training in macroeconomics or a relevant field, with most successful candidates completing a PhD shortly before or shortly after entering on duty.

Other opportunities include the Research Assistant Program (RAP) and the Internship Program. The RAP is for BA students with exceptional academic records who have recently graduated from leading universities and would like to gain useful field experience before continuing their studies or pursuing other career opportunities. Appointments are limited to two years. Internships are offered to approximately fifty graduate students each year, most taken during the summer. Interns work with IMF economists on research projects. They are typically below the age of thirty and within one or two years of completing a PhD in macroeconomics or a relevant field. The IMF hires approximately two hundred staff worldwide each year.

> International Monetary Fund
> 700 19th Street, NW
> Washington, DC 20431
> Tel.: 202-623-7422
> Fax: 202-623-7333
> e-mail: recruit@imf.org
> www.imf.org

International Telecommunications Union

The International Telecommunications Union (ITU), a specialized agency of the United Nations, is a worldwide organization that brings governments and the private sector together to coordinate the establishment and operation of global telecommunication networks and services. It is responsible for the standardization, coordination, and development of international telecommunications, including radio communications and the harmonization of national policies.

The ITU adopts international regulations and treaties governing all terrestrial and space uses of the frequency spectrum as well as the use of all satellite orbits that serve as a framework for national legislation. It develops standards to foster the interconnection of telecommunication systems on a worldwide scale regardless of the type of technology used. It also fosters the development of telecommunications in developing countries.

The ITU is divided into three sectors—Radiocommunication (ITU-R), Telecommunication Standardization (ITU-T), and Telecommunication Development (ITU-D)—whose work covers all aspects of telecommunications, from setting standards that facilitate the seamless interworking of equipment and systems on a global basis to adopting operational procedures for the vast and growing array of wireless services and designing programs to improve telecommunication infrastructure in the developing world. The ITU's work has provided the essential background that has enabled telecommunications to grow into a $1 trillion industry worldwide.

As of January 1, 2006, the ITU employed 822 people from eighty different countries, with staff members distributed between its headquarters in

Geneva and eleven field offices located around the world. In recruiting, the ITU seeks to have as many of its member countries represented as possible, in order to integrate diverse perspectives, skills, and languages. Candidates for senior counselor and professional positions must have a university degree or its equivalent in a combination of education, training, and experience and are subject to international recruitment. Vacancies are listed on the ITU website. Applications from outside may be submitted through a nation's administration or directly to the ITU on the understanding that the secretary-general would in such cases normally consult with the administrations of the nationals involved before making a final selection.

The ITU also runs a nonremunerated internship program for students who wish to improve their skills and gain experience working in an international environment. This program is open to all undergraduate and graduate students from the ITU's 189 member states. Candidates are selected in response to specific needs identified within ITU departments.

> International Telecommunication Union
> Place des nations
> CH-1211 Geneva 20
> Switzerland
> Tel.: 41-22-730-51-11
> Fax: 41-22-733-73-56
> e-mail: recruitment@itu.int
> www.itu.int/employment

North Atlantic Treaty Organization

The North Atlantic Treaty Organization (NATO) is an alliance of twenty-six sovereign nations in Europe and North America. Its objectives, as stated in the Washington Treaty of 1949, are to safeguard the freedom, common heritage, and civilization of their peoples, based on democracy, individual liberty, and the rule of law; to promote stability in the North Atlantic area; to unite efforts for collective defense; and to preserve peace and security. To this end, NATO draws up collective defense plans, establishes required infrastructure and logistical support for those plans, and arranges joint training and military exercises. NATO also pursues closer cooperation in the political, social, economic, cultural, and scientific fields. Since 1992 and 1994, respectively, the North Atlantic Cooperation Council and the Partnership for Peace Program at NATO headquarters have primarily sought to increase cooperation and consultation between

NATO and the democratic states to the east of the region made up of its member countries.

NATO headquarters in Brussels hires staff in several grades; or particular interest are the managerial/professional-level staff (A grade) and the linguistic staff (L grade). In addition to a university degree, A-grade posts require a professional experience of several years in the subject matter of the particular post (at least two or three years, not including periods of training), together with a good knowledge of the two official NATO languages (English and French). Linguistic staff in either the translation or interpretation services areas must have a degree or equivalent experience and speak English or French as their mother tongue. Candidates must apply for specific posts. NATO does not recruit for traineeships, internships or summer jobs, or temporary employment.

NATO staff positions are open only to citizens of member nations. Positions for U.S. citizens are usually filled by the Department of State by seconding U.S. government personnel to NATO or by direct hire with the concurrence of the U.S. government. A useful publication is the *NATO Handbook*, available from the U.S. Liaison Office.

> North Atlantic Treaty Organization
> 1110 Brussels
> Belgium
> www.nato.int
>
> U.S. Liaison Office
> U.S. NATO
> PSC 81
> Box 200
> APO AE 09724

Organization of American States

The Organization of American States (OAS) brings together the countries of the Western Hemisphere to strengthen cooperation and advance common interests. It is the region's premier forum for multilateral dialogue and concerted action.

At the core of the OAS mission is an unequivocal commitment to democracy, as expressed in the Inter-American Democratic Charter: "The peoples of the Americas have a right to democracy and their governments have an obligation to promote and defend it." Building on this foundation, the OAS works to promote good governance, strengthen human rights, foster peace and security, expand trade, and address the complex problems caused by poverty, drugs, and corruption. Through decisions made by its political bodies and programs carried out by its General Secretariat, the OAS promotes greater inter-American cooperation and understanding.

The OAS member states have intensified their cooperation since the end of the cold war, taking on new and important challenges. In 1994 the region's thirty-four democratically elected presidents and prime ministers met in Miami for the first Summit of the Americas, where they established broad political, economic, and social development goals. They have continued to meet periodically since then to examine common interests and priorities. Through the ongoing Summits of the Americas process, the region's leaders have entrusted the OAS with a growing number of responsibilities to help advance the countries' shared vision.

With four official languages—English, Spanish, Portuguese, and French—the OAS reflects the rich diversity of peoples and cultures across the Americas. The OAS has thirty-five member states, comprising the independent nations of North, Central, and South America, and the Caribbean. (The government of one member state, Cuba, has been barred from participation since 1962.) Countries from all around the world are permanent observers, closely following the issues that are critical to the Americas and often providing key financial support for OAS programs.

The member states set major policies and goals through the General Assembly, which gathers the hemisphere's foreign ministers once a year in regular session. The Permanent Council, made up of ambassadors appointed by the member states, meets regularly at OAS headquarters in Washington to guide ongoing policies and actions. The chairmanship of the Permanent Council rotates every three months, in the alphabetical order of countries. Each member state has an equal voice, and most decisions are forged through consensus. Also under the OAS umbrella are several specialized agencies that have considerable autonomy, including the Washington-based Pan American Health Organization; the Inter-American Children's Institute, based in Montevideo; the Inter-American Institute for Cooperation on Agriculture, based in San José; and the Pan American Institute of Geography and History and the Inter-American Indian Institute, both headquartered in Mexico City.

The OAS hires for both professional positions and consultancies. It also has an internship program for university juniors, seniors, and graduate students, which requires a good command of at least two of the organization's official languages. Vacancies are posted on the OAS website.

Organization of American States
17th Street and Constitution Avenue
Washington, DC 20009
www.oas.org

Pan American Health Organization

The Pan American Health Organization (PAHO), founded in 1902, is the world's oldest international health organization and works with its member countries to promote and protect the health and quality of life of the peoples of the Western Hemisphere. Since 1949, PAHO has served as the regional office for the Americas of the World Health Organization (WHO). Together, PAHO and five other WHO regional offices plan and coordinate health activities on a global basis and provide technical cooperation in essential areas of public health. Guided by the core principles of equity and pan-Americanism, PAHO's work focuses on the promotion of high-quality vaccination and immunization programs; the prevention and control of communicable, chronic, sexually transmitted, and veterinary diseases; the evaluation, prevention, and control of environmental risks for public health (with special emphasis on the most vulnerable populations); the promotion of health systems and services that ensure universal access to quality health care; the training and development of an effective health labor force; the provision of humanitarian and technical assistance to areas struck by disasters; and the promotion of services for mental health, nutrition, family health, and aging, among others. Recognizing the interrelationship between health and development, PAHO promotes social inclusion in health and provides technical advice and supports resource mobilization efforts aimed at ameliorating inequities in health. PAHO works closely with other development actors in the region of the Americas, including other member organizations of the Inter-American and United Nations system, other multilateral organizations, bilateral agencies, and nongovernmental organizations.

PAHO recruits experts on various areas of public health, as well as physicians, nurses, sanitary engineers, health administrators, and other professionals from the health, social sciences, and other fields. PAHO and WHO seek professionals who are competent in areas including epidemiology, policy analysis and advocacy, program planning and management, health technology, health information systems, health systems research, human resources for health, social communication, and resource mobilization.

Approximately fifty positions are open annually in the field of international public health. Requirements vary depending on the position sought, but an advanced degree in public health is highly valued, as is at least seven years of experience at the national level and at least two years of participation in technical cooperation programs and activities at the international level. For most assignments, knowledge of at least two of PAHO's four official languages is required, usually Spanish and English, though Portuguese and French are highly desired.

As a part of its commitment to strengthening leadership in the area of health, PAHO offers students and young to midcareer professionals a variety of training opportunities. Graduate and upper-level undergraduate students and young professionals can gain work experience in global public health through PAHO's nonpaid internship and practicum training program. Trainees are matched with appropriate technical units in PAHO's Washington headquarters or in one of the PAHO country offices or scientific centers in Latin America and the Caribbean. Additionally, PAHO's global health leadership development program, established in 1985, allows middle- to higher-level professionals to delve more deeply into key global health issues, including those related to trade, foreign policy, and human security, and to develop the competencies necessary to be future global health leaders in their countries. Further information on these and other opportunities are available on the PAHO website.

> Pan American Health Organization
> Pan American Sanitary Bureau
> Regional Offices of the World Health Organization
> 525 23rd Street, NW
> Washington, DC 20037
> Tel.: 202-974-3000
> Fax: 202-974-3663
> www.paho.org

United Nations Children's Fund

The United Nations Children's Fund (UNICEF) is the only United Nations agency devoted to children worldwide. Its unique mandate is rooted in the recognition that every child—regardless of ethnicity, gender, or religion—is entitled to health, equality, education, and protection. In pursuit of results for children, UNICEF works in close partnership with a range of partners, including governments, civil society, other UN agencies, and the private sector.

UNICEF plays an important role in the promotion of the basic rights of children embodied in the Convention on the Rights of the Child and in the achievement of the goals set at the 1990 World Summit for Children. UNICEF is also committed to the achievement of the Millennium Development Goals (MDGs)—six of which relate directly to children. Meeting these MDGs is most critical for children because they are the most vulnerable when people lack essential needs like food, water, sanitation, and health care, and they are the first to die when basic needs are not met.

UNICEF was created in 1946 as the United Nations International Children's Emergency Fund to help the children of war-devastated Europe. In the early 1950s, its mandate was expanded by the UN General Assembly to address the problems of children in both the industrial and developing world.

UNICEF has a diverse workforce of close to 10,000 from nationalities all around the world. About 35 percent of the UNICEF staff is located in Sub-Saharan Africa; 28 percent in South Asia, East Asia, and the Pacific; 10 percent in the Middle East and North Africa; and 8 percent in Latin America and the Caribbean. The remaining staff serve in New York, Geneva, Copenhagen, and Florence, or in offices in Central and Eastern Europe and the Baltic states. About 4,500 UNICEF staff are in the professional category, both international and national.

Candidates interested in this category must possess a minimum of a first university degree or preferably a postgraduate degree in development-related disciplines such as public health, nutrition, primary education, economics, social welfare, sociology, accounting, civil engineering, public administration, or information systems. Candidates are also expected to have professional work experience in a developing country and fluency in English and another UN language.

> UNICEF
> 3 United Nations Plaza
> New York, NY 10017
> Tel.: 212-326-7000
> www.unicef.org

United Nations Conference on Trade and Development

The United Nations Conference on Trade and Development (UNCTAD) was established in 1964 as a subsidiary organ of the UN General Assembly. It is the only body of the UN system to deal with all aspects of trade investment and development. Its main goals are to work as a laboratory of ideas and to provide on-the-ground assistance to developing countries in a number of areas related to trade, investment, and finance; and to help developing countries both to ensure development gains from trade, investment, and development opportunities, and to participate fully in the world economy. UNCTAD's main activities may be divided into five organizational groupings: globalization and development; trade and commodities; investment and enterprise development; technology; and transport, trade efficiency, and human resource development. These activities are carried out through three channels: (1) research, policy analysis, and data collection (see the main annual reports on the website); (2) a forum for discussion and consensus building (see the calendar of meetings); and (3) technical assistance (a total of 250 projects and programs were under way in 2006).

Posts at the junior professional level are filled through examinations open only to nationals of member states inadequately represented on the staff of the United Nations Secretariat. Posts above the junior professional levels usually are advertised worldwide. Given equal qualifications, candidates from underrepresented member states and women are given preference. There are about 230 professional posts at UNCTAD, most of which require advanced training and experience in economics and a few of which require a legal background. Journeymen candidates usually have a PhD or the equivalent and up to five years of relevant experience. Recruits typically are drawn from advanced university research programs or government positions in an appropriate field.

> United Nations Conference on Trade and Development
> Palais des Nations
> CH-1211 Geneva 10
> Switzerland
> www.unctad.org

United Nations Development Program
The United Nations Development Program (UNDP) is the United Nations' largest provider of grant funding for development and the main body for coordinating UN development assistance. It has offices in 136 countries to promote development advocacy, advice, and assistance to 166 countries. The UNDP's focus is on providing developing countries with knowledge-based consulting services and building national, regional, and global coalitions for change.

The UNDP has a wide range of international opportunities across its programs and hires individuals with strong cross-cultural skills from a range of backgrounds. It runs two programs for those interested in long-term UNDP careers. The first, the Leadership Development Program (LEAD), is for young development professionals interested in developing their knowledge and skills while contributing to development work. It is a four- to five-year program in which participants hold two assignments of roughly two years each, working as entry-level managers and/or as specialists in a UNDP practice area (governance, poverty, crisis prevention and recovery, environment, or HIV/AIDS) or business operations. Participants select a track—policy advice, development management, or business operations—and receive extensive feedback and career development supervision. LEAD participants have the opportunity to go through a special training and mentoring program, and their careers are closely monitored to ensure that they are exposed to opportunities that will facilitate their career progression. Candidates for the LEAD program should possess a master's degree or related equivalent in a relevant field, proficiency in English and at least one of the UN's other five official languages, and a minimum of three years' work experience in development, crisis/postconflict management, and/or consultancy, including work in developing countries and management in a multicultural environment.

The second program for which the UNDP hires is the Junior Professional Officer Program, which is for nationals of developing countries. Only citizens of the 118 countries currently listed by the Organization for Economic Cooperation and Development as least-developed countries, other low-income countries, and lower-middle-income countries and territories can apply. Candidates should be under thirty-two years of age, possess a master's degree or equivalent in a development-related discipline, have one to two years of working experience in a developing country, and have written and spoken proficiency in at least two of the UNDP's working languages (English, French, and Spanish), among other desirable skills.

There are also some internship opportunities available for graduate students in development-related fields who have a demonstrated interest in development and speak one or preferably two of the UNDP's working languages. Internships can take place in a UNDP country office or regional center, or at the headquarters in New York.

United Nations Development Program
One United Nations Plaza
New York, NY 10017

Tel.: 212-906-5000
Fax: 212-906-5364
e-mail: ohr.recruitment.hq@undp.org
www.undp.org

United Nations Educational, Scientific, and Cultural Organization

The United Nations Educational, Scientific, and Cultural Organization (UNESCO) is a specialized agency of the United Nations headquartered in Paris that seeks to promote collaboration among member states and help build their capacity in the fields of education, the sciences, communication, and culture. Its programs are organized into five major sectors: education, natural sciences, social and human sciences, culture, and communication and information. In addition to its own activities in these fields, UNESCO frequently coordinates with other organizations in the UN system, such as the UNDP, the World Bank, and UNICEF.

Competition for permanent, professional positions in UNESCO's Secretariat staff is very fierce and subject to considerations of geographical distribution. The United States, which rejoined UNESCO in October 2003, is currently classified as an "underrepresented" member state, and qualified Americans are encouraged to apply. Most candidates must have advanced degrees and extensive professional experience in one of UNESCO's fields of expertise. Fluency in either English or French is mandatory; field posts may require additional languages. U.S. citizens are encouraged to inform the U.S. National Commission for UNESCO of their application.

U.S. National Commission for UNESCO
Suite 6200, 2121 Virginia Ave, NW
Washington, DC 20037
Tel.: 202-663-0026
Fax: 202-663-0035
dsunesco@state.gov
www.state.gov/p/io/unesco

The UNESCO Secretariat may be contacted at

Bureau of Personnel
UNESCO
7 Place de Fontenoy
75700 Paris
France
Tel.: 33-1-45-68-10 00

Fax: 33-1-45-67-16 90
http://recruitweb.unesco.org

United Nations Environment Program

The United Nations Environment Program (UNEP), established in 1972, works to encourage sustainable development through sound environmental practices everywhere. Its activities cover a wide range of issues, from atmosphere and terrestrial ecosystems, and the promotion of environmental science and information, to an early warning and emergency response capacity to deal with environmental disasters and emergencies. UNEP's present priorities include environmental information, assessment, and research, including an environmental emergency response capacity and the strengthening of early warning and assessment functions; enhanced coordination of environmental conventions and development of policy instruments; fresh water; technology transfer and industry; and support for Africa.

UNEP is headquartered in Nairobi and has regional and outposted offices in Paris, Geneva, Osaka, The Hague, Washington, New York, Bangkok, Panama City, Manama, Montreal, and Bonn. There are approximately 550 professional posts in UNEP worldwide with about 50 job openings annually. The academic and employment experience required varies by position, but an advanced degree is usually required.

Vacant positions are posted on the UNEP website; interested and qualified applicants are encouraged to regularly visit this site for new vacancies. Because applicants only are considered for the positions for which they apply, interested and qualified candidates are also encouraged to apply for more than one position when their qualifications are in line with the requirements of the respective advertised positions. Unsolicited applications will not be considered.

The hiring for positions is very competitive. Successful candidates for entry-level positions typically have at least three to five years of experience in the field. UNEP pays due regard to the importance of recruiting staff on as wide a geographical basis as possible (United Nations Charter, chapter 15, article 101). Competition is especially intense among candidates from developed countries. UNEP particularly encourages qualified women to apply.

United Nations Environment Program
P.O. Box 30552
Nairobi

Kenya
Tel.: 254-2-621234
Fax: 254-2-226886, -622614
www.unep.org

United Nations Environment Program
Washington Office
Suite 300, 1707 H Street, NW
Washington, DC 20006
Tel.: 202-785-0465
Fax: 202-785-2096

United Nations High Commissioner for Refugees, Office of

The Office of the United Nations High Commissioner for Refugees (UNHCR) is mandated to lead and coordinate international action to protect refugees and resolve refugee problems worldwide. It strives to ensure that everyone can exercise the right to seek asylum and find safe refuge in another state, with the option to return home voluntarily, integrate locally, or resettle in a third country. The UNHCR engages states and international institutions to reduce situations of forced displacement and to reintegrate refugees into their country of origin. It also offers protection and assistance to refugees directly.

There are three entry paths to careers with the UNHCR. First is through the International Professional Roster (IPR) Program. Officers hired through the IPR include administration officers, program officers, protection officers, and public information officers. Applicants must be prepared to serve in field positions and to rotate. Candidates must have a university degree or an advanced university degree in a field such as international relations, international law, public administration, economics, social work, or another related field, and a minimum number of years of work experience depending on the level of the post. All candidates must have a working knowledge of English and should have knowledge of a second UN Language. After a review of their files, retained applicants will be invited to take an entry test to gauge their skills and qualifications.

The UNHCR's Junior Professional Officer (JPO) Program is open to nationals from twenty-three governments, including the United States. Candidates with expertise in law, public administration, and the social sciences are particularly strong. JPO candidates must have at least a BA or equivalent in a field relevant to the job description, two to three years of work experience, and an excellent knowledge of English and/or French;

knowledge of other official UN languages is a definite advantage. JPOs under contract as well as ex-JPOs are eligible to register in UNHCR's IPR.

Candidates may also apply through external recruitment to specific vacancies, which often have a more specific set of required qualifications. Internships are not currently offered.

UN High Commissioner for Refugees
Case Postale 2500
CH-1211 Geneva 2 Depot
Switzerland
Tel.: 44-22-739-8111
www.unhcr.org

United Nations Industrial Development Organization

The United Nations Industrial Development Organization (UNIDO) was set up in 1966 and became a specialized agency of the United Nations in 1985. As part of the UN common system, UNIDO has responsibility for promoting industrialization throughout the developing world, in cooperation with its 172 member states. Its headquarters are in Vienna, and it is represented in 35 developing countries. This representation and a number of specialized field offices, for investment and technology promotion and other specific aspects of its work, give UNIDO an active presence in the field. The broad programmatic objectives and priorities of UNIDO are given in the Business Plan on the Future Role and Functions of UNIDO endorsed by the seventh session of the General Conference in 1997.

This Business Plan grouped the activities of UNIDO into two areas of concentration:

- strengthening industrial capacities, including programs in support of the global forum function and policy advice; and
- cleaner and sustainable industrial development.

In addition, while maintaining the universal character and vocation of UNIDO, the Business Plan provided for UNIDO's activities to be focused geographically on least-developed countries, in particular in Africa; sectorally on agro-based industries; and thematically on small and medium-sized enterprises.

To meet particularly pressing development needs in line with the international development agenda and UNIDO's comparative advantages in the field of industrial development, UNIDO has launched four thematic initiatives to supplement the existing modalities of integrated programs, country service frameworks, and standalone projects: the **Trade Capacity Building Initiative**, launched at the International Conference of Financing for Development (Monterrey, March 2002); the **Rural Energy for Productive Use Initiative**, launched a the World Summit for Sustainable Development (Johannesburg, September 2002); the **Post-Crisis Initiative**, also presented in September 2002; and the **UNIDO/UNDP Joint Program of Cooperation on Private-Sector Development**, launched in September 2004.

In 2006, UNIDO advertised seventy-one professional positions—twenty for positions in the field and fifty-one at its headquarters. For its professional-level staff, UNIDO requires an advanced (master's-level) university degree in a discipline and specialization related to the position. UNIDO requires that professional-level staff should already have some relevant experience before joining the organization. The minimum number of years of relevant experience for different levels range from one to three years at the entry level to ten to fifteen years at the most senior.

Due to the high volume of applications, UNIDO unfortunately cannot respond to individual applications. Only those who are short listed would normally be contacted for a telephone interview. Following the telephone interview, the top three to five candidates would be invited to the UNIDO headquarters in Vienna, for the personal assessment program. This program includes a written assignment, the preparation of a presentation, and the delivery of the presentation to professional peers in the organization as well as a structured interview panel meeting.

United Nations Industrial Development Organization
Human Resource Management
P.O. Box 300
A-1400 Vienna
Austria
www.unido.org

New York Office
One United Nations Plaza
New York, NY 10017
Tel.: 212-963-6890
Fax: 212-963-7904
e-mail: office.newyork@unido.org

United Nations Institute for Training and Research

The United Nations Institute for Training and Research (UNITAR) was established by the secretary-general of the United Nations pursuant to General Assembly resolution 1934 (XVIII) of December 11, 1963, as an autonomous institution within the framework of the United Nations. Thirty years later, the General Assembly moved UNITAR's headquarters to Geneva, where most training programs are designed and conducted. The UNITAR New York office continues to cater to the needs of diplomats accredited to United Nations headquarters. UNITAR also has an office in Hiroshima. UNITAR's mandate is to enhance the effectiveness of the United Nations in achieving its major objectives, in particular the maintenance of peace and security and the promotion of economic and social development.

UNITAR has, as its name implies, two main functions: training and research. Recently, however, the main focus has been shifted to training; the research activities currently being undertaken concentrate on training. Training is, according to UNITAR's statute, provided at various levels to government officials, particularly from developing countries, for assignments with the UN or the specialized agencies and for functions in their national services connected to the work of the UN, the organizations related to it, or other organizations operating in similar fields.

UNITAR's training activities in New York, geared toward diplomats posted at UN headquarters, are based on three main pillars: (1) the UN system and its functioning, (2) international law and policy, and (3) skills strengthening. UNITAR is self-financed through voluntary contributions from member states and special-purpose grants provided by states as well as multilateral and bilateral development cooperation agencies, funds, foundations, and the private sector.

> United Nations Institute for Training and Research
> Chemin des Anémones 11–13
> CH-1219 Geneva
> Switzerland
> www.unitar.org
>
> New York Office
> Tel.: 212-963-9196
> Fax: 212-963-9686
> www.unitarny.org

Hiroshima Office
Tel.: 81-82-511-2424
Fax: 81-82-211-0511
www.unitar.org/hiroshima

United Nations Population Fund

The United Nations Population Fund (UNFPA) helps developing countries find solutions to their population problems. The UNFPA began operations in 1969. It is the largest international source of population assistance. About a quarter of all population assistance from donor nations to developing countries is channeled through the UNFPA. The UNFPA has three main program areas: reproductive health, including family planning and sexual health; population and development strategies; and advocacy.

The UNFPA extends assistance to developing countries, countries with economies in transition, and other countries at their request to help them address reproductive health and population issues. It also raises awareness of these issues in all countries, as it has since its inception. The UNFPA's three main areas of work are to help ensure universal access to reproductive health, including family planning and sexual health, to all couples and individuals by or before 2015; to support population programming; to promote awareness of population and development issues, and to advocate for the mobilization of the resources and political will necessary to accomplish its areas of work.

The UNFPA is guided by and promotes the principles of the Program of Action of the International Conference on Population and Development (1994). In particular, the UNFPA affirms its commitment to reproductive rights, gender equality, and male responsibility and to the autonomy and empowerment of women everywhere. The UNFPA believes that safeguarding and promoting these rights and promoting the well-being of children, especially female children, are development goals in themselves. All couples and individuals have the right to freely and responsibly decide the number and spacing of their children as well as the right to the information and means to do so.

The UNFPA is convinced that meeting these goals will contribute to improving the quality of life and to the universally accepted aim of stabilizing world population. It also believes that these goals are an integral part of all efforts to achieve sustained and sustainable social and economic development that meets human needs, ensures well-being, and protects the natural resources on which all life depends.

The UNFPA recognizes that all human rights, including the right to development, are universal, indivisible, interdependent, and interrelated, as expressed in the Program of Action of the International Conference on Population and Development, the Vienna Declaration and the Program of Action adopted by the World Conference on Human Rights, the Convention on Elimination of All Forms of Discrimination Against Women, the Program of Action of the World Summit for Social Development, the Platform for Action of the Fourth World Conference on Women, and other internationally agreed-upon instruments.

The UNFPA, as the lead UN organization for the follow-up and implementation of the Program of Action of the International Conference on Population and Development, is fully committed to working in partnership with governments, all parts of the UN system, development banks, bilateral aid agencies, nongovernmental organizations, and civil society. The UNFPA strongly supports the UN Resident Coordination System and the implementation of all relevant UN decisions. The UNFPA will assist in the mobilization of resources from both developed and developing countries, following the commitments made by all countries in the Program of Action to ensure that the goals of the International Conference on Population and Development are met.

For employment with the UNFPA, prerequisites are an advanced degree in a field pertinent to the UNFPA's program (e.g., demography, public health, and population studies) and some experience in a developing country, preferably with a development organization similar to the UNFPA. The applicant should also have the ability to take up assignments in the UNFPA field duty stations as part of his or her career development. Fluency in English is required; speaking and reading ability in one other United Nations language, preferably French or Spanish, is desirable. The UNFPA is able to respond only to those applicants in whom it has a further interest. There were approximately one hundred international professional-level job openings in 2006.

United Nations Population Fund
220 East 42nd Street
New York, NY 10017
www.unfpa.org

United Nations Relief and Works Agency for Palestine Refugees in the Near East

The United Nations Relief and Works Agency for Palestine Refugees in the Near East (UNRWA) was established in 1949 to assist refugees from the 1948 Arab–Israeli conflict. The UNRWA provides education, health, and welfare services to over 4 million registered Palestinian refugees living in Jordan, Lebanon, Syria, the West Bank, and the Gaza Strip. The UNRWA has 652 elementary and preparatory schools, 8 vocational and teacher training centers, and 123 health centers. It relies on voluntary contributions, mainly from governments, for its funding. The largest donor government is the United States, which in 2006 provided almost a quarter of the UNRWA's funds, followed by the European Union and its member governments.

The UNRWA employs more than 27,000 people, almost all Palestinian refugees. There are about 160 international positions in the areas of finance, administration, data processing, law, personnel, public relations, and supply. Since 1988, the UNRWA has been running emergency operations in the occupied West Bank and the Gaza Strip, as well as in Lebanon during episodes of crisis such as the conflict with Israel during the summer of 2006. Approximately seventy-five of the international positions are at the UNRWA's Gaza Strip and Amman headquarters; the remainders are in its five field offices. The UNRWA had approximately thirteen international vacancies in 2006. Applicants for junior positions are normally considered only if they have a minimum of three years work experience in addition to the related educational qualifications.

> United Nations Relief and Works Agency for Palestine Refugees in
>   the Near East
> Director of Human Resources
> Headquarters, Amman
> Bayader Wadi Seer
> P.O. Box 140157
> Amman 11814
> Jordan
> e-mail: unrwa-ahr@unrwa.org
> www.unrwa.org

United Nations Secretariat
The United Nations Secretariat carries out the substantive and administrative work of the United Nations as directed by the General Assembly, the Security Council, and other UN organs. It has a total staff of about 8,900, drawn from 170 countries. Duty stations include UN headquarters in New York as well as offices in Geneva, Vienna, and Nairobi. There are also regional commissions in Addis Ababa, Santiago, Bangkok, and Beirut. Special efforts are made to recruit from as wide a geographic area as

possible, in order to achieve, as closely as possible, equitable representation among member states.

Employment opportunities are available in the following occupational groups: administration, economics, electronic data processing, finance, language and related work, legal affairs, the library, political affairs, public information social development, and statistics. Staff members for entry-level positions are recruited via National Competitive Recruitment Examinations, organized as a matter of priority in countries that are inadequately represented among the staff of the Secretariat. Candidates for junior professional (P1/P2) positions must possess a first-level university degree, and be thirty-two years of age or younger. For professional (P3) positions, a candidate must have an advanced university degree, at least four years of professional experiences, and be thirty-nine years of age or younger. Fluency in either English or French is required. Candidates should also support the purposes and ideals of the United Nations, including support for human rights, the equal rights of men and women, and respect for all cultures.

Translator positions are filled as needed from a roster of qualified candidates who have passed examinations. Candidates must translate from at least two of the UN's six official languages (Arabic, Chinese, English, French, Russian, and Spanish). Interpreter positions require the ability to interpret simultaneously into one of these official languages and have full auditory comprehension of at least two other official languages.

The United Nations headquarters in New York also has an internship program offered to students currently enrolled in a graduate school and specializing in international relations, international law, economics, political science, journalism, population studies, translation and terminology, or public administration, or another field related to the work of the United Nations. Interested candidates are encouraged to visit the UN website for more information. Extensive information on the application process for all of the aforementioned positions is available at jobs.un.org.

UN Secretariat
UN Headquarters
First Avenue at 46th Street
New York, NY 10017
www.un.org

United Nations University

The United Nations University (UNU) is an international community of scholars that generates knowledge and builds capacities in areas relevant to the global problems of human security, peace, and development, with a particular emphasis on the concerns and needs of developing countries. Its position as an academic institution within the United Nations system offers the UNU unique opportunities to contribute to the advancement of knowledge as well as to its application in the formulation of sound policies. Current research and capacity building activities focus in five main areas: peace and security; good governance; development and poverty reduction; science, technology, and society; and environment and sustainability.

The UNU comprises the UNU Center in Tokyo, a global network of thirteen research and training centers and programs that focus on specific problems, liaison offices in UN headquarters and UNESCO headquarters, fourteen associated institutions, and hundreds of cooperating institutions and scholars the world over. The UNU currently has more than 350 positions and advertises numerous vacancies each year. All programmatic positions are advertised the international media; applicants for such positions should have an advanced degree and a substantial publication record in the relevant discipline, particularly on issues of relevance to the developing world. Further information can be found at the UNU website.

> United Nations University
> 5-53-70 Jingumae, Shibuya-ku
> Tokyo 150-8925
> Japan
> Tel.: 81-3-3499-2811
> Fax: 81-3-3499-2828
> mbox@hq.unu.edu
> www.unu.edu
>
> UNU Office at the UN, New York
> Room DC2-2060, 2 United Nations Plaza
> New York, NY 10017
> Tel.: 212-963-6387
> Fax: 212-371-9454
> unuona@ony.unu.edu
> www.ony.unu.edu

United Nations Volunteers
The United Nations Volunteers (UNV) program is the UN organization that supports sustainable human development globally through the promotion of volunteerism, including the mobilization of volunteers. It is

an associated program under the administration of the United Nations Development Program. UNV volunteers worldwide are supporting the efforts of the United Nations, governments, and other development partners playing a distinctive role in building the local capacity of people and institutions. In the process, UNV volunteers address the time-bound targets set out within the Millennium Development Goals. Whether they are working with village groups or policymakers, UNV volunteers help in realizing the MDGs by acting as catalysts of change in the communities they serve.

In 2006, some 7,500 volunteers were assigned to apply their knowledge and skills worldwide in fields ranging from agronomy to medicine, from engineering to humanitarian and emergency relief work. These UNV volunteers represent more than 165 nationalities and worked in more than 140 countries. The majority of UNV volunteers are nationals of developing countries or economies in transition. Since 2000, the UNV has offered the opportunity to volunteer online through its online volunteering service, www.onlinevolunteering.org.

Volunteer work demands commitment, and UNV seeks volunteers who will be dedicated to the attainment of the MDGs. Called "volunteerism for development," it is intended to ensure that volunteerism is effective in all its forms, such as building national capacities, advocating and fostering an enabling environment, and promoting gender equity, to name a few.

UNV volunteers are skilled and experienced in their fields. The average age of a volunteer was thirty-seven years in 2006, but just over one-quarter of those were under the age of thirty. Knowledge of one foreign language (English is mandatory), a master's degree, and at least three to five years' work experience are required. This emphasis on experience, coupled with the high degree of commitment and motivation inherent in volunteer service, produces an extremely efficient agency for development on an international level.

United Nations Volunteers
Postfach 260 111
D-53153 Bonn
Germany
Tel.: 49-228-815-2000
Fax: 49-228-815-2001
e-mail: hq@unvolunteers.org
www.unvolunteers.org

New York Liaison Office
New York, NY 10017
Tel.: 212-906-3639
Fax: 212-906-3659

World Bank Group

The World Bank Group works to help developing countries reduce poverty and promote sustainable development. Unlike many international aid programs, however, the World Bank Group does not make grants but rather lends money to developing countries, which must repay loans. The World Bank Group comprises five organizations.

The **International Bank for Reconstruction and Development (IBRD)** and the **International Development Association (IDA)** are commonly known as the World Bank. The IBRD lends to middle-income and creditworthy developing countries, aiming to reduce poverty and promote sustainable development through loans, guarantees, risk management products, and analytical and advisory services. It raises most of its funds on the world financial markets, generating income that allows it to fund development activities and to ensure its financial strength. It is increasingly focused on providing relevant products and services to middle-income countries. The IBRD was established in 1944 under the Bretton Woods agreement as the original organization of what is now the World Bank Group.

IDA has offered concessional loans (credits) to the world's poorest countries since 1960. It provides interest-free loans and grants for programs that boost economic growth, reduce inequalities, and improve people's living conditions. It is one of the largest sources of assistance for the world's eighty-two poorest countries.

The **International Finance Corporation (IFC)** encourages private growth enterprises in developing countries through its financial services and the provision of its expertise in legal and technical aspects of private business. The IFC lends directly to the private sector; it does not seek or accept government guarantees. The IFC, one of the few international development organizations that makes equity investments as well as providing loans, aids the private sector by providing long-term loans; equity investments; guarantees and "stand-by" financing; risk management; and "quasi-equity instruments" like subordinated loans, preferred stock, and income notes.

The **Multilateral Investment Guarantee Agency (MIGA)** promotes foreign investment for economic development by providing investors with guarantees against noncommercial risks such as expropriation and war. MIGA also provides advisory and consultative services to member countries to assist in creating a responsive investment climate and an information base to guide and encourage the flow of capital. It focuses on infrastructure development, "frontier" (high-risk and/or low-income) markets, investment in conflict-afflicted areas, and insurance services for investments between developing countries.

The **International Center for Settlement of Disputes (ICSID)** promotes increased flows of international investment by providing facilities for the conciliation and arbitration of disputes between governments and foreign investors. The ICSID also provides advice, carries out research, and produces publications in the area of foreign investment law.

The World Bank Group has some 10,000 development professionals on staff at its headquarters in Washington and its 100 country offices (roughly 30 percent). Staff have a range of backgrounds, including economics, education, environmental science, finance, anthropology, and engineering. The World Bank seeks candidates with the breadth of education and experience to take a comprehensive view of the development issues with which it is concerned. Most successful candidates for employment with the World Bank have many years of experience in the field and normally join it between the ages of thirty-five and fifty years.

Through its Young Professionals Program (YPP), however, the World Bank does seek younger candidates who show potential for building a successful career in international development. To be eligible for consideration, YPP applicants must not have reached their thirty-second birthdays as of July 1 of the selection year; must have a master's degree (or equivalent) in economics, finance, or a related field; and must have either a minimum of two years of relevant work experience or continued academic study at the PhD level. Fluency in English is required, and speaking proficiency in one or more of the bank's other working languages (i.e., Arabic, Chinese, French, Portuguese, and Spanish) is beneficial. Work experience in a developing country also is desirable. Competition for the program is strong. Each year the program receives thousands of applications for twenty to thirty positions. Interested and qualified persons should submit a self-addressed envelope requesting application forms for the program by early fall.

The World Bank also runs a Junior Professionals Program for Afro Descendants with similar criteria to the YPP; candidates must be thirty-five years of age or younger. Citizens of some donor countries may be eligible for the Junior Professional Officers Program, a partnership between these countries and the World Bank. The World Bank also hires consultants and temporary staff, who are usually hired locally.

Summer and winter internships at the World Bank are available to current graduate students (master's or PhD). Candidates with educational backgrounds in economics, finance, human development, social science, agriculture, environment, private sector development, and other fields are considered. Fluency in English is required; knowledge of other major languages and prior experience are beneficial.

> Recruitment Division
> Personnel Department
> World Bank
> 1818 H Street, NW
> Washington, DC 20433
> Tel.: 202-477-1234
> www.worldbank.org

World Health Organization
The World Health Organization is the public health arm of the United Nations. Its objective is the attainment by all peoples of the highest possible level of health, defined as physical, mental, and social well-being. WHO works in four strategic directions, aiming to reduce excess mortality, morbidity, and disability; promote healthy lifestyles and reduce health risk factors; develop responsive, fair, equitable, and effective health systems; and frame a policy and environment for the health sector while promoting an effective health dimension to social, economic, environmental, and development policy.

WHO focuses on six core functions: articulating policy and advocacy positions; managing information; catalyzing change through technical and policy support; negotiating and sustaining national and global partnerships; pursuing proper implementation of norms and standards; and stimulating the development of new technologies, tools, and guidelines.

Competition for professional staff positions is keen. Applicants should have a university degree, a postgraduate specialization, and working experience at national and/or international level in the required field of public health and development issues. Candidates are sought from a variety of health-related fields, including medical officers, health economists, and policy analysts, as well as nonhealth-related fields such as finance, legal, and general administration. Candidates should have substantial training and experience in this field before they can be considered for an assignment.

WHO also runs an Associate Professional Officers (APOs) Program. APOs are young professionals in various fields at an early stage in their career who are proposed for specific assignments identified by WHO. The funds to defray their employment costs are covered by the government or other donor concerned. WHO currently has agreements for the employment of APOs with Austria, Belgium, Denmark, Finland, France, Agence Intergouvernementale de la Francophonie, Germany, Italy, Japan, Luxembourg, the Netherlands, Norway, Sweden, Switzerland, and the United States. Generally, only nationals of the "donor countries" are considered, although certain donors occasionally sponsor candidates from developing countries. Internships are also available to graduate students with a first degree in a public health, medical, or social field related to the work of WHO and who are fluent in the working language of the office of assignment.

WHO recruits candidates who demonstrate a high level of technical knowledge, are motivated and have a strong commitment to the policies and programs of WHO, and possess good analytical skills and a keen interest in and an understanding of policy issues especially in the area of public health. Additionally, they should be able to work well on a multicultural team and be proficient in at least one of the official languages of the Organization (Arabic, Chinese, English, French, Russian, and Spanish) and have a working knowledge of a second. Additional languages are an asset. Smokers and other tobacco users are no longer recruited by WHO. Candidates are hired for either fixed-term or temporary assignments.

Interested applicants for professional or internship positions should visit WHO's employment website. Those interested in APO appointments should directly contact one of the sponsors of APOs.

> Central Human Resources Services
> World Health Organization
> Avenue Appia 20
> CH-1211 Geneva 27
> Switzerland
> Fax: 41-22-791-4773
> www.who.int/employment

World Intellectual Property Organization
The World Intellectual Property Organization (WIPO) is an international organization dedicated to developing a balanced and accessible international intellectual property (IP) system, which rewards creativity, stimulates innovation, and contributes to economic development while safeguarding the public interest. With a staff drawn from around the world, WIPO carries out many tasks related to the protection of intellectual property rights, such as developing international IP laws and standards; delivering global IP protection services; encouraging the use of IP for economic development; promoting a better understanding of IP; and providing a forum for governments, civil society, and private sector actors to debate current challenges.

With headquarters in Geneva and one main office in New York, WIPO is one of the sixteen specialized agencies of the UN system of organizations. It administers twenty-one international treaties dealing with different aspects of intellectual property protection. WIPO counts 175 nations as member states.

The recruitment of candidates for career posts at various levels with the professional and special categories (marked "P" or "D") is generally reflected through vacancies published on WIPO's website and in the *ICSC Bulletin* and also advertised in WIPO periodicals and through the appropriate administrations of its member states. Most of these posts require staff with a legal academic background and considerable professional experience in the field of intellectual property.

WIPO runs a summer school internship program and an ad hoc internship program, open to senior students and young professionals wishing to acquire a working knowledge of intellectual property and to be exposed to the work of the organization.

World Intellectual Property Organization
34 chemin des Colombettes
CH-1211 Geneva 20
Switzerland
Tel.: 41-22-730-9111
Fax: 41-22-733-5428
www.wipo.int

World Meteorological Organization
The World Meteorological Organization (WMO) is a specialized agency of the United Nations with a membership of 187 states and territories.

The WMO was established as an intergovernmental organization in 1950 as the successor of the International Meteorological Organization set up in 1873 as a nongovernmental organization. In dealing specifically with meteorology, operational hydrology, and related geophysical sciences, the WMO facilitates worldwide cooperation on the issues of weather, climate, and water cycles, which are inherently international.

There are very few professional opportunities at the WMO, and they are mostly in specialized fields. Employment opportunities are distributed to the permanent representatives of members of the WMO. Thus, they are always available in the national meteorological services of member countries. In the United States, information is available from the U.S. National Weather Service of the National Oceanic and Atmospheric Administration in Silver Spring, Maryland. It is also available from the American Meteorological Society. The WMO only accepts applications for specific vacancies.

> World Meteorological Organization
> 7bis, Avenue de la Paix
> Case Postale No. 2300
> CH-1211 Geneva 2
> Switzerland
> Tel.: 41-22-730-81-11
> Fax: 41-22-730-81-81
> e-mail: wmo@wmo.int
> www.wmo.int

World Trade Organization

The World Trade Organization (WTO), the successor organization to the General Agreement on Tariffs and Trade, seeks to liberalize and expand world trade. A total of 150 member countries now belong to the WTO, together accounting for over 97 percent of world trade. Around 30 other countries are negotiating membership. The agreements of the WTO, negotiated and signed by a large majority of the world's trading nations, underpin the multilateral trading system. They set the legal ground rules for international commerce and grant important trade rights to member countries. These agreements bind governments to implement trade policies that benefit everyone.

The WTO has a secretariat staff of 635 and is based in Geneva. The WTO Secretariat's main duties are to supply technical support for the various councils and committees and the ministerial conferences, to provide technical assistance for developing countries, to analyze world trade, and to explain WTO affairs to the public and media. The Secretariat also provides some forms of legal assistance in the dispute settlement process and advises governments wishing to become members of the WTO. The Secretariat's professional staff consists primarily of economists and lawyers specialized in international trade policy. Candidates for such positions should have a postgraduate degree in economics, international relations, or law, with an emphasis on trade issues, supplemented by no less than five years of work experience in the field with a national government, international organization, or another organization dealing with international trade policy or issues. Staff are expected to work in at least two of the three official languages of the WTO (English, French, and Spanish), with a knowledge of French particularly desirable as the language of the Geneva area, which is the sole location of the WTO.

Any applicant for a professional post must be a national of a member state and under sixty-two years old. Staff turnover is very limited. Vacancy notices are distributed to official representatives of participating governments and are posted on the WTO website. The selection and appointment process is rigorous and can last several months.

Chief Human Resources Officer
World Trade Organization
Centre William Rappard
Rue de Lausanne 154
1211 Geneva 21
Switzerland
Fax: 41-22-731-5772
www.wto.org

Starting Out at the United Nations

ALF IVAR BLIKBERG

Alf Ivar Blikberg *is a 2000 graduate of the Master of Science in Foreign Service Program at Georgetown University. He is currently a humanitarian affairs officer with the UN Office for the Coordination for Humanitarian Affairs in Zimbabwe. His earlier experience included military service in the Royal Norwegian Navy, a consultancy with the Poverty Group at the World Bank, and several years in Switzerland with the World Economic Forum.*

I JOINED THE United Nations in May 2004 as a junior program officer (JPO) sponsored by my home country, Norway. Before this, I had worked in the HIV/AIDS field for three years and traveled frequently to Africa. Witnessing the devastating impact of the HIV/AIDS epidemic first-hand was what triggered my interest in humanitarian affairs.

My experience at the UN began in the Office for the Coordination for Humanitarian Affairs (OCHA), where I have remained ever since. OCHA is an excellent posting, first because it is a relatively small entity, and as a result, one gets to know most of its 150 New York–based staff very quickly; second, because at OCHA, JPOs tend to be treated just like regular UN staff, even though JPOs have been sponsored by their respective home countries and not recruited through international competitions.

My UN career took a new path at the end of December 2004. On my way back to New York from Christmas in Norway, I heard on the radio about an earthquake in the Indian Ocean. I was working on emergencies in Africa and not Asia, so an earthquake beneath the ocean did not seem significant to me. However, by the time I arrived in New York, it was increasingly clear that, in fact, it had resulted in a very large disaster. My department is the coordinating unit for emergencies at the UN, and knowing that most of my colleagues were away over Christmas, I sent an e-mail to the officer in charge, offering to help. Five minutes later, an e-mail came back, copied to all staff in OCHA, announcing that I was now the New York–based focal point for the Indian Ocean tsunami! As is often the case in humanitarian affairs, there was no opportunity to turn down the assignment.

The next six weeks were the busiest in my life so far. The UN and its partners had to mobilize one of the largest relief operations ever undertaken, in response to one of the worst disasters of all time. For each day, the number of persons, organizations, and countries involved in providing relief grew exponentially, and the team effort at headquarters and in the field was in my view what ultimately made the operation successful.

In this situation, the drafting and presentation skills I learned at Georgetown were crucial. Several times a day, I had to pull together and analyze information from the field for senior UN officials, with very short deadlines and constant interruptions in the office. In the first few weeks, the most frequent thoughts that went through my mind, and probably those of many colleagues, were "work now, sleep later" and "implement the assignment now, complain about workload later." At one point, I was not sure if we were still in 2004 or if we had entered 2005.

After about six weeks of work on the tsunami, I returned to my regular job at the Africa desk. During my second year at OCHA, I passed the UN National Competitive Exam, which makes young professionals eligible for regular UN posts, and was formally recruited soon afterward. My third and fourth years with the UN are being spent with the OCHA field office in Zimbabwe.

My three years of working at the UN have been an inspiring, rewarding, and sometimes exhausting experience. I am part of one of the most dynamic branches of the organization, and I feel that our work is meaningful and important. As such, working at the UN is a career path that I strongly recommend to other recent graduates.

8

Banking

Careers in Banking

JEFF BERNSTEIN

Jeff Bernstein is a 1985 graduate of the Master of Science in Foreign Service Program at Georgetown University. He is the cofounder and portfolio manager at Keel Capital Management, and he has had twenty years of experience in the investment business. Before cofounding Keel, he was a partner at the Galleon Group, and before that, a managing director at Goldman Sachs. While at Goldman, he started the industry's first institutional equity sales force dedicated to selling technology equities.

RISK IS WHAT we in the investment community measure every day, and it is what the international affairs graduate is especially qualified to assess. As you contemplate how to apply your academic training and passion toward a career that will stimulate you, provide you financial security, and improve the lives of others, it is important to recognize that you have spent the greater part of your graduate study understanding and measuring the risk associated with critical decisions and recommending courses of action based on your conclusions. This is exactly what financial institutions are looking for in their new hires, and it is ultimately the skill that separates successful financiers from the pack.

In my twenty-plus years working on Wall Street, I have never seen a better or more appropriate time to seek a career in banking and finance. For decades, the United States was forced to carry the majority of the burden for financing global economic growth. The bulk of the world's population was not represented by governments whose policies encouraged capitalism. Western Europe, Japan, and the United States represented the lion's share of global consumption, especially the consumption of capital-intensive technology and innovative industrial products. Finance, banking, and money flows therefore were concentrated in these geographies, and the expertise necessary to evaluate and commit capital wisely was similarly focused. That has all changed, and with that change a dramatic shift is occurring in the skill set required by individuals in our industry. Financial globalization has placed new demands on the banking community. These demands include deep and specific country or regional knowledge. They include a much more acute awareness of the socioeconomic realities in regions of the world that most bankers over the age of thirty-five have never been trained to evaluate. They require hands-on experience and relationships with local business and government leaders who themselves are just learning to coexist in a new world flush with liquidity and opportunity. This is exactly what we, as international affairs graduates, have to offer.

> **Financial globalization has placed new demands on the banking community. These demands include deep and specific country or regional knowledge.**

But why choose this industry? Though it offers the chance for lucrative compensation, is it not tedious and filled with boring MBAs who care little about the global community? How can we, idealists all, commit to a career that appears so unemotional, so numbers oriented? Those were my thoughts twenty years ago, and yes, at times, this industry offers little in the way of empathy or creativity, but for those of us who have worked hard and been blessed with a measure of success, no career offers more opportunities to improve the lives of others on as massive a scale as this one. Your career in finance and banking can take you anywhere you want it to take you—from negotiating huge contracts on behalf of sovereign governments, to financing their economic growth, to underwriting water projects in undeveloped regions, to financing new solar technologies that will ultimately and dramatically reduce our dependence on fossil fuels.

Each of these kinds of projects will require the diplomatic and risk-assessment skills that you have honed, and each will require you to dive deeply into its details, taking you around the world and building a library of experience and knowledge that is matched by few professions. If you want this, it is there. The world changes every day, and in our industry we get paid to figure out how that change will affect the financial livelihoods of companies and countries. We may not realize it at the time, as we write our research and do our spreadsheets, but ultimately we get paid to protect these entities from harm and to help them build better lives for their employees, their shareholders, and their citizens.

So where do you begin? How do you set about getting into the business? How do you learn where you want to work or to whom you should send your resume? How do you answer the dreadful question, "Why didn't you go to business school?" There are plenty of good answers to these questions, so I focus here on what I feel are the five imperatives for international affairs graduates seeking careers in banking and finance.

The first imperative is to take some courses in finance and choose one or two companies that you can get to know reasonably well. By the time you begin the interviewing process, you must be able to present your interests in the language of basic finance. This requires understanding income statements, balance sheets, and cash flows, and how they relate to each other. Choose a company, presumably a public company where financial information is readily available, in an industry or country that interests you, and learn to describe its financial health in these terms. Be willing and able to talk about growth, leverage, margins, competition, management, and what you perceive to be the company's greatest opportunities and risks. If all this bores you, do not worry; it gets a lot more interesting, but these are the essential building blocks that interviewers are going to want to see, especially in a non-MBA student.

The second imperative is to play to your strengths. For example, even if you do not necessarily want to focus on the energy industry, if the bulk of your prior academic and work experience is in this industry, use that knowledge to gain entry by applying to the energy divisions of financial institutions. In general, investment banks, commercial banks, private equity firms, and the like will be broken down by industry expertise (or perhaps first by region and then by industry). Remember, once you have been hired, after a year or two, your ability to move within the organization and our industry will be great. The key is to get in—and to use your industry or country experience to get there. Though you may want to work on microfinance in Malaysia, it is better to get there by first playing on your four years of experience working at the Ministry of Trade in

Singapore and getting a job in the Asian Investment Banking Division, rather than by pin-holing yourself into such a narrow opportunity.

The third imperative is to be creative in your thinking. Do your research beforehand. Again, if you are interested in alternative energy (solar, wind, geothermal, etc.), think of the countries that most need assistance, then either find the financial institutions that focus on the energy industry in those regions or apply to the major banks in those countries. In the past ten years, there has been an explosion of financial boutiques and divisions within global banks that specialize in various areas. Do not confine yourself to the Citibanks, Goldman Sachs, and Credit Suisses of the world—do the research to locate where there might be a need. Often, initial entry is easiest into the smaller companies that do not have well-organized recruiting efforts.

The fourth imperative is to present something and offer something. When it comes to the interviewing process, nothing is more effective than being able to offer the recruiter something tangible. This can take two forms, and I recommend both. First, if you have written a study, for either a course or an internship, that assesses an industry, company, or country, bring a copy and offer it at the interview. Ask the recruiter to read it, and if he or she feels that it is valuable, ask them to pass it on to the company executives who might also find value in it. And attach your business card to it! Second, if you are meeting with line executives (as opposed to human resources personnel), ask them if there is some small project they have not had time to tackle and offer to do it for them. This will not only demonstrate your skills but also your creativity, your interest, and your determination to find a place in that company.

The fifth and final imperative is to be willing to compromise. Remember, it is a marathon, not a sprint. Be willing to take a position that may not meet your expectations for rank or pay.

Most banks hire analysts and associates into a generalist pool and place them in different departments after a short training program. The more important thing is who you will be working with, rather than what you will be doing for the first year or two. Try to speak with both recent and not-so-recent hires about mobility within the company. Try to assess whether the culture of the organization suits you. If you are being placed somewhere in the company where you have met or interviewed with your immediate superior, make sure you believe this is someone you can work with, can respect, and who will ultimately have your best interests in mind as you gain more experience.

A career in banking can be extremely rewarding. Face the fact that financial security will give you a tremendous amount of freedom over time. This is an industry that can, and will (if you are good at it) reward you with experience, knowledge, and wealth. These resources will allow you to make choices later in your career that might not be possible if you choose a different path. Many former bankers have made the transition to public service at a very high level later in their careers. The relationships they built during their years in finance help them achieve results in the policy world that enrich the lives of people around the world.

Finally, no matter what you choose as your career direction, it is important that you build and nurture three things. The first is relationships. Make sure that you build relationships with people you respect across a variety of industries, countries, and responsibilities. You always want to be in a position to seek counsel from the right people at the right time.

Second, know your numbers. You can only go so far in any walk of life without a keen understanding of the financial impact of your actions. Do not be afraid to supplement your education with some serious study of finance.

Third, have conviction. Without conviction in yourself, your knowledge, and your ideas, you will be doing yourself and others who rely on you a disservice. Do the work necessary to build conviction. If you do this, more often than not, your ability to measure and conquer risk will benefit more people than you can ever imagine.

A final note: Banks focus on many different clients and activities, but their core business types can be summarized as investment banks, private banking, research, asset management, and private equity. This essay has focused on investment banking, and table 8.1 outlines its major product areas.

TABLE 8.1
Major Product Areas in Investment Banking

Advisory

Mergers and acquisitions (M&A)	Work with companies on evaluating acquisitions, divestitures, mergers, sales, and other strategic transactions.
Restructuring	Restructure or refinance a company's balance sheet while it is going into, coming out of, or trying to avoid Chapter 11 bankruptcy. Includes refinancing advisory, M&A opportunities for buyers or sellers of distressed properties, debt capacity and valuation analysis, and structuring and loan syndication advice.

Capital Markets

Equities	Market and execute equity transactions for corporate clients, including initial public offerings, follow-on common stock issues, convertible issues, and private placements.
Fixed income	Arrange fixed-income financing for corporate and government clients. Instruments include syndicated loans, money market instruments (i.e., commercial paper), high-grade securities, securitized debt (i.e., asset-backed and mortgage-backed securities), emerging markets debt (sovereign and corporate bonds); project finance, private placements, structured finance, collateralized debt obligations and credit derivatives.
	Major departments: (1) Investment-Grade Debt Capital Markets, which arranges corporate bond issuance for investment-grade companies and sovereigns. (2) Global Syndicated Finance, which arranges bank loan financing for clients. Banks minimize their exposure by arranging loans that can be distributed across many other banks. The lead bank typically keeps a portion of the loan and earns a fee for the amount placed to other banks. (3) High-Yield Capital Markets, which arranges corporate bond issuance for companies rated below investment grade (BBB). There is a large and relatively liquid market for these types of bonds today. (4) Private Placements, which raises financing for companies with private investors. This financing is typically in the form of debt but also can be structured as convertible securities or equity.

TABLE 8.1 (Continued)

Sales and Trading

Sales and trading professionals interact with major investor clients (institutions, governments, hedge funds, and individuals) in day-to-day trading, portfolio recommendations, and marketing new bond or equity/equity-linked issues. There are many specialized sales and trading desks across the organization focusing on specific instruments (i.e., equities, convertible securities, and fixed-income securities). The salesperson is analogous to the client banker and delivers the bank's research, new-issue products, and trading capabilities to clients. The trader is responsible for facilitating client transactions, committing the bank's capital, and managing the bank's risk. Instruments include money market instruments (i.e., commercial paper, certificates of deposits, loan participations, and bankers' acceptances), corporate securities, high-grade and high-yield government and quasi-government securities, government agency securities and municipal bonds, emerging markets investments (i.e., sovereign and corporate bonds); structured finance obligations and securitized obligations, equities, commodities, foreign exchange and derivatives, exchange-traded futures, and options.

Risk Management

Equity derivatives

Structure, execute, sell, and trade all equity derivative hedging and investment products (single stock, baskets, index structures) for investors, private banking and corporate clients.

Foreign exchange and interest rate derivatives

Structure, execute, sell, and trade interest rate and foreign exchange hedging transactions for companies.

Commodity derivatives

Structure, execute, sell, and trade bullion, base metals, oil, natural gas and agricultural derivatives.

RESOURCE LISTINGS

Banco Santander

Banco Santander is a global financial group that offers every type of financial service to every kind of customer, from individuals to institutions. It is the world's tenth-largest financial group by market value. Santander operates primarily in continental Europe, the United Kingdom, and Latin America, mainly in Brazil, Chile, Argentina, Puerto Rico, Venezuela, and Colombia. Its main retail businesses are retail banking, wholesale banking, and asset management and insurance.

Headquartered in Madrid, Banco Santander has over 129,000 employees worldwide and 66 million customers. The bank hires for professional positions in its globally managed business areas, such as wholesale banking, consumer finance or asset management, insurance, and private banking. Specialized experience and skills are required for employment in its functional areas, which include auditing, risk, legal affairs, technology, and so forth. It also hires in its network of commercial banking offices.

Santander offers a variety of opportunities for students, including internships, work experience, and continuing higher education. Grupo Santander operates work experience programs in cooperation with over 357 universities and business schools in Spain and Latin America. In the United States, the group has several offices in New York, an office in Miami, and representational offices in Connecticut, Massachusetts, and New Jersey.

> Banco Santander International
> 45 East 53rd Street, 16th Floor
> New York, NY 10022
> Tel.: 212-350-3400
> Fax: 212-407-4560
> www.santander.com

Bank of America

Bank of America is a diverse institution that offers banking services to individuals, business, government agencies, and financial institutions throughout the world. It offers a variety of financial products and services to clients in North America, Europe, Asia, and Latin America. It is a global leader in corporate and institutional banking, serving 98 percent of the U.S. *Fortune* 500 and 80 percent of global *Fortune* 500 companies and operating offices across the United States and in twenty countries worldwide. It has specialized, global industry teams for a variety of sectors, including environmental services, financial institutions, franchises and restaurants, law firms, real estate banking, sports finance and advisory, and transportation. It offers a variety of services, from sophisticated debt and liquid products and mergers and acquisitions advisory to government and insurance services, trade services, and treasury management. This mix of financial products and services provides a diverse revenue stream and has made Bank of America the world's fifth most profitable company.

Bank of America's global operations include global consumer and small business banking, global corporate and investment banking, global risk management, global wealth and investment management, and global technology and operations. With operations in over thirty countries, there are a variety of opportunities. However, each market has a different focus and corresponding set of services offered.

Both bachelor's degree holders and master's or MBA candidates can apply for positions. Current undergraduate students or recent graduates can apply for full-time or internship-schedule analyst programs. Associate programs are available to current students or recent graduates of MBA and other advanced degree programs. Most opportunities are in the United States. Candidates for internships must have a grade point average of 3.0 or above, nongraduating status, be eligible to work forty hours a week for at least ten weeks, and have a business or technical education background. The recruitment process in the United States and Europe usually begins with an on-campus interview, from which finalists are selected for a second round. Bank of America also hires full-time analysts in Asia. Students may also apply to analyst and associate positions online at careers.bankofamerica.com.

Bank of America's corporate center is located in Charlotte. It is currently constructing a tower in New York City at One Bryant Park that will be its global corporate and investment banking headquarters and also house most of its New York employees.

Bank of America
Corporate Headquarters
100 North Tryon Street
Charlotte, NC 28255
Tel.: 704-386-1845
www.bankofamerica.com

BMO Financial Group
Founded in 1817 as the Bank of Montreal, Canada's first bank, BMO Financial Group is now one of the largest financial services organizations in North America. It offers clients a broad range of financial services across Canada and in the United States through BMO Bank of Montreal, its personal and commercial banking business; BMO Nesbitt Burns, a leading wealth management firm; BMO Capital Markets, its North American investment and corporate banking division; and Harris Bank, its Chicago-based subsidiary.

With average assets of $268 billion and more than 35,000 employees around the world, BMO Financial Group is a diversified and growing company. Career opportunities are available in all its businesses; Nesbitt Burns' Investment and Corporate Banking Team offers associate and analyst programs for new graduates. Its capital-raising activities include debt and equity security underwriting, securitization, private placements, and project-leveraged financing; its financial advisory services include mergers and acquisitions, strategic advice, restructurings, recapitalizations, takeover defense, fairness opinions, and valuations. Associates—typically, MBA graduates with prior relevant work experience—work on public underwritings, private placements, mergers and acquisitions, and advisory products, as well as analyzing financial and capital markets alternatives. Analyst positions, designed for university graduates with finance backgrounds, are two to three years in duration and involve research on specific companies, stock price analyses, discounted cash flow analyses, and financial modeling. Analysts may continue on to associate positions upon the completion of their program.

BMO Financial Group's strategy for success is guided by the principles of respect for the culture of the communities where it does business and an identity as a professional, financially secure institution with strong risk management skills. It values strong management and leadership, a client service focus, conceptual and strategic thinking, and managing for inclusion, among other candidate qualities.

> BMO Financial Group
> First Canadian Place
> Toronto, Ontario M5X 1A1
> Canada
> Tel.: 416-867-5000
> Fax: 415-867-6793
> www.bmo.com/careers

Bank of New York

The Bank of New York, founded in 1784 by Alexander Hamilton and the nation's oldest bank operating under its original name, is the sixteenth-largest bank holding company in the United States. The bank provides a complete range of banking and other financial services to corporations and individuals worldwide through its core businesses: securities and other processing, credit cards, corporate banking, retail banking, trusts, investment management and private banking, and financial market services. The Bank of New York is an important lender to major U.S. and multinational corporations and is the leading retail bank in suburban New York. The bank is also the largest provider of securities-processing services to the market and a respected trust and investment manager.

The Bank of New York hires master's degree graduates with a concentration in finance, strong writing skills, and one to three years of previous financial analysis experience for corporate banking associate positions and corporate credit analyst positions. As an associate, new hires work closely in support of the more experienced corporate finance professionals. In addition to financial modeling and credit analysis, associates participate in all aspects of business development and relationship management. They work closely with and gain knowledge of key product groups throughout the bank, including loan syndications, capital markets, securities processing, and cash management. Analysts work with relationship managers, senior credit analysts, and loan syndicators to analyze and structure credit transactions.

> Bank of New York
> One Wall Street, 13th Floor
> New York, NY 10286
> Tel.: 212-635-7717
> www.bankofny.com

Barclays Capital

Headquartered in London, Barclays Capital is the investment banking division of Barclays Bank PLC, with a balance sheet over $1.9 trillion and an AA credit rating. Serving large corporate, institutional, and government clients, Barclays Capital offers a variety of financial and risk management products, including equity derivatives, leveraged finance, and securitization.

Globally, Barclays Capital has approximately 13,200 employees in twenty-six countries in the Americas, the Asia-Pacific region, and Europe, the Middle East, and Africa. It recruits candidates at all degree levels. Holders of bachelor's and master's degrees with little or no prior experience in investment banking qualify for the analyst program. Candidates with a strong background in finance, solid communication skills, and fluency in more than one language are desired for positions across its businesses, with positions in operations, corporate communications, facilities management, and legal; wealth management; finance, global financial risk management, investment banking, and debt capital management; research; sales; trading; and others. Candidates for associate positions are expected to have or be studying toward a master's in finance or an MBA with relevant professional work experience. Associate positions are available in investment banking and debt capital markets, research, sales, strategy and planning, structuring, trading, and wealth management. Quantitative associates are typically expected to hold a PhD in a highly technical discipline such as mathematics, physics, or engineering. Positions are available in global financial risk management, quantitative analytics, research, structuring, and trading.

Barclays also offers summer internships at both the analyst (undergraduate) and associate (typically graduate) levels. They are ten weeks long, carefully structured, and can lead to an offer of permanent employment upon degree completion. Full-time and summer analyst and associate positions are available in the United States, Europe, and the Asia-Pacific region.

> Barclays Capital
> Corporate Headquarters
> One Churchill Place
> Canary Wharf
> London E14 4PA
> United Kingdom
> www.barcap.com/campusrecruitment

Brown Brothers Harriman

Founded in 1818, Brown Brothers Harriman & Co. is the oldest and largest partnership bank in America. In addition to a full range of commercial banking facilities, the firm is among the leading providers of global custody, foreign exchange, private equity, merger and acquisition services, investment management for individuals and institutions, personal trust and estate administration, and securities brokerage. It currently operates in eight domestic and seven overseas locations (including

London, Dublin, Grand Cayman, Hong Kong, Luxembourg, Tokyo, and Zurich) with over 3,000 employees. Most of its staff is located in Boston, Jersey City, and New York City. Brown Brothers Harriman is organized into nine lines of business: administration, banking, corporate finance, institutional equities, investment management, investor services, operations, systems, and treasury.

> Brown Brothers Harriman & Co.
> 140 Broadway
> New York, NY 10005
> Tel.: 212-483-1818
> www.bbh.com/careers

Calyon

Calyon is the corporate and investment bank of Crédit Agricole, a leading player in France and Europe in retail banking and related businesses. It was formed from the merger of Crédit Agricole Indosuez and Crédit Lyonnais' corporate and investment banking division, and it is now a leading player in financial markets. Two-thirds of its net banking income comes from overseas activities. Calyon specializes in capital markets, investment banking, and financing. Its international private banking activities are primarily in Europe. Calyon has 12,000 staff in fifty-five countries, and numerous internships and overseas training programs for those beginning careers. Information on internships and international placement opportunities is available on the Crédit Agricole website.

> Calyon Headquarters
> 9, quai du Président Paul Doumer
> 92920 Paris La Défense Cedex
> Tel.: 33-1-41-89-0000
> www.postuler.credit-agricole.fr
> www.calyon.com

Citigroup

The creation of Citigroup in 1998 brought together two large companies: Citicorp and Travelers. It is now the most profitable financial services company in the world, with some 200 million customers in more than a hundred countries. Citigroup offers individual and corporate customers a range of high-quality products and services. As a result, it is able to provide its employees with a breadth of career opportunities.

Citigroup is a company for people who have a sense of urgency and excitement; who are candid, insightful and creative; and who thrive in an environment of change, challenge and competition. Citigroup is composed of four distinct business divisions: Corporate and Investment Banking, Global Consumer Group, Global Wealth Management, and Citigroup Alternative Investments.

In almost all its businesses, Citigroup offers structured programs for professionals joining the banking and insurance business. These programs combine on-the-job experience with training modules and other learning tools and are intended to prepare participants for future leadership positions in the organization. In the first years at Citigroup, a new hire would typically be offered two or three rotational assignments in order to develop a broad understanding of a business field or specialty. Many programs include an overseas assignment. During this stage, recruits are called management associates.

Citigroup
399 Park Avenue
New York, NY 10043
www.citigroup.com/citigroup/oncampus/index.htm

CLS Bank
CLS Bank is a multicurrency bank based in New York that provides an efficient cross-currency settlement process, allowing for timely transaction settlements that reduce temporal risks. The unique CLS settlement process allows its settlement members and their affiliated user members to simultaneously settle transactions in real time, providing secure protection for cross-currency settlement. CLS employs staff in a range of disciplines, including finance, information technology, banking operations, and relationship management. Those interested in careers with CLS should send a statement of interest and résumé.

Human Resources Department
CLS UK Intermediate Holdings Ltd
P.O. Box 50576
London
E14 9TT
United Kingdom
e-mail: jobs@cls-group.com
www.cls-group.com

Credit Suisse
Founded in 1856 in Zurich, Credit Suisse is the oldest of the three big Swiss banks. After a reorganization and rebranding in 2006, Credit

Suisse's investment banking division is one of the world's largest securities and private banking firms. Operating in fifty countries on five continents worldwide, Credit Suisse has a presence in all major financial centers, leading industrial nations, and markets with high growth potential. Credit Suisse is a proven leader across the spectrum of investment banking, capital markets, and financial services, ranking in the top tier in virtually all major business segments. Its businesses include sales and trading, investment banking, alternative investments and private equity, financial advising, securities underwriting, asset management, and private banking. Its clients include businesses, governments, and wealthy individuals.

Candidates for positions with Credit Suisse should be energetic, flexible, team-oriented, and enthusiastic self-starters with strong communication, quantitative, computer, and problem-solving skills, along with a strong drive to succeed. Graduate students finishing MBAs or other postgraduate programs can apply for associate positions within investment banking, fixed income, equity, and private banking as well as analyst positions within equity research. Undergraduates can apply for analyst positions within investment banking, equity, and fixed income and for associate positions within equity research and information technology.

Credit Suisse Investment Banking Headquarters
11 Madison Avenue
New York, NY 10010
Tel.: 212-325-2000
www.credit-suisse.com

Deutsche Bank
Deutsche Bank is a leading global investment bank with a strong and profitable private clients franchise. A leader in Germany and Europe, the bank is continuously growing in North America, Asia, and key emerging markets. With $1.126 billion in assets and 68,849 employees in seventy-three countries, Deutsche Bank offers financial services throughout the world. The bank competes to be the leading global provider of financial solutions for demanding clients, creating exceptional value for its shareholders and people.

Deutsche Bank credits its success to the skill, determination, and creativity of its employees, who thrive on the unparalleled challenges and global career opportunities it can offer. It seeks highly motivated candidates with a proven work ethic who have demonstrated outstanding academic and extracurricular achievement, leadership, and community involvement. Deutsche Bank offers analyst internship and training programs for both graduates and undergraduates. MBAs are invited to participate in its associate programs, which include both summer and full-time training.

> Deutsche Bank AG
> Taunusanlage 12
> 60325 Frankfurt am Main
> Germany
> Tel.: 49-69-910-00
> Fax: 49-69-910-34225
>
> Deutsche Bank AG
> 60 Wall Street
> New York, NY 10005
> Tel.: 212-250-2500
> www.db.com/careers

Dresdner Bank

Headquartered in Frankfurt, Dresdner Bank AG is one of the world's major banks and a member of the Allianz Group. It is active in about fifty countries, with over 27,000 full-time staff. Dresdner Bank has trainee schemes as well as direct-entry programs, but all applicants must have fluency in German.

Dresdner Kleinwort, the bank's investment banking division, is headquartered in London and Frankfurt. It offers a fully integrated set of services in capital markets products and has a strong international cross-border advisory program. It employs approximately 6,000 people globally. Dresdner Kleinwort's major overseas offices are in Tokyo and Singapore, with other offices in Shanghai, Beijing, Hong Kong, and Kuala Lumpur.

Graduates are normally recruited into one of three business areas: capital markets, information technology, and operations. A number of recruits begin their careers in Japan, with the possibility to later move to other international operations. Approximately 270 people work in Dresdner Bank Group in Japan. Capital markets activities include global distribution—matching products with research, research, trading, and derivatives. The Singapore and Hong Kong offices do not recruit graduates. There are a limited number of positions for candidates with advanced degrees (master's and PhDs) in quantitative research, trading, and development; most other international positions are for experienced hires only.

Dresdner Bank AG
75 Wall Street
New York, NY 10005
Tel.: 212-429-2100
www.dresdner-bank.com

Dresdner Kleinwort
1301 Avenue of the Americas
New York, NY 10019
Tel.: 212-969-2700
www.dresdnerkleinwort.com/eng/careers

Goldman Sachs

Goldman Sachs is a leading international investment banking and securities firm, providing a full range of investment and financing services to corporations, governments, institutions, and individuals worldwide. Its areas of work include debt and equity trading and underwriting, merger and acquisitions advice, privatizations, currencies, commodities, bank loans, corporate banking, asset management, and fundamental and quantitative research.

Founded in 1869, Goldman Sachs is among the oldest and largest of the U.S.-based international investment banks. The firm is headquartered in New York and has over forty offices throughout the world. It seeks to hire a diverse group of individuals with various skills and professional orientations. It values a team approach, creativity, high ethical standards, and a willingness to work hard. Each year, it hires individuals from leading universities and graduate schools to work as professionals in a wide range of positions in various geographic locations.

Goldman Sachs
85 Broad Street
New York, NY 10004
Tel.: 212-902-1000, 800-323-5678
www.gs.com/careers

J. P. Morgan Chase

J. P. Morgan Chase & Co. is a leading global financial services firm with assets of $1.4 trillion and operations in more than fifty countries. The firm is a leader in investment banking, financial services for consumers, small business and commercial banking, financial transaction processing, asset management, and private equity. A component of the Dow Jones Industrial Average, J. P. Morgan Chase serves millions of consumers in the United States and many of the world's most prominent corporate, institutional, and government clients under its J. P. Morgan and Chase brands. Undergraduates and MBAs can choose from a wide range of opportunities in corporate, wholesale financial services, and consumer financial services. For more information on opportunities, including qualifications, training, and assignments, visit the J. P. Morgan careers website.

> J.P. Morgan Chase & Company
> 270 Park Avenue
> New York, NY 10017
> www.jpmorganchase.com/careers

Merrill Lynch

Merrill Lynch is one of the world's leading wealth management, capital markets, and advisory companies, with offices in thirty-seven countries and territories and total client assets of approximately $1.6 trillion. As an investment bank, it is a leading global trader and underwriter of securities and derivatives across a broad range of asset classes and serves as a strategic adviser to corporations, governments, institutions, and individuals worldwide. Merrill Lynch owns approximately half of BlackRock, one of the world's largest publicly traded investment management companies, with more than $1 trillion in assets under management. Merrill Lynch's Global Private Client Group provides advice-based wealth management services and products to individual clients and businesses. The Global Private Client business model is based on its network of more than 15,000 financial advisers in nearly 700 offices around the world and the one-to-one relationships they develop with their clients.

As a top-tier financial services firm, Merrill Lynch is an ideal place to build a career. With a breadth of business activities spanning the globe, it can offer a wide range of work experience and learning opportunities—opportunities that are constantly evolving and growing to stay ahead of the changing financial services landscape. It offers opportunities to holders of all degree levels—bachelor's, master's, and PhDs—across the globe.

> Merrill Lynch & Co., Inc.
> 4 World Financial Center
> 250 Vesey Street
> New York, NY 10080
> Tel.: 212-449-1000
> www.ml.com/careers

Morgan Stanley

With over $697 billion in assets under management and over 5.4 million individual investors, Morgan Stanley is one of the largest financial firms in the world. It is headquartered in New York but has offices in twenty-seven countries, representing the increasingly global nature of financial markets. Morgan Stanley is a market leader in its asset management, credit services, and securities businesses, and its financial services are highly regarded internationally.

The firm is organized into four main divisions: Institutional Securities, Global Wealth Management Group, Investment Management, and Discover Financial Services. Morgan Stanley Institutional Securities serves corporations, governments, and other institutional and investment banking clients, providing them with investment banking advice and managing private partnerships, among other services. The Global Wealth Management Group serves individual investors through its retail brokerage network and its tailored private wealth management service. Morgan Stanley Investment Management is a global asset management business. The firm also operates Discover Financial Services. Programs for candidates with graduate degrees are available in investment banking, investment management, private wealth management, research, sales and trading, and strategy and execution.

> Morgan Stanley
> 1585 Broadway, 14th Floor
> New York, NY 10036
> www.morganstanley.com/about/careers

Société Générale Corporate and Investment Banking

Société Générale Corporate and Investment Banking is the third-largest corporate and investment bank in the euro currency zone by net banking income and has a worldwide presence, operating in some forty-five countries across Europe, the Americas, and the Asia-Pacific region. It is headquartered in France, but more than 50 percent of its 10,000 employees work outside of France.

Société Générale Corporate and Investment Banking specializes in euro capital markets, where it is a market leader in all key debt and equity products, and it also offers mergers and acquisitions, brokerage, and cross-asset research services; derivatives, especially equity derivatives; and structured finance. It is one of Europe's leading banks and was voted the best place to work in France in 2003.

Société Générale Corporate and Investment Banking's corporate values are innovation, professionalism, and team spirit. The bank encourages both functional and geographic mobility; many of its senior managers have worked in other branches, such as asset management. It is particularly interested in hiring traders, who intervene in financial markets on the bank's behalf; persons for sales positions, who advise institutional investors or distribution networks for financial products on their investment strategies; financial analysts, who produce analyses and recommendations on companies and promote them to institutional investors; and middle and back office managers.

Société Générale Corporate and Investment Banking also offers internships to university and business students, many of whom are offered permanent positions at the end of their placement. European citizens between eighteen and twenty-eight years of age can also apply for the Voluntary Service Program, which offers six- to twenty-four-month placements throughout the international Société Générale network.

> Société Générale Corporate and Investment Banking
> Tour Société Générale
> 17 cours Valmy
> 92987 Paris-La Défense
> France
> Tel.: 33-1-42-14-20-00
> www.recrutement-societegenerale.com

Standard & Poor's

Standard & Poor's (S&P), a division of the McGraw-Hill Companies, is the world's foremost provider of financial market intelligence, including independent credit ratings, indices, risk evaluation, and investment research and data. It has approximately 8,500 employees, including those of wholly owned affiliates, located in twenty-one countries. Headquartered in New York, S&P is an essential part of the world's financial infrastructure and has played a leading role for more than 140 years in providing investors with the independent benchmarks they need to feel more confident about their investment and financial decisions. S&P does not engage in trading or underwriting activities. S&P credit analysts interact with the world's leading financial intermediaries, banks, corporations, governments, and other capital market participants. They visit the institutions they analyze. For example, they inspect the real estate used as collateral for mortgage-backed bonds and meet with government leaders. S&P analysts work closely in teams that encourage collaborative efforts to arrive at a quality rating. As developed and emerging market countries all over the world seek capital for their industrial and infrastructure growth, they increasingly turn to the U.S. capital markets, the most liquid in the world, as a guidepost for developing their own systems. Candidates for positions with S&P should be energetic team players with a demonstrated record of academic achievement—usually in fields such as business, finance, economics, and mathematics—and possess strong analytical capabilities.

> Standard & Poor's
> 55 Water Street
> New York, NY 10041
> Tel.: 212-438-2000
> www.standardandpoors.com

Standard Chartered Bank

Standard Chartered Bank PLC (SCB) is listed on both the London Stock Exchange and the Hong Kong Stock Exchange and is consistently ranked in the top twenty-five among FTSE-100 companies by market capitalization. SCB has a history of over 150 years in banking and operates in many of the world's fastest-growing markets with an extensive global network of over 1,400 branches in over fifty countries in the Asia-Pacific region, South Asia, the Middle East, Africa, the United Kingdom, and the Americas.

As one of the world's most international banks, SCB employs almost 60,000 people, representing over 100 nationalities, worldwide. This diversity lies at the heart of SCB's values and supports its growth as the world increasingly becomes one market. With strong organic growth supported by strategic alliances and acquisitions and driven by its strengths in the balance and diversity of its business, products, geography, and people, SCB is well positioned in the emerging trade corridors of Asia, Africa, and the Middle East.

SCB hires undergraduate and graduate students in a variety of disciplines to work in consumer banking, corporate and institutional banking, global markets, risk management, and other areas. Applying to SCB is a multistep process that involves psychometric testing, numerical testing, and an interview.

> Standard Chartered Bank
> One Madison Avenue
> New York, NY 10010-3603
> Tel.: 212-667-0700
> www.standardchartered.com

UBS

UBS is a leading global wealth manager, a top-tier investment banking and securities firm, and one of the largest global asset managers. In Switzerland, UBS is the market leader in retail and commercial banking. With headquarters in Zurich and Basel, UBS is present in all major financial centers worldwide. In total, UBS employs around 78,000 people, with 39 percent in the Americas, 35 percent in Switzerland, 16 percent in the rest of Europe, and 10 percent in the Asia-Pacific region. UBS's four primary businesses are wealth management, asset management, investment banking and securities, and Swiss retail and corporate banking.

UBS has career programs at all levels, from graduates to experienced professionals. All graduate training programs combine teaching, on-the-job experience, off-the-job learning, networking, support, and placement opportunities. Internships are available in many business areas and often lead to full-time position offers the following year. UBS graduate training programs and internships are available in the United States, the United Kingdom, Ireland, continental Europe, Switzerland, Asia Pacific, and Japan. There are global opportunities for MBAs in its corporate center and in its Global Asset Management, Global Wealth Management and Business Banking, and Investment Banking divisions. In Switzerland, UBS offers an apprenticeship and all-around traineeship for candidates fluent in German, French, or Italian.

> UBS
> Banhofstrasse 45
> P.O. Box CH-8098
> Zurich
> Switzerland
> Tel.: 41-44-234-11
> www.ubs.com
>
> UBS
> 1285 Avenue of the Americas
> New York, NY 10019
> Tel.: 212-713-2000

Wachovia Corporation

Wachovia Corporation is one of the top five diversified bank holding companies in the United States ranked by revenues or market value. Over the past decade, the company has grown enormously, in part through a series of successful acquisitions. It operates in four major business lines:

capital management, general banking, wealth management, and corporate and investment banking. The company provides commercial and retail banking and trust services through full-service banking offices throughout the United States, with a strong regional concentration ranging from the Middle Atlantic region through the Southeast and Southwest and California. The company also has offices in twenty major cities in Europe, Asia, and South America.

Wachovia recruits actively for master's-level graduates (mostly, but not exclusively, MBAs) for its investment banking business under the banner of Wachovia Capital Markets LLC. This investment banking business offers its clients a full range of institutional services, including an established, industry-oriented banking practice, merger and acquisitions advisory, sponsor coverage, equity and fixed-income capital markets, and leveraged capital. Though its origins are distinctly regional, today the investment bank is staffed with plenty of seasoned Wall Street veterans in all its departments, including its investment research activities. Most positions are located in the bank's headquarter city—Charlotte—but some positions are available in Manhattan in the bank's new Park Avenue location as well as in San Francisco.

In the past Wachovia has successfully recruited graduates from the Master of Science in Foreign Service Program at Georgetown University, and these candidates have been streamed with the incoming MBAs. The firm recruits competitively from the major business schools around the country. It follows the familiar schedule coordinated with all other major firms: full-time MBAs in the fall; summer interns; and both analysts and associates in January. Interested candidates should familiarize themselves with the firm's annual recruiting calendar as soon as possible but no later than mid-September.

Wachovia Corporation
Suite 4000, 301 South College Street
One Wachovia Center
Charlotte, NC 28288
Tel.: 704-590-0000
www.wachovia.com

Getting Started in Banking

Jae Lee

Jae Lee, *a 2000 graduate of the Bachelor of Science in Business Administration / Master of Science in Foreign Service Program at Georgetown University, recently moved from his position as vice president in debt markets at Merrill Lynch to Dresdner Kleinwort in Singapore. He joined Merrill Lynch in 2000, and he has been responsible for short-term interest rate trading for emerging-market Asia. Before moving to Asia, he was a member of the short-term interest rate trading team in New York, where he worked for four years. He began his career with the Merrill Lynch's Corporate Strategy Group.*

JOINING AN investment bank from a university (undergraduate or graduate) can be both one of the easiest and hardest routes for a student. It is one industry that comes to the leading schools almost every year—usually with recruiting efforts led by friendly alumni. School career centers will have the timeline for the recruiting process all set by the last week of September, with successful candidates getting offers before packing for their winter breaks. Plenty of books and websites provide insight into the firms and their process. You can even find most of the typical interview questions—and the corresponding "right" answers.

However, though the road may be well mapped out, it is definitely uphill all the way. The competition to join the leading banks is fierce. From Georgetown alone, Merrill Lynch Global Markets receives over 150 resumes from students each year for twenty interview slots, which end with only three to six offers—for summer analysts! Given the strong supply of talented individuals, the interview process is designed to go beyond identifying candidates capable of doing the job. Firms look for candidates that have the potential to excel while also being a good fit with their corporate culture.

For me, joining Merrill Lynch was both easier and harder than most. My job search started with the quest for a relevant summer internship. I dropped my resume at the career center, and after the initial round of on-campus interviews, I was introduced to the Corporate Strategy Group. From that point, however, there were a further two rounds of interviews—I ended up interviewing with nineteen different people before receiving an offer of a summer internship. Getting them to extend me a full-time offer was a lot simpler—I just had to do everything they asked of me, work more hours than the guy next to me, and try not to ask the same dumb question more than once!

And they did offer me a job after graduation from the Master of Science in Foreign Service Program. I returned to the Corporate Strategy Group, and I enjoyed spending the first two years as a management consultant with one of the world's largest investment banks. But when there were some changes in management, it was an opportunity for me to reassess where I wanted to take my career. I asked to move over to become a currency trader. This was a great opportunity—one that took advantage of my love of international relations. It was also a very exciting area of finance; currency markets are very interesting in that the markets will focus on different things at different times—everything from terrorism to central bank policy, trade numbers, equity markets, and coup d'états. Even the weather can affect how currencies trade. I have found current markets to offer great practical applications of the multidisciplinary approach to my studies at the Master of Science in Foreign Service Program (that degree saved me and my bank money on more than a few occasions).

Reflecting on my experiences—both as a candidate and an interviewer—I think a successful approach requires answering three key questions: How can I get an interview? How can I convince the interviewer that I am capable of doing the job? How can I convince them that I fit into the corporate culture?

Successfully completing that part of the interviewing and hiring process that will answer each of these questions requires a slightly different approach. First, most resumes only get about fifteen to thirty seconds of attention. Think about what you want your resume to say about you (focus on one or two "themes"), and make sure it sends that message clearly. Also, though easier said than done, work to get good names on your resume. In finance, a great internship at a company no one has heard of will probably not get as much positive attention as a less glamorous one at a prestigious institution. If interviewers spent more than thirty seconds reading the smaller print, it might be different—but they usually do not.

Second, convincing the interviewer that you are capable of doing the job is probably the easiest part of the process. There are plenty of resources that will help you find out the requirements of the job. Focus on highlighting those skills you have, and develop good answers to address any deficiencies that may be inferred from your résumé. Remember, no one expects you to be ready to produce from day one; they are just looking for candidates with the "potential" to excel.

Third, convincing interviewers that you fit into the corporate culture is challenging but crucial. At the end of the day, investment banks can afford to be highly selective. It is not enough for you to be competent; they also have to like you as a person, want to sit next to you for twelve to twenty-four hours a day, and believe that you will uphold the firm's culture and values. Do your best to understand each firm's culture before the interview (alumni are a great source) and prepare accordingly. For instance, suppose the same position is open at three different banks—a white-shoe investment bank, a boutique specialist bank, and a commercial bank. Though the title and duties of the position may be the same, each bank has a different culture, and each will want a different kind of candidate for the same job.

Do not get discouraged, because it takes both preparation and luck to complete all three of these parts of the interviewing and hiring process "correctly." However, if you succeed, you will find yourself in a dynamic industry full of opportunities.

9

Business

Careers in Business

KARLA SULLIVAN BOUSQUET

Karla Sullivan Bousquet, *a 1996 graduate of the Master of Science in Foreign Service Program at Georgetown University, is with IBM. Previously, she was with Procter & Gamble's Latin American Division in Puerto Rico; while in school, she interned with the Central Africa Foundation and the World Bank. Upon joining IBM, she held positions in corporate communications in Paris and New York, was appointed manager of workforce diversity, and is currently responsible for IBM's client services in Washington.*

AS A STUDENT of international business diplomacy, I vividly remember discussing the role of multinational corporations (MNCs) not only in shaping local economies but also in influencing societal trends and policies at both macro and micro levels. In one class we debated which had more influence on society: governments or MNCs? The class was evenly split as we discussed the balance of power between public institutions and the private sector. We studied the rise of MNCs and examined business strategies for gaining access to new markets while taking into account variables such as political risk and the dynamics of trade regulations, which could lower barriers and create free trade zones (like the North American Free Trade Agreement) or continue to protect national interests, as witnessed by current clashes in the World Trade Organization.

I now look back now on a decade of change from within IBM and can confidently predict that the MNC business models we discussed in class are headed for extinction. The new enterprises that emerge will most certainly be characterized as "global" rather than multinational, requiring new approaches to regulation, education, trade, and commerce.

Corporations have evolved from a hub-and-spokes model of home-country manufacture and international distribution to a more decentralized model of production in response to the rise of tariffs and other trade barriers. The rise of global brands that are marketed worldwide has had a dramatic impact on consumer buying behavior from Bamako to Beijing and ensured new growth opportunities for companies in emerging markets across the world.

At the same time, a revolution in information technology has allowed companies to standardize business operations, creating new links within and among companies. As individuals, corporations, and governments become increasingly interconnected, the world seems to be flattening. And in this flattened world, corporations are finding new opportunities and are responding. Rather than make foreign investments in reaction to foreign demand, companies increasingly make investments to change the way they supply the entire global market, taking advantage of new sources of knowledge and skilled labor while cutting costs.

As American and European politicians debate the consequences of "outsourcing" employment to emerging markets such as India, companies are realizing the immediate advantages of rethinking their business models, deconstructing their businesses into discrete components and functions and reconstructing them in new combinations with an array of global partners and suppliers. To illustrate this point, consider the heavy investments that IBM is making in India and the rapid development of its services business, which serves clients around the world. As the largest foreign employer in India, IBM has grown its workforce from just a few thousand employees ten years ago to over 50,000 today and announced its intention to invest a further $6 billion over the next three years to fuel growth in emerging business areas such as business transformation outsourcing. Globally integrated enterprises are leading a new wave of collaborative innovation that has profound implications for business, communities, and society at large, and that promises economic benefits for both developed and developing markets. From procurement processing centers in Manila to back office derivative transactions handled in Dublin or x-rays that travel across the globe and back for almost immediate interpretation, global integration is allowing companies to choose where they want different functions to be performed and by whom.

All of this brings me back to that classroom debate ten years ago. In a flat world, where increasing numbers of people have access to the same technology, human talent will become the only sustainable edge. Companies will tap productive talent wherever it is located, and a convergence in education will spur global growth and innovation. Ultimately, the quality of education offered by both public and private institutions and the education policies formulated by national governments will determine which countries excel and which fall behind.

In a flat world, where increasing numbers of people have access to the same technology, human talent will become the only sustainable edge.

Students interested in pursuing a career in international business will need to demonstrate the ability to work collaboratively and "virtually" in a world where teams communicate more by e-mail and instant messaging than in conference rooms. Having spent a year in Washington leading a team of thirty people in Europe, I can attest that this new virtual world is opening up unimagined opportunities for those comfortable working in multicultural environments and who can inspire trust and commitment from colleagues across the globe. So I urge you to embrace diversity and take advantage of opportunities to work with people who are different from you—the world is flat and getting smaller every day.

Developing a Successful Career

My job search started not just a few months before graduation but much earlier in my undergraduate studies as I searched for internships that would allow me to experiment with different sectors and activities. In my junior year I decided, after rooming with two business school majors, that I might want to try my hand in the world of finance. Through Georgetown's student employment office, I found an ad for an internship at Merrill Lynch Investment Services. To my surprise, during the interview my future manager said he had placed the ad at several universities but I was the first to apply. He hired me on the spot!

That summer, I interned at the U.S. Agency for International Development's Office of Democratic Initiatives in El Salvador. After my first real exposure to working in a government agency, I began to have doubts as to whether I wanted to start my career working for the U.S. government. I had just taken the Foreign Service examination, passing the written test but failing the oral. Keeping all options open, I took the exam a second time, and with the benefit of experience, I was much better prepared and passed both tests.

But I continued to be interested in the private sector. As I was now an undergraduate senior, my business school roommates and I began a friendly competition to see who could get the most interviews and ultimately secure the most interesting first job. With my eyes wide open, I looked for opportunities to differentiate myself from other applicants. I am the daughter of a Brazilian mother and Irish American father, so my passport enabled me to attend an international job fair, resumes in hand, ready to wow the interviewers with diverse internship experience and language abilities. However, I soon realized my language skills as a native English speaker with fluent skills in Portuguese and Spanish were not a great differentiator. There were many other students with equally impressive communications skills.

I also learned an important lesson at the Arthur Anderson Consulting (now Accenture) booth. Instead of reviewing my resume and asking questions about my prior experiences, the recruiter asked me what I knew about consulting and whether I had any specific industry expertise. Because I had not done my homework, I could not say that I knew very much about their business, and I scanned the brochure on the table frantically looking for some "Anderson-speak" that would make me sound informed. It did not work.

With that lesson in hand, I picked up a brochure at the Proctor & Gamble Latin America table and scanned it in the corner of the room before approaching the recruiter. We had an immediate rapport, and when she told me they were hiring for their brand management team in Brazil, I told her working papers would be no problem and my Portuguese would allow me to integrate with the local team, while my English would be an asset working at corporate headquarters. She agreed, and a week later she called to let me know that I had a job in Brazil if I was interested.

Alas, Brazil was not meant to be. With the fluctuations in the Brazilian currency, the P&G's Brazilian operations tanked one month after the interview. P&G Latin America then asked if I would apply to its Puerto Rico branch, its only other Latin American subsidiary that did not require a special work permit. I offered to meet with the managers in the P&G offices in Old San Juan, and after three rounds of interviews, I got the job. Within a month of graduation, I accepted—but I left my name on the State Department waiting list, just in case.

Lessons Learned

What lessons did I learn from these experiences? The first lesson: *Always be prepared.* Do not even bother to show up at an interview if you have not researched the position, the company, and, better yet, the industry and competitive landscape.

The second lesson I learned was: *Keep as many doors open as possible.* Even after passing the Foreign Service exam and deciding to move to Puerto Rico, I still went to New York and interviewed with a leading ad agency. By the time it offered me a job, I already had my ticket to San Juan. Nevertheless, I had gained some insights on ad agencies, which would become my business partners while I was at P&G.

My third lesson was: *Trust your instincts.* After my experience at the U.S. Agency for International Development, government seemed too bureaucratic for me, without sufficient rewards and promotions. By the time the Federal Bureau of Investigation contacted me for a security clearance, two years had passed, and I had decided to enroll in the Master of Science in Foreign Service Program at Georgetown. After receiving my degree, I did interview with another government group, only to learn that even with two years' experience and a master's degree, the most I could expect was the lowest pay grade and post. Thanks, but no thanks.

My fourth lesson was: *Network, network, network.* Moving through a series of internships and work experiences, I have made an effort to keep in touch with my former colleagues and managers. During my years at Georgetown, I attended many lectures given by outside speakers and made an effort to at least introduce myself to them and mingle with others in the audience. When it was time to look for a job after my graduate studies, I scoured the alumni lists and wrote to alums whose job titles sounded interesting or who were working for Fortune 500 companies.

In fact, my entrée into IBM came after a guest lecturer from its government affairs office on K Street in Washington came to class to share his experiences working to influence the U.S. government to take a tougher stance against Brazil during the 1970s. At that time, Brazil was trying to develop its own information technology industry and used tariffs and other trade policies to gain competitive advantage (or disadvantage foreign firms, in the eyes of this IBMer!). I knew I wanted to specialize in technology and had already studied both sides of the case. Although IBM had a right to protest high tariffs and worry about transferring technology know-how, I could also understand why a developing giant like Brazil wanted to end its dependence on foreign firms and create local competencies and skills in information technology.

Something in my arguments must have impressed the IBM lecturer, because after class he approached me and asked if I would be interested in working for IBM. When I told him I was planning to marry a Frenchman and needed a job in Paris, he offered to send my resume to Paris with a recommendation for a post in corporate communications.

In the end, I decided to buy my own plane ticket and try to get as many interviews lined up as possible during spring break of my final year. At the time, I had just finished an internship at the World Bank, contributing research and writing to the annual report and serving as the first webmaster for the Multilateral Investment Guarantee Agency. Both experiences caught the eye of the vice president for corporate communications for IBM Europe, the Middle East, Africa, and a week after returning to Washington I received an excellent job offer—by e-mail! This may seem mundane now, but in the mid-1990s, the Internet was just taking off. The e-mail helped me understand very quickly the terms and conditions of working as a "local" as opposed to an "expatriate" in France.

Now going on my eleventh year at IBM, I can genuinely say the company has given me fabulous opportunities to grow and stretch my skills and intellect. I am proud to work with people who share the same values and believe in the transformative power of information technology. Even when I have had a rough day and wonder why I bothered coming to work, my World Community Grid screensaver pops up to remind me of IBM's work with worldwide research institutions tapping unused computing power to unravel the mysteries of HIV/AIDS and cancer.

My experiences at IBM have given me the opportunity to work on public policy issues; public relations; executive, employee, and client communications; special events; and even a two-year stint building a new organization in human resources as the diversity leader for IBM Europe, the Middle East, and Africa. After those first three years in Paris, I landed an expatriate assignment to work with corporate communications in New

York City. Then I returned to France taking on a leadership communications role with IBM Global Services. Three years later, pregnant with my second child, I called on the network I had built in my diversity role (especially with leaders in human resources) to request reassignment to the United States, this time as a local, so I could work from home in Washington. My manager bent over backwards to ensure that my vision for working in the United States become a reality.

The best advice I can offer students of international relations and business who are interested in building an international career, whether within a globally integrated enterprise or a new start-up, is to do the following:

1. *Build a career plan.* Think about what and where you want to be one to two years from now, as well as five years down the road.
2. *Test your career plan.* Test it not only with your current manager but also with mentors and other potential sponsors who are interested in helping you develop. Is your plan realistic? What skills and competencies will you need to grow and demonstrate to get to the next level or position?
3. *Market your successes.* Too many people believe that as long as they are doing a good job, their work will get noticed. Yet even in more conservative Asian cultures where humility is valued, it does not hurt to understand corporate politics and find ways to make your accomplishments known (perhaps through peers or your own manager). Also, never forget that sometimes company culture trumps national culture and if you do not feel comfortable in one or both, it is a good sign that you should move on and seek new opportunities.
4. *Communicate your ambition.* Through my work in diversity, I came to realize that a common shortcoming among women professionals is a failure to communicate their career aspirations, leading to frustration when career opportunities seem to pass them by. Make sure that at least once a year, perhaps during a performance appraisal, you spend as much time discussing your strengths, how to grow professionally, and what specifically you are aiming for next as you do focusing on past performance and areas for improvement.
5. *Repeat steps 1 through 4—but be flexible.* Make sure to incorporate new insights and inputs and always keep the door open to new opportunities!

RESOURCE LISTINGS

Asea Brown Boveri
Asea Brown Boveri (ABB) is a global technology company headquartered in Zurich and with operations in more than 120 countries. The company is a global leader in power and automation technologies that enable utility and industry customers to improve performance while lowering environmental impact. Having helped countries all over the world to build, develop, and maintain their infrastructures, ABB has in recent years shifted from large-scale solutions to alternative energy and the advanced products in power and automation technologies.

ABB employs approximately 170,000 people. It runs several programs designed specifically for recent graduates of master's programs. Special trainee programs operate in Germany, Italy, Norway, Sweden, and Switzerland. The ABB Passport Program in Italy is offered to twenty young talents of different nationalities. It is a one-year program run in English, designed to give new graduates diverse competencies. It seeks recent graduates with technical backgrounds in fields such as design and engineering, project management, and marketing and sales. Business graduates should explore the Global Trainee Programs, which run from eighteen to twenty-four months and are in the fields of finance and business control, corporate development, and information systems. Generally, applicants must apply to their home countries; other applicants must speak the local language and possess a valid work permit for the country in question.

Asea Brown Boveri Group Headquarters
Affolternstr. 44
P.O. Box 8131
CH-8050
Zurich, Switzerland
Tel.: 41-0-43-317-7111
Fax: 41-0-43-317-7958
www.abb.com

Asea Brown Boveri USA
501 Merritt 7
P.O. Box 5308
Norwalk, CT 06851
Tel.: 203-750-2200
Fax: 203-750-2263
www.abb.com/us

American International Group

American International Group, Inc. (AIG), a world leader in insurance and financial services, is the leading international insurance organization with operations in more than 130 countries and jurisdictions. AIG companies serve commercial, institutional, and individual customers through the most extensive worldwide property-casualty and life insurance networks of any insurer. In addition, AIG companies are leading providers of retirement services, financial services, and asset management around the world. AIG's common stock is listed on the New York Stock Exchange as well as the stock exchanges in London, Paris, Zurich, and Tokyo.

AIG companies recruit talented people at both the undergraduate and graduate levels. Several associate programs are offered, including a summer associate program for both undergraduate and graduate students. Management associates are expected to have a master's or other advanced degree in business or another related field, have two to four years of business experience, and preferably speak another language or have international experience. Undergraduate training programs last from one to two years and are available in the fields of underwriting, accounting, actuarial, asset management, and claims. The twelve-month Global Investment Group Analyst Program in asset management may be of particular interest.

American International Group Inc.
72 Wall Street, 6th Floor
New York, NY 10270
Tel.: 877-638-4244
www.aig.com/careers
www.aig.com/college

Bechtel Corporation

Bechtel is a global engineering, construction, and project management company with more than a century of experience on complex projects in challenging locations. Privately owned and headquartered in San Francisco, it has forty offices around the world and nearly 40,000 employees. In 2006, the company had revenues of $20.5 billion and booked new work valued at $24.7 billion. Bechtel works on roads and rail systems, airports and seaports, fossil and nuclear power plants, refineries and petrochemical facilities, mines and smelters, defense and aerospace facilities, environmental cleanup projects, telecommunications networks, pipelines, and oil and gas field development.

Bechtel has global opportunities for experienced candidates and new graduates—in the Americas, Australia, and Asia as well as in Europe, Africa, the Middle East, and Southwest Asia. It offers a four-year, international Graduate Development Program in four business areas: civil; oil, gas, and chemicals; telecommunications; and corporate.

> Bechtel Corporate Headquarters
> 50 Beale Street
> San Francisco, CA 94105
> Tel.: 415-768-1234
> Fax: 415-768-9038
> www.bechtel.com/careers

Boeing

Boeing is the world's leading aerospace company and the largest manufacturer of commercial jetliners and military aircraft combined. Additionally, Boeing designs and manufactures rotorcraft, electronic and defense systems, missiles, satellites, launch vehicles, and advanced information and communication systems. As a major service provider to the National Aeronautics and Space Administration, Boeing operates the Space Shuttle and International Space Station. The company also provides numerous military and commercial airline support services. Boeing has customers in more than ninety countries around the world and is one of the largest U.S. exporters in terms of sales.

Headquartered in Chicago, Boeing employs more than 150,000 people across the United States and in seventy countries. More than 83,800 of its people hold college degrees—including nearly 29,000 advanced degrees—in virtually every business and technical field from approximately 2,800 colleges and universities worldwide. The enterprise also leverages the talents of hundreds of thousands more skilled people working for Boeing suppliers worldwide.

Boeing hires professionals, recent graduates, and interns from a range of scientific, engineering, and business backgrounds. New college graduates in business are eligible for the Business Career Foundation Program, a two-year rotational program that exposes participants to a variety of business positions within Boeing.

> Boeing Corporate Offices
> 100 North Riverside
> Chicago, IL 60606
> Tel.: 312-544-2000
> jobs.boeing.com

BP

BP is one of the world's largest energy companies, with 97,000 employees and operations in over one hundred countries across six continents. It is organized into three business segments: exploration and production; refining and marketing; and gas, power, and renewables. It is a leader in upstream activities in Alaska, the North Sea, and North America; is developing major new fields across the globe, including in the deep waters of the Gulf of Mexico; and has invested in Russian crude oil through its joint venture TNK-BP. It is active in pipelines and shipping, operates eighteen refineries, markets petroleum products through over 25,000 fuel stations worldwide, and is a leading marketer and producer of natural gas liquids in North America. With the launch of BP Alternative Energy in 2005, BP consolidated all its low-carbon activities in the power sector—solar, wind, hydrogen, and gas fired. It is also investing in activities to bring biofuels to the mainstream.

BP has received a number of employer awards in the United States and in Europe. Its graduate and intern programs in the United Kingdom are open to all nationalities. BP operates graduate and intern programs in sixteen countries; runs four programs for MBAs, PhDs, and postdoctoral researchers; and has two programs for European bilinguists and multilinguists. Its Global MBA Program, a two-month summer internship followed by a two-year Helios Fellowship, is an accelerated, internationally focused program for select MBA candidates. Remuneration can include language training.

> BP New York
> 535 Madison Avenue
> New York, NY 10022
> Tel.: 212-421-5010
> www.bp.com/careers

Brunswick Corporation

Brunswick Corporation is the world's leading manufacturer and marketer of pleasure boats, marine engines, fitness equipment, bowling equipment, consumer products, and billiards tables. Brunswick products are sold throughout North America, the United Kingdom, South America, Europe, Africa, the Middle East, Asia, and Australia. Brunswick brands include Mercury and Mariner outboard engines; Mercury MerCruiser sterndrives and outboard engines; Sea Ray, Bayliner, Maxum, Hatteras, and Sealine pleasure boats; Baja high-performance boats; Boston Whaler and Trophy offshore fishing boats; Triton, Lund, Harris FloteBote, and Princecraft fishing, deck, and pontoon boats; Life Fitness, Hammer Strength, and ParaBody fitness equipment; and Brunswick bowling centers, equipment, and consumer products.

Brunswick Corporation has a growing international presence and has opportunities for both U.S. citizens and foreign nationals throughout its operations. Candidates for these international operations are encouraged to apply for internships that afford international affairs students substantive exposure to that area of the company's operations.

> Brunswick Corporation
> 1 North Field Court
> Lake Forest, IL 60045
> Tel.: 847-735-4700
> Fax: 847-735-4765
> www.brunswick.com

Caterpillar

For more than eighty years, Caterpillar Inc. has been making progress possible and driving positive and sustainable change on every continent. With 2006 sales and revenues of $41.5 billion, Caterpillar is the world's leading manufacturer of construction and mining equipment, diesel and natural gas engines, industrial gas turbines, and a wide and growing offering of related services. Caterpillar employs more than 90,000 people worldwide. Its products and components are manufactured in fifty U.S. facilities and in over sixty other locations in twenty-three countries around the globe. Caterpillar ships products to job sites in nearly two hundred countries.

Caterpillar values global diversity—the variety of unique skills, abilities, experiences, and cultural backgrounds that enables Caterpillar to achieve superior business results. Global diversity at Caterpillar is more than ethnicity and gender. It includes areas of experience that make people unique, such as global experience, cross-functional experience, and external experience. Developing a globally diverse culture better serves an increasingly diverse global marketplace.

> Caterpillar Inc.
> 100 NE Adams Street
> Peoria, IL 61629
> Tel.: 309-675-1000
> www.cat.com/careers

Chevron

Chevron, parent company of Chevron, Texaco, and Unocal, is one of the world's largest integrated oil companies. Headquartered in San Ramon, California, and operating in about 180 countries, it is engaged in every aspect of the oil and gas industry, including exploration and production, refining, marketing and transportation, chemicals manufacturing and sales, and geothermal and power generation. It employs over 56,000 people worldwide.

Students, recent graduates, and experienced professionals all have a place at Chevron. Internships are available worldwide in a variety of business, technology, marketing, and policy fields. Chevron offers several programs geared specifically toward MBA graduates, in global marketing, finance, supply and trading, and global gas commercial skills. All these programs include rotational assignments, and most offer rotations in key international offices.

> Chevron Headquarters
> 6001 Bollinger Canyon Road
> San Ramon, CA 94583
> Tel.: 925-842-1000
> careers.chevron.com

Coca-Cola

The Coca-Cola Company, founded in 1886, is the world's leading manufacturer, marketer, and distributor of nonalcoholic beverage concentrates and syrups, used to produce more than four hundred beverage brands in over two hundred countries around the world. The Coca-Cola brand is one of the most recognized trademarks in the world, but other local and global brands also continue to contribute to the firm's success. The Coca-Cola Company, including the bottling entities it owns, employs approximately 55,000 people, over 44,000 of whom are employed outside of the United States. In 2005, it reported financial revenues of $80 billion, with 70 percent of its income coming from outside the United States. The Coca-Cola Company in North America offers internship programs for both graduate and undergraduate students.

> Coca-Cola Company
> P.O. Box 1734
> Atlanta, GA 30301
> www.thecoca-colacompany.com/careers

Dell Computer Corporation
The Dell Computer Corporation, which is headquartered in Austin, Texas, sells more systems globally than any other computer company. It is a market leader in computing products and services, ranking twenty-fifth on the *Fortune* 500 list of companies. It is active in fifty-one countries. Dell offers career paths in sales, customer service and support, information technology, engineering, business, and manufacturing and logistics. Internships are available for first-year MBA students, first-year master's students, and undergraduates with a sophomore or junior ranking. Opportunities are mainly available in the United States, although some opportunities may be available in Latin America and Canada.

> Dell Computer Corporation
> One Dell Way
> Round Rock, TX 78682
> www.dell.com

DuPont
Headquartered in Wilmington, Delaware, DuPont is a research- and technology–based global chemicals, materials, and energy. Operating in more than seventy countries, DuPont offers a wide range of innovative products and services for markets including agriculture, nutrition, electronics, communications, safety and protection, home and construction, transportation, and apparel. It has over 60,000 employees worldwide, more than forty research and development and customer service laboratories in the United States, and more than thirty-five laboratories in eleven other countries.

DuPont recruits in the fields of consulting solutions, engineering, finance, hospitality and services, human resources, information and computing technologies, legal, sales and marketing, sourcing and logistics, and research and development. For MBAs, internships are available in accounting and finance and in marketing. There are also career development programs for recent graduates of BA, MS and MA, MBA, and PhD programs. Early career development programs in finance and sales and marketing offer rotations and a special focus on development and training.

> DuPont
> 1007 Market Street
> Wilmington, DE 19898
> www.dupont.com

Eli Lilly & Company

Eli Lilly & Company is a leading, innovation-driven corporation committed to developing a growing portfolio of best-in-class and first-in-class pharmaceutical products that help people live longer, healthier, and more active lives. Lilly products treat depression, schizophrenia, attention-deficit hyperactivity disorder, diabetes, osteoporosis, and many other conditions. The firm is committed to providing answers that matter for some of the world's most urgent medical needs. Eli Lilly has approximately 41,350 employees worldwide, 7,980 of whom are engaged in research and development. Its products are marketed in 143 countries. In addition to recruiting those with science backgrounds, Eli Lilly offers internships and entry programs to candidates with backgrounds in marketing, finance, human resources, information technology, and other fields. It also has an MBA internship program.

> Eli Lilly Corporate Center
> Indianapolis, IN 46285
> Tel.: 317-276-2000
> www.lilly.com/careers

ExxonMobil

ExxonMobil is one of the world's largest energy companies, with activities in exploration, production, refining and supply, lubricants and specialties, natural gas and power marketing, fuels marketing, and chemicals. It has a development portfolio with potential investments of more than $120 billion. Career opportunities are available on five continents for those with master's degrees or PhDs in engineering and chemistry; for experienced professionals; and for recent recipients of bachelor's and master's degrees in fields ranging from science and engineering to law, finance, and public affairs.

> ExxonMobil Corporate Headquarters
> 5959 Las Colinas Boulevard
> Irving, TX 75039
> Tel.: 972-444-1000
> www.exxonmobil.com

Ford Motor Company

Ford Motor Company is a global automotive industry leader headquartered in Dearborn, Michigan, that manufactures and distributes automobiles on six continents. With about 300,000 employees and 108 plants worldwide, the company's core and affiliated automotive brands include Ford, Jaguar, Land Rover, Lincoln, Mazda, Mercury, and Volvo. Its automotive-related services include Ford Motor Credit Company. Ford Motor Company offers a range of internships, student programs, and full-time programs for recent graduates.

> Ford Motor Company
> 1 American Road
> Dearborn, MI 48126
> www.mycareer.ford.com

General Electric

General Electric (GE) is a diversified services, technology, and manufacturing company with a commitment to achieving customer success and worldwide leadership in each of its six businesses: GE Commercial Finance, GE Healthcare, GE Industrial, GE Infrastructure, GE Money, and NBC Universal. GE offers internships and coops in Canada, China, Europe, Japan, Mexico, and the United States. It also has several entry-level corporate leadership programs—in communications, engineering, finance, information technology, manufacturing/operations, and sales and marketing—as well as several business-specific programs.

> General Electric Company
> 3135 Easton Turnpike
> Fairfield, CT 06828
> www.gecareers.com

General Motors

General Motors (GM) is the world's largest automaker and has been the global industry sales leader for seventy-six years. Headquartered in Detroit, GM employs about 284,000 people around the world and manufactures its cars and trucks in thirty-three countries. In 2006, 9.1 million GM cars and trucks were sold globally under these brands: Buick, Cadillac, Chevrolet, GMC, GM Daewoo, Holden, Hummer, Opel, Pontiac, Saab, Saturn and Vauxhall. GM's OnStar subsidiary is the industry leader in vehicle safety, security, and information services.

> General Motors Corporation
> P.O. Box 33170
> Detroit, MI 48232
> www.gm.com/company/careers

GlaxoSmithKline

GlaxoSmithKline (GSK) is a world-leading research-based pharmaceutical company and the only one to tackle the three global "priority" diseases as identified by the World Health Organization: HIV/AIDS, tuberculosis, and malaria. Headquartered in the United Kingdom and with operations based in the United States, GSK is one of the industry leaders, with an estimated 7 percent of the world's pharmaceutical market. Its business employs over 100,000 people in 116 countries.

GSK career opportunities exist in the United States, United Kingdom, Canada, Africa, Asia and Australia, Europe, the Middle East, and South America. As a global leader in health care, it recruits from many different disciplines, and it offers a huge array of internships, coops, and full-time direct-entry opportunities, not just within the scientific disciplines but also across the functions of production, engineering, logistics, sales and marketing, finance, information technology, and procurement/purchasing.

> GlaxoSmithKline
> One Franklin Plaza
> P.O. Box 7929
> Philadelphia, PA 19101
> www.gsk.com/careers/index.htm

Google

Google's mission is to organize the world's information and make it universally accessible and useful. The utility and ease of use of the Google World Wide Web search engine have made Google one of the world's best-known brands almost entirely through word of mouth from satisfied users. As a business, Google generates revenue by providing advertisers with the opportunity to deliver measurable, cost-effective online advertising that is relevant to the information displayed on any given web page. Google is the number one search engine in Argentina, Australia, Belgium, Brazil, Canada, Denmark, France, Germany, India, Italy, Mexico, Spain, Sweden, Switzerland, the United Kingdom, and the United States. Google has approximately 380 global unique users per month; owns 112 international Internet domains; and as of June 30, 2006, had 7,942 full-time employees worldwide. More than 50 percent of Google's web traffic is from outside the United States.

The Googleplex in Mountain View, California, is the world headquarters for the Google organization, though the company maintains sales and engineering offices around the globe. Google's European headquarters are in Ireland. Google is rapidly growing in popularity around the world, and it seeks highly dynamic and proficient individuals with excellent sales and people skills to build its global teams. Internships and full-time opportunities are available to students and recent graduates in technical and non-technical fields such as advertising sales and management; business operations, finance, and human resources; marketing and product management; and strategy, operations, and development.

Google Headquarters
1600 Amphitheatre Parkway
Mountain View, CA 94043
Tel.: 650-253-0000
Fax: 650-253-0001
www.google.com/intl/en/jobs

Halliburton and KBR

Halliburton adds value through the entire lifecycle of oil and gas reservoirs, starting with exploration and development, and moving through production, operations, maintenance, conversion, and refining to infrastructure and abandonment. It operates in over 120 countries working in three business segments: drilling, evaluation, and digital solutions; fluid systems; and production optimization. These segments offer a broad array of products and services to upstream oil and gas customers worldwide, ranging from the manufacturing of drill bits and other downhole and completion tools to pressure pumping services.

KBR, Halliburton's engineering subsidiary, is a global leader in construction and project management, with a strong historical position in LNG and oil and gas projects. The company is a leading government services contractor as well.

Halliburton Corporate Headquarters
5 Houston Center
Suite 2400, 1401 McKinney Street
Houston, TX 77010
Tel.: 713-759-2605
www.halliburton.com/careers

KBR
601 Jefferson
Houston, TX 77002
www.kbrjobs.com

IBM

International Business Machines Corporation, or IBM, has been the world's largest computer company for most of its recent history. It employs more than 350,000 people in more than 170 countries, and it has eight research laboratories around the world. IBM holds more patents than any other United States-based company, but it has also transformed itself from a leader in computer hardware into an information technology services business providing solutions for a wide variety of enterprise needs. Its Global Business Services is the world's largest computing organization. IBM hires both graduates and experienced professionals to staff its offices in the Americas, Europe, the Middle East, Africa, and Asia and the Pacific. Its cooperative and intern programs are limited to the United States.

> IBM Corporation
> 1 New Orchard Road
> Armonk, NY 10504
> www.ibm.com/jobs

ITOCHU International

Headquartered in New York, ITOCHU International Inc. is the North American flagship company of Tokyo-based ITOCHU Corporation, with revenues of more than $19 billion a year, an employee base of 45,000, and 135 offices in more than seventy countries. ITOCHU started in 1858 as an import/export house. Today, with its diverse portfolio of more than four hundred subsidiaries whose operations complement the trading services, ITOCHU Corporation boasts one of the most extensive business networks in the world, and is a member of the Fortune Global 500. ITOCHU Corporation's trading divisions are Textiles; Machinery; Aerospace, Electronics, and Multimedia; Energy, Metals, and Minerals; Chemicals, Forest Products and General Merchandise; Food; and Finance, Realty, and Logistics Services. ITOCHU employees can be found in places as diverse as Australia, Nigeria, Romania, and Thailand.

Like its parent company, ITOCHU International began as a global trading company, importing and exporting goods around the world. Today, ITOCHU still offers trading services for 20,000 different items, and it also manages a portfolio of more than forty subsidiaries and affiliates. These subsidiaries and affiliates report to six trading divisions, all headquartered in New York: Textile; Machinery; Information Technology and Aerospace; Energy, Metals, and Minerals; Food; and Chemicals, Forest Products, and General Merchandise. In addition, ITOCHU International has an Enterprise Division, whose subsidiary operations fall outside the scope of regular trading divisions. The company's principal focus is working with its several subsidiaries and business partners to achieve growth.

ITOCHU hires people with differing levels of experience in various functions that have recently included finance and accounting, technology, and business analysis. The firm looks for people who focus on detail, are collaborative, and understand the real meaning of teamwork but who also possess the initiative to learn about a project, the aptitude to understand all the issues surrounding a project, and the ability to bring a project to completion. ITOCHU International expects individuals at every level of the organization to behave with respect and integrity. As a worldwide international company that is constantly changing, ITOCHU looks for people who thrive in a challenging and exciting environment.

> ITOCHU Corporation
> 6-1 Kita-Aoyama 2-chome
> Minato-ku, Tokyo 107-8077
> Japan
> Tel.: 81-3-3497-7295
> Fax: 81-3-3497-7296
> www.itochu.co.jp
>
> ITOCHU International
> 335 Madison Avenue
> New York, NY 10017
> Tel.: 212-818-8000
> www.itochu.com.

Johnson & Johnson

Johnson & Johnson products are sold worldwide, generating annual global revenues of more than $53 billion. The company produces and sells products to meet a wide range of human health care needs, including anti-infectives, orthopedics, cardiology and circulatory diseases, urology, diagnostics, women's health, mental health, and skin care. The more than 250 Johnson & Johnson operating companies employ approximately 121,000 men and women in fifty-seven countries and sell products throughout the world.

Johnson & Johnson companies have full-time, internship, coop, and postdoctoral fellowship opportunities for students in graduate degree programs (MS, MBA, PhD). If you have recently completed, or are about to complete, a university graduate degree program, have less than one year of regular full-time work experience since receiving your graduate degree, and have demonstrated leadership potential, you may qualify for one of Johnson & Johnson's leadership development programs, including the International Recruitment and Development Program. Johnson & Johnson International Recruitment and Development recruits high-potential MBA students for specific positions offered by Johnson & Johnson companies throughout the Asia-Pacific, Europe–Middle East–Africa, and Latin America regions. Opportunities are generally within the functional disciplines of sales, marketing, finance, operations/logistics, human resources, and information management. Development assignments run for twelve months and, based on the needs of the hiring companies, may take place at either the regional or international level. Regional assignments take place within the hiring country; international assignments typically take place outside the country in which the hiring company is located. In some instances, there may be a blend of both regional and international assignments during the development period.

Internships, coops, and leadership development programs are also available to students currently enrolled in or completing bachelor's degree programs. The Global Operations Leadership Development Program offers recent university graduates the opportunity to accelerate their career growth through a structured process that combines classroom and online training with challenging work rotations during a two-year period. The goal of the program is to develop the next generation of leaders for the engineering, operations, and quality disciplines within the Johnson & Johnson family of companies.

Johnson & Johnson
One Johnson & Johnson Plaza
New Brunswick, NJ 08933
Tel.: 732-524-0400
www.jnj.com/careers

Kraft Foods

With revenues of $34 billion, Kraft Foods Inc. is one of the world's largest food and beverage companies. It markets many of the world's leading food brands, which are sold in more than 155 countries. Kraft employs over 90,000 people and has 159 manufacturing and processing facilities worldwide. Kraft offers careers in finance, global supply chain, human resources, information systems, marketing, marketing resources, sales, and technology and quality.

> Kraft Foods Inc.
> Global Corporate Headquarters
> Three Lakes Drive
> Northfield, IL 60093
> Tel.: 847-646-2000
> www.kraftfoods.com/careers

Lockheed Martin

Lockheed Martin is a premier systems integrator and global security enterprise principally engaged in the research, design, development, manufacture, integration, and sustainment of advanced technology systems, products, and services. With growth markets in defense, homeland security, and systems / government information technology, Lockheed Martin delivers innovative technologies that help customers address complex challenges of strategic and national importance.

Headquartered in Bethesda, Maryland, Lockheed Martin employs 140,000 people worldwide. Distinguished by whole-system thinking and action, a passion for invention, and disciplined performance, Lockheed Martin strives to earn a reputation as the partner of choice, supplier of choice, and employer of choice in the global marketplace. Lockheed Martin is led by Bob Stevens, chairman, president, and chief executive officer. The corporation reported 2006 sales of $39.6 billion.

> Lockheed Martin Corporation
> 6801 Rockledge Drive
> Bethesda, MD 20817
> Tel.: 301-897-6000
> www.lockheedmartin.com/careers

Marathon Oil Corporation

Marathon Oil Corporation is engaged in the worldwide exploration and production of crude oil and natural gas, as well as the domestic refining, marketing, and transportation of petroleum products. Headquartered in Houston, Marathon is among the leading energy industry players, applying innovative technologies to discover valuable energy resources and deliver the highest-quality products to the marketplace. With operations that embrace three continents, Marathon strives to be the company of choice for investors, partners, customers, neighbors, and employees in the areas where it does business. Marathon's international locations include Equatorial Guinea, Gabon, Ireland, Norway, and the United Kingdom.

Marathon seeks talented students who thrive in an environment full of challenges and professional development prospects. At times throughout the year, there may be opportunities in geology, geophysics, engineering, information technology, finance, law, accounting, and purchasing. The company seeks talented undergraduates and graduate students who can thrive in an environment full of challenges and professional development prospects.

> Marathon Oil Corporation
> Corporate Headquarters
> 5555 San Felipe Road
> Houston, TX 77056-2723
> Tel.: 713-629-6600
> e-mail: explorewithus@marathonoil.com (college recruiting)
> www.marathonoil.com

Marriott International

Marriott International, Inc., is a leading worldwide hospitality company. Its heritage can be traced to a small root beer stand opened in Washington in 1927 by J. Willard and Alice S. Marriott. Today, Marriott International is a leading lodging company with more than 2,800 lodging properties in the United States and sixty-seven other countries and territories. Headquartered in Washington, the company has approximately 151,000 employees worldwide. Marriott International operates and franchises hotels under the Marriott, JW Marriott, Ritz-Carlton, Renaissance, Residence Inn, Courtyard, TownePlace Suites, Fairfield Inn, SpringHill Suites, and Bulgari brand names; develops and operates vacation ownership resorts under the Marriott Vacation Club, Horizons by Marriott Vacation Club, Ritz-Carlton Club, and Grand Residence Club by Marriott brands; operates Marriott Executive Apartments; provides furnished corporate housing through its Marriott ExecuStay division; and operates conference centers. Career paths with Marriott include accounting and finance, administrative and support, and sales and marketing. Marriott offers internships and a Management Development Program for new graduates.

Marriott International
Marriott Drive
Washington, DC 20058
Tel.: 301-380-3000
marriott.com/careers

Marsh and McLennan Companies

Marsh and McLennan Companies (MMC) is a global professional services firm with annual revenues of approximately $12 billion. MMC has 55,000 employees who provide analysis, advice, and transactional capabilities; and clients in more than one hundred countries. It is active in the following sectors: risk and insurance services, risk consulting and technology, consulting, and investment management. Its vision is to be the world's leading global advice and solutions firm. Through its expertise and commitment to excellence, it is dedicated to managing risk, maximizing growth, and creating value for its clients and shareholders.

Among the myriad issues and risks that MMC helps clients address are natural disasters, pandemics, terrorism, outsourcing, health and benefits, pension liabilities, business continuity, aging workforces, technology shifts, security, and global warming. MMC companies include:

- Marsh, the world's leading risk and insurance services firm, which provides risk management consulting and transfer, design and administration of insurance programs, managing of general agency, and claims management.
- Kroll, a leading risk consulting company, which provides legal technologies, background and credit screenings, corporate investigations, competitive intelligence, restructuring advice, and other services.
- Guy Carpenter, a leading risk and reinsurance specialist providing reinsurance placement, risk quantification and investment, and run-off administration.
- Mercer Specialty Consulting, a global provider of strategy and operations advices, financial services consulting, expert consulting, and other specialty services.
- Mercer Human Resource Consulting, which provides human resource and related financial advice, products, and services.
- Putnam Investments, one of the largest investment management companies in the United States, which handles mutual funds, tax-advantaged accounts, customized institutional management, quantitative investment strategies, and private equity investments.

Marsh & McLennan Companies
1166 Avenue of the Americas
New York, NY 10036
Tel.: 212-345-5000
www.mmc.com/careers

Merck & Company

Merck & Company, Inc., is a leading research-driven pharmaceutical products and services company. Established in 1891, Merck discovers, develops, manufactures, and markets vaccines and medicines to address unmet medical needs. The company devotes extensive efforts to increase access to medicines through far-reaching programs that not only donate Merck medicines but also help deliver them to the people who need them. Merck also publishes unbiased health information as a not-for-profit service.

The mission of Merck is to provide society with superior products and services by developing innovations and solutions that improve the quality of life and satisfy customer needs, to provide employees with meaningful work and advancement opportunities, and to provide investors with a superior rate of return. Merck offers rotational programs for highly motivated recent graduates, as well as special programs for MBA and MILR graduates.

Merck & Company
1 Merck Drive
Whitehouse Station, NJ 08889
Tel.: 908-423-1000
www.merck.com/careers

Microsoft

Founded in 1975, Microsoft Corporation designs, develops, markets, and supports a wide range of personal computer software systems, applications, development tools and languages, hardware peripherals, and books. The company offers a family of operating system products to satisfy any level of customer need; Microsoft Windows, introduced in 1990, is regarded as the standard operating system for personal computers worldwide. In addition to its offices in the United States, Microsoft has subsidiary offices in ninety-nine countries worldwide and operation centers in Ireland, Puerto Rico, Nevada, and Singapore. Its products appear in forty languages.

Microsoft employs more than 76,000 people worldwide. Career opportunities with Microsoft exist in worldwide operations, corporate operations, human resources, finance, legal and corporate affairs, consulting, sales, marketing, support, and technical positions. Special opportunities are available to students, including internships, programs for undergraduates, and programs for MBAs. On average, an MBA changes jobs at Microsoft every eighteen to twenty-four months. Field positions offer many opportunities for global exposure.

Microsoft Corporation
One Microsoft Way
Redmond, WA 98052
Tel.: 425-882-8080
e-mail: jobinfo@microsoft.com
www.microsoft.com

Nestlé

Nestlé Corporation is the world's largest food and beverage company, with about 260,000 employees and factories or operations in almost every country in the world. Based in Vevey, Switzerland, Nestlé is a global company; over 98 percent of its sales are generated outside Switzerland. About 1,600 employees from over seventy countries oversee Nestlé's global strategy from its headquarters. Each year, Nestlé recruits a number of top young graduates into various business areas, including engineering, the Nestlé audit group, the productivity team, and marketing and sales.

Nestlé USA
800 North Brand Boulevard
Glendale, CA 91203
www.careers.nestle.com

Nestlé Headquarters
Nestlé S.A.
Avenue Nestlé 55
1800 Vevey
Switzerland
Tel.: 41-21-924-2111
recruitment-nrcc@nestle.com

Nike

Nike, which started with a handshake between two running geeks in then-sleepy Eugene, Oregon, is now the world's most competitive sports and fitness company. Nike's world headquarters is in Beaverton, Oregon. The Pacific Northwest is Nike's home region, but it has expanded to every corner of the world. It employs approximately 25,000 people, and every one of them is significant to the company's mission of bringing inspiration and innovation to every athlete in the world. Nike also owns the Cole Haan, Bauer, Hurley, and Converse brands, as well as the Exeter brands group. Nike employs people in the United States; in Europe, the Middle East, and Africa; in the Asia-Pacific region; and in the Americas.

> Nike World Headquarters
> One Bowerman Drive
> Beaverton, OR 97005-6453
> Tel.: 800-344-6453
> www.nikebiz.com

> Nike European Headquarters
> Colosseum 1
> 1213 NL Hilversum
> The Netherlands
> Tel.: 31-35-626-6453

PepsiCo

PepsiCo, Inc., is a world leader in convenient foods and beverages, with 2006 revenues of more than $35 billion and 168,000 employees. The company consists of Frito-Lay North America, PepsiCo Beverages North America, PepsiCo International, and Quaker Foods North America. PepsiCo brands are available in nearly two hundred countries and territories and generate sales at the retail level of about $92 billion. PepsiCo employs more than 153,000 people around the world.

> PepsiCo, Inc.
> 700 Anderson Hill Road
> Purchase, NY 10577
> Tel.: 914-253-2000
> www.pepsico.com

Pfizer

Pfizer Inc., founded in 1849, is dedicated to better health and greater access to health care for people and their valued animals. Its purpose is helping people live longer, healthier, happier lives through discovering and developing breakthrough medicines; providing information on prevention, wellness, and treatment; consistent high-quality manufacturing of medicines and consumer products; and global leadership in corporate responsibility. Every day, Pfizer helps 38 million patients, employs more than 100,000 colleagues, utilizes the skills of more than 12,000 medical researchers, and works in partnership with governments, individuals, and other payers for health care to treat and prevent illnesses—adding both years to life and life to years.

At Pfizer, you may never set foot in a laboratory or work directly with scientists or health care providers, but your talent will have an impact on people worldwide. Prospective graduates have career options in marketing, market analytics, human resources, finance, field force sales, business technology, and global research and development. Pfizer offers internship opportunities to students in many fields. Some are geared toward students of science or with technical backgrounds; others are designed for current MBA, MS, or JD students.

Pfizer Inc.
235 East 42nd Street
New York, NY 10017
Tel.: 212-733-2323
www.pfizer.com/careers

Philip Morris International
Philip Morris International (PMI), based in Lausanne, is one of the largest tobacco companies in the world. It produces many of the world's best-selling cigarette brands, including the most popular brand worldwide; its brands are made in more than fifty factories around the world and sold in over 160 markets; and the company is a worldwide organization—PMI employs more than 80,000 people. Approximately 3,000 of these work at the PMI headquarters in Lausanne.

Employment opportunities range from sales, marketing, and trade practices to law and corporate affairs. PMI accepts graduates from a variety of disciplines and higher education institutions around the world. Typically, candidates are expected to have a degree from a recognized university or business school; a good command of English (written and spoken); and business experience through internships or student placements. Proficiency in more than one language is an asset, and candidates should be prepared to relocate as there may be opportunities to work in PMI offices worldwide. PMI offers a challenging work environment, international job assignments, an ongoing training and structured career development, and competitive salaries and benefits. PMI does not recruit in the United States.

Philip Morris International Management SA
107 Avenue de Cour
1001 Lausanne
Switzerland
Telephone: 41-0-21-618-6111
www.pmicareers.com

Philip Morris USA
P.O. Box 26603
Richmond, VA 23261
www.cantbeattheexperience.com (U.S. careers)

Procter & Gamble

The Procter & Gamble Company (P&G) consists of over 135,000 employees working in over 80 countries worldwide. What began as a small, family-operated soap and candle company now provides products and services of superior quality and value to consumers in 140 countries. P&G's recruiting focus in all countries is on new and recent college graduates. Career functions include general administrative, consumer and market knowledge, external relations, and intellectual property / legal. Although an international company, P&G recruits local expertise in its countries of operation.

Corporate Headquarters
Procter & Gamble Company
P.O. Box 599
Cincinnati, OH 45201
www.pg.com/jobs

Rockwell Collins

Rockwell Collins has been recognized as a leader in the design, production, and support of communication and aviation electronics for over seventy years. The company's unique balance of commercial and government customers helps it to maintain stability in a volatile marketplace. Leveraging developments across both markets enables Rockwell Collins to reduce costs, extend product viability, and enhance the capabilities of its systems. Rockwell Collins is well positioned in five key areas of high growth potential: information management, transformational defense communications, open system architecture, service and support, and next-generation global positioning systems.

Rockwell Collins is a global company that operates from more than sixty locations in twenty-seven countries. With a large portion of its sales coming from outside the United States, Rockwell Collins continues to focus on growing its business globally. You do not have to be an engineer to be an important part of Rockwell Collins's success. The company has opportunities in a number of technical and nontechnical areas where your talents can be put to use. All positions require an undergraduate or graduate degree in applicable engineering, mathematics, or science field or equivalent with demonstrated high academic and/or job performance. Rockwell Collins is especially interested in hiring individuals with demonstrated analytical thinking, team building, and communication skills.

Rockwell Collins Headquarters
400 Collins Road, N.E.
Cedar Rapids, IA 52498
Tel.: 319-295-1000
www.rockwellcollins.com/careers

SAIC

SAIC is a leading systems, solutions, and technical services company. It solves its customers' mission-critical problems with innovative applications of technology and expertise. SAIC people and technologies work in medical laboratories researching cancer cures, in the desert testing next-generation robotics, and in the ocean deploying tsunami warning systems. They also work in crime labs investigating new evidence and in Iraq helping to protect and support the men and women in uniform.

SAIC is committed to recruiting, retaining, and developing a diverse team of talented professionals. Its success depends on bringing people together to solve some of the toughest problems facing the United States and the world. SAIC actively recruits college students for paid internship and coop positions. You will join a team that is known for delivering definitive solutions that span the boundaries of government programs, national priorities, and commercial interests. Most positions are available in the summer; however, openings are also available during the school year.

SAIC Headquarters
10260 Campus Point Drive
San Diego, CA 92121
www.saic.com/careers

Shell

Shell is a worldwide group of oil, gas, and petrochemical companies with interests in biofuels, wind and solar power, and hydrogen. Shell is active in more than 130 countries and territories and employs 108,000 people worldwide. Royal Dutch Shell consists of the upstream businesses of exploration and production and gas and power and the downstream businesses of oil products and chemicals. It also has interests in other industry segments, such as renewables, hydrogen, and carbon dioxide. Because Shell operates globally, there are many international career opportunities. Shell does not recruit into a generic graduate scheme. Instead, it matches each individual to a particular role based on their skills, potential, and personal preferences. As a general guide, most graduates are likely to have commenced a second assignment within their first three years.

> Shell Oil Company
> Attraction and Recruitment
> P.O. Box 4939
> Houston, TX 77210
> www.shell.com

Siemens

Siemens, headquartered in Berlin and Munich, is one of the world's largest electrical engineering and electronics companies. With a presence in more than 190 countries, Siemens is one of the most international organizations on Earth. Founded more than 150 years ago, the company is active in the areas of information and communications, automation and control, power, transportation, medical, and lighting.

By 2025, the Earth will be home to nearly 8 billion people—2 billion more than today—and most of them will be living in cities. In addition, life expectancy is continuously increasing in both the developing and industrial nations. As a result, the world of tomorrow will be shaped in large measure by the megatrends of urbanization and demographic change. Under these circumstances, ensuring adequate supplies of energy, water, and other everyday necessities while guaranteeing mobility, security, health care, industrial production, and environmental protection will be a major challenge. Siemens—with its cross-sector portfolio, technological leadership, and worldwide presence—is better positioned than any other company to provide the solutions needed to meet the requirements of tomorrow's world. The company's innovative and future-proof solutions generate competitive advantages for its customers and lay the basis for profitable growth.

Siemens employs over 400,000 people in more than 850 locations worldwide, filling over 30,000 job vacancies annually. The Siemens career website allows you to search international jobs by country, level, and field, or to submit a general application to keep on file.

> Siemens AG
> Wittelsbacherplatz 2
> D-80333 Munich
> Germany
> Tel.: 49-89-63600
> www.siemens.com/careers

Texas Instruments

Texas Instruments Incorporated (TI) is the world leader in digital signal processing and analog technologies, the semiconductor engines of the Internet age. TI is a leader in the real-time technologies that help people communicate. It is moving fast to drive the Internet age forward with semiconductor solutions for large markets such as wireless and broadband access and for new emerging markets such as digital cameras and digital audio. With manufacturing sites, sales, and support offices located in Europe, Asia, Japan, and the Americas, TI can provide products and services to customers wherever they do business. TI has specific programs for graduates in engineering; finance, accounting, and operations; finance development, and technology sales and field applications.

> Company Headquarters
> Texas Instruments Incorporated
> 12500 TI Boulevard
> Dallas, TX 75243-4136
> Tel.: 800-336-5236
> focus.ti.com/careers

3M

3M is a diversified technology company serving customers and communities with innovative products and services. Each of its six businesses—consumer and office; display and graphics; electro and communications; health care; industrial and transportation; and safety, security, and protection services—has earned a leading market position. Its worldwide sales total $22.9 billion, over 61 percent of which are international. Its products are sold in over 200 countries. Of 3M's nearly 69,000 employees, fewer than 100 are foreign service employees not residing in their home countries. 3M offers internships to college students at its headquarters in Saint Paul.

> 3M Corporate Headquarters
> 3M Center
> Saint Paul, MN 55144
> Tel.: 888-364-3577
> www.3m.com

10

Business-Related Organizations

Careers in Business-Related Organizations

JONATHAN HUNEKE

Jonathan Huneke *is a 1988 graduate of the Master of Science in Foreign Service Program at Georgetown University. He is vice president for communications with the United States Council for International Business (USCIB), a New York–based business organization that promotes an open system of global commerce, represents American business in several worldwide industries, and provides services for companies doing business overseas. Previously, he was a U.S.-based representative of the Province of Quebec, acting as corporate liaison during the period surrounding the 1995 referendum on Quebec sovereignty and as public affairs manager thereafter. In a prior stint with the USCIB after graduating from Georgetown, he worked as a policy analyst in the organization's policy and program department.*

VOLUNTARY NETWORKS have been a hallmark of American culture since well before the 1830s, when Alexis de Tocqueville wrote of Americans' penchant for forming "associations" in their professional, social, civic, and political lives. Of course, nowadays such groups are not at all unique to the United States; virtually every imaginable type of organization has some sort of representation in Washington and other major world capitals. Among the most visible and active are business and industry associations.

Why do such organizations exist? First and foremost, they advocate laws, regulations, and policies that benefit their members' interests—in other words, they exist to lobby. This may include traditional legislative lobbying of the kind so familiar in Washington or Brussels. Or it may include "soft lobbying"—convening working groups, holding conferences, commissioning research, issuing position papers and press releases, and so on. In addition, in many industries, business organizations provide a much-needed self-regulatory role, developing standards for companies in the industry and offering training and professional certification for individuals working in it. And of course, most business associations organize periodic conventions and other gatherings for networking, while many also fulfill an educational role.

As regional and global integration has marched forward, the international activities of business organizations have mushroomed, both in the United States and overseas. At the national level, nearly every country, whatever its size, has a leading chamber of commerce and employers' federation, along with some form of "club" for chief executives, such as the Business Roundtable in the United States. Though such groups work largely to influence domestic law and policy, their international focus has grown alongside that of their members and in many countries may be their most important calling card.

Business organizations active at the global level are sometimes overlooked. The oldest of these is the International Chamber of Commerce, founded after World War I, which works closely with the United Nations and other intergovernmental organizations, maintains a leading court of commercial arbitration, and sets worldwide standards in such areas as marketing and advertising, trade terminology, and letters of credit. Some groups even have quasi-official mandates; for example, the International Organization of Employers sends voting delegates to meetings of the UN's International Labor Organization, where governments, businesses, and trade unions all take part in deliberations.

Although not, strictly speaking, a business organization, the World Economic Forum, well known for its annual high-profile get-together in Davos, Switzerland, convenes groups of executives and other experts from around the world to address specific topics. At the regional level, the European Roundtable and Business Europe (formerly known by the acronym UNICE) is the preferred provider of industry views to the European Union and its member states, whereas other transnational business bodies have sprung up around the Asia-Pacific Economic Cooperation forum, the Association of Southeast Asian Nations, the North America Free Trade Agreement, and other regional trade groupings.

Operating alongside, and often in close cooperation with, these multi-sector business groups are a seemingly endless array of "vertical" industry associations that seek to safeguard and promote the interests of companies in a particular industry. Again, some of these are quite well known—for example, at the national level, the Motion Picture Association of America, Pharmaceutical Research and Manufacturers of America, and Information Technology Association of America—while others operate largely below the radar of public perception. In many cases, the national industry federation is part of an international confederation that seeks to coordinate the industry's public and regulatory affairs work worldwide.

Furthermore, in a reflection of the "downward" distribution of economic and regulatory power, numerous business bodies at the state and local levels are actively seeking to promote trade, attract investment, and work with governments and business groups overseas. State and metropolitan chambers of commerce, along with regional world trade centers, are increasingly active in promoting business across borders.

What skills are important in the association environment? Public policy, lobbying, and diplomatic expertise are especially desirable, and those with significant legislative or executive branch experience are often in high demand. But in many associations, legal, marketing, finance, event management, public relations, and administrative skills may be equally or even more valuable. Needless to say, working in an international association environment demands tact and diplomacy, an appreciation for national and cultural differences, and the breadth of knowledge to appreciate how one's industry fits into the global scheme of things. Foreign language skills are also important, as is experience working and living abroad.

What opportunities does this sector offer for those trained in international affairs? Plenty! Though perhaps not as remunerative as working for a large company, law firm, or financial institution, a career in the business association world can provide greater visibility at an earlier stage in one's career, as well as extensive contacts in government and industry that can serve you well later on. As one of my colleagues told me when I first started out, "This is a great first job," and for many it has served as a useful stepping-stone to a job in the public sector or private industry. But it is also a great career path, offering responsibility, autonomy, and opportunities for professional growth not often found at larger, more bureaucratic organizations.

Another plus: Though the number of people working for business and trade associations may be small compared with those in government or the corporate world, the number of potential employers, especially in Washington, is enormous and growing. As mentioned at the outset, seemingly every industry and profession has its own association—there is even an association of *association* executives! And guess what? Most of these groups are keenly aware that the international dimension forms a critical aspect of their future growth and relevance. So the possibilities for lateral movement, or for moving up from one association to another, are great. Look into them!

RESOURCE LISTINGS

Advanced Medical Technology Association

The Advanced Medical Technology Association (AdvaMed) represents the interests of manufacturers of medical devices. Its members control more than 50 percent share of the $159 billion world market for these devices. AdvaMed works with, and for, member companies in key foreign countries to improve market access, facilitate regulatory approval, and demonstrate the value of their technologies for better reimbursement. Its major markets are in Western Europe, Japan, and China. AdvaMed hires only a few professionals each year. Employees have a mix of experience ranging from international trade to health care. It values academic work in international economics, foreign policy, and/or health care economics. Candidates must have strong interpersonal skills, including experience working with foreigners; foreign language ability is helpful.

> Advanced Medical Technology Association
> Health Industry Manufacturers Association
> 1200 G Street, NW
> Washington, DC 20005
> Tel.: 202-783-8700
> Fax: 202-783-8750
> www.himanet.org

American Bankers Association

The American Bankers Association (ABA) acts as a consensus-building and lobbying organization for influencing government policy affecting the banking sector. Every year the ABA sponsors an annual convention and numerous schools, conferences, and workshops. Through its American Institute of Banking, it conducts more than 1,000 courses and other educational activities each year. It publishes several periodicals concerning compliance with government regulation, current banking practices, and public information. The ABA is the secretariat for the annual International Monetary Conference. The ABA has a staff of more than 350 professionals, of whom 5 work in its International Relations Division. Its annual budget is about $50 million.

> American Bankers Association
> 1120 Connecticut Avenue, NW
> Washington, DC 20036
> Tel.: 202-663-5000
> www.aba.com

American Chemical Society

The American Chemical Society (ACS) is a self-governing individual-membership organization that consists of more than 160,000 members at all degree levels and in all fields of chemistry. The organization provides a broad range of opportunities for peer interaction and career development, regardless of a member's professional or scientific interests. The programs and activities conducted by the ACS today are the products of a tradition of excellence in meeting member needs that dates from its founding in 1876. The ACS maintains a professional staff and has a small Office of International Activities.

> American Chemical Society
> 1155 16th Street, NW
> Washington, DC 20036
> Tel.: 800-227-5558 (United States only)
> 202-872-4600 (outside United States)
> Fax: 202-872-4615
> e-mail: help@acs.org
> www.chemistry.org

American Electronics Association (AeA)

The American Electronics Association (AeA), the nation's largest high-technology trade association, works to advance the business of technology. Founded in 1943 by David Packard, the AeA has nearly 2,500 member companies, with 1.8 million employees, who represent all segments of the industry. With eighteen regional U.S. offices and offices in Brussels and Beijing, the AeA offers a unique global policy grassroots capability and a wide portfolio of valuable business services and products for the high-technology industry. Its primary purpose is helping its members' top and bottom lines by providing numerous services, including federal and international lobbying and foreign market access. Positions become available on a random basis in the Washington office in the groups' handling domestic policy, international and trade policy, small business, and research and statistics.

> Director of Human Resources
> American Electronics Association
> 601 Pennsylvania Avenue, NW
> Suite 600, North Building
> Washington, DC 20004
> Tel.: 202-682-9110
> Fax: 202-682-9111
> www.aeanet.org

American Forest & Paper Association

The American Forest & Paper Association (AF&PA) is the national trade association of the forest, pulp, paper, paperboard, and wood products industry. The AF&PA represents more than two hundred member companies and related trade associations that grow, harvest, and process wood and wood fiber; manufacture pulp, paper, and paperboard products from both virgin and recovered fiber; and produce engineered and traditional wood products.

The AF&PA's international activities include influencing trade policy at the state, federal, international, and multilateral levels; monitoring international trade developments; collecting, analyzing, and disseminating statistics on the international forest products trade; and promoting exports of U.S. forest products. The AF&PA's international staff members have varied backgrounds, with experience in economics, environment, trade policy, law, and/or languages.

> American Forest & Paper Association
> Suite 800, 1111 19th Street, NW
> Washington, DC 20036
> Tel.: 202-463-2700
> www.afandpa.org

American Iron and Steel Institute

The American Iron and Steel Institute (AISI) is a nonprofit trade association of North American companies engaged in the iron and steel industry, including integrated, electric furnace, and reconstituted mills. It comprises 125 associate member companies that are suppliers to or customers of the industry. Its 32 member companies account for more than three-quarters of the raw steel produced in the United States, half the steel manufactured in Canada and nearly three-quarters of the flat-rolled steel products in Mexico. Its international trade section monitors legislative and executive actions in import and export trade in steel, organizes research and symposia of North American and global trade law and steel trade practices, maintains contact with government officials concerned with international trade, makes recommendations for action to the institute's governing bodies, and engages in public advocacy of AISI's positions.

> American Iron and Steel Institute
> Suite 750, 1140 Connecticut Avenue, NW
> Washington, DC 20036
> Tel.: 202-452-7100
> www.steel.org

American Petroleum Institute

The American Petroleum Institute (API), founded in 1919, is the U.S. oil and natural gas industry's primary trade association. Its membership consists of a broad cross-section of oil, gas, and allied companies in exploration, production, transportation, refining, and marketing. Its mission is to promote public policies that support a strong, viable U.S. oil and natural gas industry that meets consumer needs in an efficient, environmentally responsible manner. Its membership currently includes over four hundred companies.

The API is headquartered in Washington and is represented in twenty-one state capitals. In the other twenty-nine states, the API works in conjunction with regional and state oil and gas associations. It seeks employees who want to advocate meeting the nation's energy needs while enhancing environmental stewardship. Positions are available in statistical analysis, policy analysis, government affairs, and other fields.

> American Petroleum Institute
> 1220 L Street, NW
> Washington, DC 20005
> Tel.: 202-682-8000
> www.api.org

American Society of Association Executives' Center for Association Leadership

The American Society of Association Executives (ASAE) is the membership organization and voice of the association profession. Founded in 1920, the ASAE now has more than 22,000 association chief executive officers, staff professionals, industry partners, and consultant members. The ASAE's Center for Association Leadership is the premier provider of learning and knowledge for the association community. The center was founded in 2001. The ASAE and the center serve approximately 10,000 associations that represent more than 287 million people and organizations worldwide. The staff of the ASAE and the center is small, but they run a useful career site (www.careerhq.org), which offers information on careers in associations and a job search and résumé-posting function.

> American Society of Association Executives and Center for
> Association Leadership
> 1575 Eye Street, NW
> Washington, DC 20005
> Tel.: 888-950-2723
> Fax: 202-371-8315
> www.asaecenter.org

Association of American Publishers

The Association of American Publishers is the principal trade association of the U.S. publishing industry. Its core issues include intellectual property; First Amendment rights, censorship, and libel; and the international freedom to publish. It has over 260 members located throughout the United States. It maintains offices in Washington and New York, with approximately thirty-one professional and support staff in total.

> Association of American Publishers Washington Office
> Suite 400, 50 F Street, NW
> Washington, DC 20001
> Tel.: 202-347-3375
> Fax: 202-347-3690
> www.publishers.org

> Association of American Publishers New York Office
> 71 Fifth Avenue, 2nd Floor
> New York, NY 10003
> Tel.: 212-255-0200
> Fax: 212-255-7007

Conference Board

The Conference Board is the world's leading business research and membership organization, linking executives from different companies, industries, and countries. Founded in 1916, the Conference Board has become the leader in helping executives build strong professional relationships, expand their business knowledge, and find solutions to a wide range of business problems. The Conference Board's twofold purpose is to improve the business enterprise system and to enhance the contribution of business to society. The Conference Board is a not-for-profit, nonadvocacy organization with members in more than sixty countries.

The Conference Board sponsors events in the Asia-Pacific region that focus on its core competencies of knowledge management, corporate branding and image, shared services, economics, corporate governance, and all areas of human resources. In previous years, events have been held in Hong Kong, Australia, Singapore, India, and China. With the Conference Board's growing presence in the region, it anticipates that the number of events and countries where events are held will increase substantially. Individuals in the capacity of program director for the board's international business ideally must be located in the particular region, have knowledge of the specific subject matter of the event, and have excellent writing skills and sales experience.

In the Asia-Pacific region, the Conference Board has offices in Hong Kong and New Delhi staffed with sales, logistics, and administrative executives. The Asia-Pacific office recently hired a new director. The board also has an office in Mexico City staffed with a regional director; there were no openings there in 2006. When hiring for international offices, the board looks for local individuals who have an international outlook and three to four years of experience in sales, conference programming, or administration, depending on the position.

> Conference Board
> 845 Third Avenue
> New York, NY 10022-6679
> Tel.: 212-759-0900
> Fax: 212-980-7014
> www.conference-board.org

Consumer Electronics Association (CEA)

The Consumer Electronics Association (CEA), based in Arlington, Virginia, represents more than 2,100 businesses from every segment of the

$121 billion consumer electronics industry. It works to educate consumers about consumer electronics products and technologies, create a favorable public policy environment for technology and the technology industry, track and promote emerging technologies, develop standards that make it easier to introduce new technologies, and shape the future of technology in other ways.

The CEA sponsors and manages the International CES, the annual consumer electronics industry forum, which expands, strengthens, drives, and grows the consumer technology industry. The CEA's government and legal affairs office in Washington advises, lobbies, and reports on federal, state, and international policy on behalf of its members and the industry. Full-time and internship positions are available for a variety of activities, including conferences, events, and marketing.

> Consumer Electronics Association
> Attention: Human Resources
> 2500 Wilson Boulevard
> Arlington, VA 22201
> Tel.: 703-907-7056
> www.ce.org

Council of the Americas

The Council of the Americas, an affiliate of the Americas Society Inc., is a U.S. business association dedicated to advocacy of the interests of its international corporate members doing business in the Americas. The council, broadly representative of total U.S. investment in the region, is the private sector vehicle for promoting positive change and future private sector-led development in the hemisphere. Its various member constituencies include industrial, financial, and service companies. It is a strong advocate of free trade, democracy, and the rule of law, and it works with members to promote policies in service of those goals in Washington and capitals throughout the Americas, as well as to private-sector actors. It is a strong supporter of the Free Trade Area of the Americas process. Consensus and viewpoints are communicated to Latin American government officials and U.S. policymakers as well as to the domestic Latin American private sector. The council has a staff of over thirty people, roughly a third of whom work in policy or public programs.

> Council of the Americas
> 680 Park Avenue
> New York, NY 10021

Tel.: 212-249-8950
Fax: 212-249-1880
inforequest@as-coa.org

Council of the Americas
1615 L Street, NW
Washington, DC 20036
Tel.: 202-659-8989
Fax: 202-659-7755
www.counciloftheamericas.org

Council on Competitiveness
The Council on Competitiveness was founded in 1986 to serve as a focal point for leadership efforts aimed at improving the competitive position of the United States in global markets. The council's core agenda is built on four interrelated and interdependent issues: capital formation and investment policies, science and technology, international economics and trade, and human resources. To address public policy issues, the council publishes reports and position statements developed with the assistance of council members, staff, and expert advisers. To promote public awareness, the council publishes a monthly e-mail newsletter that chronicles major trends, policies, and people affecting competitiveness. A Competitiveness Index comparing the United States' performance with that of other nations also is released annually.

At its peak, the council has seventeen staff members. New graduates usually enter at the position of council associate, which is comparable to that of a research assistant. For its council associates, the council seeks master's degree candidates with a concentration in international trade, business, economics, public policy, and/or technology. Work experience in other associations or think tanks specializing in these issues or experience on Capitol Hill is preferred.

Council on Competitiveness
Suite 850, 1500 K Street, NW
Washington, DC 20005
Tel.: 202-682-4292
Fax: 202-682-5150
www.compete.org

Electronic Industries Alliance
The Electronic Industries Alliance (EIA) is a national trade organization that includes the full spectrum of U.S. manufacturers. The EIA is a partnership of electronic and high-technology associations and companies

whose mission is promoting the market development and competitiveness of the U.S. high-tech industry through domestic and international policy efforts. The EIA, which is headquartered in Arlington, Virginia, comprises nearly 1,300 member companies whose products and services range from the smallest electronic components to the most complex systems used in defense products, the space program, and other industries, including the full range of consumer electronic products.

The EIA is the only high-tech trade association that helps members navigate the array of global environmental policy issues affecting their ability to manufacture, market, and sell their products. Its Environmental Issues Council leads the electronics industry in addressing national and international environmental policies surrounding its products. The EIA is also the only high-tech trade association that brings together members of the electronics industry, Fortune 500 firms, and e-commerce and cyber security arenas, via the Internet Security Alliance (ISAlliance). The ISAlliance was formed in April 2001 as a nonprofit collaboration between the EIA and Carnegie-Mellon University's CyLab. The ISAlliance works closely with a component of Carnegie-Mellon's CERT, known as the CERT Coordination Center (CERT/CC), a leading center of Internet security expertise to fill the void for an industry-led, global, cross-sector network focused on advancing the security and survivability of the Internet. Members of the ISAlliance represent every sector of industry. Career opportunities are available within the EIA and its sector organizations.

> Electronic Industries Alliance
> 2500 Wilson Boulevard
> Arlington, VA 22201
> Tel.: 703-907-7500
> www.eia.org

European-American Business Council

the European-American Business Council (EABC)—made up of more than seventy companies based in European Union member countries and the United States—actively promotes EU-U.S. economic integration, growth, and competitiveness. One of its key policy goals is promoting regulatory convergence through government-to-government and business-to-government consultations, thereby reducing barriers to trade. Its signature issues are twenty-first-century health care, accessibility to Internet and communications technologies, and digital rights management. The EABC holds policy roundtables on reforming the process under the U.S. Committee on Foreign Investments in the United States, transatlantic corporate governance and accounting standards, trade security, privacy and data security, and electricity and costs deregulation. The EABC's main office is in Washington and maintains a very small staff. Recruitment is done on an as-needed basis.

> European American Business Council
> Suite 500, 1325 G Street, NW
> Washington, DC 20005
> Tel.: 202-449-7705
> Fax: 202-449-7704
> www.eabc.org

International Business-Government Counsellors

International Business-Government Counsellors Inc. (IBC) is a Washington-based firm that assists companies in international government relations affecting their global operations. IBC's clients include major multinational companies based in the United States, Asia, and Europe. Established in 1972, IBC is the oldest and most prominent international government relations firm in the United States. Its staff of international trade and government relations professionals provides clients with a number of services: the monitoring of executive, legislative, and regulatory developments that may affect the client's operations; the analysis of U.S. and foreign government policies and regulations affecting the client's trade, investment, and international business operations; the development and implementation of strategic advice for worldwide corporate responses to government policies and developments; and direct client representations to the U.S. Congress and executive branch, such as the Office of the U.S. Trade Representative and the Departments of Commerce, State, Agriculture, Treasury, and Defense, as well as to foreign governments. IBC welcomes inquiries from qualified individuals seeking employment. It provides a fast-paced international affairs environment and offers excellent benefits.

> International Business-Government Counsellors Inc.
> 818 Connecticut Avenue, NW
> 12th Floor
> Washington, DC 20006-2702
> Tel.: 202-872-8181
> Fax: 202-872-8696
> e-mail: personnel@ibgc.com
> www.ibgc.com

Japan External Trade Organization

The Japan External Trade Organization (JETRO) was established by the Japanese government in 1958 as the nation's principal organization for implementing trade policy on a comprehensive basis. In the first half of the 1980s, JETRO began promoting imports to Japan, a primary mission that continues to this day. It is also actively involved in helping developing nations to nurture their supporting industries, promoting cooperation between industries in Japan and other developed nations, supporting the development of regional economies in Japan and other nations, and encouraging international exchange on a variety of levels. JETRO relies on its extensive worldwide network, which includes its headquarters in Tokyo and Osaka and thirty-eight local offices in Japan as well as seventy-three overseas offices in fifty-five countries. Of JETRO's approximately 1,660 full-time professionals, 820 are working in its overseas offices, where about 300 additional local staff at various levels support their operations.

> Japan External Trade Organization Headquarters
> Ark Mori Building, 6F
> 12-32, Akasaka 1-chome, Minato-ku, Tokyo
> 107-6006
> Japan
> Tel.: 81-3-3582-5511
> www.jetro.go.je

Motion Picture Association

From its headquarters in Los Angeles and key offices in Washington, Brussels, São Paolo, Singapore, and Toronto, the Motion Picture Association (MPA) conducts a wide range of foreign activities. Established in 1945 as the Motion Picture Export Association of America, its original goal was to reestablish American films in the world market and to respond to protectionist measures that attempted to restrict the importation of American films. Today, the MPA's activities have expanded to include diplomatic, political, and economic issues, such as government regulation, antipiracy, legal treaties, distribution enhancement, professional and student training, and ratings systems. It is the global representative of the U.S. film industry, which produces films and television products viewed in over 150 countries and the majority of home entertainment products the world over. The American branch of the MPA, the Motion Picture Association of America, offers internships in the office of its chief executive, in the worldwide antipiracy department, in worldwide antipiracy Internet enforcement, and in international box office research. International relations and political experience are helpful qualifications.

> Motion Picture Association of America
> Office of the Chairman and Chief Executive Officer
> 1600 Eye Street, NW
> Washington, DC 20006
> Tel.: 202-293-1966
> Fax: 202-296-7410
> www.mpaa.org

National Association of Manufacturers

The National Association of Manufacturers (NAM) is the nation's largest industrial trade association representing more than 11,000 companies (of which 80 percent are small manufacturers), plus 350 member associations in all fifty states. The NAM's member firms produce 86 percent of the manufactured goods and services in the United States and employ more than 14 million people. Headquartered in Washington, the NAM has eleven additional offices across the country.

The mission of the NAM is to strengthen U.S. manufacturing and improve the ability of U.S. manufacturers to compete in the global marketplace. The NAM's international activities focus on developing policy that achieves the mission of the organization, focusing on trade, tariffs, sanctions, border security, and exchange rates, plus other issues of significance to its members. Staff regularly interact with members of Congress, the administration, the Commerce Department, member companies with international operations, and the media.

Operating with a small staff of only four lobbyists, the NAM's International Economic Affairs Department was, at the time of writing, seeking to fill an opening. Qualified applicants had to have substantive expertise in a range of trade matters, a master's degree in international relations or a related field, at least six years of relevant work experience, a keen political sense, and excellent written and oral communications skills.

Challenging opportunities are available during the summer and school semesters for students who can receive scholastic credit for work experience with the NAM. Research and writing are the primary tasks, along with gaining issue exposure through member and Capitol Hill meetings. Those wishing to submit a resume or make inquiries may contact:

Director of Human Resources
Suite 600, 1331 Pennsylvania Avenue, NW
Washington, DC 20004-1790
Tel.: 202-637-3000
Fax: 202-637-3182
www.nam.org

National Foreign Trade Council

The National Foreign Trade Council (NFTC) was founded in 1914 by a group of American companies that supported an open world trade system. Today, it is the premier business organization advocating a rules-based economy and the only one to exclusively advocate international and public policy priorities such as international trade, investment, tax, export finance, and human resources. The NFTC and its affiliates now serve about three hundred member companies. It also houses the nonpartisan umbrella group Hispanic Alliance for Free Trade and USA*Engage, an organization dedicated to supporting multilateral engagement rather than unilateral sanctions as solutions to global problems. The NFTC has a total staff of fifteen, eleven in its Washington office and four in New York. Vacancies are infrequent, but interested parties should send a resume to the president, William Reinsch, at the Washington address below. Most of the NFTC's professional employees have advanced degrees and professional experience in international trade or tax issues.

National Foreign Trade Council
Suite 200, 1625 K Street, NW
Washington, DC 20006
Tel.: 202-887-0278
Fax: 202-452-8160
www.nftc.org

National Foreign Trade Council
Suite 1602, 2 West 45th Street
New York, NY 10036
Tel.: 212-399-7128
Fax: 212-399-7144

Pharmaceutical Research and Manufacturers of America

The Pharmaceutical Research and Manufacturers of America (PhRMA) is made up of the leading U.S. pharmaceutical research and biotechnology companies and a handful of international affiliates. These companies are devoted to finding new cures and inventing medicines that promote health and long life. PhRMA members alone invested an estimated $39.4 billion in 2005 in discovering and developing new medicines. PhRMA's mission is to conduct effective advocacy for public policies that encourage the discovery of important new medicines for patients by pharmaceutical and biotechnology research companies. It promotes patient access to safe and effective medicines through the free market, without price controls; strong intellectual property incentives; and transparent, efficient regulation and the free flow of information to patients. Its departments include Alliance Development, Communications, Federal Affairs, Finance and Operations, International, Legal, the Office of the President and Chief Executive Officer, Policy and Research, Scientific and Regulatory Affairs, and State Government Affairs.

> PhRMA
> Suite 300, 950 F Street, NW
> Washington, DC 20004
> Tel.: 202-835-3400
> Fax: 202-835-3414
> www.phrma.org

U.S. Chamber of Commerce

The U.S. Chamber of Commerce is the world's largest business federation. It represents more than 3 million businesses and includes over a hundred American chambers of commerce in ninety-one countries. Its members included businesses of every kind, size, and sector. Through its programs and affiliates, the chamber advances members' legal and political interests, runs a public policy think tank and a trade education program, works to lower trade barriers, and helps emerging nations develop free market practices and institutions. Headquartered in Washington, the chamber has a professional staff of over three hundred policy experts, lobbyists, lawyers, and communicators. It also maintains eight regional offices around the country, offices in New York and Brussels, and an on-the-ground presence in China. Internship opportunities are also available to graduate and undergraduate students for all semesters, and the chamber offers paid summer fellowships to currently enrolled graduate students.

> U.S. Chamber of Commerce
> 1615 H Street, NW
> Washington, DC 20062
> Tel.: 202-659-6000
> www.uschamber.com/careers

United States Council for International Business

The United States Council for International Business (USCIB) promotes an open system of world commerce in which business can flourish and contribute to economic growth, human welfare, and protection of the environment. Its membership includes about three hundred U.S. companies, professional services firms, and associations. As the American affiliate of several leading international business groups, the USCIB presents industry views to policymakers and regulatory authorities worldwide. It also provides a range of services for companies doing business overseas, including the facilitation of duty-free temporary exports and the resolution of transborder commercial disputes.

The USCIB has a staff of approximately fifty, based in New York City, with a small Washington office. It has a limited number of openings each year for individuals with backgrounds in international affairs, business, law, and related areas. Managerial positions (for which there are approximately one or two openings per year) generally require a master's degree and some specialized work or academic experience in the desired subject area. Experience with international economic policy issues and advocacy is particularly desirable, as is foreign language proficiency (especially French). Entry-level administrative and support staff positions (two or three openings per year) generally require a bachelor's degree and some work experience. Computer proficiency is required for all positions.

United States Council for International Business
1212 Avenue of the Americas
New York, NY 10036
Tel.: 212-354-4480
Fax: 212-575-0327
www.uscib.org

The US–China Business Council

Established in 1973, the US–China Business Council (USCBC) is a private, nonprofit business association supported by about 250 American firms engaged in trade and investment with the People's Republic of China. The USCBC provides information, analysis, and tailored business advisory services to individual member companies. Its meetings and programs—in the United States, China, and Hong Kong—provide highly business-relevant information and offer companies the chance to share ideas and experiences.

The USCBC also plays a central role in the analysis and advocacy of key policy issues of significance not only to U.S. businesses but also to the future of United States–China relations. To support government policies conducive to expanded United States–China commercial and economic ties, the USCBC holds educational meetings with members of Congress and congressional staff and frequently testifies in congressional and other venues. The USCBC also works to enhance media and public understanding of complex issues in United States–China relations.

The USCBC's publications include the leading U.S. periodical on China trade, the *China Business Review*; the members-only weekly electronic newsletter, *China Market Intelligence*; and numerous studies on topics of current business interest. The USCBC also maintains websites for use by the general public and members (www.uschina.org; www.chinabusinessreview.com).

Headquartered in Washington, the USCBC maintains offices in Beijing and Shanghai. Of the present staff of about thirty, more than twenty are professionals with backgrounds in Chinese, East Asian studies, international affairs, business administration, and government. The USCBC has, on average, two to three professional openings a year.

US–China Business Council
Suite 200, 1818 N Street, NW
Washington, DC 20036
Tel.: 202-429-0340
Fax: 202-775-2476
www.uschina.org/jobops

U.S.–Russia Business Council

The U.S.–Russia Business Council is a Washington-based trade association that represents the interests of three hundred member companies operating in the Russian market. The council's mission is to expand and enhance the U.S.–Russian commercial relationship. Guided by member interests, the council promotes an economic environment in which businesses can succeed in a challenging Russian market. Through a range of activities, the council contributes to the stability and development of a free market in Russia and supports Russia's integration into the global economy. To achieve its mission, the council conducts activities and provides services that fall into these categories: company-specific assistance and industry-sector efforts; Russian and U.S. government policy work; information products; Russian business relationships; and briefings, conferences, and formal/informal networking opportunities.

U.S.–Russia Business Council
Suite 520, 1701 Pennsylvania Avenue, NW
Washington, DC 20006
Tel.: 202-739-9180
Fax: 202-659-5920
e-mail: info@usrbc.org
www.usrbc.org/employment.asp

Getting Started in Business–
Government Relations

STEPHEN ZIEHM

Steven Ziehm, *a 2001 graduate of the Master of Science in Foreign Service Program at Georgetown University, joined International Business-Government Counsellors, Inc., as a counsellor and is now vice president. Before joining International Business-Government Counsellors, he held internships at the Federal Deposit Insurance Corporation, the U.S. Department of State, International Development Systems, and the U.S. International Trade Commission.*

ALTHOUGH I ONLY BEGAN to interview for full-time jobs in my second year of the Master of Science in Foreign Service Program, my job search began before I even started graduate work at Georgetown. Having narrowed my focus to international relations during my undergraduate studies, I decided to pursue several Washington internships in different settings to see what might be a good fit. I did not realize it at the time, but my choice of internships greatly affected the outcome of my career search. Not only did the internships help to supplement my academic studies by providing a real-world context for the issues I was debating in class, but the process of conducting a search (preparing a résumé, using the career center resources, and interviewing for a position) was also an invaluable experience when it came time to apply for a full-time position.

I frequently encounter students and recent graduates looking to get into the international government relations field. There are many different paths one could follow. Perhaps most fundamental is to identify how your academic interests are best translated into a career. The way I did this was to use my time away from class to try different options through internships. The internships I held at several government agencies and a private-sector consulting firm also provided the background my future employers were looking for in a candidate. Those same internships also helped to direct my coursework, because I selected a concentration and electives that corresponded to the work I most enjoyed in the field of international trade and government relations. In this way, I was able to build qualifications and contacts while weeding out particular jobs or career paths that did not appeal to me on closer inspection. The same could be accomplished through informational interviews, which I would highly recommend.

This being said, the job search itself was quite stressful. After several months of submitting applications without a response, I was quite worried that I would be unemployed after graduating. I interviewed for and was offered a research position at a law firm that, though financially lucrative, did not meet my expectations for a work environment. It can be very difficult to pass up a job when your options seem limited, but finding a position that is right for you is definitely worth the search.

It is hard to point to just one aspect of the job search that was most important, but it undoubtedly helped that one of my educators at Georgetown, an adjunct professor of business–government relations, advertised a position shortly before I graduated. Opportunities can arise from places you do not expect, so it is always good to put your best foot forward regardless of the context. Little did I know that my time in class was a sort of extended job interview! You never know when one of the contacts you make in school can result in a career opportunity. For me, it just so happened that my former professor is now my boss.

11

Consulting

Careers in Consulting

LINDSEY TYLER ARGALAS

Lindsey Tyler Argalas *is a 1998 graduate of the Master of Science in Foreign Service Program at Georgetown University. She is currently a manager with the Boston Consulting Group in San Francisco. She has also worked in their Madrid, Sydney, Chicago, and New York offices and has served as one of their recruiting directors. Previously, she interned at the U.S. embassy in Thailand for the Commerce Department, and later, with the Advisory Board Company in Washington, working on Latin American financial institutions.*

CONSULTING HAS BECOME increasingly popular over time, yet it remains one of the most ambiguously defined professions. Consulting has been described as the most "improbable business on earth" because of the paradox that the world's most successful companies and organizations hire people fresh out of school. What makes this possible? What *is* consulting, and why have consulting firms been so successful?

Broadly defined, consultants are outside advisers to organizations. A consultant can be a specialist and advise on specific areas such as finance, information technology, or negotiation strategy; alternatively, a consultant may be a generalist and advise on issues as broad as the overall strategic direction of a company. Organizations hire outside consultants for four main reasons. First, consultants bring a fresh perspective, through their industrywide view, analogs from other industries or clients, and ability to challenge the status quo. Second, consultants add value by bringing specialist tools and capabilities along with subject matter expertise. They may also bring new, ground-breaking ideas to the forefront, which is often difficult to do as an internal employee of an organization because of politics or the burden of day-to-day responsibilities. Third, the consulting industry gives organizations access to a pool of highly intelligent, motivated people, who as a result of their high-caliber talent are difficult to attract and retain as permanent employees. Consulting allows organizations to temporarily "hire" these individuals for particular projects. And fourth, consultants make change happen because of their inherent role as outside advisers: they are apolitical; they willingly challenge conventional wisdom; and they commit to achieving results for their clients.

Consulting as an industry has continued to thrive over the past decade, irrespective of the cyclicality of the economy. Consulting market growth is accelerated during times of economic expansion as companies seek to capitalize on favorable market conditions, enter new markets, and define a robust platform for growth. Conversely, during times of economic or political distress, organizations may seek consulting support to help them best maneuver difficult situations, become more efficient in their operations, or reduce costs.

Consulting as an industry has continued to thrive over the past decade, irrespective of the cyclicality of the economy.

The growth of consulting—in good times and in bad—is fueled not only by client demand but also by an increase in the supply of talented individuals that find consulting appealing as a profession. First, consulting typically allows a person to gain exposure to a diverse set of issues, industries, and clients; in other words, there is variety that many people enjoy and cannot find elsewhere. Second, consulting is regarded as excellent training for recent graduates because of the multifaceted nature of the work. Many people opt to use consulting as a platform from which to gain experience and make contacts, and then join a specific organization or company. Despite the many benefits of a consulting profession, there are potential drawbacks, including long hours (sixty-plus per week), extensive travel, less control over one's schedule, and the inability to make actual decisions—consultants only give recommendations. When evaluating career options, it is important to weigh all these considerations. Although there are drawbacks, intense competition for jobs at consulting firms reveals that many people find the benefits are still greater.

Varieties of Consulting

"Consulting" is a generic term that describes a broad spectrum of definitions and roles. It is critical to research and understand the different types of consulting to determine which interest you most. I am surprised that I receive such a high volume of calls from students interested in international development consulting given that the majority of my work in management consulting is advising large multinational companies on business issues. These are very different careers, not only in the type of clients we serve but also the type of projects for which we are hired. Both can be equally rewarding and challenging, but the distinction is important because it affects how much a person will enjoy the work. When choosing the type of consulting and specific consulting firm you will pursue, you should consider four key questions:

- *Who are the clients?* Domestic or foreign government agencies, for-profit corporations, nonprofit organizations, or public institutions? Are the clients concentrated in a particular industry, or are multiple industries served? How large are the clients served?
- *What type of project is the norm?* Broad strategic or management issues, or more narrow, specific, and/or functional issues? Are the consultants therefore hired and/or trained to be generalists or specialists?
- *How big is the consulting firm?* Boutique, medium size, or large, as determined by the number of consultants employed and the geographic reach? This greatly affects the firm's culture as well as potential opportunities for geographic mobility.
- *Do I like the feel of the firm?* Consultants spend much time with their colleagues. Therefore, it is imperative that you believe in the firm's approach and the people with whom you will be working.

After assessing macro issues regarding the consulting firm and its clients, it is important to understand the mix of projects. Numerous variables shape the type of project:

- *The nature of the client's problem.* Given the plethora of issues for which an organization hires consultants, it is critical to understand the types of problems for which a particular consulting firm is typically hired. The first-order classification is the split mentioned above between broad strategy and specific topic. Second, within that classification, a client's problem can range from functional (marketing, finance, sales, procurement) to organizational (talent management, organization structure, compensation, and incentives) to operational (processes, execution). And the work required to address each of those problems differs, including activities such as management interviews, market diagnostic, competitive benchmarking, consumer understanding, analysis of status quo (i.e., key financial and performance metrics, capabilities assessment, process mapping), and so on. Different consulting firms exhibit different mixes of such types of client problem solving.

- *The length of the engagement.* This can vary from three or four weeks to twelve, eighteen, or even twenty-four months. The length depends on the nature of the problem and the scope of the consulting firm's involvement. Consultants may be involved in any of the problem-solving stages from initial diagnostic to high-level recommendation, detailed business model, or full-scale implementation.

- *Industry.* Certain consulting firms specialize in a particular industry while others cover multiple industries, including education, health care, financial services, consumer goods and retail, energy, and information technology.

- *Team size and composition.* Teamwork is a central tenet of consulting because most firms structure a team to serve a particular client. The team can vary from two people on a more straightforward or contained piece of work to more than thirty people, particularly if the project is global in nature, is particularly complex, requires significant hands-on client management, or has a tight time frame. Although consulting firms have different titles for positions, a team is often made up of the following individuals:

  —a *senior partner*, who is responsible for managing the senior client relationship and providing thought leadership based on a wealth of experience;

  —a more *junior partner*, who is responsible for managing the overall client relationship and overseeing the success of the engagement;

  —a *project manager*, who is responsible for managing the day-to-day aspects of the project, mentoring the team of consultants, and liaising with the client; and

  —*consultants*, who are responsible for conducting the analysis and executing the work that provides inputs to form recommendations.

  Not surprisingly, the team size and composition affect team dynamics, opportunities for mentorship, and the extent of learning.

- *Degree of collaboration with the client.* Depending on the consulting firm, the clients served, and the nature of the project, the degree of collaboration with the client varies. In some instances, consultants work directly with their dedicated client counterparts every day of the week and are intimately involved with the client's internal issues. An alternate model is one in which consultants interact with the client on an as-needed basis and work more independently, checking in with the client for presentations and occasional feedback. Again, the extent of client collaboration significantly shapes the project experience for the consultant.

- *Lifestyle.* The lifestyle on an engagement is primarily a function of the number of hours, flexibility of schedule, and extent of travel required. As previously mentioned, the hours can be long in consulting, but they vary by project based on the scope of work and the time frame. The schedule is highly dependent on the client's schedule and culture (early versus late, long versus short days). If the engagement requires close collaboration with the client, the consultants should expect to have less flexibility in managing their own schedule. Finally, travel can be both one of consulting's best perks and one of its biggest drawbacks. During my first consulting project, in a span of two weeks, I had conferences in Rio de Janeiro, London, and Hong Kong. For other projects, I have traveled extensively to Milan, Paris, Bangkok, Zurich, São Paulo, New York, Buenos Aires, Melbourne, Los Angeles, Madrid, Athens, Montreal, Miami, and many more destinations, contributing to a healthy pool of frequent flyer miles and free hotel nights. Consulting can be a great way to see the world, but it has significant implications for personal lifestyle as well as the project experience. A project requiring intense travel is very different than one where consultants primarily work in their home office. Consulting can impose a very demanding lifestyle through travel and long hours, so do not underestimate this in your decision.

People often ask me to describe a "typical day" in consulting. Although this is a valid question, there simply is no typical day—regardless of a consultant's level or tenure. Table 11.1 gives one Boston Consulting Group associate's view on the variations of the "typical day." Of course, this is an illustration from one of the management consultancies, but it provides a sense of the variety consultants enjoy.

International Career Opportunities

One of the biggest draws of consulting for me after graduating from the School of Foreign Service at Georgetown was the opportunity to gain international experience. There are several manifestations of international consulting experience, and the opportunities are plentiful, particularly with large international consulting firms or when working with multinational organizations. First, you may work for a firm that has offices in multiple countries, creating the opportunity for geographic mobility and the chance to experience another personal and professional environment.

TABLE 11.1
A Day in the Life of an Associate (There Really Is No "Typical" Day)

Time	Normal Day	Intense Day	Light Day
8 a.m.		Final iterations of deck before client meetings	
9 a.m.			
10 a.m.	Market research		Catch up on e-mail
11 a.m.		Back-to-back meetings with client stakeholders	Translate findings into slides
12 p.m.			Office lunch
1 p.m.	Lunch with case team		Performance review
2 p.m.	Discuss findings with client experts by phone	Revise analysis based on feedback	
3 p.m.			Meeting with client lead about progress and next steps
4 p.m.			
5 p.m.	Case team meeting		
6 p.m.		Follow up on new stakeholder concerns	Revise deck and send to client and manager
7 p.m.	Slides on insights from research		
8 p.m.			
9 p.m.		Meet with manager to verify next steps	
10 p.m.			
11 p.m.		Update presentation	
12 a.m.			
Percent mix	75	15	10

For example, my employer, the Boston Consulting Group, has sixty-one offices in thirty-six countries, and during my tenure at this firm, I have worked in five offices, two of which have been overseas (Madrid and Sydney). Working in a foreign country firsthand provides the opportunity to work with local clients, understand the market dynamics unique to that country, and conduct work in the local language.

Second, consultants may advise a multinational organization or corporation on a project that deals with issues of globalization. I have worked on several projects of this nature, including one in which we helped a U.S.-based household goods manufacturer to redesign the way it develops products and goes to market in more than twenty-five countries. Another project was for a global duty-free retailer with stores in seventeen countries. We helped this client to design a buying organization and a negotiation strategy to take purchase goods on a global scale, rather than by region or country market. Our firm also has a partnership with one of the international agencies to combat world hunger, in which our teams help the organization to become even more effective in its programs, which serve the malnourished in countries throughout the world. It is important to understand the type of international experience to which a consultant has access on a firm-by-firm basis.

Positions Available to Graduates

Just as there are several variables to consider in what type of consulting interests you and what firms are best aligned with your interests and goals, the specific position or role for which graduates apply varies by firm. There are typically two basic types of entry-level position: one for individuals who are entering directly from a university or have little work experience (in some cases, including those with master's degrees); and one for individuals who have a graduate degree and several years of work experience. Depending on the type of consulting firm, competition for the latter type of job is intense. In the case of business consulting firms, the pool typically consists of MBAs from top business schools like Harvard, Stanford, Kellogg, and Wharton. At some of the more competitive firms, do not be discouraged by an offer for a more junior position; this often gives a new consultant a greater advantage, providing you the opportunity to hone business and management skills.

It is important to understand the career path at any firm. If it is meritocratic, the firm should allow for promotion to keep skilled employees challenged. Also, a few consulting firms offer to sponsor individuals to obtain an MBA. This is not necessarily the case, but it is worth inquiry because it can factor into your longer-term career path and professional development.

Given the variability across firms in entry-level roles, the type of work and responsibilities varies accordingly. It is important to discuss this in detail with the different consulting firms—not only with recruiters and senior partners but also with those who understand the work, activities, and responsibilities firsthand. Speaking with people in positions similar to the job for which you are applying is one of the best ways to learn if it is the right type of work for you. For example, at one firm, the entry-level position may require you to solely do research or financial modeling; at another, to manage senior client teams; at another, to present your findings to a foreign leader or the chief executive of a Fortune 500 company; and at still another, to do all the above.

Preparing for a Career in Consulting

A successful consulting career requires a unique combination of analytical abilities (both quantitative and qualitative), strong interpersonal skills (teamwork, empathy, and a commitment to clients), logical thinking in problem solving, and intellectual curiosity. Of course, specific traits vary by consulting firm, so again, you must understand what traits a particular firm values and how your strengths align with those traits. Many firms respect diverse backgrounds and do not seek any one mold. They supplement individuals' diverse backgrounds with a formal training program, in many cases tailored to the individuals' needs, and emphasize on-the-job training through mentorship.

There are three important steps to help build the skill set and to best position yourself for a job with a consulting firm. First, a very strong academic record is critical because most consulting firms consider academic achievement at top institutions a key indicator of success. Second, coursework in statistics, economics, negotiation, and business strategy (including those cross-listed with the business school) is very beneficial in helping to build analytical skills and in familiarizing students with the problem solving that is the core of consulting. Third, internships and prior work experience are incredibly important, so students should proactively seek the best work experience possible. This need not be a consulting internship per se but rather one that is with a prestigious company or organization, is part of a highly selective program, demonstrates a degree of uniqueness, or allows the individual to develop exceptional perspective or experience. Such internships are not easy to find or obtain, but I assure you that it is worth the pursuit—it is almost a "must-have" for top consulting firms.

Getting the Job

First you need to think critically about whether (1) the general nature of consulting interests you, (2) what specific type of consulting is most appealing, (3) which specific consulting firms are aligned with your goals and interests, and (4) whether your skills align with the profile and skill set those firms require. Then it is time to focus on how to secure a coveted position at these highly competitive firms. As with everything else, the recruiting process varies significantly by firm:

- Some have active, formal recruiting to attract undergraduate and graduate school candidates into a structured analyst or associate program, but others have a more flexible approach to recruiting.
- Some may recruit from your academic program, but not all.
- Some recruit nearly twelve months in advance, whereas others recruit only for positions currently open.
- Some require multiple rounds of interviews with different levels of employees; others have a less cumbersome process.
- Some conduct interviews on or nearby campus; others bring candidates into their offices.
- Some do use the case interview technique, or brain teasers, whereas others conduct more get-to-know-you interviews. If you know you will be tested with case interviews, you must practice to become comfortable with this interview technique, ideally with others who have worked in consulting. Some firms offer practice cases on their websites, and WetFeet Press has an excellent guide called *Ace the Case*.

There is no standard recruiting process, so make sure to enquire about the details for a particular firm. If caught off guard on any of the above, you may seriously decrease your chances of being as best prepared as possible.

Another important factor is timing—start early! Many firms start full-time recruiting as early as September for the following year. Even if a firm does not adhere to this schedule, it is best to reach out to potential employers in September to better understand their individual recruiting processes, contacts, and timing. All too often, students reach out to me a couple of months before or after graduation, which not only puts the student at a disadvantage because the next consulting class has most likely already been hired but also suggests that consulting is an afterthought or that the person is less organized and motivated than the thousands of applicants that reached out to our firm six to nine months earlier. As you begin the process, it is important to show your interest; attend company information sessions if possible, research the firm, reach out to school alumni, and prepare intelligent questions to demonstrate genuine interest and thoughtfulness. I encourage you to be proactive but also respectful and appreciative of these professionals' time.

An international consulting career can take many shapes and forms and prepares individuals well via the unique experiences and broad skill set that is developed. Whether international consulting is a long-term career or a shorter-term platform, it can be very rewarding and provide numerous attractive opportunities in the future.

RESOURCE LISTINGS

Accenture

Accenture is a global management consulting, technology services, and outsourcing company that works around the world to help its clients enter new markets, increase their revenues in existing markets, improve operational performance, and deliver their products and services more effectively and efficiently. With over $16 billion in annual revenues and over 152,000 employees in forty-nine countries, Accenture delivers high performance to some of the world's leading companies and governments.

Accenture hires people with a range of skills for each of its businesses. Technical, engineering, management, legal, mathematical, financial, and communications backgrounds are all desirable. Candidates with bachelor's degrees are typically sought for consulting analyst positions in the United States, and a small number join its outsourcing business offices in the United States. Advanced degree graduates may qualify either for entry-level or experienced positions. Qualified MBA students are sought for Accenture's strategy practice, its "elite force" of 2,500 professionals. Summer internships in strategy are available to both graduate and undergraduate degree candidates.

> Accenture
> 22 Victoria Street, Canon's Court
> Hamilton, HM12
> Bermuda
> Tel.: 44-1-296-8262
> Fax: 44-1-296-4245
> careers.accenture.com

APCO Worldwide

APCO Worldwide is a global communication consultancy specializing in building relationships with an organization's key stakeholders. These relationships are critical to the full range of challenges its clients face. APCO has the lowest staff turnover in the industry. The consistency of APCO's team allows it to serve clients seamlessly across international borders and ensures long client partnerships—some more than fifteen years.

APCO Worldwide's competitive advantage is the talented and experienced people it employs. The company's philosophy is to hire and retain employees who provide exceptional service to clients locally but have the capacity to think and work globally. APCO seeks to hire professionals with diverse backgrounds and experiences who are creative, intelligent, and take initiative. It employs a mix of former high-level government officials, elected politicians, business leaders, journalists, and political and communications advisers, as well as recent graduates.

Many of APCO's offices around the world offer internships to college students, graduate students, and recent college graduates, providing valuable exposure to the firm's operations and service areas. All intern applicants should have excellent written and oral communication skills, along with the ability to balance multiple work assignments. The specific skill sets for each office and position are listed individually. Internships are available in the United States and internationally.

Recruitment in the United States:
APCO Worldwide
Human Resources Department
Suite 800, 700 12th Street, NW
Washington, DC 20005
Tel.: 202-778-1000

Recruitment in Europe, the Middle East, and Africa:
APCO Worldwide
90 Long Acre
London WC2E 9RA
United Kingdom
Tel.: 44-207-526-3600

Recruitment in Asia:
APCO Worldwide
9/F, Cambridge House, TaiKoo Place
979 King's Road
Hong Kong
Tel.: 8-52-2866-2313

A. T. Kearney

A. T. Kearney is a leading global management consulting firm with a broad range of capabilities and expertise in all major industries. Of about 2,500 employees worldwide, 1,600 are consultants; A. T. Kearney employees have broad industry experience and come from leading business schools. A. T. Kearney offices are situated in major business centers in thirty-two countries across the Americas, Africa, the Asia-Pacific region, and Europe. With 2005 revenues of $798 million, A. T. Kearney is one of the largest global high-value consulting firms.

In 1992, A. T. Kearney established the Global Business Policy Council, a strategic service that helps chief executives monitor and capitalize on geopolitical, economic, social, and technological changes worldwide. Because the firm knows that its long-term success will depend upon yours, A. T. Kearney makes every effort to hasten your progress along a clearly defined career path. Depending on your education and experience, you will enter the firm as a business analyst, senior business analyst, or associate. Thereafter, you will advance along the path as rapidly as your abilities will allow.

> A. T. Kearney Campus Recruiting
> 222 West Adams Street
> Chicago, IL 60606
> e-mail: campus.recruiting@atkearney.com
> industry.resumes@atkearney.com
> www.atkearney.com

Bain & Company

Bain & Company is a global business consulting firm, founded in 1973 on the principle that consultants should deliver results—not just reports—to their clients. Since then, Bain has worked for over 3,600 clients in virtually every industry. Over 2,700 Bain consultants work in its thirty-three offices in twenty-one countries around the world.

The role that new hires play at Bain will depend strongly on their quantitative skills. Associate consultants generally join Bain directly after graduating from a college or university with a BA or similar degree. Associate consultants are a diverse group of highly qualified people with extremely broad backgrounds—from economics to literature, with and without deep analytic experience. MBA graduates and most other candidates with advanced degrees who have rigorous, relevant business and analytical experience join Bain as consultants. Consultants take responsibility for attacking the most advanced and difficult problems its clients face, including understanding specific competitor performance, assessing underlying market dynamics, and dissecting the drivers of—and potential for—financial returns. Current students should apply through their college or university web page, if applicable. All other candidates may submit applications online for positions at up to three Bain offices.

Bain & Company, Inc.
131 Dartmouth Street
Boston, MA 02116
Tel.: 617-572-2000
Fax: 617-572-2427
e-mail: recruiting@bain.com
www.bain.com

BearingPoint

BearingPoint is a leading management and technology consulting firm with expertise across a number of industries, including the public sector. It works for clients in government and industry in sixty countries to solve their most pressing challenges from strategy through execution. More than 17,000 employees provide strategic consulting, applications services, technology solutions, and managed services to government organizations, Global 2,000 companies, and medium-sized businesses in the United States and around the world.

BearingPoint's government work includes a significant emerging markets practice. In the United States, BearingPoint serves all fifteen Cabinet-level government agencies. It also works with more than sixty central, regional, and local governments of developing nations around the world. To help these markets grow, BearingPoint helps governments to accelerate public-sector reform, promote economic growth, and improve public services; to create an environment that supports private-sector growth, attracts new investment, and increases employment; and to use information technology to build capacity and become more competitive. Bearing-Point also serves major international organizations, such as the World Bank, Asian Development Bank, and Inter-American Development Bank, in addition to the aid and development agencies of the U.S., U.K., and Canadian governments. BearingPoint recruits college and university graduates and former military officers in addition to experienced professionals.

BearingPoint
1676 International Drive
McLean, VA 22102

Tel.: 703-747-3000
www.bearingpoint.com/careers

Booz Allen Hamilton

Booz Allen Hamilton, a leading global consulting firm, has 19,000 employees serving clients on six continents. Integrating the full range of consulting capabilities, Booz Allen is the one firm that helps government and commercial clients solve their toughest problems with services in strategy, operations, organization and change, and information technology.

Booz Allen has special opportunities for Americans with defense and intelligence expertise and clearances. It supports mission-critical projects across a wide range of national security, intelligence, and law enforcement agencies. Booz Allen actively recruits MBA and postgraduate students from leading colleges and universities around the world. An MBA or advanced degree candidate will typically join Booz Allen as an associate or summer associate.

Overseas opportunities in Europe and the Middle East are also available. Booz Allen consultants possess a variety of educational backgrounds—ranging from business studies, physics, and electrical engineering to psychology, linguistics, history, and law. If you have strong analytical skills, business-level fluency in the language of the region where you wish to work, international work experience, and hold a degree with an outstanding academic record from a world-renowned academic institution, you fit the profile of a Booz Allen consultant. The firm also seeks candidates who have experience working for blue-chip companies as an intern or as a professional for two to five years.

Corporate Headquarters
8283 Greensboro Drive
McLean, VA 22102
Tel.: 703-902-5000
www.boozallen.com/careers

Boston Consulting Group

The Boston Consulting Group is an international strategy and general management consulting firm whose mission is to help leading corporations create and sustain competitive advantage. Because it is a truly international firm, with over sixty offices worldwide, its strong global presence offers clients and employees a wealth of cross-cultural experience.

Most entry-level candidates begin as either associates or consultants, depending on education and experience. Associates are hired from undergraduate and sometimes from graduate programs and are exposed to a broad range of clients and industries. They develop firsthand knowledge of critical business issues while honing client-management and problem-solving skills. Most associates take two to three years to master the challenges of the role. Some master's degree and all MBAs are hired as consultants. Consultants and associates perform many similar tasks, but consultants carry more responsibility from the outset. Their work is often more complex and its scope is broader. Most consultants remain in that role for two to three years before becoming project leaders.

> Boston Consulting Group
> Global Services
> Corporate Headquarters
> One Exchange Place, 6th Floor
> Boston, MA 02109
> Tel.: 617-973-1200
> Fax: 617-973-1399
> www.bcg.com/careers

Cambridge Energy Research Associates

Cambridge Energy Research Associates, Inc. (CERA), an IHS company, is a leading adviser to international energy companies, governments, financial institutions, and technology providers. CERA delivers critical knowledge and independent analysis on energy markets, geopolitics, industry trends, and strategy. Its services help decision makers anticipate the energy future and formulate timely, successful plans in the face of rapid changes and uncertainty. CERA's expertise covers all major energy sectors—oil and refined products, natural gas, and electric power—on a global and regional basis.

CERA has over 200 staff worldwide, with offices in Cambridge, Massachusetts; Beijing; Calgary; Mexico City; Moscow; Paris; Rio de Janeiro; San Francisco; and Washington. Current job openings can be searched on its website.

> CERA Cambridge
> 55 Cambridge Parkway
> Cambridge, MA 02142
> Tel.: 617-866-5000
> Fax: 617-866-5900
> e-mail: careers@cera.com
> www.cera.com

CGI

Founded in 1976, CGI (formerly American Management Systems) is one of the largest independent information technology and business process services companies. Approximately 25,000 professionals work in more than one hundred offices serving clients in sixteen countries. CGI achieves a high client satisfaction rating by providing end-to-end services, including consulting, systems integration, management of information technology and business functions, and approximately a hundred proprietary business solutions. Providing both information technology and industry expertise, CGI works in a range of industries, including financial services; government, and health care; telecommunications and utilities; and retail, distribution, and manufacturing.

CGI is always seeking knowledgeable, creative, and committed individuals who are ready to grow with it. It hires college graduates in technical (computer science) and functional (business, testing, decision analysis, and technical writing) areas. In Canada and the United States, CGI only accepts resumes through its online application system.

> CGI Head Office
> 1130 Sherbrooke Street West, 7th Floor
> Montreal, Quebec H3A 2M8
> Tel.: 514-841-3200
> Fax: 514-841-3299
> www.cgi.com

Chemonics International

Headquartered in Washington, Chemonics International is an international development consulting firm. Founded in 1975, the company has worked in 139 countries, managing more than nine hundred projects in agricultural development, environmental resource management, private-sector development, finance and banking, democracy and governance, health, and crisis prevention and recovery. Chemonics implements projects on behalf of the U.S. Agency for International Development, the U.K. Department for International Development, international organizations, and private sector clients.

In 2004, Chemonics launched its entry-level professional program to recruit, orient, train, and develop new staff members. Program participants receive one-to-one attention to facilitate their professional development and fill positions in project management; new business development; and a wide variety of project support functions such as communications, procurement, and training. Entry-level program participants may have a bachelor's or master's degree and generally have less than five years of work experience. Most have lived or worked in a developing country and speak a relevant foreign language. All potential candidates for the program must apply through the online application system. Individuals with more than five years of experience, including some developing-country experience, are encouraged to submit their resumes to resume@chemonics.com.

Chemonics International Inc.
1717 H Street, NW
Washington, DC, 20006
www.chemonics.com

Constella Futures

Constella Futures (formerly Futures Group International) specializes in the design and implementation of public health and social programs for developing countries. Since 1971, it has worked on projects in more than a hundred countries across Africa, Asia and the Middle East, Eastern Europe, and Latin America and the Caribbean. Constella staff work collaboratively with in-country counterparts to improve policies and programs that address population issues, reproductive health, HIV/AIDS, infectious diseases, and maternal and child health.

Constella Futures' experts in disciplines such as public policy, economics and health finance, medicine, law and human rights, public health, demography, epidemiology, gender, social marketing, communications, and monitoring and evaluation employ a focused yet flexible approach to helping countries and communities build local capacity and forge public-private partnerships. Committed to the sustainability of the programs in which they participate, Constella builds the capacity of its partners to make well-informed decisions and effectively address a multitude of complex health and social issues.

Constella Futures has more than 150 employees based in the United States and the United Kingdom, and more the 260 employees and full-time consultants based in developing countries. Their broad scope of work requires expertise across a multitude of disciplines, backgrounds, and cultures. They are continually seeking exceptional talent to help achieve their vision of enhancing human health around the world, every day. Entry-level positions require a BA in a related field with two or more years of experience, midcareer positions require an MA with five or more years of experience, and senior positions are filled by candidates with an MA or PhD in a related field and ten or more years of experience. All positions require a second language.

Corporate offices are located in Washington; Glastonbury, Connecticut; and Bath, England. Constella also has twenty-five project offices around the globe. In 2006, the firm hired for seventy-five positions, including staff, consultants, and personal service contractors.

Constella Futures, LLC
Suite 200, One Thomas Circle, NW
Washington, DC 20005
Tel.: 202-775-9680
info@constellagroup.com
www.constellagroup.com

Corporate Executive Board

The Corporate Executive Board (CEB) is the premier membership organization for senior executives of leading public and private institutions worldwide who want to discover innovative strategies for addressing their most pressing challenges. In general, CEB serves a group of clients (a membership) as opposed to focusing on the needs of any one specific client. Its dedicated membership programs focus upon increasing the effectiveness of leaders within member organizations. To that end, CEB provides best practices research, decision-support tools, and executive education to a membership of the world's leading corporations and not-for-profit institutions. Its research addresses issues related to corporate strategy, operations, and general management. Its focus is on identifying management initiatives, processes, tools, and frameworks that will allow its members to avoid reinventing the wheel in addressing problems they share in common with their peers.

CEB has over twenty years of experience in managing high-quality executive memberships, with over 2,400 large corporate members around the world, and over 2,200 staff in its Washington and London offices. CEB is on a constant search for exceptional talent. Its current staff consists of people from a variety of advanced degree backgrounds, including MBAs, JDs, and PhDs. Typical positions for graduate students are in sales, content delivery, member services, or strategic research consulting.

Corporate Executive Board
Victoria House, Fourth Floor
37–63 Southampton Row
Bloomsbury Square
London, WC1B 4DR
United Kingdom
Tel.: 44-0-20-7632-6000
Fax: 44-0-20-7632-6001
www.exbd.com

Corporate Executive Board
Suite 6000, 2000 Pennsylvania Avenue, NW
Washington, DC 20006
Tel.: 202-777-5000
Fax: 202-777-5100

Dalberg

Dalberg is an international consulting firm serving clients in the public, private, and nonprofit sectors. Its mission is to provide outstanding advice to clients in the areas of globalization and sustainable international development to help them achieve breakthroughs in performance and innovation. Dalberg's work is organized along three distinct service lines: building institutions, engaging the private sector, and innovating for development. Established in October 2001 by a group of experienced private-sector consultants, today the firm employs more than thirty professionals operating from New York, Washington, Copenhagen, and Geneva.

Dalberg seeks candidates that have successfully handled complex problem-solving and project management challenges and who are open to joining a dynamic and entrepreneurial environment with many opportunities to take on significant leadership roles. Successful candidates at Dalberg typically have professional advisory experience with a leading management consulting firm, field experience in a developing country, professional or volunteer experience with a nonprofit organization or development agency, distinctive academic credentials, an entrepreneurial mindset, and long-term commitment to the development sector. Interested candidates should e-mail a curriculum vitae and cover letter, indicating the relevant role and preferred geographic location in the subject line.

Dalberg in North America
Suite 1830, 205 East 42nd Street

New York, NY 10017
Tel.: 212-867-4447
e-mail: recruitment@dalberg.com
www.dalberg.com/opportunities

Development Alternatives

Development Alternatives Inc. (DAI) is a global consulting firm providing social and economic development solutions to international development agencies, international lending institutions, global corporations, and host-country governments. Founded in 1970, DAI now includes companies in South Africa, Palestine, and the United Kingdom. After thirty-five years, DAI remains the industry leader in delivering practical solutions to social and economic development challenges. The DAI group is made up of several individual companies:

- DAI Washington offers a wide range of rewarding career opportunities for talented technical, managerial, and support professionals in the United States and overseas. Its 2,000 employees work in more than fifty countries.
- DAI Europe, based in London, has 40 permanent staff, 20 full-time associates, and more than 100 long-term project associates.
- DAI Palestine began operations in 2004 after ten years of long-term DAI project experience in the area. Headquartered in Ramallah with a branch office in Gaza City, DAI Palestine seeks to enhance the well-being of Middle Eastern societies through innovative development responses to economic, social, political, and environmental challenges. DAI Palestine currently has 60 employees in both the West Bank and Gaza.
- ECI*Africa* is an international economic development consultancy and capacity-building organization working principally in the fields of enterprise development, business linkages, development finance, governance and public sector management, agribusiness and rural development, and HIV/AIDS in the economic context. All the operational groups have a highly symbiotic relationship. ECI*Africa* has a large permanent staff and access to the expertise of affiliates and corporate partners, including a database of 26,000 consultants worldwide. Its hub is in Johannesburg, South Africa.
- DAI's Corporate Practice combines DAI's economic development capabilities with business strategy expertise to help corporate clients succeed in their developing world operations.

DAI Washington
Suite 200, 7600 Wisconsin Avenue

Bethesda, MD 20814
Tel.: 301-771-7600
Fax: 301-771-7777
Corporate recruitment/internships: jobs@dai.com
Consultant recruitment: globalcv@dai.com
www.dai.com

Deloitte & Touche Tohmatsu

Deloitte Touche Tohmatsu is an organization of member firms around the world devoted to excellence in providing professional services and advice, focused on client service through a global strategy executed locally in nearly 150 countries. Deloitte serves more than half the world's largest companies, as well as large national enterprises, public institutions, locally important clients, and successful, fast-growing global growth companies.

In the United States, Deloitte & Touche USA LLP is the member firm of Deloitte Touche Tohmatsu, and services provided by its subsidiaries are among the nation's leading professional services firms, providing audit, tax, consulting, and financial advisory services through nearly 30,000 people in more than eighty cities. Known as employers of choice for innovative human resources programs, they are dedicated to helping their clients and their people excel.

With 135,000 people in nearly 140 countries, Deloitte member firms serve more than 80 percent of the world's largest companies as well as large national enterprises, public institutions, and successful fast-growing companies.

Deloitte & Touche USA
1633 Broadway
New York, NY 10019
Tel.: 212-489-1600
Fax: 212-489-1687
www.deloitte.com

Development Associates

Established in 1969, Development Associates Inc. has headquarters in the Washington area and maintains overseas offices in Africa, Latin America, the Middle East, and Eastern Europe. The multilingual, multicultural, and ethnically diverse staff allows the firm to rapidly respond to client needs in a culturally and technically appropriate manner. To complement its staff, the firm draws on over 1,000 active consultants worldwide and maintains listings of some 8,000 other specialists in a broad range of fields. Development Associates has successfully designed and implemented projects in the United States and over a hundred countries.

Current job openings are listed at the firm's website. Development Associates Inc. also runs an online consultant database that allows consultants and others to submit their resumes and to enter or change information about their interests, skills, and experience. For informational purposes, resumes may be sent at any time.

> Development Associates Inc.
> Navy League Building
> Suite 300, 2300 Wilson Boulevard
> Arlington, VA 22201-5426
> Tel.: 703-276-0677
> e-mail: hr@devassoc.com
> www.devassoc.com

Ernst & Young

Ernst & Young U.S. is a member firm of Ernst & Young International, a leading international professional services firm dedicated to helping companies identify and capitalize on business opportunities throughout the world. Practice areas include accounting and auditing, tax, management consulting, corporate finance, restructuring and reorganization, capital markets, cash management, valuation, benefits and compensation consulting, and outsourcing services. Ernst & Young has more than 114,000 employees in 140 countries worldwide. With annual revenues of over $18 billion, Ernst & Young is one of the largest accounting firms in the world.

> U.S. Headquarters
> Ernst & Young LLP
> 5 Times Square
> New York, NY 10036
> Tel.: 212-773-3000
> www.ey.com

Eurasia Group

The Eurasia Group is the world's leading global political risk advisory and consulting firm. It covers political, social, security, and economic developments worldwide. Its coverage is organized into four geographic practices—Asia, Europe and Eurasia, Latin America, and the Middle East and Africa—plus a Global Macro Practice Group and a Transnational

Issues Practice Group. It offers clients advisory services, publications, and tailored consulting, as well as direct access to Eurasia Group analysts. These analysts cover political developments and their impact on business and financial markets on a daily basis. The Eurasia Group also provides programming services that enable multinational companies to engage in direct dialogue with leaders from around the world.

The Eurasia Group had twenty-five professional job openings in the international field in 2006 in the areas of research and analysis, business development, production, and operations. Associates at the firm are required to have at a minimum a BA in political science or relevant field, and an MA is preferred. Relevant language fluency is required, as well as at least one year's field experience in the region. Analysts at the Eurasia Group are required to have at a minimum an MA in political science or relevant field (a PhD preferred). Relevant language fluency is required, as well as three to five years of experience and at least one year of field experience in the region.

> Eurasia Group
> 475 Fifth Avenue, 14th Floor
> New York, NY 10017
> Tel.: 212-213-3112
> Fax: 212-213-3075
> e-mail: careers@eurasiagroup.net
> www.eurasiagroup.net

IHS

IHS, Inc., is one of the leading global providers of critical technical information, decision-support tools, and related services to customers in the energy, defense, aerospace, construction, electronics, and automotive industries. IHS is organized into two operating segments. Its Energy Segment provides a comprehensive suite of information services to the oil and gas industry—from well and production data to economic and consulting products and services. Energy Segment services and solutions support oil and gas professionals as they evaluate subsurface issues related to geology, technology, and reserves potential, and as they assess the economic impact of political, fiscal and environmental risks. With seventeen technical teams positioned worldwide and proficiencies in forty-two languages, IHS covers the petroleum industry in over ninety countries.

The IHS Engineering Segment develops and implements engineering, technical, and regulatory information solutions for customers in over one hundred countries. The Engineering Segment provides solutions for the following verticals: automotive, aviation/aerospace, construction, energy, government / department of defense, electronics/telecommunications, petrochemicals, and utilities.

IHS employs more than 600 people in Colorado and 2,300 worldwide. The company offers a wide range of career opportunities to exceptional candidates interested in joining one of the most successful and unique firms in the information industry. As one of the leading global providers of critical technical information, decision-support tools, and related services to customers in the energy, defense, aerospace, construction, and automotive industries, IHS is always in search of new talent to join its team. If you are seeking a position at IHS, visit the Current Openings page of the employment section of its website.

> IHS, Inc.
> 15 Inverness Way East
> MS D101
> Englewood, CO 80112
> www.ihs.com

McKinsey & Company

McKinsey & Company is a global management consulting firm that advises the world's leading businesses, governments, and institutions. Its clients include more than 70 percent of *Fortune* magazine's most admired companies and governments in more than thirty-five countries around the world. In total, McKinsey has more than eighty offices in more than forty countries. The firm also has a large nonprofit practice, typically serving over one hundred nonprofit organizations each year in the fields of arts and culture, economic development, education, global public health, international aid and development, philanthropy, and social services.

McKinsey employees come from all over the world, with rich experience and all kinds of backgrounds and areas of expertise. Collectively, McKinsey people speak over 120 languages and represent over 100 nationalities. Advancement at McKinsey is strictly based on merit—there are no tenure-based requirements. Holders of BAs and some MAs start out as business analysts (called "fellows" in some offices). MBAs, holders of other advanced degrees, and experienced professionals typically begin their careers as associates.

McKinsey is not a place that only hires people with MBAs. In fact, less than half of the people at the firm have advanced business degrees. What it looks for is people with distinctive intelligence, deep expertise, an analytical mind, and leadership potential. You will find more tips and resources when you start the application process. Students at all levels should begin the application process with their schools; experienced professionals may begin their application online.

McKinsey's Asia House, based in Frankfurt, is a key office that supports projects mainly in Europe and Asia, as well as in the Pacific Rim, the Middle East, and the Americas. During their time in Europe, consultants work in mixed teams in English. With more and more clients interested in Asian markets, consultants at Asia House are often the first points of contact, and they engage as key experts on innovative problem solving at the crossroads of Europe and Asia. Qualifications for Asia House employees are similar to those for U.S.-based consultants but include fluency in both English and at least one Asian language. To be able to liaise at an appropriate level with the client, candidates should also bring the cultural and educational background from one Asian country. Candidates preferably have already lived on both sides of the "bridge"—both in Asia and in Europe or the United States. The Asia House program last two to three years; new hires start at the Asia House for twelve to eighteen months and then move on to deepen their expertise at McKinsey in Asia and have the chance to be promoted, with further opportunities for advancement at McKinsey all the way up to partner.

McKinsey & Company
Suite 300, 600 14th Street, NW
Washington, DC 20005
Tel.: 202-662-3100
Fax: 202-662-3175
www.mckinsey.com/careers
e-mail: career_opportunities@mckinsey.com

McKinsey & Company
Recruiting "Asia House"
Lynn Schäfer
Magnusstraße 11
50672 Köln
Germany
Tel.: 49-0-221-208-7561
e-mail: asiahouse-recruiting@mckinsey.com
www.asiahouse.mckinsey.com

Nathan Associates
One of the oldest economic consulting firms in the United States, Nathan Associates Inc. has been working in developing countries and with international development and donor agencies for more than sixty years. The services of its International Division are based on an understanding of the economics of competition, innovation, and reward. Nathan Associates helps public- and private-sector leaders in developing countries formulate and execute trade and economic policies that introduce competition into sheltered or restricted markets; respond to local, regional, and international market opportunities and challenges; grasp the importance of innovation and of intellectual property rights to economic growth; study the costs and benefits improving infrastructure, liberalizing trade, investing in information technology, and adjusting policies and business strategies; and understand and prepare for the economic effects of change on employment, wages, and tax revenues.

Nathan Associates provides these services through four units: Infrastructure Planning and Economics, Trade and Investment, Economic Policy and Governance, and Enterprise and Industry Development. Each unit consists of permanent staff and consultants who work on projects in developing countries. Whether hiring new staff or consultants, Nathan Associates seeks people with a passion for development economics and who understand how that field can make a positive difference in the lives of ordinary people. Candidates should be able to share their ideas and observations in writing as well as in person. Most staff and nearly all consultants have advanced degrees and quantitative skills and are fluent in at least one language other than English. These degrees are usually in economics, international relations, international studies, international business, and political science.

In 2006, Nathan hired fifteen permanent staff for its International Division and many consultants to work on projects in Afghanistan, Angola, Armenia, Bangladesh, Bolivia, Brazil, Brunei, Burundi, Cambodia, China, Colombia, Costa Rica, Croatia, the Dominican Republic, Ecuador, Egypt, El Salvador, Ethiopia, Georgia, Guyana, India, Indonesia, Jordan, Lesotho, Mexico, Morocco, Mozambique, Nigeria, Pakistan, Panama, Peru, the Philippines, Serbia, Singapore, South Africa, Sri Lanka, Tanzania, Trinidad and Tobago, the United Arab Emirates, and the West Bank and Gaza.

Nathan Associates Inc.
Suite 1200, 2101 Wilson Boulevard
Arlington, VA 22201
Tel.: 703-516-7700
Fax: 703-351-6162
www.nathaninc.com

Oliver Wyman

Oliver Wyman (formerly Mercer Management Consulting) combines deep industry knowledge with specialized expertise in strategy, operations, risk management, organizational transformation, and leadership development. The firm works with clients to deliver sustained shareholder value growth, helping managers to anticipate changes in customer priorities and the competitive environment, and then design their businesses, improve their operations and risk profile, and accelerate their organizational performance to seize the most attractive opportunities.

Oliver Wyman has more than thirty-five years experience serving Global 1,000 clients. Its staff of 2,500 operates from offices in more than forty cities in sixteen countries. Candidates may apply for general management consulting, financial services consulting, or Delta organization and leadership consulting, staffed by professionals with extensive experience. The firm recruits for general management and financial services, consulting at more than sixty university campuses worldwide each year. If Oliver Wyman does not recruit at your school, you may submit an application online.

Oliver Wyman Recruiting
United States (Boston, Chicago, Dallas, New York, San Francisco)
John Hancock Tower
200 Clarendon Street
Boston, MA 02116
recruitingUS.gmc@oliverwyman.com
www.oliverwyman.com

PFC Energy

PFC Energy has been a trusted adviser to energy companies and governments across the globe for over twenty years. Founded in 1984, the firm has grown to over one hundred professionals, with offices in Washington, Paris, Houston, London, Lausanne, Kuala Lumpur, and Buenos Aires. PFC Energy provides in-depth analysis and forward-looking scenarios that provide the foundation for strategy development, investment evaluation, and commercial decisions at the global and regional levels. PFC Energy seeks the highest-level professionals, who are team oriented, self-directed, and able to add to its diverse perspectives. PFC Energy offers a competitive salary, bonus, and benefits package for all positions. Applications can be submitted only through the PFC Energy website or by e-mail.

> PFC Energy, Washington
> Senior Director
> Suite 800, 1300 Connecticut Avenue, N.W.
> Washington, DC 20036
> jobs@pfcenergy.com

Pragma Corporation

The Pragma Corporation is a private international development-consulting firm headquartered in Falls Church, Virginia. Since 1977, it has been working with the U.S. Agency for International Development, the Asian Development Bank, the World Bank, the Inter-American Development Bank, and other donors to provide expert technical and management consulting services for approximately six hundred development projects in seventy-five countries. Its focus is on helping countries develop the foundation for economic growth through small and medium-sized enterprise development; trade and investment facilitation; banking, privatization, and business support; capital and financial market development; pension reform and insurance; regional trade promotion; accounting reform, training, and examination; and agribusiness development. The number of professional openings in the international field varies yearly with projects.

> Pragma Corporation
> 116 East Broad Street
> Falls Church, Virginia 22046
> Tel.: 703-237-9303
> Fax: 703-237-9326
> e-mail: pragma@pragmacorp.com
> www.pragmacorp.com

Pyramid Research

Pyramid Research provides market analysis and consulting services to the telecommunications, Internet, and media industry. It helps clients to develop sound international business strategies by providing rigorous, in-depth analysis and advice on markets that span the globe. Pyramid is the only company whose core competency is covering emerging markets around the world. It has spent more than two decades building a solid understanding of the intangibles that make these markets particularly difficult to navigate, providing clients with guidance in markets filled with regulatory uncertainty, economic instability, and unclear business practices. Its coverage includes North America, Latin America, Central and Eastern Europe, Western Europe, Africa and the Middle East, and the Asia-Pacific region. Headquartered in Cambridge, Massachusetts, Pyramid Research also has offices in London and Hong Kong and has a network of a hundred specialized professionals, including consultants, analysts, and associates.

Pyramid offers a bridge between strategic consulting and proprietary research that assesses clients' individual business issues in emerging and developed countries worldwide. Companies use its services to assist with market analysis and sizing, customer segmentation and targeting, competitive tracking, global benchmarking of opportunities and risk, new license valuation, market entry strategies, and partner identification.

All Pyramid's analysts and consultants speak one or more foreign language(s) fluently and have had extensive experience living and working abroad. Although industry experience is not required to apply, a good understanding of international business issues and superior intellect are a must. Candidates with bachelor's degrees usually fill associate positions, whereas analyst and consultant positions are reserved for candidates with graduate degrees in business and international affairs.

Pyramid Research
58 Charles Street
Cambridge, MA 02141
Tel.: 617-494-1515
Fax: 617-494-8898
e-mail: careers@pyr.com
www.pyramidresearch.com

The Rothkopf Group

The Rothkopf Group LLC draws on a considerable depth of experience in international business, economic, and security issues to provide consulting services and information products for clients worldwide. Areas of special competence include emerging markets, intelligence, U.S.

national security, international trade, and science- and technology-related projects.

Divisions of the Rothkopf Group include C-Level Solutions, a Washington-based company that specializes in turnkey solutions; the Global Leadership Series; the Tradable Intelligence Company; and the Scenario Group.

Rothkopf Group LLC
Suite 500, 1330 Connecticut Avenue, NW
Washington, DC 20036
Tel.: 202-457-7920
Fax: 202-457-7921
www.therothkopfgroup.com

SRI International

SRI International is an independent, nonprofit research institute conducting client-sponsored research and development for government agencies, commercial businesses, foundations, and other organizations. SRI also brings its innovations to the marketplace by licensing its intellectual property and creating new ventures.

For more than sixty years, since its beginnings when it was called Stanford Research Institute, SRI's strengths have been its staff's world-leading expertise and passion for working with clients on important challenges. SRI is well known for its legacy of innovations in communications and networks, computing, economic development and science and technology policy, education, energy and the environment, engineering systems, pharmaceuticals and health sciences, homeland security and national defense, and materials and structures.

Based in Washington, SRI's Center for Science, Technology, and Economic Development has crafted development strategies for more than a hundred countries and regions around the world, from Lebanon to Hong Kong and San Francisco. The center is staffed with seasoned professionals who conduct research, analysis, program evaluation, and strategic planning for private and public sector clients. The center's multidisciplinary approach gives it a unique perspective that allows it to integrate skills from different disciplines for each client assignment.

Headquarters
SRI International
333 Ravenswood Avenue
Menlo Park, CA 94025-3493

Tel.: 650-859-2000
www.sri.com/jobs

Center for Science, Technology, and Economic Development
SRI International
Suite 2800, 1100 Wilson Boulevard
Arlington, VA 22209
Tel.: 703-524-2053
Fax: 703-247-8569
www.sri.com

12

International Development and Relief

Careers in International Development

Kristi Ragan

Kristi Ragan, *a 1989 graduate of the Master of Science in Foreign Service Program at Georgetown University, is an international development professional with more than twenty years of experience working in Africa, Asia, Latin America, the Middle East, and the Pacific. Her career includes over a decade with the United Nations Development Program, service as Peace Corps country director in Cotê d' Ivoire, and an adjunct faculty position in the Master of Science in Foreign Service Program at Georgetown. She is currently director of the Business Advantage Group at Development Alternatives, Inc., where she builds public–private partnerships that leverage donor and private sector resources for development.*

TODAY, 3 billion people live on less than $2 a day, 1.3 billion have no access to clean water, 3 billion lack basic sanitation, and 2 billion live without access to electricity. These figures, which will double by 2050, provide concrete evidence of the continued need for international development professionals. However, international development, like everything else, is being dramatically changed by the forces of globalization, and it is not the same industry that it was for the past forty years. When rock stars like Bono are writing the foreword to major development tomes like Jeffrey Sachs's *The End of Poverty*, it is clear that the actors and the issues around development are moving into new territories.

320

Likewise, the traditional international development career path has evolved. Twenty years ago, the typical route to a job in international development meant spending two years as a Peace Corps volunteer, followed by a graduate degree in international affairs that got you a job with the U.S. Agency for International Development (USAID). These are no longer the primary or only career paths for individuals seeking to work on global economic and social development. A career in international development today involves a growing array of opportunities that include business firms, nonprofits, and nongovernmental organizations (NGOs), think tanks, bilateral and multilateral donor organizations, foundations, and consulting firms. Whether you decide to market cellular telephones in rural Africa, promote human rights with NGOs in the former Soviet states, or buy local agricultural products for Wal-Mart superstores, you can tangibly contribute to the objectives of international development. A senior USAID official interviewed for this chapter said: "The challenge of a career in international development is to find a way to work at the nexus of government, civil society, and business."

THE PUBLIC SECTOR

The public sector has always been and will continue to be a major employer of international development experts. The term "public sector" refers to government agencies, and also to any bilateral government or multilateral governmental organization that delivers foreign aid to poor countries. Most of the development jobs in the public sector—whether with bilateral organizations such as USAID, the U.K. Department for International Development, or the German Deutsche Gesellschaft für Technische Zusammenarbeit (known as GTZ); or with multilateral agencies like the World Bank, the United Nations, or the International Finance Corporation—largely deal with the administration of aid. They involve overseeing the projects and contracts that the public sector has approved for funding. The important difference to be aware of when considering a job in these institutions is that most donors fund projects but do not implement them. As a result, they need job skills focused on program strategy, project design, contract administration, and monitoring and evaluation, in addition to government representation, rather than the hands-on project management required by other development actors.

Significant shifts are taking place in the public sector's development objectives and operating modalities. Today, foreign assistance is being increasingly aligned with the foreign policy objectives of the governments that deliver it. This shift is most apparent in the case of the U.S. government, and it has had a significant impact on the objectives and geographical focus of U.S. development aid. The close linking of aid and foreign policy is bringing new challenges and job opportunities for development workers. New actors such as the Millennium Challenge Corporation, the State Department, and the Department of Defense are entering the development arena for the first time. Their program focus on governance and on transformational development aimed at nation building is requiring new skills from development professionals. The goals of peace and security and their corresponding wide-ranging skill sets are key aspects of development work today. Iraq, Afghanistan, and the Middle East are a major geographical focus for much of this assistance, and skills in Arabic, conflict mitigation, infrastructure rehabilitation, and small grants management are just a few of those emerging as highly valued.

Significant shifts are taking place in the public sector's development objectives and operating modalities.

If you are interested in working for a government agency on a particular development topic, you have a wide range of possibilities and should look beyond the larger entities already mentioned and consider smaller agencies like the Environmental Protection Agency, the U.S. Trade and Development Authority, the U.S. Department of Labor, and the U.S. Department of Agriculture. These agencies and many others have their own, albeit small, international programs that are funded with their own resources. It is clear that development assistance is no longer delivered by any single government entity. This situation creates new opportunities if you are prepared to put in the time to understand these new actors and their program goals.

Business

International development and international business have significant points of intersection today. Many would argue that the answer to solving the toughest development issues lies with the private sector, whether it is health service delivery in Botswana or clean water in Bangladesh. Most agree that the fundamental objective of international development is poverty alleviation and that solving this issue means promoting economic growth through jobs and other sustainable livelihoods. Enterprise development, trade, and competitiveness projects continue to require professional experts to implement them.

International development and international business have significant points of intersection today.

On the other side, global businesses find themselves moving into countries they would never have dreamed of working in ten years ago as a result of the need to extract critical resources, source lower-cost products, and open up new markets. The business challenges facing global corporations in these poor countries are the same challenges that have absorbed the energies of development professionals—for example, private-sector competitiveness, gender promotion, advancing rule of law, anticorruption efforts, poverty reduction, national capacity building and skills development, and regulatory and policy reform, just to name a few.

Multinational corporations with major brand recognition have a great deal at stake when they do business in developing countries. The rule of law is infrequently enforced, and running afoul of communities can mean significant delays and loss of revenue. Oil companies have been sued for human rights violations committed by a national government that was using the local population to build roads that would be used by companies, even though the company was not present or even connected to the work. Apparel companies have been sued for the poor working conditions of garment workers in factories that were not owned or managed by the multinational but merely sold their products to them. As a result, multinational corporations are increasingly engaging in development activities as part of their "social investment strategies" or the local content requirements agreed to in their contracts with national governments (e.g., supply chain training, community development projects, and health and education provision). These private sector initiatives help manage their risk in developing countries and build positive relationships with the local communities that own the resources they are removing or making the products they are selling.

Some of these initiatives are categorized as "corporate social responsibility," and there is a growing number of jobs in companies with these groups. Opportunities for NGOs abound as these companies hire local nonprofit partners to implement their social programs. As businesses move into these countries, they undertake development projects to help deliver the message that they are a good global citizen helping to reduce their environmental footprint, improving the lives of the workers who make their products, and caring about the economic well-being of the countries where they are selling their products.

NGOs and Nonprofits

NGOs and nonprofits at both the international and local levels in developing countries are key actors in designing and implementing development projects. These groups work on a range of critical issues and have increasingly moved from awareness raising and advocacy to supplementing the service delivery capacity of the national governments in areas of basic needs like health and education. NGOs work to ensure that HIV/AIDS medicines reach the most remote village, that poor women have opportunities to launch their own business, that the child solider is demobilized and given skills that can earn him an income and keep him off the streets. There are over 60,000 international NGOs working around the world today—a number that roughly equals the number of multinational corporations. NGOs cover the full gamut of development issues and sectors. Working in an NGO can offer significant field-based opportunities and a higher level of responsibility than one might have in a donor organization or large private sector company. The NGOs today are made up of extremely large organizations like CARE or Save the Children, along with a sizable number of smaller, very specialized NGOs that work in select geographies or sectors.

Associations like the American Chamber of Commerce, the Center for International Private Enterprise, and Business for Social Responsibility are all actively engaged in looking at issues that address developing countries and, as such, offer job opportunities to work on policy-level advocacy as well as pilot demonstration interventions. Joining an industry association or other industry-related group can offer great networking options for young professionals looking to enter the development arena as well as job opportunities down the road. These organizations organize industry members around key issues, often involving developing country trade policies as well as corporate social responsibility.

FOUNDATIONS

The announcement that Warren Buffet gave $31 billion to the Bill and Melinda Gates Foundation drives home the role of nongovernmental actors in development. This single contribution exceeds the annual total U.S. government spending on foreign development and humanitarian assistance and signals the importance of philanthropy as a new actor on the scene of international development. The Gates Foundation has already expanded its initial focus beyond global health and stopping the spread of HIV/AIDS to include other key development issues like microfinance, enterprise promotion, agriculture, and gender. Strategic philanthropy goes far beyond one or two wealthy individuals. Traditional foundations that have been active in international development—including Ford, Kellogg, MacArthur, Rockefeller, and George Soros's Open Society Institute—join new actors like the Packard Foundation, begun by one of the cofounders of Hewlett Packard; Omidyer, set up by the founder of eBay; the Wellcome Trust, the largest medical and life science charity in the world; and the Schwab Foundation, created by the founder of the World Economic Forum to promote social entrepreneurs. Work in these institutions often involves looking for innovative new approaches to solving development problems and the strategic allocation of grant monies to spur the impact and scale of such projects.

THINK TANKS AND ACADEMIA

Think tanks have taken up the cause of development in many of their various policy analyses. The Center for Global Development in Washington is one example of a think tank that is significantly involved in development issues, covering topics that range from the impact of mega-supermarkets on poverty to supporting Liberia's new political leadership. These think tanks have significant input into development issue. One example is their key input into the establishment and design of the Millennium Challenge Corporation as a new aid delivery mechanism for the U.S. government. Some think tanks are deeply involved in a wide range of analysis that includes well-thought-out recommendations on the future of U.S. foreign assistance policy. Others, like the Carnegie Endowment for International Peace, engage heavily on analyzing the impact of free trade and other policies that significantly affect development policy and foreign aid allocations in Congress. Internships and employment opportunities exist in these organizations at junior and senior levels.

ACADEMIC PATHS

Education is a key qualification for any career in international development. However, looking at the wide array of opportunities, it is clear that no one particular degree is valued more than another by the industry. Among major donors, generalist degrees continue to be valued. At the same time, the rise of local staffing capacities is contributing to a tightening of the number of international positions in these organizations.

Beyond the donors, there is a growing emphasis on the technical skills needed for development work. The leading universities around the world now include an international content in most degree programs along with offering specific international degrees in a range of fields (e.g., politics, economics, international affairs) at the undergraduate and graduate levels. These degrees, combined with proficiency in a language, continue to offer useful qualifications for work in international development. If you are considering working at the upper levels of development—for example, as a manager of a development project for a major donor or with a global business expanding into emerging markets—you will be expected to have a graduate-level degree. Programs like the Peace Corps offer special arrangements with some of the best academic institutions to pursue graduate degrees after the completion of Peace Corps service. Many private-sector companies will cover graduate tuition for their employees in relevant areas of study that could include international studies.

EDUCATION FOR DEVELOPMENT

Increasingly, persons looking at a career in international development want to combine the versatility of the international affairs degree with the focus and technical training that comes with a more specialized degree. As a result, university dual-degree programs are becoming increasingly popular. Students can combine their work in international affairs with international business, public administration, or international law, to name just a few. These dual-degree programs provide a solid general understanding and framework for understanding international development as well as a set of skills that development professionals need to be able to deal effectively with specific issues. An MBA has become an extremely relevant degree for development work because promoting economic markets and jobs is at the heart of international development; and this degree offers job possibilities with development entities as well as private sector corporations.

There is stiff competition for jobs in international development because it is an increasingly attractive job choice for young job seekers who envision an exciting career of travel and adventure in far-flung countries while at the same time doing good and serving broader humanitarian objectives. To be competitive in this job market, you need to differentiate yourself from the other job seekers—so you can leverage your education in five ways that will help you stand out.

First, take business courses in addition to international economics and politics courses. Whether you are managing a community project, running an NGO, or working in a large donor bureaucracy, you need to have good business skills. Measuring impact, cost/benefit analysis, and strategic planning are all business tools that you will employ in your day-to-day development work. Managerial, communication, and marketing skills are key to successful development work. Implementing a project can not be done with technical expertise alone but requires organization and team-building approaches, budget management, and communication skills for both internal and external audiences.

Second, build your networks. Your fellow students and university faculty will be an invaluable network as you move through your career in international development. Alumni networks are useful for informational interviews, contacts, and insights that can help position you for jobs. University professors are increasingly called upon to advise and consult on issues pertaining to international development and thus have a good sense of donor and other organizational needs around development issues. Maintaining contact with these individuals can be extremely helpful and will give you much more than just providing you with references. Universities continually host speakers and luminaries in the field of development, and these are good opportunities to engage thought leaders on the topic and get their business contacts for possible future follow-up.

Third, use internships strategically. Most universities have a considerable range of intern possibilities that can be used to expand your networks and your practical experience. Using internships to gain exposure to a range of development organizations—including donors, businesses, NGOs, foundations, and think tanks—can facilitate your decision making on where the best fit might be for you. These internships expand your network of contacts for future job searches while at the same time opening up possibilities for permanent employment with that organization.

Many companies like to use internships to test out a young hire to see if there is a good technical and organizational fit.

Fourth, gain technical and developing country experience. Academic programs can often provide study or work abroad opportunities that will fill gaps in your technical skills or give you that much-needed field experience that is a prerequisite for work in development. Having diverse geographical experience makes you more employable and also allows you to bring best practices from one region to another.

Fifth, achieve fluency in languages. Academic study can be used to expand your facility with languages through a wide range of offerings that include foreign language groups, housing, field trips, research projects. Donors, companies, and NGOs all need individuals who can speak French, Portuguese, Spanish, and Arabic. Managing local partners and interacting with national governments can be done more effectively and with higher levels of trust when the expert has local language skills.

Skill Sets

The skills needed to work in international development have been significantly evolving. No matter whether you are working for a donor, a business, or a nonprofit, management skills are increasingly valued. Both large and small development projects require expertise in management, including leadership, strategic planning, team building, budgeting, and human resource management. Good management has been found to be a key element of successful development work. In addition, there is a priority on imparting these skills to the national staff and development project counterparts.

No matter whether you are working for a donor, a business, or a nonprofit, management skills are increasingly valued.

A second key skill set is communication and marketing. Development professionals need to effectively communicate with the wide range of actors that will be affected by any development project. Written and verbal skills are essential and highly valued. Gone are the days of the isolated development worker in the bush and off the radar screen of everyone. All projects are required to have an impact and are heavily monitored. Reporting on impact has become a key part of the work of an international development professional. This requires excellent analytical skills along with report writing and public presentation skills. Donors no longer want to be totally invisible about what they are doing. USAID developed a comprehensive communication strategy over the last several years that has been rolled out to every mission in the world. This effort included training all international and local staff on how to get the word out and tell the positive story of development. It helped staff identify who the audience was and how to adapt the message to them. Good communication skills are needed to improve the image of American foreign assistance both abroad and at home among the American taxpayers who provide the funding.

Cultivating specific areas of technical expertise during your academic study will be useful in pursuing a career in development. Though the broad-based skills of a generalist development professional are still valued by many, there are few job opportunities for this type of work. Donors, businesses, and nonprofits are all looking for advice from specialists in areas that include human rights, the rule of law, avian influenza, global trade standards, clean technologies, water and sanitation, decentralized government, and conflict mitigation. When designing new strategies and initiatives in these areas, donors will look to experienced technical experts to supplement the ideas of their own generalist program staff.

> **One skill requirement that has not changed over the years is the need for individuals who can build trust across cultures and organizations.**

One skill requirement that has not changed over the years is the need for individuals who can build trust across cultures and organizations. Development success only comes where trust has been fostered. A significant amount goes into this, including good listening skills, cross-cultural sensitivity, and humility. Attitude is always a key quality in the hiring of any development professional. The people who do the best in this field are those with a deep commitment to the issue and a willingness to work continually to refine approaches until they yield success.

GLOBAL TRENDS AFFECTING INTERNATIONAL DEVELOPMENT

In the coming years, six issues will have a significant impact on developing countries and will offer interesting new job opportunities. The first issue is *global business*. Companies are going global and spawning enterprises that will go after the grassroots markets. GE and IBM will make over half their products overseas within the next three years. Procter & Gamble and Unilever are targeting the markets in poor developing countries to bring them growth rates of over 30 percent. Countries like Rwanda are laying nationwide fiber-optic systems to help launch Internet-facilitated government and business. Developing countries are getting considerable attention as venues for both production and new consumers, and this will continue to grow.

The second issue is *environmental crisis and global warming*. It is commonly acknowledged that we are fundamentally changing our planet. These environmental changes are bringing about a critical need for clean technologies, clean water, and alternative sources of renewable energy. The megacity phenomenon mentioned below will bring such problems to a crisis level in major urban areas with dense populations of poor people. There will be a need for urban planning, urban engineers, water and sanitation experts, transportation experts, and other experts who can help deliver well-managed public services.

The third issue is *increasing global health threats*. SARS, HIV/AIDS, and avian influenza all signal the increasing number of unanticipated global health risks that will sweep large parts of the world before they are contained. Existing preventable illnesses like malaria and diarrheal diseases that currently claim over 13 million lives a year will get even worse as pollution, a lack of clean water, and increasing urban population density all contribute to rising mortality. Health will be an area critical to international development objectives and needed new expertise, ideas, and technologies.

The fourth issue is *the rise of the megacity*. By 2007 over half the world's population will live in cities and, more starkly, one-third of the world will be living in urban slums. Of the world's twenty megacities, fourteen will be in the developing world and will be desperately in need of basic health and education services, energy, and jobs to maintain any hope of a decent life. Opportunities to help support these cities in meeting the needs of their growing poor populations will abound.

The fifth issue is *remittances*. Over $250 billion is sent back home by migrant workers around the world. Much of this goes back to developing countries. Development will continue to focus on how these remittance transfers can be harnessed to build a better life for the recipients and bring them access to capital and hopefully a more sustainable livelihood. Efforts will be made to reach these recipients with banking services aided by cellular technology. Africa is already one of the fastest-growing cell phone markets in the world. India is adding millions of cell phone users and bank accounts each year.

The sixth and final issue is *peace and security*. The rise of religious fundamentalism and ethnic conflict will create the need for significant assistance aimed at relief and reconstruction as well as conflict prevention and mediation. The staggering figures for unemployed youths will fuel tension and have a negative impact on security for both civilians and global business. NGOs and businesses that can help build peace and rebuild communities will be greatly needed.

International development is merging with globalization to create new challenges and new opportunities. It is an important and exciting career path to consider, and one that brings individual growth, expansive networks, and significant job satisfaction.

Careers in Relief

PATRICIA L. DELANEY

Patricia L. Delaney, *a 1990 graduate of the School of Foreign Service at Georgetown University and the recipient of a PhD in anthropology from the University of California, Los Angeles, is an assistant professor of sociology and anthropology at Saint Michael's College, Vermont. She has also taught as an adjunct professor in the Master in Foreign Service Program at Georgetown University; was a country director in the Peace Corps in East Timor; and served as social science adviser to the Office of Foreign Disaster Assistance and as technical adviser to the Office of Population, Health, and Nutrition, both at the U.S. Agency for International Development.*

ALTHOUGH THERE ARE major differences between the effects of natural disasters and those of complex humanitarian emergencies, the six major sectors of assistance are largely the same. The first is *search and rescue.* This activity takes place during the first hours or days after a disaster event. Typically, highly trained professionals such as firefighters and emergency medical technicians are involved in this phase. As in any emergency situation, logisticians must also ensure the rapid arrival of staff, equipment, and supplies.

The second sector of assistance is *health care.* The provision of emergency health care can take the form of triage, providing immediate assistance to combatants and noncombatants during conflict. It also includes the temporary provision of regular health care for those persons who are temporarily relocated (in evacuation centers, refugee camps, or other shelters). Water and sanitation is an especially important component in these situations. Many emergency health workers are trained as nurses or doctors, or are recipients of master's in public health degrees, although other support staff are often needed to provide logistical, financial, or information-gathering assistance.

The third sector is *shelter*. The provision of emergency shelter (tents, plastic sheeting, communal facilities) also takes place in the immediate aftermath of a disaster. People who are displaced from their homes, due to political violence or natural events such as earthquakes and floods, receive shelter or the materials to construct shelter. They often also receive necessary household goods such as linens and cooking supplies. Shelter staff workers tend to need a strong background or skill base in logistics and often have some training in construction or engineering.

The fourth sector is *food security*. The provision of emergency rations, cooking oil, grains, and supplemental feeding for the malnourished are the most typical activities in the food security area. In some long-term emergencies, food security programs often resemble agricultural development projects, with the distribution of seeds and tools. Many of the staff who work in food distribution are generalists, although persons with skills in logistics and social assessment are also needed (to determine the types of rations and culturally appropriate mechanisms for distribution).

The fifth sector is *conflict resolution and protection*. These projects are most often seen in the wake of complex humanitarian emergencies, although the protection of women and girls from sexual violence, the prevention of looting, and the like also take place after natural disasters. Typical projects include community workshops in conflict resolution, counseling services for victims of violence, and the capacity building of local security enforcers. Many staff in this sector have experience in law, law enforcement, counseling, or political science. Protection is also a cross-cutting theme that many generalists incorporate into all projects.

The sixth sector is *long-term relief*. These are the development activities such as education or capacity building that often are needed in protracted emergencies such as civil wars. Quite often, the target population is refugees or internally displaced persons. Although these activities are implemented by relief agencies, they often more closely resemble development than traditional relief. They aim to decrease dependency on external assistance and to ease the transition for beneficiaries after the emergency ends. Many staff members working on these projects have been trained as development practitioners and may have little experience with the provision of relief per se.

CROSS-CUTTING THEMES IN RELIEF AND DEVELOPMENT

In addition to the various sectors in relief and development, a variety of cross-cutting themes are important in virtually every development project. Sometimes organizations rely on technical experts to integrate these important issues. More often, however, generalists are expected to incorporate these principles themselves or to call on colleagues who can do so. Three of the most common themes are gender, participation, and sustainability.

In years past, the issue of gender was often addressed as Women in Development, an approach that aimed to correct past mistakes of exclusion through the explicit inclusion of women. Some programs, such as Girl's Education and Women's Empowerment projects, continue to follow this model. Increasingly, however, development practice is moving toward the inclusion of a Gender and Development (GAD) approach. Projects using a GAD lens look carefully at the roles and responsibilities of women and men, and girls and boys, before and during project activities. The goal is to include culturally and gender-appropriate activities. In one example, this has meant the training of both men and women to serve as peer educators about family planning (instead of the previous pattern of only working with women). In relief work, GAD activities have included distribution of food relief to women, because they are likelier than men to provide resources to children and the family. Technical experts in this area do things such as gender analysis and gender training.

The issue of participation is sometimes also referred to as stakeholder consultation (by groups such as the World Bank) or client-oriented design (e.g., by USAID). This issue is a result of the growing awareness that earlier development activities often failed to reach their objectives because they did not meet the real needs of people on the ground. Most development projects now include some form of stakeholder involvement and participation, although the quality and quantity of such participation varies widely. The goal of participation is both to increase "buy-in" on the part of beneficiaries and also to better target interventions. Activities stemming from this concept include participatory rural appraisal and other participatory diagnostic tools. Though direct participation is often difficult during the acute emergency phase, relief agencies are increasingly incorporating participatory methods in disaster planning and disaster prevention activities. Technical experts in this area often conduct institutional analyses for implementing agencies and also conduct training sessions for field and headquarters staff.

The need for sustainability, or the ability of a program to continue to operate after donor agencies have finished their work, is increasingly seen as a given in international development. Donors and implementing agencies now regularly incorporate mechanisms such as cost recovery (e.g., fees for services at health clinics) in order to work toward long-term sustainability. In the relief field, most agencies have worked toward building national capacity in disaster-prone countries, including famine early warning systems, climate forecasting, and the training of local search-and-rescue teams.

WHERE IS YOUR BASE? HEADQUARTERS VERSUS THE FIELD

Virtually every actor in international relief and development maintains a presence at both the field level and headquarters. Not surprisingly, the work that staff members are expected to do and the skills that are required vary greatly in these different environments. Despite the differences, many workers move back and forth between headquarters and field positions over the course of their career. Some development agencies explicitly require this kind of rotation so that people have a chance to observe both perspectives.

> **Many workers move back and forth between headquarters and field positions over the course of their career.**

Although they are sometimes located at the village or community level, staff working "in the field" are most often located in the national capital or in a provincial center or town. Nonetheless, these positions usually feel much closer to "the field," and most staff members spend extended periods of time immersed in the culture in which they are working. Staffing profiles usually include both expatriates and local hires. Daily work is often conducted in the local language, although reports to headquarters are usually in the official working language of the home organization (often English). Field workers typically report that their biggest challenges are managing relationships with headquarters and adapting to the frequent scarcity of resources. Conversely, they report that the biggest benefit to working at this level is their deep relationship with beneficiaries and other stakeholders. They also enjoy seeing the often-immediate positive impact of their work at the local level. There is no such thing as typical work in the field, and good problem-solving skills and flexibility are key. Field staff are expected to do everything from receiving and processing equipment and supplies (e.g., making sure computers for a training project make it through customs) to conducting periodic evaluations of ongoing projects.

Staff members at headquarters tend to find themselves in a larger, more specialized, and compartmentalized environment. Though they sometimes feel somewhat removed from "the field," they are much closer to the decision-making and policy-setting processes. They spend most of their time at headquarters, attending meetings and preparing reports. They also conduct periodic visits to the field for training, oversight, and new project development activities. These headquarters staffers often report that their biggest challenge is managing what is often a vast bureaucracy and staying focused on the ultimate client: the beneficiary. Conversely, they report that the most rewarding part of working at headquarters is the ability to closely observe, and sometimes influence, the policymaking process. The greater scale on which most headquarters staff members work guarantees that any decisions they do make are likely to have an impact on far greater numbers of people than their colleagues in the field. Important skills for headquarters staff include excellent writing and data synthesis skills, strong oral presentation skills, and adeptness at navigating the complex institutional environment. Typical duties include strategic planning, monitoring and evaluation, work plan development, and oversight of portfolios of development projects.

WHAT DO YOU ACTUALLY DO? THE PROJECT CYCLE IN RELIEF AND DEVELOPMENT

The actual cycle of a relief project depends on many things, including the sector, region, and previous experience of development. Nonetheless, four key steps are common to most projects. The first step is *needs assessment*. Assessments can take a variety of forms, such as epidemiological studies for child health projects, detailed participatory appraisals for natural resource management activities, or "windshield" assessments of damages immediately following a natural disaster. Stakeholder analysis is a critical component in any needs assessment.

The second step is *project design.* Following the needs assessment process, staff members, usually working in teams, complete the actual project design, work plan, and budget. They work to reach consensus among the many stakeholders on topics such as project objectives, risk assessments, and performance monitoring plans.

The third step is *implementation.* This is usually the longest phase in the development cycle, the period in which services or benefits are actually delivered to clients and beneficiaries. For health projects, this phase might include both training of HIV/AIDS outreach staff and the refurbishment of laboratory facilities in a local hospital. Important elements of any implementation include realistic scheduling and budgeting, clear roles and responsibilities, and open mechanisms for feedback and readjustment.

The fourth step is *monitoring and evaluation.* Monitoring generally refers to the oversight of activities during the actual phase of project implementation, whereas evaluation refers to the ex-post analysis of effects, challenges, and lessons learned. This work can be either qualitative or quantitative, or both. The work at this phase is often conducted by a combination of field and headquarters staff members as well as objective outsiders such as consultants.

FINAL THOUGHTS

As you move forward in your career as a relief professional, I encourage you to remember that one feeling, event, or experience that led to your involvement. Your work as a professional will be much easier and, in my experience, far more rewarding if you are true to your ideals, hopes, and aspirations, for both yourself and the endeavor at hand.

13

Nonprofit and Educational Organizations

Careers in Nonprofits

Denis Dragovic

Denis Dragovic *is a 2000 graduate of the Masters of Science in Foreign Service Program at Georgetown University. He is currently serving as the country director for CHF International in Iraq, his third posting to that country. Since graduating from Georgetown University, he has worked with not-for-profit contractors, for-profit development companies, and humanitarian organizations in Asia, the Middle East, and Africa.*

THE NOT-FOR-PROFIT WORLD has undergone a transformation over the past decade and in particular over the last few years. The sector has seen a tremendous growth spurt, combined with a much-needed infusion of professionalism, while at the same time being confronted by a number of ethical challenges that will forge the face of the industry in the coming decades. Entering the field now, upon graduation, is a far more daunting challenge then five or fifteen years ago. Employers' expectations and competition from other applicants are far more rigorous. Whereas a bachelor's degree was all that was required "back in the day," now a master's degree from a well-known university along with some field experience is considered bare minimum.

As more money continues to pour toward humanitarian and development aid efforts, the organizations implementing these projects have grown into big businesses; some, such as the United States–based World

Vision, see their annual revenue exceed $1 billion. Hand in hand with such growth comes the need to develop institutional structures and systems that rival those of similar-sized corporations, particularly the need to recruit more qualified professionals and fewer well-intentioned idealists. Not only have existing organizations grown and turned professional but many new entities also have emerged as players. These new not-for-profits, although competing for the same nongovernmental organization (NGO) pool of funds, are adopting more aggressive "corporate" tactics in an effort to win projects. The result is a divided industry with many different and sometimes hidden facets that are often hard for an outsider to negotiate. This essay attempts to decode the industry for newcomers. It is written to help the reader make well-informed decisions before deciding to apply for jobs in the not-for-profit field.

Entering the field now, upon graduation, is a far more daunting challenge then five or fifteen years ago. Employers' expectations and competition from other applicants are far more rigorous.

In general there are five distinctly different groupings of NGOs:

1. humanitarian organizations (e.g., International Committee of the Red Cross, CARE, IRC, Save the Children, MSF),
2. development NGO (e.g., Malaria Consortium, Planned Parenthood),
3. not-for-profit contractors (e.g., International Relief and Development, Research Triangle Institute),
4. advocacy organizations (e.g., Human Rights Watch, Freedom House, Amnesty International), and
5. donor organizations (e.g., Ford Foundation, Bill and Melinda Gates Foundation).

The character, salary, institutional structure, career prospects, and type of work are very different from one to the other. Knowing what you are after will help you choose the category for which you are best suited.

Humanitarian Organizations

The humanitarian organization is often the face of the not-for-profit world. We are all familiar with household names such as CARE, Oxfam, and World Vision. These organizations are often embedded in our own communities; they raise money through public campaigns, hold advocacy positions, and send young people out to high-profile humanitarian crises to "do good." They are truly international, with subsidiaries or member organizations established throughout—mainly—the Western world. Over the years, the level of professionalism has increased, resulting in higher employer expectations as well as higher salaries. Of the humanitarian organizations, there are two types: those that value the concept of volunteerism, and those that seek career professionals.

Over the years, the level of professionalism has increased, resulting in higher employer expectations as well as higher salaries.

The volunteer agencies, such as Médecins Sans Frontières and GOAL (an Irish NGO), take on large numbers of eager, young, well-qualified but inexperienced people to work in their far-flung operations. The pay is dismal, starting as low as several hundred dollars a month, though the spirit of camaraderie, the training opportunities, and the organizational support are great (food and shared accommodations are provided). These organizations are a good stepping-stone for people who want to get into the field or for those concerned about the ethics that their organization will uphold.

Iraq is a prime example of a humanitarian mission fraught with ethical issues that has divided the NGO community. Some NGOs chose not to accept U.S. government funding, feeling that to do so would be tantamount to being party to the conflict. Other NGOs, recognizing the humanitarian imperative, chose to leave as soon as it became clear that there would not be a humanitarian crisis resulting from the initial invasion. Still others accepted U.S. government funds and signed on to projects that required them to be "force multipliers" and provided intelligence for the military, believing that the results on the ground are what count.

The second type of humanitarian organization seeks career professionals. These organizations pay monthly salaries ranging from $2,000 to $3,500 for those at starting levels to $8,000 to $9,000 for experienced professionals. Over the years, this group of organizations—which includes the International Rescue Committee, Save the Children, and Mercy Corps—has worked to improve its staff retention rates by providing retirement packages, permanent job placement, and training opportunities. As a result, the caliber of applicants and new hires has substantially increased. Technical expertise is required for most program positions in sectors such as health, water, sanitation, and shelter as well as a master's degree either in the relevant field or a general degree such as international relations or public policy.

For aspiring managers, the situation is not as clear-cut. The greatest failing of the industry to date and one that has led to multimillion-dollar losses is a lack of strong management skills. Promotions based simply upon years of experience, rather than specific managerial experience, can result in poor leadership, low levels of oversight, and big losses. Some organizations have been reluctant to recognize management as a specialty, but this is changing. Today, more and more donors are wary of funding poorly run operations.

To find postings for job vacancies in humanitarian organizations, ReliefWeb (www.reliefweb.org/vacancies) is the one-stop shop. Alternatively, many organizations also advertise in the *Guardian Weekly*. Not every job of each organization is posted on ReliefWeb. Sometimes, due to the sheer number of postings, job advertisements are hard to find. Visiting an organization's official job website is another way to find the right job.

DEVELOPMENT NONGOVERNMENTAL ORGANIZATIONS

There are two main differences between development and humanitarian organizations—the countries where they work, and the type of work. Development organizations often work in safer locations on longer-term projects, helping a country or community to help itself in fields such as good governance, human development, and civil society. Most such jobs are multiyear family postings, which result in fewer job opportunities for newcomers into the field. Also, often due to the higher capacity of local staff, development jobs are highly specialized and require several years of experience and/or substantial educational qualifications. Nevertheless, for qualified candidates with interests in a particular country or field, opportunities do exist—if not through direct employment, then through internships or volunteering, potentially as interns or volunteers, a great way to enter a field that often leads to permanent positions (to be discussed below).

To find jobs with development organizations, there are a number of websites that require subscription, but www.developmentex.com or www.dev-zone.org are good places to start. Another approach is to check government websites, such as those for the U.S. Agency for International Development (www.usaid.gov) or the U.K. Department for International Development (www.dfid.gov.uk), see which projects are currently being implemented, and write directly to the implementing organization.

NOT-FOR-PROFIT CONTRACTORS

This category of organizations is the newcomer to the field. Most successful not-for-profit contractors are less than a decade old, have roots in the for-profit field, and are aggressive in their approach. These organizations are often funded from U.S. government departments, and therefore they do not do a great deal of fund-raising. They rarely hold an advocacy position. Nevertheless, these are the organizations that often remain in areas of insecurity and deliver results when others have left. Though humanitarian organizations eschew the use of armed guards or military escorts, not-for-profit contractors that work in highly insecure environments adopt whatever security protocols are required to get the job done. While I worked in Iraq, I moved from a humanitarian organization that decided to close its offices to a not-for-profit contractor. Whereas with the humanitarian organization our security entailed good relations with neighbors, a guard down the road armed with a whistle and some regular practice runs over the back fence; the not-for-profit contractor purchased armored sport utility vehicles, used a close protection security detail, and installed large concrete walls around the compound.

For people looking to combine a corporate experience with the chance to make a positive difference in the lives of people in far-flung places, not-for profit contractors may be the best bet. Salaries with these organizations are often high—but they are based on experience and the willingness to risk life and limb! In Iraq, remuneration for senior staff can reach as high as $200,000 to $300,000 a year. Jobs with these contractors are advertised on the same websites listed above.

ADVOCACY ORGANIZATIONS

Advocacy organizations offer a completely different experience. Freedom House, Transparency International, International Crisis Group, Human

Rights Watch, and Amnesty International as well as indigenous single-issue advocacy organizations provide opportunities for those interested in political analysis, report writing, and research. These organizations work hand in hand with humanitarian organizations to ensure that human rights violations are brought to the attention of the international community. Advocacy organizations also work independently in many countries, pursuing their own mandate of reducing corruption or highlighting environmental issues. The list is long, given that in every country there are civil society groups tackling local issues. Working for a small advocacy groups as a volunteer is a good way to obtain the experience necessary for application to larger international groups.

DONOR ORGANIZATIONS

Donor organizations are experiencing many changes that arise simply from their sheer size. The Bill and Melinda Gates Foundation, for example, manages a portfolio of over $30 billion. Its size gives it unprecedented influence in tackling specific issues holistically. For example, it is foreseeable that a cure for malaria will be found through research funded by the Gates Foundation. Large foundations, unlike humanitarian or development agencies, can tackle the root causes of problems rather than responding piecemeal or short term. However, working for a donor will not necessarily bring you face to face on a daily basis with the people or the communities you hope to serve. What they do permit is an opportunity to have a foot in both worlds—some short-term field opportunities alternating with strategic planning in a major urban area.

EXPECTATIONS

Given the changing environment in the international not-for-profit field, expectations can differ greatly from reality. The old perception of the typical aid worker as a free spirit distributing food to the hungry no longer applies. Today's reality is very different, even for entry-level jobs. A large portion of a typical day consists of office work—writing reports, attending meetings, reviewing proposals, and working on budgets. Though the day-to-day reach into a community is still a core aspect of this career, in some cases it can be overwhelmed by huge budgets and large expatriate staff. In such situations, sometimes the opportunity to respond to grassroots-driven requests is missed. Newcomers to field posts must be clear about what they are seeking—relative isolation and grass-roots experience, or the adrenaline of a high-profile emergency and expertise in that arena.

One particular frustration in the field is the need for men and women who are jacks-of-all-trades. Those posted in remote locations need many skills beyond their "job description"—and that includes the usual security savvy, first aid techniques, vehicle management, budget oversight, and radio usage; or the unusual, such as kidnap and ransom response, attendance at staff funerals, and dealing with local and foreign governments. Only within government and United Nations postings is the institutional structure so robust that international staff are not required to move beyond their job description. And that can be a frustration, too.

COMPENSATION AND CAREER PATH

The compensation for entry-level personnel can vary from several hundred dollars a month to hundreds of thousands of dollars a year. Most organizations also offer a pension plan, comprehensive insurance coverage (and high-risk insurance in countries such as Iraq and Afghanistan), regular training opportunities (both internal and external), and rest and relaxation leave (up to every two months) as well as home leave. Although entry-level salaries may not compare well with Wall Street, once one considers tax-free income (depending upon your nationality and income level), accommodation allowance, cost of living (I have lived in places where the monthly expenditure was no more than $60), and rest-and-relaxation leaves, overall compensation packages are very competitive—and possibly more necessary! Given the lifestyle, however, there is a high turnover, especially in the humanitarian field, and there are plenty of opportunities for promotion.

APPLICATION ADVICE

Breaking into the not-for-profit world has become a very difficult proposition. The competition is fierce, and many people applying have Peace Corps or similar field experience, language skills, and technical qualifications. Without some field experience, it is now almost impossible to get that first job. This explains the popularity and frequency of volunteering in the not-for-profit world. Volunteering is a great way to get a taste for the work, gain some experience, and become a known quantity by demonstrating skills. Many organizations have structured volunteer or internship programs.

Without some field experience, it is now almost impossible to get that first job. This explains the popularity and frequency of volunteering in the not-for-profit world.

Sending out application letters can sometimes help with smaller organizations, but with larger organizations, knowing someone who will support your application is a big help. Because most interviews for entry-level field positions are held over the telephone, being a known quantity helps people feel comfortable with a hiring decision that may have to be made sight unseen. A more radical approach is to simply save enough cash, make your way out to the field, and present yourself in the hope that you will be the right person at the right time!

ARE YOU THE RIGHT PERSON FOR THE JOB?

One of the larger costs associated with the international aid industry is the recruitment, training, and placement of expatriate staff. Finding the right person who will stay and contribute for the duration of the contract can be very difficult. Some years ago, I was posted to Wau, Sudan, where I lived alone in a decrepit old house, with sparse furniture, cement floors, no kitchen, no electricity, no running water, and a curfew at 7 p.m. The town was surrounded by opposition forces, making food scarce; there was poor medical care; sanitation consisted of a pit latrine; and water for washing had to be trucked to my house. Living alone with only a book and kerosene lantern for entertainment can be challenging but also very rewarding and even life-changing.

Each posting is unique, and you should not hesitate to ask the recruiter what life is like or whether there are opportunities to get away. Being able to take time away from work is the key to remaining focused and being effective. In some circumstances, particularly high-profile emergencies, entertainment overload can arrive via busloads of young Western expatriates who create a social life unmatched anywhere. It is not only comfort, or the lack thereof, that can make or break someone. While visiting the offices of another organization in Sudan, several dozen horseback riders, known as the *murahaleen*, returned from a slave and cattle raid, surrounded the compound, and began to shoot into the air and into the walls. We lay on the floor of the office for a quarter of an hour. The gunmen were not a direct threat, but they were clearly intent on harassing foreigners. One person in our group was so traumatized by the incident that she was evacuated two days later and has not returned to this line of work since. It is hard to know in advance whether you can work under fire, so to speak, until it actually happens, but being honest about your threshold for insecurity will certainly help to determine what jobs to apply for, and where.

Living alone with only a book and kerosene lantern for entertainment can be challenging but also very rewarding and even life-changing.

Your interest in and acceptance of other cultures is the key to being successful and enjoying your post or being attacked or expelled. Doing background research on the local culture before applying is a must, if only to learn the norms and avoid "surprises"—such as discovering that alcohol is illegal or women drivers are frowned upon. Too often, new hires arrive expecting to create change in a people or a culture rather than being willing to simply adjust and work within the systems that exist and doing what can be done, one step at a time.

For all the challenges, working in the nonprofit world is a great experience—enjoyable and rewarding. I encourage people to give at least some years of their life to this line of work. The people you meet, the places you see, and the insights you gain will last the rest of your life.

RESOURCE LISTINGS

Academy for Educational Development

Founded in 1961, the Academy for Educational Development (AED) is an independent, nonprofit service organization committed to addressing human development needs in the United States and in 150 other countries throughout the world. The AED's major activity issues include health, education, the environment, and youth development. The AED's activities are supported through grants and contracts from international organizations, U.S. and foreign government agencies, foundations, and private contributions. Under these contracts and grants, the AED operates programs in collaboration with policy leaders, NGOs and community-based organizations, businesses, governmental agencies, international multilateral and bilateral funders, and schools, colleges, and universities.

In partnership with its clients, the AED seeks to meet today's social, economic, and environmental challenges through education and human resource development; to apply state-of-the-art education, training, research and technology, management, behavioral analysis, and social marketing techniques to solve problems; and to improve knowledge and skills as the most effective means for stimulating growth, reducing poverty, and promoting democratic and humanitarian ideals.

When the AED hires, it looks for excellent organization and analytical skills, several years of international or domestic experience related to its programs, good language ability, solid research and writing skills, and a master's degree in international relations, education, journalism, communications, or a similar field.

> Academy for Educational Development
> 1825 Connecticut Avenue, NW
> Washington, DC 20009
> Tel.: 202-884-8000
> Fax: 202-884-8413
> www.aed.org

Africa-America Institute

The Africa-America Institute (AAI) was founded in 1953 to help Africans build human capacity through education and training programs. Today, the AAI continues to pursue this vision through a portfolio of programs aimed at both educating Africans and educating Americans about Africa. The AAI's African Higher Education and Training programs have provided university, graduate-level, and professional training scholarship programs for Africans in fundamental capacity-building fields, including agriculture, business and finance, education, government, health care, science, and technology. The AAI's education, outreach, and policy programs have created opportunities for policymakers, business executives, government officials, and opinion leaders from Africa and the United States to gain a more complete understanding of each other and to explore, debate, and work collaboratively on issues of mutual interest.

The AAI is a multiracial, multiethnic, nonprofit organization with headquarters in New York and offices in Washington, South Africa, and Mozambique. Through its alumni, it has an on-the-ground presence in over fifty African countries. Its work is made possible through funds provided by the U.S. government, African governments, private foundations, corporate donors, multilateral institutions, and individuals.

> Africa-America Institute (Headquarters)
> Suite 1706, 420 Lexington Avenue
> New York, NY 10170-0002
> Tel.: 212-949-5666
> Fax: 212-682-6174
> e-mail: aainy@aaionline.org
> www.aaionline.org

> Suite 400, 1625 Massachusetts Avenue, NW
> Washington, DC 20036
> Tel.: 202-667-5636
> Fax: 202-265-6332

Africare

Africare works in partnership with African communities to achieve healthy and productive societies. Over the course of its history, Africare has become a leader among private, charitable U.S. organizations assisting Africa. It is the oldest and largest African American organization in the field.

Africare's programs address needs in two principal areas: food security and agriculture, and HIV/AIDS. Africare also supports water resource development, environmental management, literacy and vocational training, microenterprise development, civil society development, governance initiatives, and emergency humanitarian aid. Since its founding in 1970, Africare has delivered more than $675 million in assistance—over 2,000 projects—to thirty-six countries Africa-wide.

Africare is headquartered in Washington but has more than twenty field offices in Africa. The most commonly available overseas positions with Africare overseas are country representatives, project coordinators, and administrative assistants. Africa also uses short-term consultants, especially in the areas of child survival, HIV/AIDs, and evaluation and monitoring. Vacancies are listed on Africare's website; qualified candidates may also send their resumes for Africare's databank to be considered when specific vacancies do occur.

Director of Human Resources
Africare
440 R Street, NW
Washington, DC 20001-1935
e-mail: resumes@africare.org
www.africare.org

AIESEC

The International Association of Students in Economics and Business Management (AIESEC) is the international platform for young people to discover and develop their potential. Present in over 1,100 universities in 100 countries, AIESEC is one of the world's largest student organizations, and its members strive to have a positive impact in society. Toward this aim, AIESEC runs more than 350 conferences, provides over 4,000 work abroad opportunities, and offers over 5,000 leadership positions to its members each year. Together with a focus on building personal networks and exploring the direction and ambition of their future, AIESEC has an innovative approach to engaging and developing young people.

AIESEC's Global Internship program runs internships anywhere from two to eighteen months in any of AIESEC's hundred-country network for students or recent graduates. Positions are in one of four categories: management (e.g., business, finance, marketing, and human resources), technical (e.g., engineering, information technology), education (e.g., teaching a second language) and developmental (e.g., government or NGOs).

AIESEC National Staff
127 West 26th Street, 10th Floor
New York, NY 10001
Tel.: 212-757-3774
Fax: 212-757-4062
www.aiesecus.org

American Baptist Churches in the USA

An evangelical denomination founded in 1814, American Baptist Churches in the USA, through its Board of International Ministries, provides a variety of services designated to help meet basic human needs in developing countries. Assistance is extended in community development, food production, public health and medicine, family planning, social welfare, and disaster relief. The overseas mission programs of the Board of International Ministries use about $15 million and employ about 120 people in development-related positions. New hires are expected to have at least a master's-level academic background plus some professional experience.

American Baptist Churches in the USA
Board of International Ministries
P.O. Box 851
Valley Forge, PA 19482
Tel.: 610-768-2000 or 800-ABC-3USA
www.abc-usa.org

American Council on Education

Founded in 1918, the American Council on Education (ACE) is the nation's unifying voice for higher education. ACE serves as a consensus leader on key higher education issues and seeks to influence public policy through advocacy, research, and program initiatives. ACE's areas of focus include access, success, equity, and diversity; institutional effectiveness; lifelong learning; and internationalization.

American Council on Education
One Dupont Circle, NW
Washington, DC 20035
Tel.: 202-939-9300
e-mail: resume@ace.nche.edu
www.acenet.edu

American Friends Service Committee

The American Friends Service Committee (AFSC) carries out service, development, social justice, and peace programs throughout the world. Founded by Quakers in 1917 to provide conscientious objectors with an opportunity to aid civilian war victims, AFSC's work attracts the support and partnership of people of many races, religions, and cultures. The AFSC thus is a Quaker organization that includes people of various faiths who are committed to social justice, peace, and humanitarian service. Announcements of job openings in various locations throughout the organization are posted on its website. Internships and paid fellowships are also available.

AFSC National Office
1501 Cherry Street
Philadelphia, PA 19102
Tel.: 215-241-7000

Fax: 215-241-7275
e-mail: afscinfo@afsc.org
www.afsc.org

American Society of International Law

The American Society of International Law (ASIL) is a nonprofit, nonpartisan, educational membership organization. It was founded in 1906, chartered by the U.S. Congress in 1950, and has held Category II Consultative Status to the Economic and Social Council of the United Nations since 1993. ASIL's mission is to foster the study of international law and promote the establishment and maintenance of international relations on the basis of law and justice. ASIL's 4,000 members (from nearly a hundred countries) comprise attorneys, academics, corporate counsel, judges, representatives of governments and NGOs, international civil servants, students, and others interested in international law.

ASIL provides a forum for the exchange of views on international law; it publishes books, periodicals, and occasional papers; and it sponsors research on a broad range of current international law topics. Outreach to the public and press is another main focus of ASIL's activity. It cosponsors the Philip C. Jessup International Law Moot Court Competition.

ASIL has a permanent, full-time staff of thirteen, and in 2006, it had five job openings. With some departmental exceptions, ASIL looks for a background in international law, a law degree (in some cases a JD), and at least two to three years' relevant experience. The ASIL internship program enables students to acquire practical experience in international law research and outreach activities.

American Society of International Law
2223 Massachusetts Avenue, NW
Washington, DC 20008
Tel.: 202-939-6000
www.asil.org/careers/jobopportunities.html

Amnesty International

Amnesty International (AI) is a Nobel Peace Prize–winning organization dedicated to the defense of human rights throughout the world. It maintains a global network of affiliated volunteer organizations and counts more than 2.2 million members, supporters, and subscribers in more than 150 countries. AI's mission is to undertake research and action focused on preventing and ending grave abuses of the rights to physical and mental integrity, freedom of conscience and expression, and freedom from discrimination, within the context of its work to promote all human rights.

Employment opportunities are with the International Secretariat of AI and are mostly based in the United Kingdom. The International Secretariat is AI's global center for research, campaigning, legal, lobbying, and membership work. The Secretariat works with AI's national sections and structures in over fifty countries (including the United Kingdom), together creating a worldwide movement promoting human rights for all and actively opposing human rights violations.

> Amnesty International USA
> 5 Penn Plaza, 14th Floor
> New York, NY 10001
> www.amnestyusa.org/jobs.

Arab American Institute

The Arab American Institute (AAI) represents the policy and community interests of Arab Americans throughout the United States and strives to promote Arab American participation in the U.S. electoral system. The AAI focuses on two areas: campaigns and elections and policy formation and research. The AAI strives to serve as a central resource to government officials, the media, political leaders, and community groups and a variety of public policy issues that concern Arab Americans and U.S.–Arab relations.

As the only national organization that promotes Arab American participation in the U.S. electoral system, the AAI has developed a host of services, from voter education to liaison with the national parties, to support the Arab American community's activities. It is also the leading policy and research organization on the domestic and policy concerns of Arab Americans. Through ongoing meetings with members of the administration and Congress, a variety of publications and issue briefs, media, and direct member mobilization, the AAI maintains a strong presence among policymakers who have an impact on the issues of concern to Arab Americans.

> Arab American Institute
> Suite 601, 1600 K Street, NW
> Washington, DC 20006
> Tel.: 202-429-9210
> Fax: 202-429-9214
> www.aaiusa.org/about/employment

Ashoka

Ashoka is the global association of the world's leading social entrepreneurs—men and women with system-changing solutions for the world's most urgent social problems. Since 1981, it has elected over 1,800 leading social entrepreneurs as Ashoka Fellows, providing them with living stipends, professional support, and access to a global network of peers in more than sixty countries. In addition to supporting social entrepreneurs as individuals, Ashoka brings them together in communities to help leverage their impact and helps build the infrastructure and financial systems needed to support the growth of the citizen sector and facilitate the spread of social innovation globally.

People at Ashoka work on highly complex, long-term projects focused on social change. They are constantly inventing new approaches, forging new partnerships, and creating new institutions—all aimed at transforming the global citizen sector. For entrepreneurial people at all career and life stages, Ashoka offers opportunities to address social change on a big scale, and it affords the chance to develop and grow as a member of a global team. Ashoka is designed to be a long-term professional home for entrepreneurial people who care about enabling the strongest networks and partnerships for social change. Ashoka's internal structure is designed to mirror the life stages of entrepreneurial development that team members are expected to move along over time. Ashoka allows staff at all career stages to move within the organization, as the needs of the institution and their own interests and abilities dictate.

> Ashoka Global Headquarters
> Suite 2000, 1700 North Moore Street
> Arlington, VA 22209
> Tel.: 703-527-8300
> Fax: 703-527-8383
> e-mail: info@ashoka.org
> www.ashoka.org/careers

Asia Foundation

The Asia Foundation is a nonprofit NGO committed to the development of a peaceful, prosperous, just, and open Asia-Pacific region. The foundation supports programs in Asia that help improve governance, law, and civil society; women's empowerment; economic reform and development; and international relations. Drawing on fifty years of experience in

Asia, the foundation collaborates with private and public partners to support leadership and institutional development, exchanges, and policy research.

With a network of seventeen offices throughout Asia, an office in Washington, and a headquarters in San Francisco, the foundation addresses these issues on both the country and regional levels. In 2006, the foundation provided more than $53 million in program support and distributed 920,000 books and educational materials valued at $30 million throughout Asia. Employment opportunities in the United States and overseas are posted on the organization's website.

> Asia Foundation
> P.O. Box 193223
> 465 California Street, 9th Floor
> San Francisco, CA 94104
> Tel.: 415-982-4640
> Fax: 415-392-8863
> www.asiafoundation.org

Asia Society

The Asia Society is an international organization dedicated to strengthening relationships and deepening understanding among the peoples of Asia and the United States. Founded in 1956 by John D. Rockefeller III, the society reaches audiences around the world through its headquarters in New York and centers in Houston, Los Angeles, San Francisco, Washington, Hong Kong, Manila, Melbourne, Mumbai, and Shanghai. A nonprofit, nonpartisan educational organization, the society provides a forum for building awareness of the more than thirty countries broadly defined as the Asia-Pacific region. Job opportunities are posted on the Asia Society website.

> Asia Society
> 725 Park Avenue
> New York, NY 10021
> Tel.: 212-288-6400
> e-mail: hr@asiasoc.org
> www.asiasociety.org

CARE

CARE is a leading humanitarian organization fighting global poverty. It places special focus on working alongside poor women because, equipped with the proper resources, women have the power to help whole families and entire communities escape poverty. Women are at the heart of CARE's community-based efforts to improve basic education, prevent the spread of HIV/AIDS, increase access to clean water and sanitation, expand economic opportunity, and protect natural resources. CARE also delivers emergency aid to survivors of war and natural disasters, and helps people rebuild their lives.

The CARE family employs over 12,000 people worldwide. CARE employees can be found in more than sixty-five countries across the globe and the staff at CARE USA headquarters office represent over forty different nationalities. Applications are only accepted online.

> CARE
> 151 Ellis Street
> Atlanta, GA 30303
> www.care.org/careers

Carter Center
The Carter Center is a nonprofit NGO devoted to advancing peace and human rights worldwide. Founded by former U.S. president Jimmy Carter and his wife, Rosalynn, in 1982, it is an independently governed part of Emory University in Atlanta. More than 150 staff members implement projects to advance peace and health in more than sixty-five nations. Areas of specialty include human rights, conflict resolution, Latin American and Caribbean affairs, democratization and election monitoring, food production and disease prevention in developing nations, and mental health.

The center's staff are primarily located at its Atlanta offices; however, field offices are occasionally established. Programs are directed by resident experts with intense, specialized preparation in their specialties. A strong academic background, experience addressing real-world problems, foreign language proficiency, and strong communications skills are desired. In the global health programs, many staff have medical or public health training. In addition, staff work in fund-raising, administration, public information, and conferencing.

> Carter Center
> One Copenhill
> 453 Freedom Parkway
> Atlanta, GA 30307
> Fax: 404-420-5145
> www.cartercenter.org

Catholic Relief Services

Catholic Relief Services (CRS) has been the international humanitarian agency of the U.S. Catholic community for over sixty years. Working through local and international offices and an extensive network of partners, CRS operates on five continents and in ninety-nine countries. In helping the poor by first providing direct assistance where needed, and then encouraging people to help with their own development, CRS strives to foster secure, productive, and just communities that enable people to realize their potential.

From its origin as a response to the call to help rebuild a shattered Europe during World War II, CRS has since expanded its programming to provide relief in times of disaster, while also laying the foundation for developing stronger communities for the future. Its overseas programming includes agriculture, community health, education, emergency response, HIV/AIDS, microfinance, peace building, and safety nets. Woven within these programs are common themes that guide CRS decisions and action. These themes—capacity building, food security, gender, and justice—teach communities how to become self-sustaining through tolerance, understanding, and solidarity. In 2005, more than 94 percent of the money CRS spent went to programs that benefit the poor overseas.

In 2006, CRS had 140 international and 115 domestic open positions. The standard qualifications for many of those positions include a master's degree in international development or an equivalent field and at least two to three years experience working in development programs overseas. Program management experience in a developing country—which generally includes implementing and monitoring programs, team management and supervisory experience, and/or financial management—is a plus. Special consideration is given to applicants with advanced foreign language skills in Spanish, French, or Portuguese. Specific job responsibilities vary greatly from one country to another depending on the country program's focus. CRS also offers a one-year fellowship program that places twenty to thirty candidates overseas with various country programs. Many of these fellowships lead to regular positions with CRS.

Department of Human Resources
Catholic Relief Services
209 West Fayette Street
Baltimore, MD 21201
www.crs.org

Church World Service

Founded in 1946, Church World Service (CWS) partners with churches and organizations in more than eighty countries, working to meet human needs and foster self-reliance. CWS works worldwide on behalf of thirty-five Protestant, Anglican, and Orthodox denominations in the United States in programs of social and economic development, emergency response, assistance to refugees, education and advocacy, and ecumenical relationships. In addition to its corporate offices and support services in New York City and Elkhart, Indiana, CWS has regional program offices throughout the United States and Southeast Asia, Africa, Europe, and Latin America.

CWS employs about 350 people in positions both domestically and overseas. Currently, 74 staff and volunteers are working overseas. Additionally, local offices worldwide employ over 900. A sampling of positions includes caseworkers, who work in refugee processing and resettlement, both within the United States and overseas, and country representatives and regional directors, who work in social and economic program development throughout the world. In addition, CWS partners with the Amity Foundation, providing valuable educational development in China. Overseas experience is often necessary, especially in social and economic development, as is appropriate cultural and multilingual ability and experience. Bachelor's and graduate degrees are also preferred.

> Human Resources Department
> Church World Service
> 28606 Phillips Street
> P.O. Box 968
> Elkhart, IN 46515
> Tel.: 574-264-3102
> Fax: 574-266-0087
> e-mail: cwshr@churchworldservice.org
> www.churchworldservice.org

Committee to Protect Journalists

A group of U.S. foreign correspondents created the Committee to Protect Journalists (CPJ) in response to the often-brutal treatment of their foreign colleagues by authoritarian governments and other enemies of independent journalism. By publicly revealing abuses against the press and by acting on behalf of imprisoned and threatened journalists, the CPJ effectively warns journalists and news organizations where attacks on press freedom are occurring. The CPJ organizes vigorous public protests and works through diplomatic channels to effect change. The CPJ publishes articles and news releases; special reports; a biannual magazine, *Dangerous Assignments*; and *Attacks on the Press*, the most comprehensive annual survey of press freedom around the world.

CPJ has a full-time staff of twenty-three at its New York headquarters, including area specialists for each major world region. The CPJ has a Washington representative and consultants stationed around the world. A thirty-five-member board of prominent journalists directs the CPJ's activities.

> Committee to Protect Journalists
> 330 Seventh Ave, 11th Floor
> New York, NY 10001
> Fax: 212-465-9568
> e-mail: jobs@cpj.org.
> www.cpj.org

Council on International Education Exchange

The Council on International Educational Exchange (CIEE), is a nonprofit NGO dedicated to helping people gain understanding, acquire knowledge, and develop skills for living in a globally interdependent and culturally diverse world. Founded in 1947, the CIEE has developed a wide variety of programs and services for students and faculty at secondary through university levels and related constituencies. With professionals in approximately thirty-five countries working to deliver diverse programs and services, the CIEE has become one of the world's leading operators of international exchange programs and related services. Today, the CIEE operates in four broad business areas: college and university programs, secondary school programs, work and travel programs, and teach-abroad programs.

The CIEE is always looking for highly motivated staff members with a strong mission commitment who thrive in a fast-paced, multitasking environment and are energetic and internationally focused. The CIEE frequently has openings for administrative clerical support staff. Entry-level applicants with excellent organizational and communication skills, foreign language ability, and international study or work experience are preferred. Travel opportunities are sometimes available. Most positions are in the Student Services of the Work and Travel divisions; duties include processing program applications and handling information requests. Second languages, overseas experience, and office skills are viewed positively. In September 2007, the CIEE combined its Boston and Portland offices in a new building in Portland, Maine.

Council on International Educational Exchange
7 Custom House Street, 3rd Floor
Portland, ME 04101
Tel.: 800-40-STUDY
Fax: 207-553-7699
www.ciee.org/about/careers.aspx

Ford Foundation
The Ford Foundation aims to advance public welfare by identifying and contributing to the solution of problems of national and international importance. It makes grants primarily to institutions for experimental, demonstration, and development efforts that are likely to produce significant advances within the field of interest. The major portion of the foundation's international budget is devoted to programs in developing countries. These programs include Asset Building and Community Development (economic development and community resource development); Peace and Social Justice (human rights and governance and civil society); and Knowledge, Creativity, and Freedom (education, sexuality, and religion; and media, arts, and culture).

The Ford Foundation has assets of over $12 billion and expends more than $500 million annually in program activities. Work in the international arena takes place in twelve field offices, employing approximately 200 people. These twelve offices in Africa, Asia, Latin America, and Russia enable staff to address problems by supporting those living and working closest to them. Since 1950, to be near the people and organizations it supports, the foundation has maintained overseas offices staffed by a mix of local and foreign nationals. About one-half of its staff is in New York and the rest is overseas. The foundation generally remains in locations outside the United States for an extended period, making grants to people who are running innovative programs in their own societies.

Ford Foundation
320 East 43rd Street
New York, NY 10017
Tel.: 212-573-5000
Fax: 212-351-3677
www.fordfound.org

Freedom House

Founded in 1941, Freedom House is a nonprofit, nonpartisan organization that promotes an engaged U.S. foreign policy, evaluates global human rights conditions, sponsors public education campaigns, facilitates training and other assistance to promote democracy and free market reforms, and provides support for the rule of law, free media, and effective local governance. Headquartered in Washington, Freedom House has affiliate offices in Hungary, Romania, and Ukraine.

Freedom House has domestic, overseas, and intern appointments available. Non–U.S. citizens applying for regular positions based in the United States must possess work authorization, which does not require sponsorship by the employer for a visa. Qualifications vary by position, but generally, a balance of education, work, and field experience and a passion for international affairs, democracy, and human rights issues are sought. Foreign language skills are also required for many positions.

Freedom House
1301 Connecticut Avenue, NW
6th Floor
Washington, DC 20036
Tel.: 202-296-5101
Fax: 202-293-2840
www.freedomhouse.org

German Marshall Fund

The German Marshall Fund of the United States (GMF) is a nonpartisan American public policy and grant-making institution dedicated to promoting greater cooperation and understanding between the United States and Europe. The GMF does this by supporting individuals and institutions working on transatlantic issues, by convening leaders to discuss the most pressing transatlantic themes, and by examining ways in which transatlantic cooperation can address a variety of global policy challenges. In addition, the GMF supports a number of initiatives to strengthen democracies.

Founded in 1972 through a gift from Germany as a permanent memorial to Marshall Plan assistance, the GMF maintains a strong presence on both sides of the Atlantic. In addition to its headquarters in Washington, the GMF has six offices in Europe: Berlin, Bratislava, Paris, Brussels, Belgrade, and Ankara.

German Marshall Fund of the United States
1744 R Street, NW
Washington, DC 20009
Tel.: 202-745-3950
Fax: 202-265-1662
www.gmfus.com/about/jobs.cfm

Human Rights First
Human Rights First believes that building respect for human rights and the rule of law will help ensure the dignity to which every individual is entitled and will stem tyranny, extremism, intolerance, and violence. Human Rights First protects people at risk: refugees who flee persecution, victims of crimes against humanity or other mass human rights violations, victims of discrimination, those whose rights have been eroded in the name of national security, and human rights advocates who are targeted for defending the rights of others. These groups are often the first victims of societal instability and breakdown; their treatment is a harbinger of wider-scale repression. Human Rights First works to prevent violations against these groups and to seek justice and accountability for violations against them.

Human Rights First is a nonprofit, nonpartisan international human rights organization based in New York and Washington. However, its work is global. Qualifications for positions vary but are listed under the job descriptions posted on the website.

Human Rights First
New York Headquarters
333 Seventh Avenue, 13th Floor
New York, NY 10001
Tel.: 212-845-5200
Fax: 212-845-5299
www.humanrightsfirst.org

Human Rights Watch
Since its founding in 1978, Human Rights Watch has grown to become the largest and most influential U.S.-based organization seeking to promote human rights worldwide. Human Rights Watch is known for its impartial and reliable human rights reporting, its innovative and high-profile advocacy campaigns, and its success in affecting the policy of the United States and other influential governments toward abusive regimes. Human Rights Watch conducts regular, systematic investigations of

human rights abuses in approximately seventy countries around the world. It addresses the human rights practices of governments of all political stripes, geopolitical alignments, and ethnic and religious affiliations. In internal wars, it documents violations by both governments and rebel groups. It is an independent NGO supported by contributions from private individuals and foundations worldwide; it accepts no government funds, directly or indirectly.

Headquartered in New York, Human Rights Watch maintains offices in Washington, Los Angeles, London, Brussels, Berlin, Geneva, and Moscow, with staff based in various other locations around the world. There are five regional divisions covering Africa, the Americas, Asia, the Middle East and North Africa, and Europe and Central Asia. In addition, there are eleven thematic divisions on arms, business and human rights, children's rights, emergencies, HIV/AIDS, international justice, lesbian-gay-bisexual-transgendered people, refugees, terrorism/counterterrorism, and women's rights. With a staff of more than 240 worldwide, there are approximately 40 openings each year. Candidates for administrative positions must have a bachelor's degree, preferably in international relations; researchers should have a master's, law, or other advanced degree. Applicants should have a working knowledge of human rights issues; foreign language skills are highly desirable.

Human Rights Watch
350 Fifth Avenue, 34th Floor
New York, NY 10118-3299
Tel.: 212-290-4700
Fax: 212-736-1300
hrwnyc@hrw.org
www.hrw.org

Institute of International Education

An independent nonprofit founded in 1919, the *Institute of International Education* (IIE) is among the world's largest and most experienced international education and training organizations. Its mission is to promote closer educational relations between the people of the United States and those of other countries, to strengthen and link institutions of higher learning globally, to rescue threatened scholars and advance academic freedom, and to build leadership skills and enhance the capacity of individuals and organizations to address local and global challenges. A total of 18,000 men and women from 175 nations participate in IIE programs each year. It has offices in New York, Washington, Chicago, Denver, Houston, and San Francisco, as well as in thirteen international locations.

> Institute of International Education
> Headquarters
> 809 United Nations Plaza
> New York, NY 10017
> Tel.: 212-883-8200
> Fax: 212-984-5452
> www.iie.org

InterAction

InterAction is the largest alliance of U.S.-based international development and humanitarian NGOs. With more than 160 members operating in every developing country, it works to overcome poverty, exclusion, and suffering by advancing social justice and basic dignity for all. InterAction convenes and coordinates its members so that, in unison, they can influence policy and debate on issues affecting tens of millions of people worldwide and improve their own practices.

Current positions available at InterAction are listed at www.inter action.org. InterAction also provides a subscription-based weekly e-mail listing of extensive employment and internship opportunities in the international development and assistance field. There is a fee for this service. To sign up, visit www.interaction.org/pub.

> InterAction
> Suite 210, 1400 16th Street, NW
> Washington, DC 20036
> Tel.: 202-667-8227
> Fax: 202-667-8236
> www.interaction.org

International Committee of the Red Cross

The International Committee of the Red Cross (ICRC) is a neutral, impartial, and independent humanitarian organization. Its nature and membership are nongovernmental. Its mandate to protect and assist the victims of armed conflicts and other situations of violence has been conferred on it by member nation-states through the four Geneva Conventions of 1949 and their Additional Protocols of 1977 and 2005, as well as the Statutes of the International Red Cross and Red Crescent Movement. The ICRC's mission includes these tasks: visits to prisoners of war and civilian detainees; search for missing persons; transmission of messages between family members separated by conflict; reunification of dispersed families; provision of food, water, and medical assistance to civilians without access to these basic necessities; spreading knowledge of international humanitarian law (IHL); monitoring compliance with that law; and drawing attention to violations and contributing to the development of IHL.

The ICRC has delegations in some eighty countries around the world and employs about 1,400 expatriate field staff (of which about 200 are from National Red Cross or Red Crescent Societies) and 10,000 nationals of the countries in which it works. About 800 people provide the essential support and back-up to the field operations from its headquarters in Geneva. In 2006, the ICRC recruited over 120 delegates, 42 interpreters in critical languages, and over 100 other staff in administration, technical support, humanitarian assistance, logistics, and health specialties.

Candidacy for delegate positions requires a master's-level university degree and a minimum of two years of professional experience. Other specialists need a master's or similar technical diploma and at least three years of profession experience in their field. Medical staff need a master's or relevant diploma and at least five years of professional experience. For more information about these posts, visit the ICRC website at www.icrc .org and browse under "jobs at the ICRC" for "skills always in demand" or "vacancies." Recruitment for all expatriate staff is centered in Geneva. The ICRC recruits year round. Interested candidates should visit the ICRC website or e-mail the recruitment unit at rh_rec.gva@icrc.org.

International Crisis Group
The International Crisis Group is an independent, nonprofit NGO, with some 130 staff members on five continents, working through field-based analysis and high-level advocacy to prevent and resolve deadly conflict. The Crisis Group's approach is grounded in field research. Teams of political analysts are located within or close by countries at risk of an outbreak, escalation, or recurrence of violent conflict. Based on information and assessments from the field, it produces analytical reports containing practical recommendations targeted at key international decision makers. The Crisis Group also publishes *CrisisWatch*, a twelve-page monthly bulletin, providing succinct regular updates on all the most significant situations of conflict or potential conflict around the world.

The Crisis Group's international headquarters are in Brussels, with advocacy offices in Washington (where it is based as a legal entity), New

York, London, and Moscow. The organization currently operates twelve regional offices (in Amman, Bishkek, Bogotá, Cairo, Dakar, Islamabad, Istanbul, Jakarta, Nairobi, Pristina, Seoul, and Tbilisi) and has local field representation in sixteen additional locations (Abuja, Baku, Beirut, Belgrade, Colombo, Damascus, Dili, Dushanbe, Jerusalem, Kabul, Kampala, Kathmandu, Kinshasa, Port-au-Prince, Pretoria, and Yerevan). The Crisis Group currently covers nearly 60 areas of actual or potential conflict across four continents. Applications (resume, cover letter, and any other requested documents) should be sent by e-mail to open_positions @crisisgroup.org to the attention of the human resources director.

> Brussels Office (Headquarters)
> 149 Avenue Louise
> Level 24
> B-1050 Brussels
> Belgium
> Tel.: 32-2-502-90-38
> Fax: 32-2-502-50-38
> www.crisisgroup.org
>
> Washington Office
> Suite 450, 1629 K Street, NW
> Washington, DC 20006
> Tel.: 202-785-1601
> Fax: 202-785-1630

International Executive Service Corps

The International Executive Service Corps (IESC) is a not-for-profit economic development firm that uses volunteer experts, paid consultants, and professional staff to promote prosperity and stability through private enterprise development. Since its founding in 1964, it has completed more than 25,000 technical and managerial assistance consultancies in more than 130 countries and implemented complex development programs across every economic sector.

Within its four major practices—trade and competitiveness, information and communication technology, financial services, and tourism development—the IESC provides a broad range of services. They include technical and managerial assistance, training programs, workshops, and seminars, trade facilitation, and grants management. Job openings with the IESC are posted on its website and include many overseas postings in addition to jobs at its Washington headquarters.

International Executive Service Corps
Suite 1010, 901 15th Street, NW
McPherson Building
Washington, DC 20005
Tel.: 202-589-2600
Fax: 202-326-0289
e-mail: iesc@iesc.org
www.iesc.org

International Institute for Environment and Development

The International Institute for Environment and Development (IIED) is an independent, nonprofit research institute working in the field of sustainable development. In alliance with others, it seeks to help shape a future that ends global poverty and delivers and sustains efficient and equitable management of the world's natural resources. Based in London, the IIED currently has sixty-three staff members from sixteen countries and an annual budget of £7 million. The IIED accepts applications only for specific vacancies, which are listed on its website.

International Institute for Environment and Development
3 Endsleigh Street
London
WC1H 0DD
Tel.: 44-20-7388-2117
Fax: 44-20-7388-2826
www.iied.org

International Republican Institute

The International Republican Institute (IRI) is a private, nonprofit, non-partisan organization dedicated to advancing democracy worldwide. In its infancy, the IRI focused on planting the seeds of democracy in Latin America. Since the end of the cold war, the IRI has broadened its reach to support democracy and freedom around the globe. It has conducted programs in more than one hundred countries and is currently active in more than sixty-five countries. *The IRI does not accept unsolicited resumes.*

International Republican Institute
Suite 700, 1225 Eye Street, NW
Washington, DC 20005
Tel.: 202-408-9450
Fax. 202-408-9462
www.iri.org/employment

International Rescue Committee

Founded in 1933, the International Rescue Committee (IRC) is a global leader in emergency relief, rehabilitation, protection of human rights, postconflict development, resettlement services, and advocacy for those uprooted or affected by violent conflict and oppression. The IRC is on the ground in twenty-five countries, providing emergency relief, relocating refugees, and rebuilding lives in the wake of disaster.

From emergency response through postconflict development work, in a great variety of roles around the world, the IRC's 8,000-plus staff is a force for humanity and hope. Careers at the IRC are wide ranging and far reaching. Encouraging staff development through promotion, transfer, and rehire, the IRC nurtures long-term career paths and helps employees grow within the organization.

Each job requires a different set of skills and work experience depending on the focus and level of the position. Jobs in the United States range from entry level with a broad, general skill set to senior level with very specific expertise. Jobs in international programs generally require at least three to five years of experience and very specific expertise. The ability to work in different languages is not essential but desirable. For example, the IRC always seeks people who can speak French for positions in French-speaking African countries. Open positions are listed on its website. A limited number of internships and fellowships with the IRC in international and U.S.-based programs are posted along with career opportunities on the job search page.

> International Rescue Committee
> 122 East 42nd Street
> New York, NY 10168
> Tel.: 212-551-3000
> www.theirc.org/jobs

International Research and Exchanges Board

The International Research and Exchanges Board (IREX) is an international nonprofit organization providing leadership and innovative programs to improve the quality of education, strengthen independent media, and foster pluralistic civil society development. Founded in 1968, IREX has an annual portfolio of $50 million and a staff of over four hundred professionals worldwide. IREX and its partner IREX Europe deliver cross-cutting programs and consulting expertise in more than fifty countries.

IREX has employment opportunities at headquarters in its Washington office as well as international opportunities in Europe, Eurasia, the Middle East and North Africa, and Asia. All interested applicants are invited to submit their resume and cover letter to resumes@irex.org.

> International Research and Exchanges Board
> Suite 700, 2121 K Street, NW
> Washington, DC 20037
> Tel.: 202-628-8188
> www.irex.org/careers

Japan Foundation Center for Global Partnership

The Center for Global Partnership (CGP) was established within the Japan Foundation in April 1991 with offices in both Tokyo and New York. To carry out its mission, the CGP operates grant programs in three areas—intellectual exchange, grassroots exchange, and education—as well as self-initiated projects and fellowships. The CGP supports an array of institutions and individuals, including nonprofit organizations, universities, policymakers, scholars, and educators, and its staff believes in the power of broad-based, multichannel approaches to effect positive change.

> Japan Foundation Center for Global Partnership
> New York Office
> 152 West 57th Street, 17th Floor
> New York, NY 10019
> Tel.: 212-489-1255
> Fax: 212-489-1344
> e-mail: info@cgp.org
> www.cgp.org

Japan Exchange and Teaching Program

The Japan Exchange and Teaching (JET) Program is aimed at promoting grassroots international exchange between Japan and other nations. The number of countries sending participants has risen over the years, as has the number of participants. In 2006, the JET program welcomed 5,508 participants from forty-four countries. Program participants come to Japan as one of the following positions: assistant language teacher, coordinator for international relations, or sports exchange adviser. For more information or to apply, visit www.jetprogramme.org.

Médecins Sans Frontières

Médecins Sans Frontières (MSF) is an international humanitarian aid organization that provides emergency medical assistance to populations in danger in more than seventy countries. In countries where health structures are insufficient or even nonexistent, MSF collaborates with authorities such as ministries of health to provide assistance. MSF works on the rehabilitation of hospitals and dispensaries, in vaccination programs, and on water and sanitation projects. MSF also works in remote health care centers and slum areas and provides training for local personnel. All this is done with the objective of rebuilding health structures to acceptable levels. Most employment opportunities are posted on the specific national websites for MSF.

U.S. Headquarters
333 7th Avenue, 2nd Floor
New York, NY 10001
Tel.: 212-679-6800
Fax: 212-679-7016
www.doctorswithoutborders.org/employment

Mercy Corps

Mercy Corps works amid disasters, conflicts, chronic poverty, and instability to unleash the potential of people who can win against nearly impossible odds. Since 1979, Mercy Corps has provided more than $1 billion in assistance to people in ninety-four nations. Supported by headquarters offices in North America, Europe, and Asia, the agency's unified global programs employ nearly 3,200 staff worldwide and reach more than 13.5 million people in nearly forty countries. Mercy Corps is searching for those "best of class" candidates who will help grow its vision. It seeks individuals who are entrepreneurial, creative, positive, team oriented, personable, bright, self-motivated, flexible, and reliable.

Mercy Corps
3015 SW First Avenue
Portland, OR 97201
Tel.: 800-292-3355
www.mercycorps.org

National Democratic Institute

The National Democratic Institute for International Affairs (NDI) is a nonprofit organization working to strengthen and expand democracy worldwide. Calling on a global network of volunteer experts, the NDI provides practical assistance to civic and political leaders advancing democratic values, practices, and institutions. The NDI works with democrats in every region of the world to build political and civic organizations, safeguard elections, and to promote citizen participation, openness, and accountability in government.

> National Democratic Institute
> 2030 M Street, NW
> Fifth Floor
> Washington, DC 20036-3306
> Tel.: 202-728-5500
> Fax: 202-728-5520
> www.ndi.org/employment/currentemploy.asp

National Endowment for Democracy
The National Endowment for Democracy (NED) is a private, nonprofit organization created in 1983 to strengthen democratic institutions around the world through nongovernmental efforts. NED is governed by an independent, nonpartisan board of directors. With its annual congressional appropriation, it makes hundreds of grants each year to support prodemocracy groups in Africa, Asia, Central and Eastern Europe, Latin America, the Middle East, and the countries of the former Soviet Union. The NED website lists both internships and positions at headquarters and in the field. Education, experience, and language skills are critical for most positions.

> National Endowment for Democracy
> Suite 800, 1025 F Street, NW
> Washington, DC 20004
> Tel.: 202-378-9700
> Fax: 202-378-9407
> e-mail: info@ned.org
> www.ned.org/employment.html

Nature Conservancy
The Nature Conservancy is a leading conservation organization working around the world to protect ecologically important lands and waters for nature and people. The mission of the Nature Conservancy is to preserve the plants, animals, and natural communities that represent the diversity of life on Earth by protecting the lands and waters they need to survive.

The Nature Conservancy works in all fifty states and more than thirty countries. Based in Arlington, Virginia, the worldwide office hosts the majority of staff connected to the key institutional support functions of the organization including. However, positions are available in many

Nature Conservancy offices. If you are interested in working with the Nature Conservancy, please review jobs by using the online search function. Once you have identified the jobs that you are interested in, submit your resume and cover letter directly to the contact person listed.

International Headquarters
The Nature Conservancy
Suite 100, 4245 North Fairfax Drive
Arlington, VA 22203
Tel.: 703-841-5300
www.nature.org/careers

Open Society Institute
The Open Society Institute (OSI) works to build vibrant and tolerant democracies whose governments are accountable to their citizens. To achieve its mission, the OSI seeks to shape public policies that assure greater fairness in political, legal, and economic systems and that safeguard fundamental rights. On a local level, the OSI implements a range of initiatives to advance justice, education, public health, and independent media. At the same time, the OSI builds alliances across borders and continents on issues such as corruption and freedom of information. The OSI places a high priority on protecting and improving the lives of marginalized people and communities.

The investor and philanthropist George Soros created the OSI in 1993 as a private operating and grant-making foundation to support his foundations in Central and Eastern Europe and the former Soviet Union. Those foundations were established, starting in 1984, to help countries make the transition from communism. The OSI has expanded the activities of the Soros foundations network to encompass the United States and more than sixty countries in Europe, Asia, Africa, and Latin America. Each Soros foundation relies on the expertise of boards composed of eminent citizens who determine individual agendas based on local priorities.

In addition to the network of Soros foundations, the OSI has offices in New York, Baltimore, Brussels, Budapest, London, Paris, and Washington that develop and administer programs addressing key civil society, human rights, public health, law and governance, education, media, and information issues.

OSI offices, particularly the larger ones in New York and Budapest, typically offer program assistant, program associate, program coordinator, program officer, and associate director positions. The academic and prior experience requirements for each position differ, depending on the responsibilities it entails, as described in the description for the position. At the level of program assistant, an undergraduate degree and at least some prior office experience would be sufficient. Proficiency in a foreign language may also be necessary. The other positions may require graduate degrees, experience working with an international program, firsthand knowledge of the region in which the program operates, foreign language fluency, and possibly experience working with NGOs or nonprofit organizations.

> Open Society Institute
> 400 West 59th Street
> New York, NY 10019
> www.soros.org

Physicians for Social Responsibility

Physicians for Social Responsibility (PSR) is a national nonprofit membership organization of more than 20,000 health professionals and supporters working to promote nuclear arms reduction, international cooperation, protection of the environment, and the reduction of violence. PSR was founded in 1961 and is the U.S. affiliate of International Physicians for the Prevention of Nuclear War, which was awarded the Nobel Peace Prize in 1985. PSR supports the downsizing of the nuclear weapons complex and cleanup of radioactive contamination at Department of Energy sites. In addition, PSR promotes an end to nuclear testing, the forging of new arms reduction treaties, a shift in federal budget priorities away from military spending and toward meeting human needs, preservation of the environment, and the reduction of violence and its causes.

PSR's activities include public education about the health effects of nuclear weapons production and testing, the social costs of the arms race, and the links between pollution and public health. PSR's programs range from citizen advocacy with Congress, speaker tours, media work, and educational publications. A background or interest in nuclear weapons and security issues and related legislative policy, as well as an interest in PSR's goals, is sought in prospective hires and interns.

> Physicians for Social Responsibility
> Suite 1012, 1875 Connecticut Avenue, NW
> Washington, DC 20009
> Tel.: 202-667-4260
> Fax: 202-667-4201
> www.psr.org

Population Services International
Population Services International (PSI) is a nonprofit organization based in Washington that harnesses the vitality of the private sector to address the health problems of low-income and vulnerable populations in more than sixty developing countries. With programs in malaria, reproductive health, child survival, and HIV/AIDS, PSI promotes products, services, and healthy behavior that enable low-income and vulnerable people to lead healthier lives. Products and services are sold at subsidized prices rather than given away in order to motivate commercial-sector involvement. PSI is the leading nonprofit social marketing organization in the world.

PSI operates in the private sector, with a bottom-line orientation that is rare among nonprofit organizations. The success of its approach is reflected in its consistent growth and impact. It currently operates in more than sixty countries in Africa, Asia, the Americas, and Eastern Europe. It is constantly expanding its portfolio of products and services for reproductive health, HIV/AIDS prevention, malaria control, child survival, and safe water. With the assistance of donors, government counterparts, and partner organizations, PSI employees are saving lives.

PSI's headquarters positions are in Washington. Positions with its offices and affiliates are based throughout Africa, the Americas, Asia, and Eastern Europe. Whether you seek work as an accountant or a program manager, PSI encourages innovation and offers continual opportunities for professional growth. Most overseas positions require experience in the field and fluency in a relevant second language.

> Population Services International Recruitment
> Suite 600, 1120 19th Street, NW
> Washington, DC 20036
> Tel.: 202-785-0072
> www.psi.org/employment

Project HOPE
Since 1958, Project HOPE has worked to make health care available for people around the globe—especially children. Its name stands for Health Opportunities for People Everywhere. The project's work includes educating health professionals and volunteers, providing medicines and supplies, strengthening health facilities, training community health workers, and fighting communicable diseases such as tuberculosis and HIV/AIDS.

As an organization with a proud history and a bright future, Project HOPE offers rewarding and challenging work opportunities in professions ranging from health education to finance. With programs in over thirty countries around the world, Project HOPE has opportunities for employees, consultants, volunteers, and interns. The organization values diversity and encourages all qualified individuals to apply. Positions are listed on the Project HOPE website.

> Project HOPE Recruitment
> 255 Carter Hall Lane
> Millwood, VA 22646
> Fax: 540-837-9052
> recruitment@projecthope.org
> www.projecthope.org

Rockefeller Foundation
The Rockefeller Foundation was founded in 1913 to "promote the well-being" of humanity by addressing the root causes of serious problems. This approach has produced such breakthrough work as the professionalization of public health; the development of a vaccine against yellow fever; the "Green Revolution" in Latin American, Asian, and Indian agriculture; and the creation of public-private partnerships to develop promising new vaccines. The foundation's "Innovation for Development" initiative is of particular interest to students of international affairs. The foundation encourages job seekers to apply for specific job openings only. Given the volume of unsolicited inquiries, resumes not linked to current job openings will not be retained by the foundation and will not receive a response.

> Rockefeller Foundation
> 420 Fifth Avenue
> New York, NY 10018
> Tel.: 212-869-8500
> www.rockfound.org/about_us/careers/jobs.shtml

Save the Children
Save the Children is the leading independent organization creating lasting change in the lives of children in need in the United States and around the world. Save the Children works in more than fifty countries, including the United States, and serves more than 33 million children and 32 million others working to save and improve children's lives, including

parents, community members, local organizations, and government agencies. Save the Children hires professionals with a minimum of three to five years' experience, especially gained in the field or overseas, in health, education, microfinance, or areas of crisis.

> Save the Children
> 54 Wilton Road
> Westport, CT 06880
> Tel.: 203-221-4030
> www.savethechildren.org/about/jobs

United Nations Association of the United States of America
The United Nations Association of the United States of America is a not-for-profit membership organization dedicated to building understanding of and support for the ideals and vital work of the United Nations among the American people. Its educational and humanitarian campaigns, along with its policy and advocacy programs, allow people to make a global impact at the local level. Its programs include Adopt-A-Minefield, Global Classrooms: Model UN, and HERO.

> United Nations Association of the United States of America
> 801 Second Avenue
> New York, NY 10017
> Tel.: 212-907-1300
> www.unausa.org

U.S.-Asia Institute
The U.S.-Asia Institute, founded in 1979, is a national nonprofit, nonpartisan organization devoted to fostering understanding and strengthening ties between the people and governments of the United States and Asia. Through conferences, congressional staff delegations to key Asian countries, policy research, symposiums, international exchanges, and consulting with various East Asian embassies, the U.S.-Asia Institute promotes the examination of the economic, political, and cultural issues vital to United States–Asia relations.

The U.S.-Asia Institute currently has three professional staff positions and selects two to three staff interns each semester and during the summer. Employment opportunities are rare and competitive. These professional internships are for American undergraduate and graduate students as well as international young professionals. The U.S.-Asia Institute internship duties include assisting staff in organizing various programs;

conducting policy research; and attending and disseminating congressional hearings, seminars, and State Department and NGO policy lectures.

Though academic training in the area of East Asia is certainly preferred, the U.S.-Asia Institute has hired individuals with economic, political science, public policy, and international relations backgrounds who have an interest in Asia. Successful applicants must have a minimum of a BA or BS and usually one to two years of international work experience. They must be well organized and able to communicate effectively in both written and oral form. It is vital that they recognize the importance of team work and be willing to do a variety of tasks.

> U.S.-Asia Institute
> 232 East Capitol Street, NE
> Washington, DC 20003
> Tel.: 202-544-3181
> Fax: 202-543-1748
> e-mail: usasiainstitute@verizon.net
> www.usasiainstitute.org

U.S. Committee for Refugees and Immigrants

The mission of the U.S. Committee for Refugees and Immigrants (USCRI) is to address the needs and rights of persons in forced or voluntary migration worldwide by advancing fair and humane public policy, facilitating and providing direct professional services, and promoting the full participation of migrants in community life. Founded in 1911, the USCRI now has a network of organization in twenty-six states.

> U.S. Committee for Refugees and Immigrants
> Suite 200, 1717 Massachusetts Ave, NW
> Washington, DC 20036
> Tel.: 202-347-3507
> Fax: 202-347-3418
> www.refugees.org

Winrock International Institute for International Development

The Winrock International Institute for International Development is a nonprofit organization that works with people in the United States and around the world to increase economic opportunity, sustain natural resources, and protect the environment. Winrock matches innovative approaches in agriculture, natural resources management, clean energy, and leadership development with the unique needs of its partners. By linking local individuals and communities with new ideas and technology, Winrock is increasing long-term productivity, equity, and responsible resource management to benefit the poor and disadvantaged of the world. Winrock staff members are part of a global team that works together to help people help themselves, no matter where they work or what position they fill.

Winrock International Institute for International Development
2101 Riverfront Drive
Little Rock, AR 72202
Tel.: 501-280-3000
Fax: 501-280-3093
e-mail: jobs@winrock.org
www.winrock.org

Women in International Security

Women in International Security (WIIS) is dedicated to increasing the influence of women in the field of foreign and defense affairs and enhancing the dialogue on international security. WIIS offers a comprehensive set of programs designed to foster and promote women in all fields related to international security, and in a variety of sectors. Established in 1987 by a small group of women experts in foreign and defense affairs, today WIIS has more than 1,400 members—women and men—in forty-seven countries and from a wide variety of fields: academia, think tanks, the diplomatic corps, the intelligence community, the military, government, NGOs, international organizations, the media, and the private sector. Members work on and are interested in diverse issues affecting international security, ranging from nonproliferation of weapons of mass destruction to terrorism, human rights, sustainable development, environmental security, and conflict resolution. There are very few professional staff positions, but WIIS does offer a limited number of internships and fellowships.

Women in International Security
Center for Peace and Security Studies
Edmund A. Walsh School of Foreign Service
Georgetown University
3600 N Street, NW
Lower Level
Washington, DC 20007
Tel.: 202-687-3366

Fax: 202-687-3233
e-mail: wiisinfo@georgetown.edu
http://wiis.georgetown.edu

World Concern

World Concern is a Christian humanitarian organization dedicated to providing life, opportunity, and hope in the most neglected and impoverished places on earth. World Concern has fieldworkers and professionals in eighteen countries whose people are under siege by HIV/AIDS, hunger, natural disasters, oppression, war, and disease. In 2005, it served 4 million people in thirty-two countries in Africa, Asia, and the Americas.

World Concern works with tribal people, marginalized farmers, orphans, and vulnerable women and children, partnering with local communities to provide resources, encouragement, and opportunity for food, better health, shelter, and meaningful work.

In 2006, World Concern hired for sixty-six openings. There are two main types of positions: short-term disaster positions for responding to international humanitarian disasters, and community workers. Short-term disaster employees must have prior technical or managerial experience in a field such as water and sanitation, treating severe malnutrition, logistics, security/risk assessment, financial management, program management/camp management, food security, livelihoods, grant writing, or psychosocial care. Community development workers need to have at least two years of international community development experience in a developing country working on agriculture or food security, NGO program management, health education, civil engineering (water and sanitation programs), microloans and economic development, or livelihood training. There are also support positions available in human resources, finance, communications and marketing, and grant writing for candidates who have domestic experience that can be transferred to an international setting. More information can be found on World Concern's employment website, reachable through its home page. Development workers must sign a two- to three-year contract.

World Concern
19303 Fremont Avenue North
Seattle, WA 98133
Tel.: 800-755-5122
e-mail: hr@worldconcern.org
www.worldconcern.org

World Learning

World Learning is a private nonprofit international organization with both academic and field project capabilities. Through its three program units—the Experiment in International Living, the School for International Training, and World Learning for International Development—World Learning is a leader in the fields of international exchange, study abroad, sustainable development, teacher education, language training, peace building, and NGO management.

World Learning promotes international and intercultural understanding, social justice, and economic development through education, training, and field projects around the globe. In the fulfillment of this mission, World Leaning prepares individuals, institutions, and communities to be inspiring and effective leaders of change. Headquartered in Brattleboro, Vermont, World Learning also has offices in Washington, Texas, and California, as well as in more than fifty locations around the world.

> World Learning
> Kipling Road, P.O. Box 676
> Brattleboro, VT 05302
> Tel.: 802-257-7751
> e-mail: info@worldlearning.org
> www.worldlearning.org/hr/jobs.html

World Vision International

World Vision International is a Christian relief and development organization working for the well-being of all people, especially children. Through emergency relief, education, health care, economic development, and the promotion of justice, World Vision helps communities help themselves. Established in 1950 to care for orphans in Asia, World Vision has grown to embrace the larger issues of community development and advocacy for the poor in its mission to help children and their families build sustainable futures. Working on six continents, World Vision is one of the largest Christian relief and development organizations in the world.

World Vision functions as a partnership of interdependent national offices, overseen by their own boards or advisory councils. A common mission statement and shared core values bind the partnership. By signing the Covenant of Partnership, each partner agrees to abide by common policies and standards. Partners hold each other accountable through an ongoing system of peer review. The partnership offices, in Geneva, Bangkok, Nairobi, Cyprus, Los Angeles, and San José, coordinate the strategic operations of the organization and represent World Vision in the international arena. Each national office, regardless of how big its programs are, enjoys an equal voice in partnership governance, erasing the usual distinctions between the developed and developing world.

World Vision International
International Liaison Office
6 Chemin de la Tourelle
1209 Geneva
Switzerland
www.wvi.org

WorldTeach

Based at the Center for International Development at Harvard University, WorldTeach is a well-established international NGO with over two decades of experience in training, placing, and providing support for volunteers who serve as teachers in host countries throughout the developing world. WorldTeach has local partnerships, field staff, and volunteers in Latin America, Africa, Asia, the Pacific Islands, and Europe. Year-long programs are available in Bangladesh, Chile, China, Costa Rica, Ecuador, Guyana, Marshall Islands, Mongolia, Namibia, Pohnpei, and Venezuela. In addition, shorter summer programs are available in China, Costa Rica, Ecuador, Namibia, Poland, and South Africa. Last year WorldTeach employed fifteen field staff members who set up programs and coordinated in-country operations for over four hundred volunteers who lived either with host families or in teacher accommodations in communities across the developing world.

Alongside a commitment to education and international development, prospective volunteers for WorldTeach's year-long programs are expected to hold bachelor's degrees or the equivalent and to be native English speakers. Non–U.S. citizens are also encouraged to apply. Once accepted, volunteers must before their departure complete twenty-five hours of teaching experience in English as a Foreign Language/English for Speakers of Other Languages. For summer programs, undergraduate students over the age of eighteen years with a demonstrated interest in cultural exchange and service projects are also welcome. Prospective volunteers should begin their applications online. There is a rolling admissions process, so candidates will be notified of their acceptance within two to four weeks of receipt of all application materials.

WorldTeach
c/o Center for International Development
Harvard University
79 John F. Kennedy Street
Cambridge, MA 02138
Tel.: 800-483-2240
e-mail: info@worldteach.org
www.worldteach.org

14

Research Institutes

Careers in University Research Institutes

ELIZABETH GARDNER

Elizabeth Gardner, *a 1988 graduate of the Master of Science in Foreign Service Program at Georgetown University, is the associate director for administration and external affairs at Stanford University's Center for International Security and Cooperation. She previously worked for the U.S. Department of State, U.S. Senate Committee on Foreign Relations, and Pacific Council on International Policy.*

I F YOU ASKED a group of young university employees to name the best parts of their jobs, what answer would surprise you the most? It would not be a surprise to hear that an invigorating intellectual environment is a big draw at a university research institute (in this case, Stanford University's Center for International Security and Cooperation, or CISAC). Faculty, students, and staff are all attracted to a place where world-class, rigorous scholarship is the basic stock in trade.

University international affairs research centers are a special breed; they are not think tanks but they are not purely academic institutes, either. At the finest universities, the core mission of the international institutes is identical to that of the universities themselves: to conduct research, publish, and teach.

Many international affairs centers, however, reach beyond campus into the halls of governments. Faculty members choose research topics with important, real-world ramifications. They advise government and international organization officials, sometimes forging enduring partnerships as the "brain trust" for elected and appointed leaders. They work in government and international organizations, often making a career of going back and forth between the academic and policy worlds. The CISAC professor William J. Perry, for example, was secretary of defense in the Bill Clinton administration, and CISAC's Condoleezza Rice served as secretary of state in the George W. Bush administration.

Many international affairs centers reach beyond campus into the halls of governments.

All these efforts in research, teaching, publishing, and policy advising rely on the hard work of a cadre of highly capable people, many of them young professionals getting to know the international affairs field. Younger workers at a research center come in two flavors: student or staff. Graduate students are employed for short periods of time to assist faculty with research, usually while laboring on their PhDs. Staff employees have responsibilities that are either purely administrative—managing a visiting scholars program, for example—or a combination of research and administrative work.

Research affords staff members the chance to delve deeply into an international topic and explore it under the tutelage of a faculty member. Some staff will draft lectures or essays for professors or edit work the professors authored themselves. Administrative work can be highly demanding, requiring a strong strategic sense, outstanding leadership, and great problem-solving abilities. Younger employees will have an opportunity to hone their business communication skills, plan complex events, and manage long-term, complicated projects. But some administrative work may prove mundane and routine. There are moments of "underachievement" when the work is not challenging enough.

Like any job, though, university staff positions are what you make of them. An administrative job can be much more than the formal job description states. For those who display an interest in what is going on around them and a willingness to take on new challenges, their superiors will gladly respond and delegate more responsibility.

There are two advancement paths within a university research center. The most senior positions require a PhD and often an appointment as a professor. For those without a PhD, the career ladder moves up administrative rungs. Younger administrative employees often will have relatively short tenures of two to three years, getting their feet wet in the field, determining what it is they want to do next, and then moving on to more schooling or greater responsibility elsewhere. They leave with a greatly enhanced knowledge of international affairs and a cell phone filled with important contacts.

For those who pursue a longer career in a research institute, an advanced degree is highly desirable and common, although not mandatory. More senior administrative employees will typically have professional experience in international affairs, having worked for the government or an international organization, for example, in addition to a professional specialization, such as financial management or public affairs. These employees can expect long careers in universities, where their interests and expertise match nicely with the institution's needs.

I am fortunate to be one of those people whose background matched well with a university's needs. My own career started at the U.S. Department of State just three days after receiving my degree from the Master of Science in Foreign Service Program at Georgetown. Through the Presidential Management Internship Program, I was hired by the State Department's Bureau of European Affairs to work on an arms control negotiation. While there, I spent a few months on Capitol Hill, handling defense and foreign policy issues for Senator Al Gore. The Hill's fast pace and intensely politicized atmosphere was intoxicating, and I returned there to work for Senator Joseph Biden once the Presidential Management Internship term ended. Subsequent executive positions with two nonprofit public policy organizations back in my home state of California provided me with managerial experience and continuing involvement in international issues. After about ten years of executive experience, I learned that Stanford's CISAC was looking for someone with a background in international policy and organizational leadership, and it turned out to be a natural match.

Regardless of how one arrives in a university, employees are attracted by a number of striking features. The caliber of one's university colleagues is uniformly high and often stratospheric. Conversations in an institute, whether by the water cooler or in the seminar room, are invariably fascinating. For young people thinking about a career in academia or government, universities are peopled with many living, breathing illustrations of how those sorts of careers unfold. Complementing all those real-life examples of different career paths is the revered tradition of mentoring, where faculty are eager and willing to counsel young people, whether employees or students, on their own professional plans.

One of the most powerful features of an international affairs institute is the shared allegiance to a common cause. Whether a center works on peace and security, economic development, or human rights, its employees are united by their dedication to that cause and, consequently, to one another. This makes for a deeply shared bond among colleagues and to the organization itself.

One of the most powerful features of an international affairs institute is the shared allegiance to a common cause.

Universities also offer a combination of other attractions not typically found elsewhere. Work hours are often flexible and the environment casual. Students are not the only ones who get to wear jeans and sandals. Campuses are awash with a rich array of activities: continuing studies courses, lectures, concerts, and other pleasures are usually only a short walk away from the office. At some research institutes, hierarchies are fairly flat. The quality of a good idea is more important than who produces the good idea. Geography also makes university jobs desirable. For people who do not live in the Washington–New York corridor, universities offer substantive, exciting international affairs careers at locations around the country.

Many U.S. universities have outstanding international research institutes: Carnegie-Mellon, Cornell, Harvard, the Massachusetts Institute of Technology, Ohio State, Princeton, Stanford, and the University of Maryland are just some of the institutions to explore. If you are interested, read their websites and send a letter to the director, asking for an informational interview.

And so, what is the answer to the question that started this essay: If you asked a group of young university employees to name the best parts of their jobs, what answer would surprise you the most? The good salaries! Large, private universities can offer competitive salaries and an excellent array of benefits. It is not necessarily what you would expect from a nonprofit job. Are you intrigued? Research institutes are always looking for good people.

RESOURCE LISTINGS

American Enterprise Institute

The American Enterprise Institute (AEI), founded in 1943, is a private, nonpartisan, not-for-profit institution dedicated to research and education on issues of government policies, economics, politics, and social welfare. AEI's purposes are to defend the principles and improve the institutions of American freedom and democratic capitalism—limited government, competitive private enterprise, individual liberty and responsibility, vital cultural and political institutions, and vigilant and effective defense and foreign policies—through rigorous inquiry, debate, and writing. AEI is home to some of America's most renowned economists, legal scholars, political scientists, and foreign policy specialists.

AEI employs approximately seventy resident scholars. There are about thirty-five full-time research assistant positions in the disciplines listed here, with three or four new foreign policy vacancies filled, on average, throughout the year. All open positions are listed on AEI's website, and holders of bachelor's and master's degrees are eligible to apply.

> American Enterprise Institute
> 1150 17th Street, NW
> Washington, DC 20036
> Tel.: 202-862-5800
> Fax: 202-862-7177
> www.aei.org

Arms Control Association

The Arms Control Association (ACA), founded in 1971, is a national nonpartisan membership organization dedicated to promoting public understanding of and support for effective arms control policies. Through its public education and media programs and its magazine, *Arms Control Today*, the ACA provides policymakers, the press, and the interested public with authoritative information, analysis, and commentary on arms control proposals, negotiations and agreements, and related national security issues. In addition to the regular press briefings the ACA holds on major arms control developments, its staff provides commentary and analysis on a broad spectrum of issues for journalists and scholars both in the United States and abroad.

The ACA currently has nine full-time positions and two internships in its Washington office. Job openings are rare. Information about internships is available on its website, which also lists arms-control-related employment and fellowships, as does the print edition of *Arms Control Today*.

> Arms Control Association
> Suite 130, 1313 L Street NW
> Washington, DC 20005
> Tel.: 202-463-8270
> e-mail: aca@armscontrol.org
> www.armscontrol.org/employment

Aspen Institute

Founded in 1950, the Aspen Institute is an international nonprofit organization dedicated to fostering enlightened leadership and open-minded dialogue. Through seminars, policy programs, conferences, and leadership development initiatives, the institute and its international partners seek to promote nonpartisan inquiry and an appreciation for timeless values. The institute is headquartered in Washington and has campuses in Aspen, Colorado, and on the Wye River on Maryland's Eastern Shore. Its international network includes partner Aspen Institutes in Berlin, Rome, Lyon, Tokyo, New Delhi, and Bucharest, as well as leadership programs in Africa, Central America, and India. Full-time employment opportunities are listed on the Aspen Institute website. To apply, submit your resume online or send your resume with cover letter to:

> Human Resources
> Aspen Institute
> One Dupont Circle, NW
> 7th Floor
> Washington, DC 20036
> e-mail: resumes@aspeninstitute.org
> Fax: 202-736-2524
> www.aspeninstitute.org

Atlantic Council of the United States

The Atlantic Council of the United States promotes constructive U.S. leadership and engagement in international affairs based on the central role of the Atlantic community in meeting the international challenges of the twenty-first century. The council embodies a nonpartisan network of leaders who aim to bring ideas to power and to give power to ideas by

- stimulating dialogue and discussion about critical international issues with a view to enriching public debate and promoting consensus on appropriate responses in the administration, Congress, the corporate and nonprofit sectors, and the media in the United States and among leaders in Europe, Asia, and the Americas; and

- conducting educational and exchange programs for successor generations of U.S. leaders so that they will come to value U.S. international engagement and have the knowledge and understanding necessary to develop effective policies.

> Atlantic Council of the United States
> 1101 15th Street, NW
> 11th Floor
> Washington, DC 20005
> Tel.: 202-463-7226
> Fax: 202-463-7241
> e-mail: info@acus.org
> www.acus.org

Brookings Institution

The Brookings Institution is a private, nonprofit organization devoted to independent research and innovative policy solutions. For more than ninety years, Brookings has analyzed current and emerging issues and produced new ideas that matter—for the nation and the world. For policymakers and the media, Brookings scholars provide the highest-quality research, policy recommendations, and analysis on the full range of public policy issues.

Research at the Brookings Institution is conducted to inform the public debate, not to advance a political agenda. Scholars are drawn from the United States and abroad—with experience in government and academia—and hold diverse points of view. More than 140 resident and non-resident scholars research issues; write books, papers, articles, and opinion pieces; testify before congressional committees; and participate in dozens of public events each year. Over two hundred research assistants and support staff contribute to the institution's research, publishing, communications, fund-raising, and information technology operations. Brookings maintains an employment page on its website. The list of openings is updated weekly. All jobs remain posted until filled. To apply for a position, submit your resume to

> Brookings Institution
> HR—Job #_____
> 1775 Massachusetts Avenue, NW
> Washington, DC 20036

Fax: 202-797-2479
e-mail: hrjobs@brookings.edu
www.brookings.edu

Carnegie Endowment for International Peace

The Carnegie Endowment for International Peace is a private, nonprofit organization dedicated to advancing cooperation between nations and promoting active international engagement by the United States. Founded in 1910, its work is nonpartisan and dedicated to achieving practical results. With operations in Moscow, Beijing, Beirut, Brussels, and Washington, the Carnegie Endowment is the first truly multinational—ultimately global—think tank.

As an operating, rather than grant-making, foundation, the Carnegie Endowment conducts programs of research, discussion, and education through publications and events in international relations and American foreign policy. Although its program activities adjust to address the shifting global relations, emphasis has been on regional and country studies, including the Middle East, China, United States–Russia relations, and South Asia. The endowment's Global Policy Program focuses on nuclear nonproliferation; trade, equity, and development; democracy promotion; and the role of the United States in the world. The organization also engages in joint programs with other tax-exempt organizations to invigorate and enlarge the scope of dialogue on international issues. The endowment also publishes *Foreign Policy*, one of the world's leading magazines of international politics and economics, which reaches readers in more than 120 countries and several languages. The endowment employs about a hundred people, including about forty senior associates who are leading experts in their fields. Additional positions include professionals associated with research, administration, communications, publications, and support activities.

The endowment offers highly competitive and prestigious fellowships for graduating college seniors. Each year, it offers eight to ten of these one-year fellowships to uniquely qualified graduating seniors and individuals who have graduated during the past academic year. They are selected from a pool of nominees from close to three hundred colleges. These Carnegie Junior Fellows work as research assistants to the endowment's senior associates. Students who have started graduate studies are not eligible to apply. The endowment's nomination deadline is January 15 of each year. See your career services or placement office to learn more about the college application process.

Carnegie Endowment for International Peace
1779 Massachusetts Avenue, NW
Washington, DC 20036
Tel.: 202-483-7600
Fax: 202-483-1840
e-mail: jrfellowinfo@carnegieendowment.org
www.carnegieendowment.org

Cato Institute

The Cato Institute is a nonprofit public policy research foundation head-quartered in Washington. Founded in 1977 by Edward H. Crane, the institute is named for *Cato's Letters*, a series of libertarian pamphlets that helped lay the philosophical foundation for the American Revolution.

The Cato Institute seeks to broaden the parameters of public policy debate to allow consideration of the traditional American principles of limited government, individual liberty, free markets, and peace. Toward that goal, the institute strives to achieve greater involvement of the intelligent, concerned lay public in questions of policy and the proper role of government. The institute undertakes an extensive publications program dealing with the complete spectrum of public policy issues. Books, monographs, briefing papers, and shorter studies are commissioned to examine issues in nearly every corner of the public policy debate. Policy forums and book forums are held regularly, as are major policy conferences, which Cato hosts throughout the year, and from which papers are published thrice yearly in the *Cato Journal*. All these events are taped and archived on Cato's website. Additionally, Cato has held major conferences in London, Moscow, Shanghai, and Mexico City. The institute also publishes the quarterly magazine *Regulation* and a bimonthly newsletter, *Cato Policy Report*.

Cato Institute
1000 Massachusetts Avenue, NW
Washington, DC 20001
Tel.: 202-842-0200
Fax: 202-842-3490
www.cato.org/jobs/jobops.html

Center for International Security and Cooperation

The Center for International Security and Cooperation (CISAC), part of the Freeman Spogli Intitute for International Studies at Stanford

University, has a mission to produce policy-relevant research on international security problems, to train the next generation of security specialists, and to influence policymaking in international security. Its work is interdisciplinary, linking scientists and engineers with political and social scientists to address today's complex policy challenges. CISAC has a vibrant fellowship program at various postgraduate and midcareer levels. Its conferences and workshops are attended by scholars, students, and policymakers. Information about events and available fellowships is available on its website.

> Center for International Security and Cooperation
> 616 Sierra Street, E200
> Stanford University
> Stanford, CA 94305
> Tel.: 650-723-9625
> http://cisac.stanford.edu

Center for Strategic and International Studies
Since 1962, the Center for Strategic and International Studies (CSIS) has advanced global security and prosperity by providing strategic insights and practical policy solutions to decision makers. John J. Hamre, a former deputy secretary of defense, has served as its president and chief executive officer since April 2000. CSIS is guided by a board of trustees chaired by former senator Sam Nunn and consisting of prominent individuals from both the public and private sectors.

The nearly two hundred researchers and support staff at CSIS focus primarily on three subject areas. First, CSIS addresses the full spectrum of challenges to national and international security. Second, CSIS maintains resident experts on all the world's major geographical regions. Third, CSIS is committed to helping develop new methods of governance to address the transnational challenges of a global age, including those presented by technology, trade, aging, and energy.

> Center for Strategic and International Studies
> 1800 K Street, NW
> Washington, DC 20006
> Tel.: 202-887-0200
> Fax: 202-775-3199
> e-mail: employment@csis.org
> www.csis.org

Chicago Council on Global Affairs

The Chicago Council on Global Affairs, founded in 1922 as the Chicago Council on Foreign Relations, is a leading independent, nonpartisan organization committed to influencing the discourse on global issues through contributions to opinion and policy formation, leadership dialogue, and public learning. The council brings the world to Chicago by hosting public programs and private events that feature world leaders and experts with diverse views on a wide range of global issues. And through task forces, conferences, studies, and leadership dialogue, the council brings Chicago's ideas and opinions to the world. The council has a staff of approximately forty people.

> Chicago Council on Global Affairs
> Suite 1100, 332 South Michigan Avenue
> Chicago, IL 60604
> Tel.: 312-726-3860
> Fax: 312-821-7555
> www.thechicagocouncil.org

Council on Foreign Relations

Founded in 1921, the Council on Foreign Relations is the leading nonprofit membership organization, research center, and publisher dedicated to increasing America's understanding of the world and contributing ideas to U.S. foreign policy. Its headquarters is in New York City, and it has an office in Washington and programs nationwide. The council's more than 4,000 members are prominent leaders in international affairs and foreign policy. The council publishes *Foreign Affairs*, the preeminent journal on global issues, and it provides up-to-date information about the world and U.S. foreign policy on its award-winning website.

The Council on Foreign Relations offers exceptional opportunities for recent graduates interested in pursuing a career in international relations. These graduates are typically hired as research associates or program associates, whose responsibilities consist of research, writing, editing, program development and coordination, budget management, and administration. Research and program associates are encouraged to attend meetings of council members to hear from a wide array of influential foreign policy and business leaders. The council also sponsors a professional development training program to enhance and build skills for associates' current and future work in the field. The council offers a benefits package that is among the best offered by nonprofit institutions today, including generous leave policies and health insurance program, some tuition reimbursement, and professional development training.

Council on Foreign Relations
58 East 68th Street
New York, NY 10021
Tel.: 212-434-9400
Fax: 212-434-9800
e-mail: humanresources@cfr.org
www.cfr.org

Council on Foreign Relations
1779 Massachusetts Avenue, NW
Washington, DC 20036
Tel.: 202-518-3400
Fax: 202-986-2984

East-West Center
The East-West Center is an education and research organization established by the U.S. Congress in 1960 to strengthen relations and understanding among the peoples and nations of Asia, the Pacific, and the United States. The center contributes to a peaceful, prosperous, and just Asia-Pacific community by serving as a vigorous hub for cooperative research, education, and dialogue on critical issues of common concern to the Asia-Pacific region and the United States. Funding for the center comes from the U.S. government, with additional support provided by private agencies, individuals, foundations, corporations, and the governments of the region.

On September 1, 2001, the center opened a Washington branch, whose primary function is to further the center's mission of strengthening relations and understanding among the governments and peoples of Asia, the Pacific, and the United States. The Washington office advances this mission and the center's institutional objective of helping to build a peaceful, prosperous, and just community in the Asia-Pacific region through substantive programming activities focused on the theme of conflict reduction.

Employment opportunities at the East-West Center include a variety of positions which contribute to multinational, multidisciplinary research, education, and seminar activities that support the institutional objective of fostering the development of an Asia-Pacific community. The human resources office does not maintain a mailing list or keep resumes on file for future vacancies. Applications are accepted only for announced position vacancies. Vacancy announcements with information about the position, required qualifications, and application requirements will be posted on the center's website. The center has many opportunities for internships and fellowships.

> East-West Center
> Human Resources
> 1601 East-West Road
> Honolulu, HA 96848-1601
> Fax: 808-944-7270
> e-mail: hrrecrut@EastWestCenter.org
> www.eastwestcenter.org

> East-West Center Washington
> Suite 200, 1819 L Street, NW
> Washington, DC 20036
> Tel.: 202-293-3995
> Fax: 202-293-1402
> washington.eastwestcenter.org

Foreign Policy Association

The Foreign Policy Association (FPA) is a nonprofit organization dedicated to inspiring the American public to learn more about the world. Founded in 1918, the FPA provides independent publications, programs, and forums to increase public awareness of, and foster popular participation in, matters relating to those policy issues. The FPA maintains a job board on its website of employment opportunities in the field of foreign policy.

> Foreign Policy Association
> 470 Park Avenue South
> New York, NY 10016
> Tel.: 212-481-8100
> www.fpa.org

Foreign Policy Research Institute

The Foreign Policy Research Institute is an independent, nonprofit organization devoted to scholarly research and public education on international affairs. Current research focuses on American foreign policy; American defense and national security issues; Western Europe; East Asia, particularly the role of China in the region; the Arab–Israeli peace process; and terrorism and political violence. The institute publishes *Orbis*, a quarterly journal of world affairs; operates a Middle East Council and an Asia Program; and administers the Marvin Wachman Fund for International Education.

Foreign Policy Research Institute
Suite 610, 1528 Walnut Street
Philadelphia, PA 19102
Tel.: 215-732-3774
Fax: 215-732-4401
www.fpri.org/about/jobs.html

Fritz Institute

The Fritz Institute is a nonprofit organization dedicated to improving global disaster relief by creating innovative approaches to ensure that help arrives when and where it is needed most. It mobilizes private-sector expertise and academic research to strengthen the standards and operations that support effective preparedness and front-line response. The institute was founded in 2001 by Lynn Fritz, a social entrepreneur and philanthropist, who recognized that effective front-line humanitarian operations must be supported by strong backroom capabilities: effective operational processes, efficient uses of technology, objective performance metrics, and institutionalized learning across the humanitarian sector. Its program areas include logistics and supply chain solutions, humanitarian technology solutions, the Bay Area Preparedness Initiative, capacity building, and humanitarian impact evaluation.

Fritz Institute
Suite 1150, 50 Fremont Street
San Francisco, CA 94105
Tel.: 415-538-8300
Fax: 415-538-1406
www.fritzinstitute.org

Heritage Foundation

Founded in 1973, the Heritage Foundation is a research and educational institute—a think tank—whose mission is to formulate and promote conservative public policies based on the principles of free enterprise, limited government, individual freedom, traditional American values, and a strong national defense. The foundation's staff pursues this mission by producing research, generating solutions consistent with their beliefs, and marketing these findings to Congress, the executive branch, the news media, and others. Several professional positions are filled annually, and openings are listed on the careers page of the foundation's website. The foundation also maintains a job bank that places qualified conservative and classical-liberal applicants in policymaking positions throughout the administration and Congress.

Heritage Foundation
214 Massachusetts Avenue, NE
Washington, DC 20002
Tel.: 202-546-4400
Fax: 202-546-8328
www.heritage.org/About/Careers

Hoover Institution

The Hoover Institution on War, Revolution, and Peace within Stanford University is a public policy research center devoted to advanced study of politics, economics, and political economy—both domestic and foreign—as well as international affairs. Founded in 1919 by Herbert Hoover, the thirty-first president of the United States, the institution houses one of the world's largest private archives and most complete libraries on political, economic, and social change in the twentieth century.

The roughly 250 people at the Hoover Institution consist of approximately 100 scholars; nearly 70 librarians, curators, archivists, and other specialists; and over 80 research support staff, ranging from research assistants to top administrators, who assist and support the scholars in their work and help further the objectives of the institution.

Hoover Institution
434 Galvez Mall
Stanford University
Stanford, CA 94305-6010
Tel.: 650-723-1754
www.hoover.org

Hudson Institute

The Hudson Institute is a nonpartisan policy research organization dedicated to innovative research and analysis that promotes global security, prosperity, and freedom. It challenges conventional thinking and helps manage strategic transitions to the future through interdisciplinary and collaborative studies in defense, international relations, economics, culture, science, technology, and law. Hudson's publications, conferences, and policy recommendations are aimed at global leaders in government and business.

Hudson's current research agenda includes the war on terror and the future of Islam, the rise of Asia and U.S.–Asian relations, human rights in Asia and Africa, civil justice reform and judicial policy, agricultural and biotechnology policy, civil society and global philanthropy, market reforms and the twenty-first-century welfare state, and Latin American studies. Much of Hudson's research and analysis occurs through its various centers.

Hudson's Center for Future Security Strategies seeks to explore evolving, emerging, and imaginable international security environments, as well as to assess the implications of possible alternative futures for security strategies. Using a variety of innovative tools and techniques, the center aims to identify the trends, attitudes, ideas, and other forces that will contribute to the shape of the future but also to go far beyond forecasts that simply project visible trends. It seeks further to analyze critical variables that might alter the trajectory of influences and events, especially the potential impact of powerful nonlinear forces, or wildcards, that might radically change outcomes.

Current center projects include Pakistan Futures, Asia 2030, Nuclear Futures, and Radical Islam: A Net Assessment. Interns typically research current and future security issues, write both short memorandums and longer papers, analyze public policy debates, attend public and private briefings, and interact with visiting experts, political leaders, and representatives of the media. Although interns work independently, their performance is always supervised by a senior scholar, who provides constant feedback. Career employees are normally hired from the intern pool.

The Hudson Institute takes seriously its responsibility to train and educate interns and researchers. The results of any research findings will not benefit Hudson. Its alumni have gained admittance to graduate programs in a number of excellent universities. Other former researchers are contributing to improving public policy by working in various government agencies, media organizations, or think tanks (including Hudson) throughout the world.

Hudson Institute
Suite 6000, 1015 15th Street, NW
Washington, DC 20005
Tel.: 202-974-2400
www.hudson.org

International Institute for Sustainable Development

The International Institute for Sustainable Development (IISD) is in the business of promoting change toward sustainable development. Through its research and through the effective communication of its findings, the IISD engages decision makers in government, business, nongovernmental organizations, and other sectors to develop and implement policies that are simultaneously beneficial to the global economy, to the global environment, and to social well-being. In the pursuit of sustainable development, it promotes open and effective international negotiation processes. And it believes fervently in the importance of building its own institutional capacity while helping partner organizations in the developing world to excel.

> International Institute for Sustainable Development
> 161 Portage Avenue East, 6th Floor
> Winnipeg, Manitoba, R3B 0Y4
> Canada
> Fax: 204-958-7710
> e-mail: info@iisd.ca
> www.iisd.org
> www.iisd.org/about/employment.asp

International Peace Academy

Since its establishment in 1970, the International Peace Academy (IPA) has become a leading policy and research institution specializing in multilateral approaches to peace and security issues, working closely with the UN Secretariat and member states of the United Nations. IPA's primary objective is to promote effective international responses to new and emerging issues and crises through research, analysis, and policy development. Its research spans regional and thematic issues and strives to provide thoughtful analysis and insight for international policymakers and practitioners and for the broader research community. Job openings are listed on it website.

> International Peace Academy
> 777 United Nations Plaza
> New York, NY 10017
> Tel.: 212-687-4300
> Fax: 212-983-8246
> e-mail: employment@ipacademy.org
> www.ipacademy.org

McKinsey Global Institute
The McKinsey Global Institute (MGI) was established in 1990 as an independent private economics research group within McKinsey & Company. Its primary purpose is to undertake original research and develop substantive points of view on critical economic issues facing businesses and governments around the world. MGI investigations are conducted with the goal of improving business performance and competitiveness while establishing a fact base for sound national and international public policymaking.

One hallmark of MGI research is a deep microeconomic analysis at the sector level. This enables it to go beyond the broad macroeconomic indicators to examine the actual drivers of performance. MGI has applied this approach extensively across many industrial and developing countries around the world and across a large number of industry sectors.

The current MGI research agenda builds on this unique micro-to-macro approach to derive perspectives that help inform the global forces shaping business and society, from demography and technology to consumer preferences and regulation. It seeks to understand these forces from a supply perspective that explores the integration of product, labor, capital, and resource markets, and from the demand perspective of households and consumers.

Each research project includes a team of McKinsey consultants from around the world and is supported by the firm's network of knowledge-management professionals. Under MGI's director, Diana Farrell, they serve six- to twelve-month assignments and then return to client work. For more information on employment with McKinsey & Company consulting, see the separate listing in chapter 11.

Middle East Institute
Since 1946 the Middle East Institute has been an important conduit of information between Middle Eastern nations and American policymakers, organizations, and the public. It strives to increase knowledge of the Middle East among U.S. citizens and to promote understanding between the peoples of the Middle East and America. Today it plays a vital and unique role in expanding the dialogue beyond Washington and actively with organizations in the Middle East. Its Public Policy Center and Department of Programs present programs with top regional experts and officials from the U.S. and foreign governments. The George Camp Keiser Library has the largest English-language collection on the Middle East

outside the Library of Congress. Quarterly, it publishes one of the most prestigious journals on the Middle East, *The Middle East Journal.* Its Department of Language and Regional Studies offers courses in Arabic, Hebrew, Persian, and Turkish and seminars highlighting the history, literature, and culture of the Middle East.

Each year, the Middle East Institute selects students from colleges and universities across the United States and the Middle East to participate in its internship program. This program is a critical tool for developing a new generation of policy leaders committed to a rigorous, balanced, and informed view of the Middle East.

Internship Coordinator
Middle East Institute
1761 N Street, NW
Washington, DC 20036-2882
e-mail: internships@mideasti.org.
www.mideasti.org

National Bureau of Economic Research
Founded in 1920, the National Bureau of Economic Research (NBER) is a private, nonprofit, nonpartisan research organization dedicated to promoting a greater understanding of how the economy works. The NBER is committed to undertaking and disseminating unbiased economic research among public policymakers, business professionals, and the academic community.

The NBER is the nation's leading nonprofit economic research organization. Sixteen of the thirty-one American Nobel Prize winners in economics and six of the past chairs of the President's Council of Economic Advisers have been researchers at the NBER. The more than six hundred professors of economics and business now teaching at universities around the country who are NBER researchers are the leading scholars in their fields. These NBER associates concentrate on four types of empirical research: developing new statistical measurements, estimating quantitative models of economic behavior, assessing the effects of public policies on the U.S. economy, and projecting the effects of alternative policy proposals. In addition to its research associates and faculty research fellows, the NBER employs a support staff of forty-five. Its main office is in Cambridge, Massachusetts, with additional offices in Palo Alto, California, and New York City.

National Bureau of Economic Research, Inc.
1050 Massachusetts Avenue
Cambridge, MA 02138
Tel.: 617-868-3900
Fax: 617-868-2742
www.nber.org/jobs

Peterson Institute for International Economics

The Peterson Institute for International Economics is a private, non-profit, nonpartisan research institution devoted to the study of international economic policy. Since 1981, it has provided timely, objective analysis and concrete solutions to key international economic problems. It attempts to anticipate emerging issues and to be ready with practical ideas to inform and shape public debate. Its audience includes government officials and legislators, business and labor leaders, management and staff at international organizations, university-based scholars and their students, other research institutions and nongovernmental organizations, the media, and the public at large. It addresses these groups both in the United States and around the world.

The Peterson Institute's staff of about fifty includes more than two dozen researchers, who are conducting about thirty studies at any given time. Its agenda emphasizes global macroeconomic topics, international money and finance, trade and related social issues, investment, and the international implications of new technologies. Current priority is given to China, globalization and the backlash against it, outsourcing, the reform of the international financial architecture, and new trade negotiations at the multilateral, regional, and bilateral levels. Institute staff and research cover all key regions—especially Asia, Europe, the Middle East, and Latin America as well as the United States itself.

Peterson Institute for International Economics
1750 Massachusetts Avenue, NW
Washington, DC 20036-1903
Tel.: 202-328-9000
Fax: 202-659-3225
www.iie.com/institute/jobs.cfm

Population Council

The Population Council, an international, nonprofit, nongovernmental organization, seeks to improve the well-being and reproductive health of current and future generations around the world and to help achieve a humane, equitable, and sustainable balance between people and resources. Its major areas of expertise are HIV/AIDS; poverty, gender, and youth; and reproductive health. It has offices in New York and Washington and in seventeen developing countries.

> Population Council
> One Dag Hammarskjold Plaza
> New York, NY 10017
> Tel.: 212-339-0500
> Fax: 212-755-6052
> www.popcouncil.org/opportunities

Potomac Institute for Policy Studies

The Potomac Institute for Policy Studies is an independent, not-for-profit public policy research institute. It identifies and aggressively shepherds discussion on key science and technology issues facing society—providing, in particular, an academic forum for the study of related policy issues. From these discussions and forums, it develops meaningful science and technology policy options and ensures their implementation at the intersection of business and government. The institute's current endeavors have required the formation of special efforts in terrorism and asymmetry, emerging threats and opportunities, national health policies, science and technology forecasting, and national security.

> Potomac Institute for Policy Studies
> Suite 200, 901 North Stuart Street
> Arlington, VA 22203
> Tel.: 703-525-0770
> Fax: 703-525-0299
> www.potomacinstitute.org

RAND Corporation

From its inception in the days following World War II, the RAND Corporation has focused on the nation's most pressing policy problems. The institution's first hallmark was high-quality, objective research and analysis of national security issues, and it began addressing problems of domestic policy in the 1960s. Today, RAND's broad research agenda helps policymakers around the world find solutions to some of the greatest challenges they face in the areas of defense, health care, education, criminal and civil justice, and other areas. RAND employs more than 1,500 full- and part-time staff; 85 percent of RAND's research staff hold advanced degrees. Most researchers work in RAND's Santa Monica head-quarters. Several hundred are also based in Washington, Pittsburgh, Cambridge, and Doha.

> RAND
> 1776 Main Street
> P.O. Box 2138
> Santa Monica, CA 90407
> Tel.: 310-393-0411
> Fax: 310-393-4818
> www.rand.org

Resources for the Future

Resources for the Future (RFF) is a nonprofit, nonpartisan organization that conducts independent research—rooted primarily in economics and other social sciences—on environmental, energy, and natural resource issues. Although RFF is headquartered in Washington, its research scope comprises programs in nations around the world. Today, RFF's staff includes about forty researchers, most of whom hold doctorates in economics. But RFF analysts also hold advanced degrees in engineering, law, ecology, city and regional planning, U.S. government, and public policy and management, among other disciplines. In addition to its research staff, RFF has a development office, a communications office, a book publishing operation, and various research support functions, including a specialized library. It also offers a variety of professional internships and academic fellowships and internships.

> Resources for the Future
> 1616 P Street, NW
> Washington, DC 20036
> Tel.: 202-328-5000
> Fax: 202-939-3460
> www.rff.org

Stimson Center

The Henry L. Stimson Center offers practical, nonpartisan, creative solutions to the problems of national and international security through research projects of the highest quality. Its current projects focus on reducing weapons of mass destruction and transnational threats, including global health security and space security; building regional security, particularly in East Asia, South Asia, Southwest Asia, and the Gulf region;

and strengthening institutions for peace and security, including peace operations and homeland security.

Employment opportunities at the Stimson Center are very limited; seven professional positions were open in 2006. The center seeks academic backgrounds ranging from bachelor's degrees through doctorates and/or policy-based research with direct security field experience. It hires interns throughout the year to assist with its various research projects. Any inquiries regarding employment can be sent to resume@stimson.org, and inquiries regarding internships can be sent to internships@stimson.org.

> Henry L. Stimson Center
> Suite 1200, 1111 19th Street, NW
> Washington, DC 20036
> Tel.: 202-223-5956
> Fax: 202-238-9604
> www.stimson.org

United States Institute of Peace

The United States Institute of Peace (USIP) is an independent, nonpartisan, national institution established and funded by Congress. Its goals are to help prevent and resolve violent conflicts, promote postconflict stability and development, and increase peace-building capacity, tools, and intellectual capital worldwide. The USIP does this by empowering others with knowledge, skills, and resources, as well as by directly engaging in peace-building efforts around the world. Among the USIP's many programs are an education program, three centers of innovation—the Center for Conflict Analysis and Prevention, the Center for Mediation and Conflict Resolution, and the Center for Post-Conflict Peace and Stability Operations—the bipartisan Iraq Study Group, and the Task Force on the United Nations. Applicants to the USIP must apply for a specific vacancy. There are relatively few vacancies. Though the USIP only considers U.S. citizens for direct employment, very highly qualified noncitizens may be engaged through contracts or other procedures to provide services.

> United States Institute of Peace
> 1200 17th Street, NW
> Washington, DC 20036
> Tel.: 202-457-1700
> Fax: 202-429-6063
> www.usip.org/jobs

Woodrow Wilson International Center for Scholars

The Woodrow Wilson International Center for Scholars was established as a living memorial to Woodrow Wilson, the twenty-eighth president of the United States, to commemorate his lifelong commitment to uniting scholarship with public affairs. The center is a nonpartisan institute for advanced study and a neutral forum for open, serious, and informed dialogue. It brings preeminent thinkers to Washington for extended periods of time to interact with policymakers through a large number of programs and projects. The center seeks to separate the important from the inconsequential and to take a historical and broad perspective on the issues.

The Woodrow Wilson Center is administered by a staff of scholars and administrators, program specialists, and support staff. In addition to these, the center offers a wide range of internships for current, recent, and returning students—approximately seventy work at the center at any given time. The center also awards approximately twenty to twenty-five residential fellowships annually to individuals with outstanding proposals for research projects on national and international issues in a broad range of the social sciences and humanities. For most positions, application materials can be submitted via e-mail to jobs@wilsoncenter.org, by fax to 202-691-4028, or mailed to:

> Woodrow Wilson International Center for Scholars
> One Woodrow Wilson Plaza
> 1300 Pennsylvania Avenue, NW
> 3rd Floor
> Washington, DC 20004
> Tel.: 202-691-4000
> www.wilsoncenter.org

World Security Institute

The World Security Institute (WSI) is a nonprofit organization committed to independent research and journalism on global affairs and security. Given the extraordinary growth of global interdependence, the WSI provides innovative approaches to communication, education, and cooperation on the social, economic, environmental, political, and military components of international security. Through a variety of publications and services, the WSI provides news and research-based analysis to the public and policymakers around the globe—from decision makers in Washington and Moscow to scholars in the Farsi- and Arabic-speaking world to scientists in China. The WSI serves as an authoritative and impartial monitor of security issues, while continuing to meet the increasing worldwide demand for information and independent ideas.

The WSI's divisions include the Center for Defense Information; International Media; Pulitzer Center on Crisis Reporting; Azimuth Media; and International Programs, with offices in Washington (founded in 1972), Brussels (2002), Cairo (2006), Moscow (2001), and Beijing (2002). The *Defense Monitor,* one of the WSI's best-known publications, is published six times per year. Other publications include three quarterly policy journals: *China Security, Arab Insight,* and *Caucasus Context.* The WSI's Azimuth Media produces the weekly television series *Foreign Exchange with Fareed Zakaria* and videos for educational purposes, as well as housing an independent documentary film production unit.

Staff members of the WSI include retired U.S. military officers, former Pentagon officials, and civilian experts with a background in a wide variety of international security issues, foreign journalists, and research analysts in four international locations. An internship program employs undergraduate students, graduate students, and recent graduates with strong interests in security affairs, related public policy questions, and journalism. Interns can serve in research, media, television production, communications, or Web production positions.

World Security Institute
Suite 615, 1779 Massachusetts Avenue, NW
Washington, DC 20036
Tel.: 202-332-0900
Fax: 202-462-4559
www.worldsecurityinstitute.org

Worldwatch Institute

The Worldwatch Institute is a nonprofit research organization dedicated to informing policymakers and the public about emerging global trends and the complex links between the world economy and its environmental support systems. The institute is dedicated to fostering the evolution of an environmentally sustainable society—one in which human needs are met in ways that do not threaten the health of the natural environment or the prospect of future generations. The institute seeks to achieve this goal through the conduct of interdisciplinary, nonpartisan research on emerging global environmental issues, the results of which are widely disseminated throughout the world.

The institute believes that information is a powerful tool for social change. Human behavior shifts in response to either new information or new experiences. The institute seeks to provide the information to bring about the changes needed to build an environmentally sustainable economy. In a sentence, the institute's mission is to raise public awareness of global environmental threats to the point where it will support effective policy responses.

Worldwatch Institute
1776 Massachusetts Avenue, NW
Washington, DC 20036-1904
Tel.: 202-452-1999
Fax: 202-296-7365
www.worldwatch.org

Getting Started in Research Institutes

Emile El-Hokayem

Emile El-Hokayem *is a 2004 graduate of the Master of Science in Foreign Service Program at Georgetown University. He is a research fellow in the Henry L. Stimson Center's Southwest Asia and Middle East Program. His previous experience includes serving as a research assistant position at the International Crisis Group, working as a publications assistant for* The Middle East Journal *at the Middle East Institute, and working as a research analyst on the Middle East at Nouveaux Droits de L'Homme in Paris and Beirut.*

WORKING AT A THINK TANK can be both intellectually satisfying and professionally fulfilling when done under the right conditions and with a strategic objective in mind. Think tanks provide original ideas and analysis, act as a bridge between different audiences (academia, the media, government, foreign governments, and the public), and play a key role in informing the public debate. Being part of this idea industry can boost one's career and help establish research and policy credentials on which to build future employment in government, the private sector, and the nonprofit world.

Major think tanks hire master's-level associates and analysts, but their work responsibilities vary considerably depending on the mission, size, and organization of the research center. Often, new hires are expected to provide substantive and administrative support for the research and work of senior analysts. Opportunities for independent analysis and writing are limited, especially at major, corporate-like institutions. These centers provide excellent work environments and opportunities to interact with top scholars, but they limit the autonomy of their junior analysts.

Candidates with a master's degree will understandably seek exposure and involvement in the policy debate. To achieve this, it is critical to develop a unique area of expertise and to be capable of translating this expertise into original written work for publication by the center and outside institutions.

It is crucial that candidates identify their areas of expertise and, even better, a research niche that makes them unique. For example, many candidates with a Middle East background focus on the Arab–Israeli conflict, but the crucial need is for candidates with real knowledge of Persian Gulf issues. Candidates should therefore ask themselves what their value added would be to a saturated policy community.

Early in graduate school, I identified think tanks as my top choice for a job after graduation. I knew the Middle East well, and I was interested in understanding the formulation and implementation of U.S. foreign policy in the region. Because government work was not an option (I am not an American citizen), think tanks were a good fit for my career plans.

I was particularly lucky with my internship and job search. I knew my area of expertise (Middle East security), I had written research papers on topics of relevance (Iran, Gulf security, Syria, Hezbollah), and I had studied with professors active in the Washington policy scene. This combination, together with my background (I am a French and Lebanese national) and my pre-master's experiences (I had researched political and human rights issues in the Middle East for years), strengthened my profile as a credible analyst. Indeed, my internship and job searches came surprisingly easily.

In the summer and fall of 2003, I interned at the Washington bureau of the International Crisis Group, assisting its Middle East Program director with research and writing. I also traveled to the Middle East with him on a research trip.

In February 2004, four months before graduating, I learned about a job opening at the Henry L. Stimson Center from a friend who had interned there. The newly created position with the center's Southwest Asia and Middle East Program offered significant autonomy because of the program's small size and the intellectual openness encouraged by its director. At the same time, the program director provided ample guidance and feedback. This unique environment (at least by Washington standards) allowed me to establish myself as an independent analyst while contributing significantly to the program's activities. A number of factors made both searches easy; aside from my qualifications (including languages), what worked to my advantage were my academic and professional references (in Washington's lexicon, my network), my own research interests, and my writing skills.

At the time I write this, I still work at the Stimson Center. Over time, the range and depth of my responsibilities have grown. This job has offered me opportunities available to few young analysts at think tanks: I have initiated and managed projects; given presentations at prestigious institutions; met with key policymakers; published a number of analyses, papers, and book chapters; and traveled to the Middle East and Europe for workshops and conferences.

Nevertheless, in the immediate future, my career is limited by my lack of government experience and lack of a PhD. These are two essential ingredients for those who want to make a career in the think tank world or move between this world and government or academia. Thankfully, given the need to comprehend how international politics affects business, economic, social, and cultural relations, there are new job opportunities emerging at the nexus of the research world and the private sector. Think tanks are excellent places to gain the expertise, exposure, and experience needed to position yourself to take this kind of career path.

Index